Practical Fraud Prevention

*Fraud and AML Analytics for Fintech
and eCommerce, Using SQL and Python*

Gilit Saporta and Shoshana Maraney

Beijing · Boston · Farnham · Sebastopol · Tokyo

Practical Fraud Prevention

by Gilit Saporta and Shoshana Maraney

Published by O'Reilly Media, Inc., 1005 Gravenstein Highway North, Sebastopol, CA 95472.

O'Reilly books may be purchased for educational, business, or sales promotional use. Online editions are also available for most titles (*http://oreilly.com*). For more information, contact our corporate/institutional sales department: 800-998-9938 or *corporate@oreilly.com*.

Acquisitions Editor: Michelle Smith	**Indexer:** Sue Klefstad
Development Editor: Corbin Collins	**Interior Designer:** David Futato
Production Editor: Kate Galloway	**Cover Designer:** Karen Montgomery
Copyeditor: Audrey Doyle	**Illustrator:** Kate Dullea
Proofreader: Charles Roumeliotis	

March 2022:   First Edition

Revision History for the First Edition

2022-03-16:   First Release

See *http://oreilly.com/catalog/errata.csp?isbn=9781492093329* for release details.

978-1-492-09332-9

[LSI]

To our moms and dads, who kept us safe when we crossed the road.
Now it's our turn to make it safe for you to surf the Net.

Table of Contents

Part I.   Introduction to Fraud Analytics

Part V.   AML and Compliance Analytics

Foreword

Very few people who identify as "fraud fighters" in the digital world began their careers with the intention of fighting fraud. Apart from one or two universities around the world, there isn't a standard course of study or a major that will prepare a young person for what they need to understand in the "real world" of identifying cybercrime. And until now, there hasn't been a book that provides practical knowledge or advice on how to get started or refine current strategies. Most of us learned our craft through on-the-job training and continual trial and error. As such, the need for a training manual of foundational knowledge across the various sectors of our emerging industry is very real.

Billions of dollars are lost to online payment fraud annually, often without much recourse for victim companies. This makes it critically important to identify suspicious and fraudulent behavior in advance, prior to bad actors committing the crime. Those outside this niche industry may assume that fraudulent orders or accounts present themselves in red blinking lights, or some other obvious form. The truth is that bad actors have the sole intention of having their online activity blend in with that of legitimate users. It is our job as fraud fighters to home in on the anomalies of their information, devices, and human behavior to identify risk indicators.

To add to the challenge (but also the fun), there is no one way to identify risky activity across multiple business models, verticals, price points, consumer bases, and so on. However, there are common behavior patterns and risk indicators that multiple companies will experience. Moreover, companies with similar business models, price points, and so forth are likely facing the same bad actors as their competitors.

That is why sharing information within the larger fraud prevention industry is so valuable and necessary. Over my career, I have had the immense privilege of introducing some of the biggest companies' fraud teams to one another. Whether they worked for big-box stores, online gaming companies, online travel agencies, or retailers, it was an honor to make these introductions and facilitate these conversations. The fraud teams know that while their brands may compete against each other, they cannot, because failing to work together against common "enemies" could be detrimental to their organization and its bottom line. When I get the opportunity to facilitate fraud-focused conversations among companies that would traditionally be competitors, there is a common understanding that the shared enemy is important enough to warrant allying with one another. Because we rally together for a common cause, the community within our industry is strong. It is because of this level of collaboration and information sharing that we have made strides in technology and strategic process improvements.

This book is another form of collaboration within the industry. The authors worked with many experts in the field, and they themselves are brilliant in the world of fraud prevention. As cyber fraud continues to grow and technology innovation continues to bring more opportunities for fraud, it is more important than ever to work together and learn what we can from one another.

I've lost count of the numerous occasions over the past decade that someone asked me to recommend a book exactly like this one. Some wanted to train new fraud fighters or learn more about a specific type of fraud or industry. Some were looking to move from banking to ecommerce, or vice versa, and wanted to prepare by learning about the similarities and differences between these fields. Others were highly experienced fraud fighters looking to expand their depth of knowledge. I've even had people ask because they're looking for a source they can share with other departments as a way to introduce them to the complexities of fraud prevention and how it impacts users as well as other elements of the organization.

It's a pleasure to see that this book finally exists. The bad actors are successful because they work together and share both information and a broader understanding of their field. It's imperative that we do the same.

— Karisse Hendrick, founder and principal
consultant at Chargelytics Consulting and
host of the popular Fraudology *podcast*

Preface

"With commerce comes fraud," wrote Airbnb cofounder Nathan Blecharczyk back in 2010, and it's safe to say that the maxim has proven itself over and over in the years since then.[1] Global online sales reached nearly $4.29 trillion in 2020, with more than $1 out of every $5 spent online. Fraudsters follow the money, making online fraud bigger, smarter, and bolder than ever (Figure P-1).

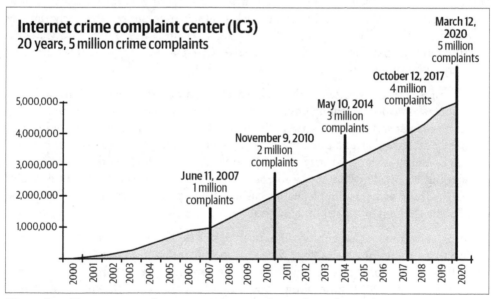

Figure P-1. Twenty years of internet crime complaints from the IC3[2]

---

1 Nathan Blecharczyk, "Hard Problems, Big Opportunity" (*https://oreil.ly/txK4b*), *The Airbnb Tech Blog*, November 7, 2010.

2 FBI, "Internet Crime Complaint Center Marks 20 Years" (*https://oreil.ly/UTQHc*), May 8, 2020.

Fraud fighters, with their heads down in the data, excel at identifying new suspicious patterns and tracking down perpetrators. The constant pressure of fraud prevention means that often, day-to-day activities prevent fraud fighters from taking a breath, putting their head above the parapet, and looking around to see what's happening outside their company or their industry. The purpose of this book is to provide a wider and more strategic perspective as well as hands-on tips and advice.

During our time in fraud prevention, we have been privileged to have the chance to talk to and see data and trends from a wide range of merchants and organizations. It's that breadth that we want to share in this book.

Introduction to Practical Fraud Prevention

Online fraud has been around almost as long as online banking and online commerce: fraudsters go where the money is and wherever they can spot an opportunity. It's worth noting right at the start that when we refer to fraudsters, we're talking about threats external to a business; this book does not discuss internal fraud or risk or employee integrity issues. There's certainly enough to be said about external fraud online—a problem that businesses have been worrying about for decades now. Julie Fergerson, CEO of the Merchant Risk Council, remembers the early days of ecommerce 20 years ago, when she'd help clients set up stores online and watch in horrified awe as fraud attacks would hit the very first week—or sometimes even the first day—of a shop's existence.

At that time, there was often a physical aspect to online fraud. Card skimming was common as a means of stealing physical card information, perhaps carried out during a legitimate transaction or at an ATM. The card information might be used online to make purchases, or fake cards might be created to attempt transactions in physical stores. Sometimes the card data ended up online, on the forums that were quickly developing to enable criminals to interact with one another on the internet. Other times, the fraud was very simple, with a cashier just copying the card information and attempting to use it to make purchases online.

Card-present fraud hasn't entirely disappeared, but there's no question that a combination of chip and pin technology for card-present transactions and the sheer scale of online interactions and commerce has put card-not-present fraud center stage (Figure P-2). One 2021 study found that 83% of all fraud attacks involving credit, debit, or prepaid cards occurred online.[3] That's the world in which fraud prevention teams now live and breathe.

---

3 Feedzai, *Financial Crime Report: The Dollar Takes Flight* (*https://oreil.ly/ViIQI*), Q2 2021 edition.

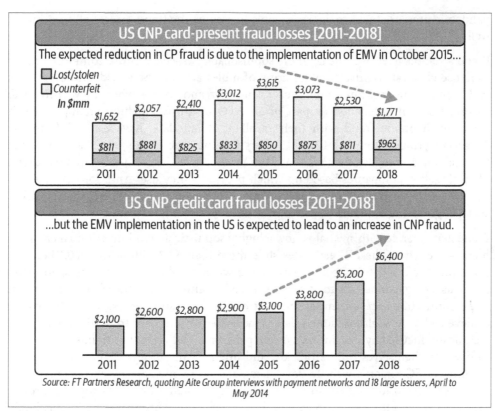

US CNP card-present fraud losses [2011-2018]

The expected reduction in CP fraud is due to the implementation of EMV in October 2015...

☐ Lost/stolen
☐ Counterfeit
In $mm

2011	2012	2013	2014	2015	2016	2017	2018
$1,652	$2,057	$2,410	$3,012	$3,615	$3,073	$2,530	$1,771
$811	$881	$825	$833	$850	$875	$811	$965

US CNP credit card fraud losses [2011-2018]

...but the EMV implementation in the US is expected to lead to an increase in CNP fraud.

2011	2012	2013	2014	2015	2016	2017	2018
$2,100	$2,600	$2,800	$2,900	$3,100	$3,800	$5,200	$6,400

Source: FT Partners Research, quoting Aite Group interviews with payment networks and 18 large issuers, April to May 2014

Figure P-2. Credit card fraud and ID theft in the United States from 2011 to 2018[4]

The onset of the COVID-19 pandemic in early 2020 accelerated digital transformation of all kinds as people adapted to the convenience and temporary necessity of shopping and interacting online. One report found that in 2020, 47% of people opened a new online shopping account, while 35% opened a new social media account and 31% opened an online banking account.[5] All of this presents financial opportunities for online companies—but not without fraud risks. Nearly 70% of merchants said chargeback rates rose during the pandemic, and many reported high levels of account takeover (ATO) attempts as well.[6] Given that consumers report the intention to continue their online purchasing and banking habits even once there's no

---

4 Emmanuel Gbenga Dada et al., "Credit Card Fraud Detection using k-star Machine Learning Algorithm" (*https://oreil.ly/LODqT*) (paper, 3rd Biennial Conference on Transition From Observation To Knowledge To Intelligence, University of Lagos, Nigeria, August 2019).

5 James Coker, "A Fifth of Consumers Affected by Identity Fraud in 2020" (*https://oreil.ly/T8k51*), *Inforsecurity Magazine*, November 23, 2020.

6 DJ Murphy, "Covid Changed Chargebacks for E-Commerce Merchants, Says Report" (*https://oreil.ly/SCFpT*), Card Not Present, June 3, 2021.

pandemic pressure to do so, it's reasonable to assume the fraud threat will continue as well.

Fraud attempts have become far more sophisticated, as well as more common. Fraudsters use elaborate obfuscation, an army of mules around the world, and even tools that capture information about a user's browser and device when they visit a site so that this can be echoed as part of an ATO disguise. Phishing attempts, which drive much online fraud with their resultant stolen data, have evolved from the "Nigerian prince" scams of 10 or 15 years ago into subtle missives that mimic the tone, layout, and logos of emails sent from providers to the companies that use them, often targeting companies based on which providers they use. And don't even get us started on the intricacies of romance scams, IT repair scams, catfishing, and other social engineering schemes.

Fraudsters operate within what is now a highly sophisticated online criminal environment—one which the FBI estimates stole more than $4.2 billion in 2020.[7] Fraud is sometimes referred to as being part of the wider world of cybercrime, and other times as being connected to it but separate. In either case, there's no doubt that these connections are an important part of the scale and success many fraudsters achieve today. A wealth of stolen data is available for purchase to use in attacks, and technically focused cybercriminals create programs and apps that fraudsters can use to disguise themselves online quickly, and often in an automated fashion. Graphic designers, SEO experts, website developers, and more all support schemes involving fake sites created to trick consumers into giving up their data or placing fake orders. We won't delve into the complex world of cybercrime more generally in this book, but we will mention aspects of the cybercriminal ecosystem when relevant.

Fraud attacks have evolved within the banking and fintech worlds too (Figure P-3). Quite early on, fraudsters developed an appetite for higher profits. Attacks on individual consumers have existed from the beginning, but fraudsters who were able to carry out malware-based cyberattacks quickly became a more serious threat. Social engineering tactics focused on business email compromise (BEC) fraud, in which a fraudster could cash in big with a single unauthorized transfer, if they were lucky enough to succeed. Over the years, banks built up stronger defenses against the attacks of the early days, and many fraudsters "migrated" to targeting younger fintech companies and/or exploiting the vulnerabilities on the consumer side of banking. More recently, malware has been combined with social engineering, as discussed in Chapter 14.

---

7 Ionut Ilascu, "FBI: Over $4.2 Billion Officially Lost to Cybercrime in 2020" (*https://oreil.ly/WmQ2q*), Bleeping Computer, March 18, 2021.

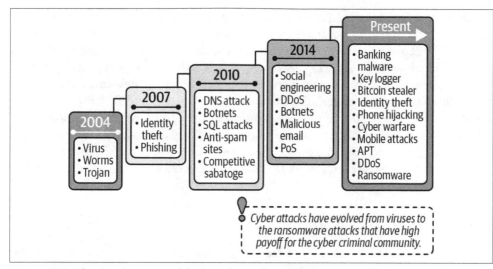

Figure P-3. The development of fraudster attack methods and sophistication within a banking context

Of course, online fraud prevention has increased in sophistication as well. Where once the industry was dominated by rules engines, now machine learning supplements most systems to add its speed and excellence at spotting patterns to a fraud system's efforts. This has enabled more decisions to be automated, more quickly. Diverse vendors of data enrichment for many kinds of data have sprung up, though as a number of these have been acquired by larger players in recent years, it will be interesting to see how this field develops.

The relationship between fraudsters and fraud prevention is often described as an arms race, with each side continually attempting to create or uncover new vulnerabilities or tools that will give them an edge. Sometimes one side appears to have the upper hand, and other times the other side does. Fraudsters are unlikely to give up the battle while there is so much money to be made, and fraud prevention teams can never afford to take their eyes off the game knowing that fraudsters will pounce on any weakness.

One advantage that fraud prevention teams can develop is strong, collaborative relationships, both with fraud fighters at other companies and with other departments in their own company. While working on this book, we were surprised how many times the topic of collaboration came up, and in how many different contexts. Working with fraud teams from other companies, or within other departments, or convening and sharing ideas, new trends, and tips through forums, roundtables, reports, and so on, was key to the way many fraud managers keep track of what's going on in the industry and ensure that their teams are not falling behind.

Similarly, developing close, trusting relationships with departments such as customer support, marketing, sales, legal, and logistics/supply can give fraud prevention teams a real advantage in spotting and preventing the development of fraud trends, and in understanding and preparing for changes in the business or market approach. In the same way, educating other departments and upper management about fraud prevention and the challenges of balancing between friction and fighting fraud helps fraud teams look and stay relevant to the needs of the business and position themselves appropriately within the organization. All of this increases interdepartmental collaboration and makes it more likely that fraud teams will get the budget they need and the key performance indicators (KPIs) that make sense for both themselves and the company.

How to Read This Book

Ohad Samet, cofounder and CEO of TrueAccord and author of *Introduction to Online Payments Risk Management* (O'Reilly), mentions "lack of data" as a common reason for failing to understand "what is going on" (*https://oreil.ly/VqIkn*) in fraud analytics. He clarifies that this is often because "maintaining event-based historical data is not anywhere near the top of these engineers' minds" (once again, note the importance of educating other departments and management). Samet gives the example of point-in-time analysis (e.g., being able to train a predictive system using only data that was available at the time of the fraud attack, long before the financial loss became evident).

The authors of this book strongly agree with Samet that "lack of data" can be catastrophic, but not just because of its negative impact on the quality of your training sets. We see the urge of digging into event-based historical data as the *key* to a successful fraud prevention operation. A passion for root cause analysis, with an emphasis on behavioral analytics and "storytelling" research methodologies, is our creed.

Therefore, we encourage you to read this book with the curiosity of a data addict. Like Alice in Wonderland, the historical data of your organization should be a rabbit hole that you should gladly jump into, feeling curiouser and curiouser and enticing others in your company to join the ride. We believe that robust fraud prevention solutions are built mainly by researchers who can explain the fraud from the perspectives of the attacker and the victim. To learn how to do so, one should definitely have broad horizons and a healthy dose of curiosity (sometimes you need to think like a fraudster to catch a fraudster) regarding the shockingly wide array of manipulative schemes out there. Open source researchers may gain some of this insight through web research (including the deep web and dark web), but we believe a good analyst can learn a lot from the combination of their imagination and their data (Figure P-4).

Surface web
- Google
- CNN.com
- Bing
- Yahoo
- Facebook
- Instagram
- Reddit

}4%

Deep web
- Government records
- Scientific records
- Academic information
- Financial records
- Medical records
- Legal documents

Dark web
- Tor-encrypted sites
- Political protest
- Drug trafficking and other illegal activities

}96%

Figure P-4. Breakdown of the different parts of the internet (left); the continually curious Alice (right)[8]

In this book, you won't find a checklist of steps you can take to stop fraud. Every business and every industry is different and has different priorities, needs, and structure. Fraud prevention must take all of them into account. Moreover, we have tried not to be too specific about particular tricks that can be used to catch fraudsters, because we know perfectly well that if we were, this book would become a favorite on fraudster forums within a month and the tricks would become useless soon afterward. Instead, we have tried to provide concepts and best practices that are helpful in different situations. We have also tried to make suggestions using features that are inherent to the nature of the challenge being faced, rather than ones that could be gamed and circumvented.

On a technical note, we wrote all the query examples in SQL, but they can easily be translated to PostgreSQL if necessary. Of course, you must adapt the queries to the specific tables of the database you're working with (e.g., replace the generic hypothetical table we called CUSTOMERS with the name of the table that holds the relevant data for your use case). We have tried to present the queries throughout

---

8 Sir John Tenniel, *Drink Me* (*https://oreil.ly/gNzgB*), in *The Nursery "Alice"* by Lewis Carroll, illustrations by John Tenniel (London: Macmillan and Co., 1889), via Wikimedia Commons.

the book in a way that is easy for the reader to adapt to their own company's setup and preferred technologies. For example, we happen to like DataGrip and MySQL Workbench for working with SQL and Jupyter Notebook for working with Python, but whatever your company's or team's preferences are will work just as well when it comes to using the suggestions in this book.

We organized many of the chapters by attack type, under the industries for which they are most relevant. For example, we placed the chapter on stolen credit card fraud in the part of the book on ecommerce, even though stolen credit card fraud touches many other elements of the online criminal ecosystem and is part of many other attack methods. Similarly, the chapter on account takeover is in the part of the book covering banking.

Our main motivation for this structure is to make it easy for fraud analysts specializing in a particular industry to find the chapters most relevant to them. We do encourage you to look at the sections in every chapter of the book, though, to see which parts may be of interest, even if they are not in the part of the book pertaining to your industry. We have done our best to ensure that although the examples given relate to the industry in whose section the chapter falls, the discussion, suggestions, and mitigation techniques are relevant across industries.

In the same spirit, we have discussed different data points, or prevention tactics, within the context of the problem they are typically used to solve. So, for example, physical address analysis and reshipper detection are discussed in the chapter on address manipulation, while login analysis and inconsistency detection are discussed in the chapter on account takeover. We did initially consider keeping the "attack" and "defense" elements separate—so that, for example, address manipulation and physical address analysis would each have their own chapter—but we felt that pairing the elements gave a much richer context for each part and kept the context far closer to what fraud prevention teams work with on a daily basis.

For the purposes of clarity, in each chapter we explore a data point separately, breaking each one down in the way that we hope will be most helpful. But in reality, when using this knowledge and the techniques suggested in analyzing user actions and profiles, you would put everything you learn about the individual data points together in order to form a story—often, two stories side by side: the legitimate story and the fraudulent story. Ultimately, you decide which is more plausible.

Context is absolutely crucial here. Say you have analyzed the IP and found a proxy, and the email address includes a lot of numbers. Perhaps the shipping address is that of a known reshipper. There's a clear fraud story there. But what if the numbers are ones believed to be lucky in China, and the reshipper is one that reships to China? Then the proxy makes sense—this is a strong legitimate story.

Making the data points analysis an integral part of the fraud types discussion, rather than splitting it off into a separate section, will, we hope, act as a constant reminder that these data points must been seen in the full context of the other data points involved, the business, the industry, and of course, the type of fraud attack.

Table P-1 is a guide to which data points are analyzed and which tactics are discussed in each chapter. You should feel free to skim or skip to the parts of chapters that discuss the mitigation techniques you are most interested in, though we do recommend that each of you reads Chapters 1 through 5 first, regardless of your industry.

Table P-1. Guide to chapter breakdown, showing which data points are analyzed in which chapter

Chapter	Topic	Examples
Part I: Introduction to Fraud Analytics		
Chapter 1, "Fraudster Traits"	An introduction to walking a mile in the fraudster's shoes	Address verification service (AVS) manipulation examples
Chapter 2, "Fraudster Archetypes"	The basics of understanding the different types of attacker you're likely to see	Manually evaluating four transactions originating from a single IP
Chapter 3, "Fraud Analysis Fundamentals"	The basics of the practical analytics approach used throughout the book	Login density anomaly; SQL to generate user's histogram of abnormal number of daily logins
Chapter 4, "Fraud Prevention Evaluation and Investment"	Building frameworks for strong fraud prevention teams	
Chapter 5, "Machine Learning and Fraud Modeling"	A discussion about the place of modeling in fraud fighting	
Part II: Ecommerce Fraud Analytics		
Chapter 6, "Stolen Credit Card Fraud"	Typical flow of stolen credit card monetization, followed by a general discussion on comparing IP data to user data	IP analysis: proxy detection, including data source examples; IP categorization using traffic breakdowns with SQL and Python
Chapter 7, "Address Manipulation and Mules"	Physical goods theft via shipping manipulation	Address misspelling; SQL to find common typos or variations on city names Python to spot reshipping services by velocity of address repetition
Chapter 8, "BORIS and BOPIS Fraud"	Fraud associated with Buy Online, Return In Store (BORIS) and Buy Online, Pick up In Store (BOPIS) programs	Linking analytics; detecting a fraud ring Analyzing potential mule operations with SQL
Chapter 9, "Digital Goods and Cryptocurrency Fraud"	Fraud associated with digital goods, including fiat-to-crypto transactions; note that anti–money laundering (AML) and compliance relating to cryptocurrency are discussed in Chapter 22	User profiling: age bucketing to spot potential social engineering

Chapter	Topic	Examples
Chapter 10, "First-Party Fraud (aka Friendly Fraud) and Refund Fraud"	First-party fraud, aka friendly chargebacks, with a focus on ecommerce	Refund request word clouds and supporting tools for customer care teams with SQL and Python
Part III: Consumer Banking Fraud Analytics		
Chapter 11, "Banking Fraud Prevention: Wider Context"	Wider context for banking fraud	
Chapter 12, "Online Account Opening Fraud"	Reasons to open fraudulent accounts and ways to catch those accounts; includes references to money muling	Applying census data to fraud prevention
Chapter 13, "Account Takeover"	Types of ATOs and how to catch them	Login analysis and inconsistency detection with SQL
Chapter 14, "Common Malware Attacks"	Malware attacks, particularly as used in conjunction with social engineering	
Chapter 15, "Identity Theft and Synthetic Identities"	Complexities of identifying and combating cases of actual stolen identity (rather than stolen and misused individual data points connected to a real identity)	Personal identifiable information (PII) analysis and identity discrepancy detection
Chapter 16, "Credit and Lending Fraud"	Credit fraud and abuse, including stimulus fraud	Email domain histogram with SQL
Part IV: Marketplace Fraud		
Chapter 17, "Marketplace Attacks: Collusion and Exit"	Collusion and exit fraud; that is, when more than one account colludes to defraud the marketplace	Peer-to-peer (P2P) analysis; seller-buyer detection with SQL and Python
Chapter 18, "Marketplace Attacks: Seller Fraud"	Forms of fraud carried out by marketplace sellers leveraging their position in the ecosystem	Seller reputation analysis and feedback padding detection using Python
Part V: AML and Compliance Analytics		
Chapter 19, "Anti–Money Laundering and Compliance: Wider Context"	Wider context for AML and compliance	
Chapter 20, "Shell Payments: Criminal and Terrorist Screening"	Concealing money movement in various ways, including money muling; also looks at criminal and terrorist screening	Credit scores and transaction analysis for money mule detection with SQL
Chapter 21, "Prohibited Items"	Prohibited items and the wide variety of thorny issues associated with dealing with them	Standard deviation/RMSE analysis for product popularity with SQL
Chapter 22, "Cryptocurrency Money Laundering"	Why cryptocurrency has become popular for money laundering	Blockchain analytic data sources
Chapter 23, "Adtech Fraud"	Bot fraud identification	Hijacked device identification
Chapter 24, "Fraud, Fraud Prevention, and the Future"	Collaboration	

Who Should Read This Book?

Primarily, fraud analysts! The main audience we had in mind as we wrote this book was the smart, dedicated, and creative collection of folks we know who fight the good fight against fraud in their organizations, and in some cases lead fraud operations in those organizations. We hope the wider context provided in this book helps you see your own work in the context in which it belongs. We also hope the structure and framework we provide for different types of fraudsters, attack methods, and identification and mitigation efforts help you get things clearer in your own head—something that can be challenging when you're always focused on making sure chargebacks remain low while approval rates remain high. We hope this book is, as it says on the cover, practical and useful. And we hope it reminds you that, whatever today's challenges are, you are never alone; you are part of a community of passionate fraud fighters who want to catch fraud, protect their companies, and *get things right* as much as you do.

We also hope this book will be valuable in training new fraud analysts, introducing them to the field, and giving them practical tips and even code to run. Having a wider understanding of online fraud, in a variety of contexts and through a variety of attack methods, will help new analysts immeasurably as they come to grips with their new challenges.

The nonfraud folks you work with regularly, such as software engineers or data scientists, who may have some working understanding of fraud prevention but who don't live and breathe fraud fighting in the way that your own team does, may also find this book interesting and beneficial, giving them valuable additional context for the work you engage in together. We hope it makes your partnership stronger, smoother, and even more successful.

As well, we hope you'll find this book helpful in introducing key concepts of fraud and fraud prevention to others in your organization who have no experience in fraud. As we emphasize repeatedly throughout this book, both collaboration with other departments and representing fraud prevention efforts appropriately to upper management are crucial in achieving true success as a fraud prevention department.

The context in which fraud analysts work is, frankly, cool—even if most fraud fighters don't recognize that or think about it day to day. You're fighting cybercriminals who use a range of ingenious techniques to try to trick you and steal from the business. Once others in your company understand this and some of the context behind it, they will care a whole lot more about what you do and will want to help you do it.

It is important to note that in general, this book reflects and speaks to the *perspective* of a fraud prevention professional or team, and also an AML professional or team in the sense that AML traces patterns, detects anomalies, and acts to prevent them. The compliance-focused side of AML, the perspective of data scientists or compliance experts or financial analysts, is not reflected here. There are other books that focus on these domains and aim to talk to and help the experts within them.

It was important for us to focus firmly on the fraud prevention side of things because in some ways, the fraud prevention industry is underserved in terms of educational opportunities. There are numerous excellent higher education courses and certifications (and even YouTube videos) that individuals can use to further their understanding of data science and become qualified in its use. ACFE runs diverse courses that enable participants to become Certified Fraud Examiners so that they can help businesses fight money laundering, insider fraud, financial fraud, and so forth. But there is no equivalent organization, course, or set of materials to help fraud analysts learn and stay up to date with fraud prevention within ecommerce, online marketplaces, or fintech. (Though the Merchant Risk Council is working on training materials and tests for junior fraud analysts, so watch that space!)

There is one advantage fraud fighters have that does balance out this lack to some degree. Fraud prevention, as an industry, has a particular advantage in that its professionals are unusually willing to collaborate, sharing experiences, tips, and even data with one another. This plays out in conferences, forums, and roundtables. Just as fraudsters work together sharing information about sites' weaknesses and how they can be leveraged, and sometimes work together to form combined attacks, so fraud fighters work together to combat their shared enemy. As Karisse Hendrick, founder and principal consultant at Chargelytics Consulting and host of the popular *Fraudology* podcast (*https://oreil.ly/q67RZ*), says, this really is a "superpower," and fraud fighters who draw on this community spirit and nurture relationships within the industry can have a powerful advantage in fighting fraud.

This drive for collaboration is, in a sense, only logical, since it extends the understanding and effectiveness of fraud fighters and helps outweigh the extent to which criminals often work together to defraud companies. It's also a reflection of the drive for justice that many of the fraud prevention experts we quote in this book feel animates their work and that of their team. Carmen Honacker, head of Customer and Payment Fraud at Booking.com, offers a delightful story about the time her card details were stolen and the bank called to inform her of the suspicious activity. Using her fraud prevention background and skills, she tracked down the thieves and then sent the police to arrest them. The bank managers, when she told them, were astonished and impressed. Fraud fighters can't manage that for every suspicious case they encounter, but the drive for justice is definitely strong in the industry.

Domain expertise is hard-won knowledge for fraud fighters. This is partly because of the lack of courses and certifications, but also because, from a data perspective, there just aren't that many fraudsters. It's a tiny minority of users who have an enormous impact. You can't fight the problem purely with data or machines (though as we will discuss in the book, data and machine learning can be extremely helpful). You simply need to know a lot about how fraudsters work and how your company works. This takes time, research, and ongoing effort; a fraud prevention expert's perspective must evolve as consumer behavior, fraudster behavior, and company priorities do.

We sincerely hope this book will help fill in a little of that information gap in the fraud prevention industry. Whether you're just starting out in your career and looking for an overview, or you're an expert with decades of experience wanting to dig into various issues or patterns, build a framework for your accumulated knowledge, or look for new ways to combat challenges, we hope you enjoy this book and find it helpful. And we wish you the best in the ongoing, ever-evolving battle against crime that characterizes the fraud prevention profession.

Conventions Used in This Book

The following typographical conventions are used in this book:

Italic
> Indicates new terms, URLs, email addresses, filenames, and file extensions.

`Constant width`
> Used for program listings, as well as within paragraphs to refer to program elements such as variable or function names, databases, data types, environment variables, statements, and keywords.

`Constant width bold`
> Shows commands or other text that should be typed literally by the user.

> This element signifies a tip or suggestion.

> This element signifies a general note.

> This element indicates a warning or caution.

O'Reilly Online Learning

O'REILLY® For more than 40 years, *O'Reilly Media* has provided technology and business training, knowledge, and insight to help companies succeed.

Our unique network of experts and innovators share their knowledge and expertise through books, articles, and our online learning platform. O'Reilly's online learning platform gives you on-demand access to live training courses, in-depth learning paths, interactive coding environments, and a vast collection of text and video from O'Reilly and 200+ other publishers. For more information, visit *https://oreilly.com*.

How to Contact Us

Please address comments and questions concerning this book to the publisher:

O'Reilly Media, Inc.
1005 Gravenstein Highway North
Sebastopol, CA 95472
800-998-9938 (in the United States or Canada)
707-829-0515 (international or local)
707-829-0104 (fax)

We have a web page for this book, where we list errata, examples, and any additional information. You can access this page at *https://oreil.ly/practical-fraud-prevention*.

Email *bookquestions@oreilly.com* to comment or ask technical questions about this book.

For news and information about our books and courses, visit *https://oreilly.com*.

Find us on Facebook: *https://facebook.com/oreilly*

Follow us on Twitter: *https://twitter.com/oreillymedia*

Watch us on YouTube: *https://youtube.com/oreillymedia*

Acknowledgments

We've had so much support from many amazing people throughout the process of writing this book. Thank you so much to everyone who helped make it a reality! We would like to give an especially big thank-you to the following people.

Our greatest thanks go to the queen of collaboration, Karisse Hendrick, who originally suggested us for this project when the O'Reilly editors decided they wanted a book about fraud prevention, and who encouraged us throughout. We're indebted to her for her enthusiasm, her willingness to share her experiences, and her conviction that we could cover all the topics we wanted to in a single book. (It seems she was right.)

We would also like to thank our wonderful technical experts and reviewers: Alon Shemesh, Ben Russell, Brett Holleman (whose excellent technical review was matched by the excellence of his additional and very relevant anecdotes), Gil Rosenthal, Ken Palla, Mike Haley, Netanel Kabala, Jack Smith, and Yanrong Wang. They helped us polish and clarify our explanations, pointed out things that needed to be added, and generally made sure our content matched the trends they had observed in their fraud-fighting work. Any remaining mistakes are, of course, our own.

This book could not have happened without the conversations and interviews we were lucky enough to carry out with a number of experts from the fraud-fighting space, who so generously shared their time, experience, and advice. Our thanks go to Aamir Ali, Arielle Caron, Ben Russell, Carmen Honacker, Dave Laramy, Elena Michaeli, Gali Ellenblum, Gil Rosenthal, Professor Itzhak Ben Israel, Jordan Harris, Julia Zuno, Julie Fergerson, Ken Palla, Keren Aviasaf, Limor Kessem, Maximilian von Both, May Michelson, Maya Har-Noy, Mike Haley, Nate Kugland, Nikki Baumann, Noam Naveh, Ohad Samet, Rahav Shalom Revivo, Raj Khare, Sam Beck, Soups Ranjan, Tal Yeshanov, Uri Lapidot, Uri Rivner, and Zach Moshe; to Arik Nagornov, Yuval Rubin, Lia Bader, and Lisa Toledano from DoubleVerify whose research we discuss in Chapter 23; and to Uri Arad and Alon Shemesh, without whose years of support and guidance we would not have been in a position to write this book in the first place.

We're grateful to DoubleVerify and Identiq for being not only willing to let us write the book, but also actively supportive of our efforts.

We'd like to thank the fantastic team at O'Reilly, and particularly our editors—Corbin Collins, Kate Galloway, and Audrey Doyle—who picked up on and fixed all the little errors and lacunae that we would never have noticed ourselves.

And we're especially grateful to our respective spouses, Ori Saporta and Ben Maraney, both of whom learned far more about fraud prevention as a result of this book than they'd bargained for. Without their encouragement, patience, and support, this book would not have happened—or at least, it certainly wouldn't have been written by us.

## PART I

Introduction to Fraud Analytics

The following five chapters cover the basic elements of fraud analytics, as well as the wider context that is shared across the various verticals of the ecosystem. The first two chapters break down the phenomenon of fraud into behaviors that characterize fraudsters and the typology of attacker personas. We believe it's crucial for every researcher to be able to envision the fraudsters' mindset. Fraudsters are definitely persona non grata in your system, but they do still have a persona. They are people driven by very human needs, and understanding where they come from can be a big step in your evolution as a researcher (and a human being).

The next two chapters focus on the more practical tactics that every fraud researcher keeps in their toolbelt (which is almost as cool as Batman's utility belt)—for example, being able to spot anomalies and figure out whether they may be seasonal, or being able to assess the risk of fraud in the context of your profit margins and then deciding whether it's worth it to develop an in-house solution or invest in working with a third-party provider. Without these fundamentals, it's virtually impossible to go into the business of risk management.

Finally, Chapter 5 is devoted to opening the black box (and sometimes Pandora's box) of fraud modeling. This chapter cannot be used to teach machine learning, but it can certainly start an important (and fun!) discussion with your data scientists.

We recommend reading these five chapters as an introduction, then skipping to the parts that are most relevant to your use case and the types of attacks you face. Consider also reading Chapter 6 before skipping ahead, since it shows basic examples of IP analytics that may be relevant to all verticals.

## CHAPTER 1

Fraudster Traits

That voodoo that you do so well...
—Cole Porter[1]

Aristotle said that something should be described as "good" if it fulfills its purpose. A good knife, for example, would be one that cuts well. With all due respect to the ancient philosopher, we're going to completely break with this way of looking at things.

It's common in fraud fighting to talk about a *bad card*, *bad IP*, *bad address*, and so on, and it's an easy way to communicate. Everyone knows what you mean: you're saying a card (or IP or address) has been linked in the past to fraudulent activity. But cards, IPs, addresses, and so on *aren't* really bad, and talking about them as though they are can be confusing in the long run and may lead to unnecessary friction or false declines for good customers. The real user may still be using their credit card legitimately, even if it's also being used fraudulently. That IP may be public, or it could be that it's now being used by someone new. An address might have many people associated with it, most of them legitimate, or a good citizen might have moved to an address recently vacated by a fraudster.

As fraud fighters, what we're interested in is the identity behind a transaction or an action taken online. Is this identity a real one? Is the person using it the one to whom it belongs? That's the question at the center of almost all the key questions fraud fighters face, and it's the context behind looking into impersonation techniques, deception techniques, card and account testing, and so on, informing all the elements we'll be exploring in this chapter (and in most of the rest of the book as well).

---

1 Cole Porter, "You Do Something to Me," in *Fifty Million Frenchmen*, music and lyrics by Cole Porter, book by Herbert Fields (1929).

Fraudsters try to blend into the background successfully (much like the moth on this book's front cover) by attempting to look plausible in a variety of ways.

In this chapter, we'll look at some of the most common traits shared by fraudsters and fraud attacks, regardless of their chosen target industry or preferred attack method. Some of these traits will be covered in greater detail in dedicated sections later in the book but are included here to set the scene, to get all readers on the same page at the start, and to establish clarity about definitions since there are some terms and distinctions, such as *abuse* versus *fraud*, which are used in different ways by different companies.

As we go through different techniques and traits, bear this one thing in mind: at the end of the day, you don't care about *what* (the IP, address, email, etc.). You care about *who*.

Impersonation Techniques

When a fraudster is trying to steal from your company, there are three likely scenarios. In the first scenario, they may pretend to be someone else, using a legitimate identity as cover for their fraud and to make their payment method look plausible. In the second, they may try to appear completely fresh, using a fake or synthetic identity, in which case obfuscation is important. In the third scenario, they may be a so-called *friendly fraudster* using their own identity and planning to file a fraudulent chargeback.

Impersonation techniques are the bread and butter of fraudsters engaged in the first scenario. In general, the impersonation is built around the payment method. The reason they want to craft the rest of their apparent identity to look like someone else is to convince you or your system that they are the real owner of the card, electronic wallet, or other payment method. The stolen payment information is usually purchased, together with details about the victim's name and address and often with the victim's email address and perhaps phone number, so that the fraudster has a good base on which to build their impersonation convincingly. The address gives both billing and shipping details, and also provides assistance with IP.

Device ID and behavioral information are far harder to spoof than other elements of a person's online presence, unless the attack is being carried out not with bought data but with malware being used to skim the information from live visitors. But since people do legitimately use multiple devices and behavioral information varies depending on circumstances, these signals are often overlooked. Though they can be helpful in confirming a good user, the absence of a known device or common behavior is not enough to pinpoint a fraudster, and relying on them in this way would cause false positives to skyrocket, with high numbers of good customers being mistakenly rejected. For accuracy, these signs must be combined with other signals from the user which can help piece together the story to show whether the user is legitimate or fraudulent.

Where emails are concerned, fraudsters will either take over the victim's account if they've stolen their password and other information, or create a new email address that appears to match the victim's real one, their name, or known facts about them. Some fraudsters will incur the risk of using the victim's real phone number, if known, because even though this leaves open a risk that the site will call the number and discover the trick, in practice that rarely happens. Others simply use disposable SIM cards that are a match for wherever the victim lives, whereas still others rely on Voice over IP (VoIP)-based phone numbers (though such numbers, which can sometimes be identified, can prove to be a weakness for the fraudster and thus an opportunity for a fraud prevention team).

For physical orders, the shipping address is typically the most difficult part of the impersonation. The fraudster can risk using the real address if they feel confident they or an accomplice will be able to carry out a bit of porch piracy, but this certainly leaves open the possibility that the victim will in fact receive the package, leaving the fraudster with nothing after all their hard criminal work. More commonly, fraudsters using the victim's real address to foil detection will try to call customer support after the order has gone through to change the address. (For more on shipping address manipulation, see Chapter 7.) The click-and-collect option, in which customers can buy online and then pick up the goods in the store or at a designated pickup point, which has become popular as a result of the COVID-19 pandemic, is another way of getting around the address challenge (and is covered in Chapter 8).

There are also more involved alternatives, notably address verification service (AVS) spoofing, which is a good example of why fraud teams can't rely too much on even the most commonly used tools. The purpose of AVS is to check that the address being given as part of the transaction matches the address the bank has on file for that card. It does not check whether that address really exists and does not provide the merchant with protection in case of a chargeback. It's also limited: AVS spoofing relies on the fact that AVS, which is used by many fraud teams to verify addresses in the countries in which it works, only checks the numbers in the address, not the letters. So, a fraudster could trick a system into thinking that 10 Main Street, zip code 12345, was a match for 10 Elm Avenue, zip code 12345. On Main Street, the fraudster would need to have a presence of their own—an office space, PO box, or residence—or they could use a *mule* (an associate assisting them with their activities, in this case by providing a safe delivery address and, often, reshipping services) with an appropriate address.

Here's an example to illustrate this point:

Address on file:
    10 Elm Avenue, Emeryville, zip code 12345

Possible addresses to fool AVS systems:
    10 Main Street, Oakland, zip code 12345 → FULL MATCH

    10 I-AM-A-FRAUDSTER Street, MOONVILLE, zip code 12345 → FULL MATCH

    1 Elm Avenue, Emeryville, zip code 12345 → ZIP MATCH (a partial match, like this, is often enough to satisfy a fraud prevention system)

In more subtle cases, fraudsters sometimes play with the fact that some towns share the same zip code but may each have a Main Street (for example). Even manual review may fail to pick this up at first glance.

Another option for evasion is muling. Mules have been a fraudster staple for years and have grown in popularity as a result of the economic uncertainty surrounding the COVID-19 pandemic, which necessitated work that could be done from home. Some mules know what they're a part of, while others are themselves victims of the scheme, sometimes being cheated of their salaries and any outlay they have taken on themselves when the fraudster drops their services. There are other dangers too, as noted in Chapter 20.

Mules are often used outside of the AVS spoofing use case, as they're valuable in many ways. For example, even if the address isn't a perfect match, if the mule lives in the right area a fraud prevention team might consider the address to be legitimate. Also, mules expand a fraudster's reach through click-and-collect dramatically. They can be relied upon to reship goods, meaning that fraudsters from a country in Eastern Europe can easily receive packages via a respectable-looking address in the United States. They can even set up accounts or place orders, to make the IP a good match for the identity being impersonated. Chapter 7 discusses shipping manipulation and mules in greater detail.

As fraud fighters, it's our job to analyze and make the most of every piece of data we have and can collect or source to piece together the story, whether fraudulent or legitimate. Ultimately, we must bear in mind that it's not the data points themselves that are being judged, but what they mean within the context of all the information we have in this case, and how it fits together.

Deception Techniques

Deception techniques can be part of a successful impersonation, especially in the case of fraudsters using sophisticated malware to scrape customers' online appearances, but they are also vital when carrying out a *blank slate* attack using a fake identity. The point of these obfuscatory tricks is to conceal the real location, device, and so on of the fraudster; they are distinct from impersonation techniques, which aim to ape the details of a real and specific person.

With enough determination and tech savvy, anything and anyone can be manipulated. Experienced fraud fighters who have seen state-run or state-funded malicious actors at work can attest to the fact that when the attackers are really motivated, they can look indistinguishable from good customers. We won't go into the deeper and darker forms of manipulation here because, as mentioned in the Preface, we suspect that more than one fraudster will read this book at some point. In any event, junior fraud fighters are generally introduced to the nuances of deception techniques early on in their careers.

However, we'll pick out a few of the most common ones, largely to make the point (not for the last time!) that most of the suspicious elements here can also have innocent explanations. Fraud analysts are often better at unmasking obfuscation than they are at remembering to consider potential legitimate scenarios in conjunction with the masking behavior. That road leads to unnecessary false positives and frustrated customers.

Consider IP masking (more on this in Chapter 6). Virtual private networks (VPNs) and anonymous proxies (mostly Socks or HTTP) are the most common methods, though you do see Tor used from time to time. There are even services that allow fraudsters to shuffle through fresh IPs for each new attack, and some allow the fraudster to match the IP to the address of the cardholder. That said, there are also plenty of reasons for a good customer to use VPNs or proxies: notably, privacy and avoiding content restrictions (which, while perhaps a form of abuse, is not fraudulent in the sense that we'll be using the term in this book). Now that working from home is common, VPNs are popular with many companies seeking to make it safer for their employees to work remotely. Even Tor browsers are used by particularly privacy-conscious but entirely legitimate individuals (in fact, fraudsters rarely use Tor because they know it looks suspicious, to the extent that seeing a Tor browser in use can actually almost be a positive sign).

Even the simplest kind of obfuscation, such as a disposable email address, can have good explanations, though this is a matter of context. A real customer is unlikely to use a *mickeymouse101@gmail.com*-style email address for their bank—but they are likely to use it for a site they visit rarely to protect themselves from spam. That's even more true following Apple's introduction of Hide My Email (*https://oreil.ly/PUnEJ*). So, depending on whether you're working at a bank or an online reviews site, this may or may not be a relevant signal. Fraudsters also know that customers use good email addresses for their banks, so if they're creating a new one it will likely be very plausible, perhaps simply substituting a 0 for an o or mixing up the first name/last name pattern in a different way. These tricks make an email more suspicious...except, of course, that real customers sometimes do this too.

Additionally, it's vital to be sensitive to the different kinds of emails seen in different cultures; depending on the profile of the user, an email address with certain numbers in it may be a good sign or a bad sign. For example, numbers that are considered lucky are often used in Chinese email addresses, and if the rest of the purchase story also suggests a Chinese shopper, this is a positive sign of a consistent legitimate story. But the same number does not have the same meaning in European countries and is far less likely to be part of a legitimate story there.

The same point can be made about changes made to a device's *user agent* (the string of characters that contains information about a device). This is a mine of valuable information for a fraud analyst, giving information about the operating system, what kind of device it is, which browser the user is employing, which languages the browser has, and so on. Sometimes there will be signs that the user is playing with their user agent. You might see an apparently different user agent profile coming from exactly the same IP several times over an hour. On the one hand, this is suspicious. On the other, these settings are easy to manipulate, and sometimes good users do this too—notably, developers, web designers, and marketing professionals trying out different settings to see how their product looks on different devices, browsers, and so on.

Social Engineering

As a deception technique, social engineering perfectly masks the identity of the fraudster. When it is achieved successfully, the fraudster becomes a puppeteer (i.e., puppet master, not the headless chrome node, although some fraudsters do favor it). The victim—being the puppet—waltzes through the checkout process with their own email, IP, device, and so on. It is only through strong behavioral analytics and/or a rich prior knowledge about the victim's habits that such an attack can be completely mitigated.

We discuss the impact of social engineering at length in Chapters 9 and 14. For now, we'll settle on boosting your motivation to tackle social engineering by calling attention to the FBI's latest Internet Crime Report, which names social engineering traits as the number one scheme in the United States in 2020 (Figure 1-1).

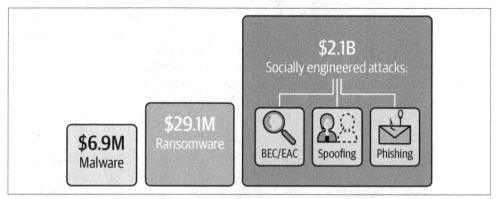

Figure 1-1. Visualization of total attack volume in 2020, as reported by the FBI in its IC3 report[2]

 It's important to analyze (and have your system analyze) every aspect of a user's online persona. The more information you have, the richer the picture you can build of that user. What a fraud analyst needs to remember, though, is that each of these details contributes to the picture—none of them alone is "good" or "bad." A good fraud analyst can develop both the legitimate and the fraudulent stories in their mind as they examine all the details, thinking of both good and bad reasons for the details to be as they are. Only once the picture is complete can the decision be made as to whether the identity behind the transaction is legitimate or not.

The Dark Web

Since we've already mentioned stolen data that can be used in impersonation and we're about to mention bots, this seems like a sensible point to talk about the dark web. Unlike the deep web, which is simply the unindexed internet (i.e., sites and pages you can't find with a search engine) and which includes lots of outdated pages, old websites, orphaned pages and images, and so on, the dark web represents online forums, marketplaces, and sites that are actively concealed from search engines, for anonymity. Typically, access is only possible through something like a Tor browser,

---

2 FBI Internet Crime Complaint Center, *2020 Internet Crime Report* (*https://oreil.ly/blsA7*), accessed March 4, 2022.

and many dark web sites have extra restrictions to make it more difficult to access unless you're in the know.

A lot of the online criminal ecosystem functions through the dark web—particularly through forums, where different attacks are discussed and planned and advice and bragging mix together, and marketplaces, where the tools of the trade are bartered. Some marketplaces specialize, while others are broader. For instance, one marketplace might only sell stolen consumer data, perhaps with a particular emphasis on payment information such as credit cards and PayPal accounts. Another might have a wealth of apps designed to make fraud easier and faster, such as apps that quickly change the details of your online persona (IP, language on the computer, time zone, etc.). Yet another might focus on illegal goods of various types. Some cover all of the above, and more.

We'll mention the dark web from time to time, generally in the context of how it enables certain fraudster attacks or techniques, and it's certainly an important factor in understanding the online criminal world. Some companies, and some vendors, have fraud fighters dedicated to spending time on the dark web in order to get advance notice of new techniques or tools and to try to get advance warnings of an attack being planned against their own business.

That said, it's also important to recognize that a lot of criminal chatter, planning, scamming, and even selling takes place on sites that are far more familiar to the average citizen, like social media sites and messaging apps. Telegram has become particularly popular with many fraudsters due to its higher-than-average levels of privacy, and Signal is sometimes used as well for the same reason. Refund fraud, which we talk about in Chapter 10, is a good example of how Telegram enables criminals and ordinary folks to interact for the profit of both (though to the detriment of the merchants they attack). Discord has also become a popular forum for gaming-focused fraudsters to congregate and run their schemes. Reddit is popular with fraudsters of all kinds, sharing tips, tricks, and boasts.

Fraud Rings/Linking

Fraud ring is the term used to describe multiple accounts or transactions that appear on the surface to be unrelated, but are actually part of a wider fraudulent pattern carried out by a single fraudster or a group of fraudsters working together and/or copycatting one another. The term *linking* is frequently used fairly synonymously with the term *fraud ring*, and you can assume in this book that when we use either term we're talking about the same thing.

Finding the details that point to a pattern indicating the presence of a fraud ring is valuable for fraud teams because you can then protect your ecosystem from future attacks of the same nature carried out by the same ring, or from further actions taken by accounts that are part of the ring but haven't yet done anything themselves that would get them blocked as fraudulent. *Linking* is so called because it finds the links that show similarity between entities. Once you've identified a strong pattern, you can see the pattern of the accounts or transactions that match it, and act accordingly.

When a fraud ring is revealed, most organizations favor short-term protection. For example, if a fraud ring originates from Ecuador, a bank may decide to route all cross-border activity in Ecuador for manual inspection for several months. An ecommerce retailer may even choose to decline all orders from a certain country or region for a while. This type of solution, besides being technologically easy to implement, relies on the common fraudster trait of "if it works, repeat it." Fraudsters typically produce the same type of fraud over and over again until they are interrupted.

However, it's important to note that for every fraud ring you've kept at bay, there's a more sophisticated version that has evolved from its predecessor. It's not a "solve and forget" sort of challenge. Your fraud prevention teams should also keep in mind that "surgical precision" in flagging fraud rings bears the inherent risk of overfitting (see Chapter 5 for fraud modeling best practices if you're not familiar with the term). As with other elements of fraud fighting, what your team needs to aim for is balance: between the risk and the likelihood of false positives, and between the fear of loss from fraud and the certainty of loss of good business if broad blocks are put in place.

Volatility

It's a truth universally acknowledged that fraud analysts shouldn't go to work expecting every day to be like the one before it. Fraud attacks have fashions like anything else, and are sensitive to different times of the year—mirroring the behaviors of legitimate shoppers—and of the shifts and events in your own business.

In addition, fraud fighters never know where a fraudster or a fraud ring will strike next; you might have a reassuringly consistent level of fraud attacks for a month, and then out of the blue get hit by a tsunami of brute-force attacks, whether human or bot generated. And the trouble is that the fraudster trait associated with volatility is a "rinse and repeat" mentality; the second they find a weakness in your ability to handle volatility, they'll double down and capitalize on it as long as the vulnerability is there. They may even tell their friends, gaining street cred for the tip and boosting their reputation, and opening the option of a mass attack where that can be effective.

If your system isn't set up appropriately, it may take a long time for you to notice the problem while you're dealing with a flood of customers during a busy period. That can lead to significant loss.

Your store may experience fluctuations every year from Valentine's Day traffic, Mother's Day and Father's Day traffic, back-to-school traffic, and year-end holiday traffic—which may itself begin or end earlier or later, depending on the year. This natural volatility comes with its own challenges for your models, but unfortunately on top of that, fraudsters will try to exploit it to the fullest as well.

Fraudsters know which items are popular at different times of the year and will target those, blending in with the rush of good customers. Similarly, if you're a business that holds flash sales, fraudsters will be as aware of that as all your legitimate users are, and they'll use the knowledge to their advantage. They may also mimic a real pattern of last-minute orders, or first-millisecond orders (as when customers try to hit the Buy button the second desirable tickets or goods go on limited sale), a tactic that's especially popular with fraudsters who act as ticket scalpers. Fraudsters also explore the possibilities of attacking at different times of the day; some boast of keeping track of customer behavior trends as reported in the news and by reports from companies that study these things so that they can leverage this knowledge to help them fly under the radar.

What is crucial from the fraud-fighting perspective is that your system is able to cope with all the variety that fraudsters can throw at it. Rules must be adjusted for different times of the year, machine learning systems must be able to scale quickly as necessary, and manual review teams must be prepared and ramped up for busy times of the year.

Sensitivity to fluctuations is important on both the fraud-fighting side (you want to stop fraudsters from attacking your site) and the customer experience side (you don't want to be so averse to risk that you add unnecessary friction, delay, or false positives for good customers).

Take simple *velocity*—when a single user tries to make several purchases in a short period of time. That might be a fraudster, capitalizing on their success or trying different points of attack or refusing to believe they've been caught and blocked (depending on the situation). Or it might be a good customer, returning for more items after having discussed it with a friend or family member and deciding they need something else, or a customer who is ordering in careful batches to avoid import taxes, or a customer who was blocked once, mistakenly, and is determinedly trying again. Once again, it's about the whole context—the identity, the story—and not the specific data points.

Relatedly, *bot attacks*, which occur when a fraudster uses an automated program to attack your site repeatedly, trying different data each time, can dramatically increase the number of transactions (and usually the number of attacks) your system has to handle in a short period of time. The same can be true of *brute-force attacks*, in which a human is likely behind a similar ramming effect. You may be a business that sees a nonfraudulent use case, for bots if not for brute-force attacks (it's hard to think of a good reason to try multiple attempts to hack into different accounts with stolen information). If you're in an industry where resellers are part of the ecosystem and you know they sometimes put great effort into getting the latest items, then bots are not out of the question when a hot new item is about to hit. How you react to that depends on your company's policy toward resellers, but from a fraud analytics perspective, what matters is that you know what's going on, and when it's the same people trying again.

Your team will need separate training sets for different models, whether you're using rules or machine learning or both. For instance, you'll need a training set that's sensitive to average volatility so that you can catch a fraud ring when it appears out of the blue one fine, ordinary day. But you'll also need a model that's more volatility agnostic, which would be a fit for Black Friday–Cyber Monday. This would need to be more forgiving of volatility, and your team would need to be more present to analyze and guide as necessary. In the same way, you would want to work with the chargeback team to develop a model that works for January and perhaps February, when the chargebacks come in after the holidays.

Fraud prevention is not a one-size-fits-all type of business. You—and your models—need to be able to adapt to different times of the year and different situations. Much of this can be prepared for, but it's also important to carry out continual assessments during volatile times in order to make changes as necessary on the fly. That's true even if your manual review team is overwhelmed by a flood of orders. Making time for bigger-picture analysis, even during busy periods, will take some of the weight off the manual reviewers and make sure your system is far more robust against the threats it faces.

Dramatic Volatility Becoming Normal

Your team also needs a plan for dealing with times when dramatic volatility becomes "the new normal." We're thinking of the COVID-19 pandemic as we write this, and we'll use that as an example to illustrate the point, but it doesn't take a pandemic to create this sort of challenging situation for the fraud team. It's important to have a way of handling it, whatever the cause. Learning from the COVID-19 period and what was done well on your team, and analyzing what could be done better on another occasion, is a good way to use the experience to strengthen your company and your team for the future.

During the pandemic, it didn't matter which vertical you were working in—your business was bound to see spikes at one time or another. If you were working in travel, your business would see a spike in refund requests and chargebacks when lockdowns were announced—but at the same time, you'd see explosions of bookings relating to people trying to get home before a lockdown kicked in. Then, when restrictions eased, you might see a flood of speculative bookings. If you were working in accommodation—hotels, hostels, apartment rentals—you'd have seen the same wave of cancellations, but then you'd have had to contend with a spike in domestic demand. If you were working in physical goods, you likely saw an overall spike, probably of dramatic proportions, but perhaps not in goods your business typically sells that many of during more ordinary times. And the spikes, along with the goods that were most popular, would have been influenced by the imposing of restrictions in addition to the time of year. And so on.

This kind of volatility is very difficult to prepare for from the machine learning/artificial intelligence perspective. Chapters 4 and 5 discuss this further, but in essence, the way these systems work is by looking for *anomalies*—they are trained on what "normal" looks like, based on the past, and then they can compare the present to that and notice when it doesn't match. But during the pandemic, erratic behavior became normal. Things looked volatile all the time. Chapter 3 covers the challenges of a crisis of this nature in greater detail, but here we'll mention the importance of having a plan in place for what to do about volatility specifically. Some tools will cope better than others—some forms of data enrichment, for instance, are unaffected by volatility, or may even be improved by an overall spike in user engagement online.

The team should be aware of which tools can be relied on more, at times when other parts of the system are struggling with extreme changes in user behavior. In the same way, you may want to develop a model that is designed for these situations, with the risk parameters and appetite different from your norms. You may need to lean heavily on manual reviews, and manual changes to rules, to protect your system while machine learning abilities can be trained to adjust to the new situation. You'll also need a plan—and a timeline—in place for that training exercise.

Card and Account Testing

Not all uses of a stolen card or hacked account are for fraudsters' immediate profit. It's common for fraudsters to test whether they'll be able to leverage a card or account by making a small purchase or taking a small step in the account, like adding a new address. If they're blocked right away (perhaps the card has been reported as stolen already), they'll give up and move on to the next one, having only spent a minute or two on the burnt one. If it's smooth sailing, they'll be willing to invest effort in setting up a richer profile to leverage the card or account for larger amounts.

The nature of card and account testing means fraudsters generally gravitate toward sites or apps that will have fewer defenses against their low-value attack, either because they're in an industry that has not traditionally invested in fraud prevention (such as nonprofit organizations) or because their goods are low value but must be delivered under time pressure (such as food delivery or low-value gift cards and other digital goods), which means the fraud team may not be able to invest much effort into small-ticket purchases. However, other kinds of sites also experience testing, sometimes as part of a fraudster's investigation to map out the typical purchase process and sometimes to build up a little bit of a legitimate-seeming profile on the site before attempting larger-scale fraud.

Keeping track of card and account testing is valuable for a fraud prevention team because, if identified, it can help to profile the fraudster or fraud ring behind the attempts, making them easier to identify in the future. Remember, it's not what, it's who. You may also be able to identify patterns between the timing or type of testing and larger monetization efforts.

Abuse Versus Fraud

The distinction between abuse and fraud is a tricky one, and there isn't widespread consensus among fraud prevention teams and the companies they protect about where to draw the line.

In general, *fraud* is a more professional affair, carried out mainly by actors who specialize in this form of crime. It's likely to include the impersonation or deception techniques we've discussed, and fraudulent attempts will often reflect knowledge—sometimes quite deep knowledge—of the site's products, processes, and vulnerabilities.

Where the gain involved is directly financial, *abuse* tends to be more the province of normal customers who want to get a bit more than they're entitled to by cheating. Sometimes this cheating goes so far as to become really fraudulent, taking it into the realm of *friendly fraud*, discussed in Chapters 2 and 3, and more deeply in Chapter 10. Consider programs set up to attract new customers, either directly or through referrals; sometimes credit with the store is offered as part of the incentive. Really motivated abusers can set up multiple accounts, cashing in on the offer for what is effectively cash. When they leverage this credit to buy items for free (at least as far as they're concerned) the business loses out, sometimes substantially.

In this and similar cases, whether or not these activities count as fraud and fall into your lap as a problem is up to how your company views them, and in many cases where they fall on the spectrum between a focus on stopping fraud and a focus on customer satisfaction. If the company prefers to optimize for customer experience, it may take many repeated instances of severe friendly fraud before it's willing to block a real customer. If it is risk averse, you may be charged with preventing friendly fraud—something that is almost impossible on the user's first try, unless you're collaborating directly with other merchants, preferably in your space, who may have seen their tricks before. Repeated offenses can stack up quickly, though, and it's important to be clear about your company's policy regarding when and how to deal with these abusers.

There's another kind of abuse that isn't quite so severe and which, unfortunately, may sometimes be carried out by your most enthusiastic customers. It's usually referred to as *promo abuse* (abuse of promotions). If your site is offering coupons, a discount on the first purchase, or a similar offer, customers who like your site or the products you offer may consider setting up a new account (or accounts) to take advantage of the offer multiple times. Or if you have a generous returns policy, customers may use an item and then return it. These activities aren't exactly fraud, they're…cheating. The industry generally refers to it as abuse.

Whether or not your fraud prevention team is responsible for catching this sort of activity is often a reflection of how fraudulent your company views these behaviors to be. Marketing or sales may request your help in protecting their coupon offer, so it's good to be prepared for the need, but it's unlikely to be a standard part of your responsibilities unless it becomes a real drain on the business. In that case, judicious friction can sometimes be enough to deter these abusers. When they go further and start using the sorts of tactics we might expect from a more professional fraudster—IP obfuscation, burner wallets, emails and phones, and so on—you can fall back on the defensive tactics you usually take against career fraudsters. Being allowed to use your skills in these cases depends on whether you can persuade your company that it's warranted. You need strong relationships with growth-driven departments to be able to give them the context they need to understand the loss, appreciate that it doesn't serve their real goals, and have your back when you try to stop it.

There are other forms of abuse, however, that do not lead to a direct financial benefit to the abuser and can be part of wider fraud attacks. Even if your team doesn't have formal responsibility for stopping them, you'll probably want to be tracking this sort of behavior because it can often help you to prevent fraud later down the line. It can also help you protect the business in wider terms, which is something you should make sure upper management is aware of and appreciates.

Account creation is a good example of this kind of abuse. A fake account might be part of straightforward coupon abuse—but it might well be the first step in aging an account that will, after some period of time, be used for fraudulent purposes.

Catching this sort of abuse is similar to identifying fraud; you'll want to look for patterns between the identity that's setting up the new accounts, or posting the reviews, and so forth, to show you that the same person is ultimately behind them all. If you can get a useful profile of this actor, you can use it to ensure that they don't succeed in more direct fraud later on. Beyond that, identifying these accounts is valuable because it means your business leaders won't have a mistaken view of its users or number of accounts, which could lead them to make problematic decisions based on bad data.

Content abuse, or review abuse, fits a similar pattern. Fake reviews can be from real customers trying to boost their profile or a friend's product or service, or they can be part of a wider fraud scheme. Fake reviews can make certain businesses, which are perhaps merely fronts, look legitimate. They can also help a fake account look more substantial. They pollute your ecosystem, undermining customers' trust in your site and its products or services.

Click Fraud

Click fraud is when someone repeatedly clicks on something, usually an ad, for no purpose other than the click—that is, they have no interest in what they get from the click. It's usually the province of *click farms*, where large groups of low-paid workers are employed to use different devices and SIM cards to surf sites and apps, looking like real users, and click on ads from time to time. Some will even set up accounts or use the service to add verisimilitude. When you factor in that these workers are paid something like $1 per 1,000 clicks, you can imagine the scale at which these operations work. Click farms can also be automated, increasing the speed and scale of the operation, although as with other bots, this can often be detected more easily because the pattern of the abusive behavior doesn't match typical human behavior; it may be much faster, with fewer breaks, and with more regularly spaced clicks or typed keys than a human would show, and so on. The newest bot programs are better at mimicking human behavior, however; the arms race continues.

Technically speaking, click fraud probably falls into the abuse category because it's not illegal, unlike the theft carried out by fraudsters. On the other hand, it also falls into a lot of the categories fraud fighters would be inclined to call fraudulent; click fraud causes direct financial loss to whoever is paying for the ads, it's carried out by cookie-cutter fraudsters (more on this in Chapter 2) using the sorts of masking techniques usually associated with fraudsters, and it occurs at enormous scale. Those businesses affected by it are likely to want to prevent it, in the same way others take steps to guard against other types of fraud.

Click fraud is carried out for three main purposes. The site with the ads might be owned by a fraudster, who gets paid per click by whomever is running the ads and thus wants to increase clicks as much as possible. Or one company will employ a click farm in order to drain the budget of a competitor. Or a firm will claim to be able to increase a company's social presence (likes, shares, etc.) or click-through rate, but instead of employing legitimate means will simply use a click farm.

Fraud analysts trying to prevent click fraud rely on much the same tool set as analysts in other fields: blocking bots, piercing proxies, identifying obfuscated IPs, connecting the dots between manipulated user agents, behavioral analysis, and so forth. For this reason, we'll rarely call it out as a separate use case, but we mention it here because of its delicate position between fraud and abuse, and we devote more in-depth coverage to it in Chapter 23.

Money Laundering and Compliance Violations

Money laundering is a natural concern for banks, fintechs, and other financial institutions, and in those contexts there are generally teams dedicated to stopping it—not to mention, of course, regulations and tools dedicated to its prevention.

Anti–money laundering (AML) work has been a concern of banks and financial institutions for many years, certainly, and as fintechs and cryptocurrencies have joined the financial ecosystem, battling money laundering has become an important part of fraud prevention in those organizations as well. In fact, the booming market for cryptocurrency has boosted money laundering efforts—and prevention work—everywhere, especially now that a number of banks allow customers to turn cryptocurrency into other forms of currency. Setting up new accounts for this purpose has become fairly commonplace, which has added urgency to the need to prevent money laundering in cases where the money is not legitimate. Since it is so difficult to tell where cryptocurrency is coming from, the emphasis must be placed on the person setting up the account. Is this a real identity? Is the person setting up the account the person that identity belongs to?

Fortunately, banks have had considerable experience authenticating identities of customers who want to set up new accounts, and most have streamlined processes in place to verify identity documents and ensure they are authentic and belong to the individual trying to set up the account. In-depth and often AI-assisted document validation has been joined in recent years by liveness checks and selfie authentication to ensure that the person involved really is present and not a photo or a deepfake (see Chapter 11 for a discussion of deepfakes in this context), even if the onboarding process is being done entirely online. There are, of course, also manual processes that help ensure that no tampering has been attempted with either the document or the photo, to support the work to prevent successful impersonation.

More difficult to identify are schemes that involve using real customers, with real identities and real accounts, who allow those accounts to be used by money laundering agents. In some countries, it is illegal to prevent a citizen from opening an account if their identification is in order and legitimate, even if your team suspects the motivation of the individual concerned. In these cases, fraud teams can only track these accounts and their activities particularly carefully once they are set up. This restriction puts considerable pressure on the fraud team and gives the criminals an added advantage.

It's worth noting in this context that the criminals involved with this sort of financial muling scheme are typically involved in large-scale organized crime, and are not small-time actors. On the one hand, this means they are well funded, organized, and difficult to catch, but on the other hand, it often means that finding one vulnerability will open up a whole scheme to a fraud team. Collaborating with other financial institutions can also bear fruit quite effectively, since organized crime usually attacks multiple targets.

Money laundering, and AML work, is commonly understood within the context of banks and financial institutions, and we discuss this in greater depth in Part V of the book. What is less often recognized is that money laundering is also possible in online marketplaces—and in some ways is much easier to do there because the defenses against it are less robust and marketplaces do not have the same compliance responsibilities as financial institutions. The principle is simple. In a marketplace, buyers and sellers interact. (We use the terms *buyer* and *seller* to refer equally to the actors involved in ride-sharing, apartment rentals, car rentals, or anything for which there may be an online marketplace.) A buyer will send money to a seller. The seller receives the money, which can be cleanly laundered in this way.

For example, let's say a fraudster wants to clean their ill-gotten gains and is using an online marketplace to do it. If one fraudster (or one fraud ring) acts as both buyer and seller, they can place orders for perfectly legitimate products or services, and pay for them. The payment, of course, goes back into their own pocket—as the seller. In their seller capacity, they have acquired the money completely legitimately…except for the small fact, of course, that the product or service was never sent or received. In general, the product or service is nonexistent, with the seller account existing purely for the purpose of laundering money.

In the same way, perhaps a criminal wants an easy, safe way to collect payment for illegal items online. They can set up an account as a seller on an online marketplace and use it to receive payment. Different items in the store can correspond to different illegal items they sell. For example, if they were selling drugs but pretending to sell apparel, heroin might correspond to a designer handbag while cocaine might be a cashmere sweater, and so on.

To be sure, there's a small fee to the marketplace, but it's really a very small amount when you consider the benefit the fraudster is reaping here: freshly laundered money, an easy and unsuspicious way for customers to pay for illegal items, and all so simple. They don't even need to impersonate anyone or use deception techniques.

We bring this up to show the relevance of money laundering to the wider online ecosystem as a concern, since fraud analysts are not always aware of this factor. More than that, though, we want to make a point that is fundamental to successful fraud prevention and one we will try to make more than once during the book.

We—the fraud fighters, the good guys, the ones on the side of the light—tend to think of the different aspects of both fraud and fraud prevention in terms of helpful categories that give us clarity and a framework. We distinguish account takeover (ATO) from stolen credit card fraud, and both from AML. We distinguish between trends in ecommerce, in marketplaces, and in banks. We consider different kinds of fraudsters. This book does this too—one look at the contents page will show you this. It's a useful way to understand the scope and levels of the challenges facing us, appreciate different aspects of different types of fraud and fraudsters, and see how they fit together. But fraudsters don't think that way. They are out to defraud your company, and any other company out there. They don't care about our categories, and if we're too wedded to those categories, they'll exploit them as vulnerabilities.

Fraudsters move smoothly between stolen cards, ATO, social engineering, money mules, shipping manipulation, and even money laundering, pulling out whichever trick might work in the circumstances in which they've found themselves. AML professionals and fraud fighters would both benefit from an awareness of each other's categories and concerns. (This is, in fact, the primary reason we combined both aspects in this book.)

Summary

This chapter sketched out definitions and distinctions relating to fraudster traits and types of attacks, which are some of the key building blocks of understanding fraudsters for the purposes of fraud prevention. We also emphasized the importance of the identity behind a transaction, something a fraud analyst should bear in mind even when focusing on the details such as IP or email analysis. The next chapter explores the other half of the picture: the different types of fraudsters, their skill sets, and their motivations.

## CHAPTER 2

Fraudster Archetypes

Getting to know you, getting to know all about you...
—Rodgers and Hammerstein[1]

If you were trying to pin down the main difference between an analyst who works extensively with data, and a data scientist, you'd likely touch on the concept of domain expertise as a key value that analysts bring to the table. Data is enormously valuable, but it won't give you the results you're looking for if you don't have a deep understanding of its context. This is particularly important with fraud fighting, since you're fighting an enemy who actively fights back, who changes their techniques and patterns to evade detection and tries to reverse engineer and thus avoid the traps you've created to catch them. You don't want to delay investigating a new attack type or new fraud ring until you have a lot of data about it. You want to catch the enemy before that.

Fraud domain experts are often the ones to provide the "secret sauce"—those impactful variables that really boost the performance of a fraud prediction model. If we had to narrow down that secret sauce, that domain expertise that every fraud analyst should hone to perfection, we'd say it ultimately comes down to *fraudster profiling*. A good analyst helps their team understand that not all fraudsters are created equal. Some of them are amateurs; others are pros. Some of them are native speakers of the language of their victims; others rely on auto translate. Some are very tech savvy, so trying to beat them with checkout barriers would be futile (e.g., if they're using brute-force bots, CAPTCHA would be counterproductive).

---

1 Richard Rodgers and Oscar Hammerstein, "Getting to Know You," in *The King and I*, music by Richard Rodgers, lyrics and book by Oscar Hammerstein (1951).

Therefore, it's essential to learn how to group fraud attacks based on the guesstimated profile of the human being behind them. It's worth mentioning that user profiling in general is a powerful analytics practice. Many departments seek to better understand their target audience by breaking down the group they're speaking to into approximate groups, each of which has specific characteristics, behaviors, and pain points. Discussing the groupings they're using with marketing, sales, or product teams on a regular basis can actually be a good way for fraud teams to get together with other departments and build lasting, mutually beneficial relationships. It can also help your team work to avoid false positives.

That said, a fraud team's key target audience is rather different. A fraud analyst is primarily focused on fraudsters. Breaking down the types of fraudsters your team is facing and which characteristics each is likely to show helps the team identify and block each type, working out which ones most regularly attack your business. This should contribute to your strategy for how to prevent fraud both now and in the future; may help you work out where to invest most of your research, resources, or new tools; and can even lead to insights about how and why your business is most vulnerable to fraud—and therefore what you could do to make yourself a less attractive target.

In this chapter, we cover some of the most common fraudster archetypes. We hope this will provide you with a useful mental framework for understanding the online criminals you work against. Some will be more or less relevant to you depending on your industry (e.g., banks are more likely to be targeted by psychological fraudsters than by amateur fraudsters), but there are no hard and fast rules for this, and we encourage you to be aware of all of these archetypes so that you can protect yourself against them should they attack you.

It is important to bear in mind, however, that we're discussing archetypes, not actual people, so don't expect every single fraudster to conform to type in every single way, every time. In particular, you need to remember that these days fraudsters rarely work alone, so you may often have more than one archetype in play as part of a large coordinated attack. Even amateur fraudsters work in groups or spend time on online forums learning from and sharing experiences with other fraudsters in training, and they benefit from guides and *burnt cards* (payment cards whose credit has almost expired) made available by more experienced fraudsters. Cookie-cutter–style fraudsters are only really a threat because they operate as cogs in a larger fraud machine, guided by managers and fueled with data stolen by other criminals.

Many fraudsters, particularly those for whom fraud is their profession, work as part of an organized crime initiative, with colleagues who specialize in areas such as botnets, phishing campaigns, or design (to create convincing fake websites and ads), to name just a few. Larger organizations boast their own financial and even HR officers. There are also consultants who can be hired. Online fraud is a big business.

Amateur Fraudster

The most common type of fraudster, and the easiest to spot, is the *amateur fraudster*. This is either someone who has only recently entered the world of online fraud or someone who engages in fraud as a side job or hobby rather than a profession. This can include young people attempting a bit of fraud without really understanding the criminal nature of the enterprise (it's something they've seen on TV) or attempting to steal items currently popular among their cohort but which are out of their price range.

The amateur approach, by nature, tends to be somewhat slapdash, and this type of fraudster will rarely think through all the implications of their online appearance. For example, they may not try to match their apparent IP to the victim's IP, or if they do, they may not remember to ensure that other details of their profile match that location. On the other hand, amateur fraudsters can come from anywhere, and if they're local to your country or area, they have the advantage of local knowledge; they can easily take advantage of specific holidays and are less likely to make mistakes in language, time zone, and so forth. This can make it easier for them to slip by if you're not careful.

Even fairly simple rules are usually enough to catch out this kind of fraudster, but make sure you actually have a mechanism in place to catch them, because if you don't, even an amateur fraudster can cost you money. This is particularly the case because amateurs share information and tips constantly on forums, social media, and messaging apps. The better the tips, the higher the street cred of the tipster, making this a good way to start building up a reputation online. So, if a tipster does find a vulnerability, you might be in for a flood of fraudsters coming your way.

Amateur fraudsters are also sometimes used as a cat's-paw by more sophisticated fraudsters. For instance, a fraudster carrying out targeted, carefully concealed, high-value attacks using a stolen credit card might also post this credit card on the dark web as a burnt card for free or at a very low cost. The resultant low-quality attacks using the card then conceal the work of the experienced actor. So, it's worth making sure your system is designed to correlate this sort of data, in case a flood of amateur fraud has a pattern that can lead you to more sophisticated and damaging fraud elsewhere.

The other interesting thing about this persona is that some amateurs go on to polish their method and master the finer points of fraud. If you've managed to get a really good lock on their location, IP, profile, and so on while they're new and careless, it'll be far easier to reidentify and stop them when they're more advanced. So, don't dismiss this category as irrelevant to your efforts; think of it as part of your long-term investment in fighting fraud.

Cookie-Cutter Fraudster

Cookie-cutter fraudsters are similar to workers in a sweatshop. Typically found in developing countries, they are poorly paid individuals who sit tightly packed in a small space and, using a laptop, run through lists of designated sites and stolen data given to them by their manager.

With this type of fraudster, you won't see the idiosyncratic aspects that make other fraudsters stand out to fraud teams. Effectively, these are brute-force attacks at scale, but with the human element built in, avoiding the traps that automated attacks can fall into because they're machines.

Each fraudster essentially follows a "script" of predefined actions each time and repeats the actions until they succeed, at which point control may be handed to a more experienced fraudster. So, as with amateur fraudsters, be sensitive to this pattern, which can help stop more sophisticated attacks as well. Often, apps or programs are used to automate actions like cleaning the browser or device, or swapping to an appropriate IP—which can make cookie-cutter fraudsters extremely fast at their jobs but also means you can look for signs of this happening to identify them.

It's these sorts of attempts that sometimes make fraud teams want to block entire regions or even countries, simply due to the sheer scale of the attacks involved. For this reason, it's important to retain perspective; the attacks are rarely that sophisticated, and the scale is due to the sweatshop setup and not the population of the surrounding area. Don't throw the baby out with the bathwater!

Gig Economy Fraudster

The gig economy has had a huge positive impact on transportation, food delivery, holiday rentals, and much more. What's less often appreciated is that a similar setup also now helps drive fraud schemes. As Identiq cofounder Uri Arad, formerly the head of analytics and research in PayPal's risk department, says in an online article on gig economy fraud:[2]

> Increasingly, people all over the world are willing to take on small jobs which ultimately contribute to a fraud scam. Placing orders, picking up packages, reshipping, setting up accounts, beating CAPTCHAs and other bot detections—any part of a fraud scheme which can be easily outsourced, doesn't require criminal expertise, and can be presented as a (typically low paying) job is now open to a dark gig economy.

---

2 Uri Arad, "Gig Economy Fraud: The Hidden Threat of the 2020 Holiday Season" (*https://oreil.ly/YQfFU*), About-Fraud.com, December 29, 2020.

The catch is, many of these people don't realize they're helping a fraud scheme or scam. All they did was answer an ad online for an innocent/legitimate-looking part-time or freelance job. For example, they think they're being paid to receive packages, wrap them very nicely, and resend them as gifts presented with an extra-special touch, or they think they're acting as the local branch of a business that largely operates overseas or out of state. Others have a sense that something fishy is going on but they close their eyes to the reality because the work is easy, and they need the job. Or they have a good idea of what's going on but they don't care, knowing that they're unlikely to get caught or punished for their role in the scam. These people still don't think of themselves as fraudsters, though. They're just doing gig work. It's just a job.

Some types of gig economy fraudsters are exceptions to this rule—in particular, those who lend their own bank accounts for money movement/money laundering in return for keeping some percentage of the proceeds (more on this in Chapter 20). They do typically know what's going on, and they may perhaps have greater knowledge of the larger criminal scheme being played out than other gig economy fraudsters. Though some of them are willfully blind to this and would be righteously horrified to have been tricked if the police did come knocking on their door one day.

This type of fraudster isn't new, and you probably know them as *mules* (i.e., they do the heavy lifting). But the number of mules, the ease with which they can be found and hired, and the scale at which they now operate have grown so significantly in recent years that "gig economy" now feels more appropriate as a term. As Arad says, "The pandemic has lifted [gig economy fraud] to a new scale. It's now global. Fraudsters can easily find helpers anywhere in the world, giving them far greater geographical scope to play with."[3] Bear this in mind when we discuss mules, particularly in Chapters 7, 8, and 20.

Psychological Fraudster

You might think of this type of fraudster as a social engineer. The *psychological fraudster* has a very different personality and mentality from those we've described so far. This is the fraudster who is behind victim-assisted fraud schemes and authorized push payment scams, in which victims are tricked out of their money by a plausible stranger with a lie tailored to their situation.

Think of elderly people scared into believing their bank account has been hacked and they have to set up a new one immediately—they just need to give the nice young person on the phone all their login and security information and it'll be taken care of right away. Authorized push payment fraud is a matter under much debate in the

---

3 Arad, "Gig Economy Fraud."

banking industry and beyond, and this is the fraudster archetype behind it. More on psychological fraudsters in the context of APP fraud can be found in Chapter 11.

Another common attack by a psychological fraudster is the romance scam, in which the fraudster pretends to be romantically interested in the victim and then persuades the victim to send them money—in the form of a gift card, cryptocurrency, or even direct bank transfer—to meet some imagined urgent need. More on the psychological fraudster in this kind of scheme can be found in Chapter 9.

In retail or travel, the fraudster might be offering a deal that's almost too good to be true, with some rational explanation for the great price—and a reason you need to decide immediately whether to take advantage of the supposed deal, rather than taking time to think about it. They may even have set up ads for similar products so that they know they're targeting the right audience.

Hitting your business or financial institution itself, the psychological fraudster might send phishing emails that purport to come from suppliers you actually use; the emails, the website URLs they contain, and the websites the URLs bring you to all look almost identical to those of your suppliers. Or they might pretend to be your own IT support, calling at a particularly busy time of day to fix an urgent problem— you just need to give them remote access to your computer and they'll take care of it all in the background. And so on.

In contrast to the archetypes described so far, this fraudster takes time to conduct their schemes. Often, considerable research goes into targeting an individual in a way that will leverage their particular weak points, and which uses supporting evidence to make them sound more legitimate.

These attacks are harder to catch but worth watching out for because the attacks are often carried out for high value. And unfortunately, the techniques are highly repeatable, so you'll want to catch any patterns before they become seriously problematic. Once you know what you're facing, you can invest in taking steps against them.

For instance, if it's victim-assisted fraud that's draining your business, you can put effort into knowing your customers and matching current behaviors to past typical behaviors—inconsistencies would raise a flag for you to investigate. If duplicates of your app or store are being used for nefarious purposes, get them shut down, communicate with your customers, and keep an eye out for repeats.

In general, combating psychological fraudsters requires fraud teams to take a wider view of their role, almost stepping into a trust and safety mindset. Collaboration with other departments may be necessary in blocking the vulnerabilities you unearth. It's worthwhile to keep this in mind, because when these criminals are successful, the results often flow downstream to become the fraud team's problem.

Product-Savvy Fraudster

Product-savvy fraudsters are among the few people in the world who actually bother to read the fine print of your user agreement. They know all the ins and outs of your returns and refunds policies. They sometimes even take the time to get to know your customer service reps individually, so as to most effectively target whoever picks up the phone.

In essence, the superpower of this fraudster is a deep working knowledge of your business, how you relate to customers, and your products. If you have different policies for different types of products, or different price ranges, they'll know.

Some product-savvy fraudsters focus on a specific business. For instance, there are those who specialize in defrauding a particular retailer, marketplace, or payments company. Others target a specific track common to many businesses; for example, there are fraudsters who master refund scams, others who are kings of coupon abuse, and yet others who are experts in leveraging stolen loyalty points.

Product-savvy fraudsters may target your call centers, your online chat, or the customer service you run by email. Many have preferences as to mode of communication, but equally many do not. Similarly, while many product-savvy fraudsters operate at a remove, some commit attacks using the Buy Online, Pick up In Store/Buy Online, Return In Store (BOPIS/BORIS) trends, picking up or returning goods themselves and in person, or using a mule.

This diversity of approach can lead fraud teams to treat each channel separately, as a different type of attack. This is a mistake. The value of seeing fraudsters according to their archetype is that you can see the patterns of attack across channels.

Fraudsters do not distinguish by channel, except when they're pinpointing vulnerabilities. They will exploit weaknesses wherever they find them. They are channel agnostic. You need a similarly neutral perspective when you take a big-picture view of who's targeting your business, and how.

Some fraud teams dismiss product-savvy fraudsters as a "customer support problem" or something which "can be solved with policies." While this is understandable, we feel it is shortsighted and can leave your business vulnerable.

First, as with the psychological fraudster, these are problems that ultimately impact the fraud prevention team. Even when there's no chargeback, fraud focusing on loyalty, coupons, and refunds causes significant loss to the business, and when questions are asked about fraud they'll typically be asked to the fraud team. Second, these fraudsters may work in more direct forms of theft as well, and if you can't make the connections, you'll find it harder to identify them accurately.

Third, the risk posed by a malicious actor who knows your business so well is simply too high to ignore. Many fraud-protection thought leaders in the industry will argue that it's always best to keep parts of your product, especially the authentication and verification side, in the dark. Noam Naveh, consultant and founder of FraudStrategy.com and chief analyst for Identiq, calls this "the detection paradox," referring to the fact that if you block fraud attacks too quickly, too successfully, you might be providing too many opportunities for fraudsters to study your system and practice—and we all know that practice makes perfect. In his article, "The Detection Paradox: How Not to Reveal Your Cards to Fraudsters" (*https://oreil.ly/02yX2*), Naveh offers several counterintelligence measures that should throw even product-savvy fraudsters off the scent. Figure 2-1 shows one example of a possible approach (Naveh mentions more in the article).

Figure 2-1. Example technique to avoid spilling the beans on your fraud detection[4]

---

4 Noam Naveh, "The Detection Paradox: How Not to Reveal Your Cards to Fraudsters" (*https://oreil.ly/02yX2*), *Fraud Strategy* (blog), December 12, 2018.

SQL injection attacks are a compelling example for product-savvy fraudsters, who do their homework and learn your system (they are also quite tech savvy, to make matters worse). In a particular example from the early 2000s, a fraudster was almost able to bring down a large retailer, after they had worked out that this retailer allowed all types of special characters in the "customer name" field. Well-acquainted with every aspect of the retailer's customer service practices, this fraudster also knew that when a customer support representative was asked to delete an account, the standard practice was for the rep to copy and paste the account details, including the "customer name" field, to a request form.

Putting these two things together, they signed up for a new account under a name that included the SQL `drop table` syntax command. (This fraudster may have been a fan of XKCD (*https://bobby-tables.com*).) The logic, of course, was that the details of the request form would likely be automatically copied and pasted into a backend script, which would execute the `drop table` command. Now, this attack is of the malicious cyber variety rather than fraud specifically, likely as part of a blackmail attempt. But with a slight alteration, a similar sort of attack could be carried out as part of a fraud campaign (we'll leave the details to your imagination, since we haven't seen this in the wild yet and don't want to give anyone any ideas). Fraud teams need to have this broader awareness as well, just in case.

Luckily, this attack was caught in time, thanks to a wonderfully paranoid developer who had already thought of this possibility and had guarded against it. But not every company has developers who think like criminals. The point of this story is that product-savvy fraudsters have the potential to cause real and lasting harm to your business. That's inherent in their in-depth knowledge of how you operate. So, watch out for them.

Tech-Savvy Fraudster

Tech-savvy fraudsters are behind the automated attacks that have been such a painful feature in fraud fighters' lives since the mid-2010s. We'll split this fraudster archetype into two categories based on the objective of the criminal concerned: the bot generator and the hacker.

Bot Generator

This fraudster is one with decent scripting abilities and is able to generate lots of reasonably convincing transactions on your system. Sometimes the only tell might be something like the fact that the emails are composed of random dictionary words or the addresses follow an alphabetical pattern. (It's automated; the content needs to come from *somewhere*.) Watch out for these attacks because they come fast and furious.

The fact that the attack is scripted means that playing a game of cat and mouse with this type of fraudster can escalate quickly (if they're clever enough they can fix their mistakes far faster than a manual fraudster, and once they've crafted the perfect attack they can do it instantly at scale).

It's best to find honeypot-based defenses against this fraudster so that they are initially drawn in, rather than instantly bouncing off to look for alternative vulnerabilities; for example, instead of declining orders too soon, try to make the fraudster burn through their resources by asking for two-factor authentication (2FA). If your process takes too long and commands too many resources, they'll likely look for an easier target. It's all about return on investment (ROI).

 It can be tempting to assume that, because bots can generate a lot of volume in fraudulent orders, AI-based models are the best defense, as they're best able to keep up. This is a dangerous approach.

Keep in mind that any attempt to use machine learning when the training set is heavily tilted toward bots will result in wild overfitting. As a basic example, your model might learn that only payments made at 3 a.m. should be deemed fraudulent, simply because the tech-savvy fraudster wrote a script that submits bad orders every day at 3 a.m. If you train a model to tackle this attack, you'll be playing into the hands of the fraudster, who will simply make a small adjustment to their script and leave you with a model that needs lengthy retraining.

Don't think fraudsters don't plan that far ahead; they do. You can see discussions about exactly this kind of many-staged attack on fraudster forums. They're not just trying to defraud you; they're trying to outwit you. Don't play into their hands.

Hacker

This category reaches beyond a fraud team's standard parameters, but we think it's important for fraud analysts to bear it in mind—and not only because an appreciation of the bigger picture is useful. Sometimes the consequences of their work will affect your job as well.

In the hacker category, we're including offenders whose aim is to access and, in some cases, take over your servers. Some of them hope to blackmail you or force you to pay a ransomware fee for the recovery of your data. Others aim to collect a bounty from a competitor who would benefit from a distributed denial-of-service (DDoS) attack on your operation. (It's not a nice thought, but it happens.) Many of them aim to obtain your own customers' personal identifiable information (PII), which they then sell to the highest bidder.

Certainly, these hackers are mostly the concern of your chief information security officer (CISO), and these types of attacks, while extremely serious, do not fall under a fraud team's remit. What is relevant to a fraud team, however, is that sometimes these attacks will include an influx of fake transactions, which might blind your volatility-based or velocity-based fraud detection models/heuristics. This is why preparing for hacker attacks should not be just a CISO's job. A fraud analyst's responsibility here does not end with good online security hygiene and practices, making sure not to fall for phishing scams or click on dubious links. It should also be your responsibility as a fraud manager to prepare for malware-induced spikes in traffic, which will otherwise throw off your detection processes.

Organized Crime Fraudster

Organized crime fraud is an international affair, and such organizations may be based in any country in the world—or, indeed, in several. Simply put, fraud has become an appealing way for people with either few good options or a love of the illicit (or both) to ensure a good and reliable income.

The difficulty of pursuing crime across borders, the "fuzziness" over legal jurisdiction for online crimes, and the relatively low amounts of money often involved in specific instances of crime all combine to make online fraud a fairly "safe" industry for criminals. Moreover, certain types of fraud, such as adtech fraud, remain in a gray area, where it is not yet universally agreed what is criminal and what is not. Similarly, bear in mind that initial coin offering (ICO) scams were legal until 2018.

The law is always far behind technology, and fraud is no exception. Fraudsters, for whom "I don't care about the law" is practically in their job description, have a natural advantage over companies that take care to adhere to regulations. Their creativity has no boundaries. Within this context, it's no wonder that some fraudster operations have become more and more institutionalized.

Some common forms of organized fintech fraud are mafia operations trafficking PII, forcing or paying shell companies/money mules to open bank accounts in order to launder dirty funds by buying crypto or precious metals, or to make peer-to-peer (P2P) payments for made-up services, and so on and so forth. These groups are of most relevance to banking and anti–money laundering (AML) fraud fighters, but they may also be seen attacking ecommerce or marketplaces.

Distinction Between Organized Crime and Cookie-Cutter Fraudsters

In our categorization, we are distinguishing between organized crime fraud setups and cookie-cutter sweatshops, even though the latter are often a part of the former—an early stage in the lifecycle of a wider organization. For fraud analysts, however, the distinction is important, because they work differently and the identification process is necessarily different as well.

In particular, note that organized crime operations tend to be well funded, and therefore can afford top-notch tech. For example, the virtual private network (VPN) or hosting services they use can be easily and automatically matched to the location of the stolen credit card being leveraged. Of course, that can become a weakness for them if you become able to spot telltale signs that that's happening.

Similarly, these groups can afford to operate at scale, which can also affect their impact. Adtech fraud fighters, for instance, need to bear this in mind when analyzing click farm fraud, and fraud analysts more generally should consider it when balancing the risks of SIM farms.

Small But Organized Crime

So-called "small but organized crime" also deserves a mention here. This type of fraud is less well funded, though generally meticulously planned and quite well staffed. Examples here would be work-from-home schemes, where two to six mules are (often unwittingly) commanded by a single arch fraudster. Travel agencies fit the same pattern, with agents often unaware that the spreadsheet of customer details they're converting into flight ticket orders is using stolen cards. SIM farms and click farms may also fall into this category when they operate on a smaller scale. Here the reason behind the scam is important: for instance, is the click farm being used to monetize incentivized browsing, or to sustain fake social media profiles that will be used to fuel fake news?

Fraud analysts are more likely to be able to spot the patterns here, since smaller groups like this often have a set way of working; this is particularly necessary for the manager when mules are unaware of what they're really doing. You need to be able to spot patterns even when multiple individuals are involved. For example, trying to identify the same obfuscated IP won't help you, but being able to identify a set pattern of actions or movements will.

Friendly Fraudster

You'll see that *friendly fraudsters* are not a primary focus in this book, except in areas where they're specifically relevant, such as here, in Chapter 3 where we discuss crises, and in Chapter 10 where we discuss friendly fraud and refund fraud. That's certainly not because there isn't enough to say about friendly fraud; we could write an entire book on this topic alone.

Rather, it's because, to an extent, friendly fraudsters don't fit the model we're discussing here. First, a friendly fraudster is typically someone using their own genuine identity, credit card, and so forth who then submits a chargeback claiming fraud, rather than honestly paying for the goods. Some do move to more sophisticated (though still basic) levels, setting up throwaway electronic payment accounts and using proxies and so forth, and we would classify them as shifting to the amateur category.

Second, and relatedly, the methods you use to combat other kinds of fraud won't work against friendly fraud. It won't help you to uncover their real identity and confirm that their name, address, email, and phone number belong together. Even if you have what seems to be cast-iron proof that this real person made the purchase, you may not be able to fight the chargeback; the customer is always right.

Third, not all fraud teams are responsible for fighting friendly fraud. It may be classified as a service, customer support, or chargeback problem. You might be asked to provide evidence so that your business can contest the chargeback, but you may not be expected to prevent these instances. It is, after all, very difficult to know the intention of a real buyer at the time of the transaction.

That said, all fraud chargebacks count toward your company's fraud chargeback limit, so you may be looking for ways to stop this kind of fraud. Working with other retailers or financial organizations, especially in your own industry, may be the most effective way to identify friendly fraudsters—at least before they've run up many chargebacks on your site, since this is often a repeat offense across multiple sites. We're not suggesting sharing personal user information in the form of lists, which may have data privacy implications, particularly in the European Union, but you can employ a form of privacy enhancing technology as part of the collaborative effort to ensure that no personal data is shared (more on this, sometimes called *providerless* technology, in Chapter 4).

Despite all this, we are including friendly fraudsters in this chapter, and elsewhere in the book where they are relevant, because of the time in which we're writing this book. Friendly fraud has been on the scene for over a decade, and has been steadily growing as a concern during that time. But 2020–2021 saw a notable increase as a result of the economic situation and general uncertainty and stress.

The friendly fraudster is sometimes genuinely mistaken, which can happen, especially when people are under stress. Or they may be acting on the infamous buyer's remorse, a trend that increases in times of crisis because people find they have less money than they had anticipated. They may be reacting angrily to receiving the wrong product or receiving the goods late and incorrectly filing a fraud claim rather than a service chargeback because that's a more reliable way to get the refund, or they may have intended to try to get the item for free all along because they want it to cheer themselves up by buying it but can't afford to pay for it—tactics which also increase in frequency during times of crisis. Underlying all this is a sense of betrayal, since people are suddenly unable to afford or receive things they had come to expect as a normal part of their lives, and this makes them less considerate about the difference between service and fraud chargebacks or what it might mean to a retailer.

The economic and psychological factors behind this trend are likely to be with us for some time, and it's for this reason that we are including friendly fraudsters as a category here, with some discussion of the factors influencing friendly fraudsters' actions and decisions. Consumers who learned how easy it is to file a fraud charge-back as a result of the COVID-19 pandemic may be more likely to do so again, even after the crisis has passed.

Different businesses have different levels of tolerance for this behavior, with policies to match, and some differentiate between cases in which this behavior was planned and becomes repetitive and cases in which a buyer originally had legitimate intentions but acts on buyer's remorse when the bill comes through. In some ways, this is more a matter for policy than for fraud analysis, but at a time when friendly fraud has grown significantly and is likely to stay with us for some time to come, it's worth working with your policy decision-makers and ensuring that you're part of that loop, because the more serious this trend becomes, the more likely it is to affect your department.

Pop Quiz

Do you think the payments shown in Table 2-1 were the work of a single bot, a random group of amateurs, or an organized operation of cookie-cutter fraudsters?

Table 2-1. Orders placed by four allegedly different customers, using a single IP

Name on card	Time of day (EST)	Email	IP	Amount in USD
Shoshana Maraney	01:12:03	shomar1993@gmail.com	102.129.249.120	30
Gilit Saporta	02:26:03	gilsap83@gmail.com	102.129.249.120	30
Amelia Blevins	09:05:59	ameblev23@gmail.com	102.129.249.120	30
Winnie T. Pooh	16:45:14	winpoo1926@gmail.com	102.129.249.120	30

The honest answer is, obviously, that one would be reluctant to make a decision solely based on five pieces of data, and we strongly recommend that you work off far more than this! That said, the very simplification of this example highlights something important: even with this limited data set, you probably have an intuition about the set of payments.

This is a very valuable ability that should not be overlooked, because it's based on your substantial experience with past transactions and interactions, both fraudulent and legitimate. Sometimes, when you have only seconds to make a decision, this intuition can be one of the most valuable tools you have. More than that, as Alon Shemesh, cofounder of Difftone, cofounder of Forter, and veteran analytics leader at

Fraud Sciences and PayPal, pointed out, "Good analyst intuition will tell you not only which questions to ask, but even before that, when there's a question that needs to be asked in the first place."

Here are a couple of pointers to help when you want to test your intuition. These are relevant even when you have far more data to work with.

First, repetition in IP, amount, and email domain naturally points to a single fraudulent entity behind all the purchases. The IP is most likely a proxy (or VPN, or manipulated traffic, etc.). This points us to the fraudster profiles that like to work en masse: cookie cutter, organized crime, and tech savvy.

Second, you can break down this apparent identity into data points and analyze each one to work out which persona its characteristics suggest. For example, to narrow it down even further, consider the comparison in Table 2-2.

Table 2-2. Analyzing which archetypes match the data points in Table 2-1

	Cookie cutter (low-paying jobs for up to ~10 mules/juniors guided by a single fraudster, usually in developing nations)	Organized crime (operations of dozens of employees, usually well funded, not just in developing nations)	Tech-savvy fraud (scripted bot, designed to automatically complete checkout/sign-up)
IP 102.129.249.120: US IP, free proxy	The low-grade proxy matches the low budget of most cookie-cutter–style operations.		
Amount: $30	The low ticket price might match the low expectations of some cookie-cutter–style operations.		The low ticket price might match the tech-savvy fraudster, since it's fairly easy for this fraudster to generate a large volume of small orders. This fraudster may also imagine that such ticket orders might be more likely to pass unexamined.
Winnie T. Pooh		A fake name might match the trait of shell identities, which is typical for organized crime.	A fake name might match the trait of beta testing, which many tech-savvy fraudsters attempt before they launch a final script.
Gmail	A Gmail account might match the sweatshop style of working; one member of the group may be told to create such accounts, or it might simply be part of a "script" they all follow.		Gmail accounts are somewhat harder to create automatically, so they are less suitable for most script attacks. However, the emails might be bought/scraped from an external source.

Partially repetitive email pattern	The email usernames show a pattern of three letters of first name + last name + digits. Some of the emails show an alleged year of birth, though using an inconsistent date format. This partial consistency suggests that different people submitted the orders, and that while they were instructed to stick to a uniform format, they weren't professional enough to do so properly.
Time frames	The orders are mostly submitted during off-hours for the United States, which might indicate that they are coming from elsewhere.
Pace	The orders are submitted in changing intervals, which is usually not the work of a script.

Summary

In this chapter, we explored the distinctions between different fraudster archetypes, and discussed how to use this framework in practical fraud identification and prevention as well as within a wider framework of understanding the fraudster fraternity and the threat they pose to businesses. In the next chapter, we'll look at the characteristics that all of these archetypes have in common: a results-driven mindset; a creative willingness to exploit any weakness, including crises; and a holistic view of the customer journey when it comes to attacking it.

## CHAPTER 3

Fraud Analysis Fundamentals

Look for the bare necessities...
—Terry Gilkyson[1]

In this chapter, we'll cover the fundamentals of fraud analysis, elements that are relevant to every fraud-fighting team, regardless of industry. These topics—foremost among them thinking like a fraudster, but including others such as the distinction between account and transaction in fraud prevention, practical anomaly detection, and crisis planning and response—are important to understand when combating a wide variety of fraud types, and also to bear in mind when developing a wider strategy of fraud prevention for your organization.

We won't be able to mention all of these everywhere they're relevant throughout the rest of the book. They're relevant to practically *everything* in the book. They're the fundamentals you need to keep in mind while reading, and the context in which everything else takes place.

Thinking Like a Fraudster

The most fundamental skill for a fraud analyst is thinking like a fraudster. The technical aspects of fraud detection and analysis are vital, but real success requires the right mindset: the mindset of a fraudster.

Fraudsters look for vulnerabilities everywhere and attack where they see a way in. You can't rely on them behaving as they have done until now; their whole MO is based on trying to trick your business. Predicting fraud is not like predicting most

---

1 Terry Gilkyson, "The Bare Necessities," in *The Jungle Book*, directed by Wolfgang Reitherman (Walt Disney Productions, 1967).

trends, because fraudsters fight back. To outthink them, both day to day and when you're working on high-level strategy, you must know how they think.

A Professional Approach to Fraud

Crucially, fraudsters focus on return on investment (ROI). Their aim is to gain as much as possible (i.e., to steal as much as possible) with as little effort as possible. These are not dramatic, state-sponsored bad actors or malicious hackers from films. These are professional thieves. They're more like the head of a small business, whose eye is always on the business's key performance indicators (KPIs), than like anything you've seen in a film.

This trait lies behind many of the things about fraudsters we take for granted. For example, if one target hardens against their attacks, they move to an easier one, because otherwise, they're putting in greater effort for potentially reduced returns. Similarly, they often attack particularly popular items, because they're harder to catch among the flood of legitimate interested buyers and because the items themselves will be easy to resell for a good price.

It's important to understand the mindset behind these trends because in that way, you can fully understand the evolution of the techniques and tools used for fraud. Some years ago, fraudsters were most likely to try to get the highest priced items on a site. When rules were put in place to guard against this trend, they moved to ordering multiples or combinations, or to placing many separate orders for cheaper goods. When fraud protection systems started to flag automated form fills, fraudsters began adding random breaks into the "typing" to make the automation look more human. For them, it's all about finding the optimal balance between the easiest, fastest method and the largest payoff.

Similarly, internalizing this mindset will enable you to move between industries in your career and apply all the things you've learned until now, even though they're given different expression in different industries. Fraudsters attacking clothing sites will often pretend to need bulk orders for groups, clubs, and so forth—a perfectly normal use case in this context. The same fraudster on an electronics site will cleverly pair a laptop with a keyboard, mouse, and headphone because they know this looks normal in that context. You'll know it's all the same move. In the same way, the same fraudster will attempt authorized push payment fraud against a bank and victim-assisted fraud against an online gift card store. And you can think of new ways those same trends might play out, and prepare for them.

Treat Categories with Caution

It's also important to remember that while we will be breaking types of fraud attack, obfuscation techniques, and so forth into categories for convenience and clarity, fraudsters don't think like this. For instance, fraudsters do often specialize in a particular industry; this is down to ROI again. Specialization maximizes the value of the research they do into which products can be stolen most easily, how to best leverage the results of the thefts, and so on.

However, fraudsters don't limit themselves; one report found that 86% of fraudsters commit fraud in more than one industry.[2] They need another arrow in their quiver for when the industry they specialize in is going through a slow time or they've made it too hot to hold them for a while, having attacked the same few sites so often and with such determination that each site has put measures in place specifically designed to catch and stop them.

This comes down to ROI again; a fraudster who has taken time to perfect a particular attack might find that the ecommerce sites they try it against have all learned how to block it. But the same might not be true of banking websites. So, they'll try it there to get the most out of the technique before they have to invest in revising it.

It's the same for fraud attack types. We'll distinguish between account takeover (ATO) and transaction fraud, and your department probably does too—but fraudsters don't. The same report found that 92% of ATO fraudsters commit another type of fraud as well.[3] For a fraudster, it's about the result, not how they get there. Taking over an account is one way to trick a site into letting you use someone else's details to make a purchase. Stealing and using loyalty points and using stolen credit card info might seem very different, but to a fraudster they're very similar: they're using something that doesn't belong to them to steal something they can monetize.

The tricky thing is that for fraud teams, catching ATOs, spotting stolen credit card fraud, and protecting loyalty points requires different methods. In some organizations, each responsibility is owned by a different team. But if you don't bear in mind that for fraudsters these are all different moves in the same game, your fraud prevention strategy will fail to combat the mindset of the enemy.

Account Versus Transaction

One division that is often employed in fraud detection circles is that between analyzing and decisioning accounts, and analyzing and decisioning transactions. It's a practical distinction, because it reflects the differences between two very different types of online interaction from the consumer side. Transactions can be carried out as guests on a site, without an account, and are primarily about payment. On the other hand, there are many things that can be done with an account (adding details, resetting passwords, using loyalty points, storing up coupons, etc.) that are not directly connected to making a transaction.

---

2 Sift, *Fraud Aftershock Index* (*https://oreil.ly/jTgxj*), accessed March 4, 2022.

3 *Fraud Aftershock Index.*

The harm a fraudster can cause by attacking an account and attacking the point of transaction is different, too. Transaction is primarily a financial risk; get it wrong, and you'll get a chargeback. Account liability is related to the trust of the customer, their loyalty to your brand, and the overall trustworthiness of your ecosystem (since the more fake or ATOed accounts you have, the weaker and less trustworthy your ecosystem becomes). This reflects a fundamental difference in the question you're asking in each case. With accounts, you're asking: Is the person behind the identity the person it belongs to? With transactions, you're really asking: Is this payment legitimate?

For all of these reasons, in many larger companies different teams are responsible for account protection and transaction protection. There is, however, an increasing tendency to place these teams under the same leader or executive, working as part of a wider trust and safety team or risk management team. The increased mutual learning and cooperation this encourages is very valuable, because the work on accounts and on transactions can be mutually beneficial, and we recommend ensuring a similar level of collaboration even if your internal structure means the teams don't work together.

Account protection should be informed by transaction knowledge and decisioning; if an ATO was so ingenious that it slipped through until checkout, then at checkout, when more information is provided, you need to act at once to protect the account, as well as decline the transaction. On the other hand, your transaction protection will be far more effective if it benefits from the deep understanding of users and their identities that you get from their accounts.

As we said, for a fraudster these approaches are not that different. The same fraudster will happily carry out ATO and checkout-focused fraud on the same site, sometimes even on the same day. It just depends on the details they have and the different ways they have found to exploit vulnerabilities. So, if the ATO team identifies a fraud ring or a repeat fraudster, the transaction team needs to know what to look for in order to catch them too. Working in silos is dangerous because fraudsters spend a lot of time analyzing your fraud prevention efforts. Once they've identified a silo, they'll leverage it.

 In general, the analysis techniques we discuss in this book are relevant to both account and transaction protection, though there may be times when we emphasize one over the other, depending on which is the more dominant use case.

The Delicate Balance Between Blocking Fraud and Avoiding Friction

This delicate and continuous balancing act is one that is reflected through every part of a fraud team's role, and throughout every section of this book. We won't call it out in every section, since that would get rather repetitive, but we can't stress enough how important it is to keep it in mind.

Fintech strategist and serial entrepreneur Maya Har-Noy, who is currently vice president of Financial Strategy at Nuvei, puts this very neatly: "The way online business works, accepting some fraud risk is inevitable. If you want zero fraud, just don't sell online. You'll be totally safe, but your business will die. If you want to sell, you have to accept that you'll have some fraud."

Ten years ago, fraud prevention teams were measured on chargebacks: their job was simply to stop fraud. Businesses were, by and large, not fully aware of the impact the fraud department had on customer experience and related success and growth.

Now, that's no longer the case. Julie Fergerson, CEO of the Merchant Risk Council, explained this evolution:

> When online fraud became organized, it was initially like a flood—merchants were routinely dealing with chargebacks on a scale that would be unimaginable today, crushing chargeback rates that might get as high as 3%. Merchant fraud teams and vendors worked together to bring the situation under control, and once that more stable point was reached, with chargebacks on the sort of scale we know them today, fraud fighters could take a breath and begin to focus on friction and false positives. That's where a lot of the work and focus comes today.

That means there's pressure on fraud departments to prevent fraud and keep chargebacks low, as well as to minimize the impact of their work on good customers. This generally means two key areas of concentration: avoiding overt friction such as email verification or two-factor authentication (2FA), and avoiding false declines in which a legitimate customer is mistakenly rejected or blocked.

Ultimately, the answer to both challenges is the same: accuracy. The more accurate you can make your system, the more precisely it will avoid irritating good customers. In that sense, the solution to this problem is the same as the one for catching fraudsters: you want to be very good at distinguishing between good and bad users.

Profit Margins

When it comes to balancing the cost of fraud appropriately, you need to be thinking about profit margins. It's all very well and good to want to accept a higher cost of fraud so that you can prioritize the customer experience, but what can you actually afford? Effectively, how many fraudulent transactions can you afford while remaining profitable?

To understand this, you need to know how much you lose per fraudulent transaction. This varies considerably depending on the nature of your business. If you lose the full cost of the item plus shipping plus chargeback handling and any related fines, that's a high cost per fraudulent transaction. If you're in gaming or software, for instance, you may have minimal costs. Unless you're a reseller, in which case it depends on your licensing agreements...and so on. All of this must be weighed against your profit margins, which, again, vary enormously from business to business. As in so many areas of fraud prevention, you need to know your business inside and out to make the right call. Likely, you'll need to build strong relationships between your department and growth-focused departments such as sales, marketing, product, and so on so that both sides understand the trade-offs and their consequences and can make informed decisions with collective buy-in.

Here is a simple example to illustrate the point. Let's say you lose $100 on average on a single fraudulent transaction. However, for every fraudulent transaction, you see 100 other transactions, each worth $100. Assuming you have a 1% profit margin, you come out even in this case. So, you know how much incoming fraud you can afford to risk. Essentially, it's an ROI calculation.

Maintaining Dynamic Tension

Since perfect accuracy is more of a holy grail than a realistic goal, it's important to be clear about other tactics you can use as well. Friction should be used dynamically and applied judiciously in appropriate circumstances. False declines can be avoided using forms of positive validation to identify good customers. Where that doesn't succeed, have steps in place to analyze the cases where a customer tries a second or third time after a decline; is it a fraudster trying to trick your customer service department, or a legitimate customer who was misunderstood? Ongoing research into account activity and transactions, separate from the decision analysis you need in the moment, can also help identify false positives and ways to avoid them.

Tactics aside, the crucial point is that in every decision you make in your fraud team—whether it's about which transactions to approve, which tools to invest in, which rules to add to deal with new situations, or how to train or retrain a machine learning system—will include balancing between the need to stop fraud and the need to provide a great experience for good customers.

That dynamic tension is at the heart of what makes fraud prevention so challenging—and so fascinating. It's also an opportunity. The Merchant Risk Council's Julie Fergerson has many years of experience working with merchants across a variety of industries and helping fraud fighters from different organizations collaborate for their mutual benefit. This means she has gained a clear view of the evolution of how fraud and payments professionals are perceived within their companies. As Julie noted:

> Payments and fraud prevention professionals have a seat at the executive table now. There's a real understanding—which wasn't there even five years ago—that these elements are crucial to creating positive customer experiences and to the whole financial framework of the company. Ecommerce and online payments and interactions aren't a checkbox to show relevance anymore. They're essential to a modern business.

Fraud prevention professionals often need to educate other parts of the organization about the intricacies of their work, but the result is better interdepartmental collaboration and better results for both sales and fraud prevention.

The Psychological Cost

Finding the right balance between fraud and friction can be one of the most intricate, interesting, and engaging aspects of fraud prevention. However, because every decision comes with such an obvious financial cost attached, if it's the wrong decision, fraud teams—and especially manual reviewers, who are on the front lines deciding whether to approve or decline transactions—sometimes feel the tension getting to them.

It's important not to overlook this aspect of fraud fighting. On the contrary, it should be a factor in planning and strategy each fiscal quarter. Having a fantastic plan on paper won't help if it puts your team under so much pressure that some of them crack and burn out or quit. Fraud analysts often feel a deep sense of responsibility for protecting the company. They know their mistakes can be easily identified and brought home to them by upper managers who may not really understand what their role entails, and they frequently work under pressure to keep review times down. They're also constantly juggling between the need to block fraud and the need to maintain high approvals. A strong sense of camaraderie among the team can be very valuable, and overt signs of appreciation from the company for their hard work (especially in times of high stress) can also be hugely impactful.

Julia Zuno, director of fraud at Newegg, noted that one of her greatest priorities as a manager is to find ways to take the burden off the members of her fraud teams:

> When things get stressful, as they do during particularly busy times like sales or holiday periods, they can get *very* stressful—*fast*. That means overtime, worry, and way too many energy drinks. There are things managers can do to mitigate all this. It's important to help your team keep their perspective, and just as important to make sure they know you have their back. You need the right policies in place, thought through sensibly during times when you have the leisure to dive into strategy. You need to continuously educate upper management about the issues involved. And you need to provide your fraud fighters with all the tools they need to do a good job.

A lot of the mitigation strategies Julia suggests represent investment that needs to come all year long. During particularly stressful periods, though, fraud managers need to be especially sensitive to the psychological impact of this high-pressure job. As Julia said, "In the moment, sometimes you need to be a counselor as well as a manager. And that's part of the job."

Tiers of Trust

When it comes to friction, it's important to flag the concept of dynamic friction. Not all levels of trust are equal, so your friction options shouldn't be either.

Aamir Ali, formerly with YouTube and now the lead product manager of trust and safety at Zoom, noted:

> It's really a question of trust tiers. You might think of transactions as binary—approve or decline. But risk is a spectrum, and friction can reflect that. Imagine a new user is signing up for an account. If you're very confident in this customer, based on your signals and information you have, you can make sure they have a great experience right away and give them access to every service and option on your platform. If you're slightly suspicious, you can maybe give them restricted access, and monitor them a little, and then decide. If you're more suspicious, or just need more information, you can add judicious friction. There's a whole range, from CAPTCHAs to email verification to SMS verification to phoning them up to making small deposits into an account. Financial institutions can even request documentation. You need to match your friction steps to the trust tier in which the user belongs.

3-D Secure

Within the context of the balance between fraud prevention and friction, it makes sense to mention 3-D Secure (3DS), which consumers often know best through its application by the card networks in forms such as Verified by Visa and Mastercard's SecureCode.

3DS inherently involves friction; that is, interrupting the purchase to ask the customer to prove they are who they say they are by providing something like a password, dynamic code, or biometric authentication.

For this reason, its first incarnation, 3DS1, which demanded a fairly complex password, remained unpopular except in the UK, with most non-UK merchants eschewing the option because of the high dropout rate it caused in purchases; customers (outside the UK, for some reason) simply weren't willing to take the extra step.

3DS became far more relevant with the advent of 3DS2, which included biometric authentication options and the sort of 2FA consumers have become accustomed to in recent years. PSD 2, the European regulation for electronic payment services, also drew attention to 3DS as an option, since it is the most obvious way to fulfill the Strong Customer Authentication (SCA) requirement. However, merchant adoption

---

has been bumpy, and once again the question of balancing friction with fraud prevention has been raised and debated.

The Merchant Risk Council has been actively involved in negotiations with the relevant parties to ensure that the authorities involved understand the real impact on merchants, and that merchant fraud prevention teams, in turn, are aware of what's involved from their side. It is likely that the process of finding a procedure that both provides strong customer authentication and does not put undue pressure on merchants and fraud teams will be one that continues at the pace of government for a long time to come. You can follow updates on this issue on the MRC Advocacy page (*https://oreil.ly/xtbAn*).

Anomaly Detection

Generally, one can argue that the bread and butter of most analysts and data scientists out there is detecting abnormal data trends. The realm of fraud analytics does not escape this reality, albeit with somewhat unique challenges. We'll state the obvious and say that every risk/fraud team should vigilantly monitor the traffic trends of their product in order to spot and react to anomalies as soon as possible.

It is only natural (and wonderful) that there are ample resources online for visualizing and monitoring traffic trends in your system. You will probably be working with a business intelligence (BI) dashboard or tailoring open source Python scripts to plot your data.

 Pandas and the Matplotlib.pyplot countplot can be helpful; see, for example, "Customize Dates on Time Series Plots in Python Using Matplotlib" (*https://oreil.ly/2phzT*) from Earth Lab.

In a perfect world, anomalies in traffic (e.g., a spike in incoming orders to an ecommerce retailer) would quickly be identified and analyzed in order to establish whether they are a result of a fraud attack or a blessed increase in sales. Sadly, our imperfect world does not usually grant us the comfort of easy-to-explain anomalies. Two major factors make it difficult to tie traffic anomalies to fraud attacks:

- Most fraud attacks are only discovered, or at least confirmed, due to victim complaints (chargebacks, customer disputes, etc.). Victim complaints take their time to come in, usually arriving several weeks or months after the occurrence. If the victim hasn't noticed the false charge, they never arrive. This means anomaly detection can never truly provide us with the full picture of a fraud attack. At best, it will merely highlight the subset of traffic where we should start our deep-dive fraud investigation.

- Despite the fact that fraud attacks can be very dramatic financially for ecommerce retailers who end up paying for the cost of stolen goods, their share of the total traffic volume rarely reaches double digits. It is common to hear ecommerce retailers in high-risk verticals discussing incoming fraud rates of around 2% (e.g., see "What Does eCommerce Fraud Really Cost Your Business?" (*https://oreil.ly/6nCp3*) by Rafael Lourenco). It's great that fraud rates don't go wild; otherwise, ecommerce wouldn't be able to survive. However, this reality makes fraud data sets imbalanced; that is, usually there just wouldn't be enough fraud cases to "move the needle" and teach you that a fraud ring is emerging, until it's way too late.

An exception to the factors just mentioned can be found in the exquisite field of adtech fraud analytics. Adtech fraud is almost an oasis of big data for anomaly detection–based analytics, because attacks in this field tend to grow to huge scale very quickly. For example, as shown in Figure 3-1, it is not unheard of to see attempted attacks in the field of connected TV (CTV) impressions (i.e., how many advertisements are being viewed on smart TVs, streaming devices, etc.) reaching even 40% of traffic volume (for the full analysis, see *Falsifying Devices: New Fraud Scheme Targets CTV* (*https://oreil.ly/HRLKD*) from DoubleVerify's Fraud Lab).

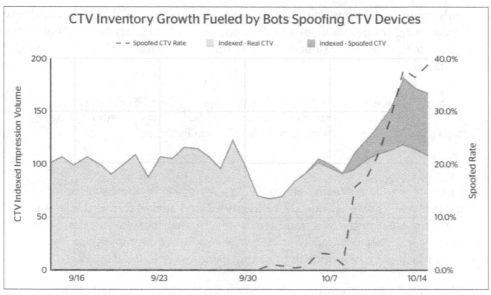

Figure 3-1. CTV traffic anomaly expressed as a sudden 40% increase[4]

4 DoubleVerify, *Falsifying Devices: New Fraud Scheme Targets CTV* (*https://oreil.ly/HRLKD*), November 15, 2018.

The traffic anomaly depicted in Figure 3-1 is a clear example of using a countplot for fraud detection. There could be no legitimate explanation for this explosion in CTV traffic. Indeed, once fraud researchers took a deep-dive approach into the traffic, they were able to classify 40% of the traffic measured for October 13–14 as fraud.

To recap, anomaly detection as a fraud analytics method should be used only as a "teaser" for triggering deep-dive investigations. If you're working in ecommerce or banking, it's worth taking anomalies with a grain of salt, realizing that the data needs to age in order for victim complaints to arrive and remembering that fraud rates are often too low to be noticeable. Having said that, anomalies can point you to where a fraud trend is emerging, or at least help you measure the impact of fraud after it's happened.

Practical Anomaly Detection: Density Case Study

A more granular form of considering anomalies is not to look for high-level trends, but rather, to spot abnormal behavior coming from specific users. The following case study assumes that for a certain bank, "normal" users would log in up to once a day. The query aims to spot users who demonstrate abnormal login metrics. First, the query generates the daily-login histogram shown in Table 3-1.

Table 3-1. Daily-login histogram

UserID	LoginDate	Count_Logins
1111	January 1	1
1111	January 2	2
2222	January 1	1
2222	January 2	30
2222	January 3	1

The `daily_logins_per_user_count` is as follows:

```
WITH daily_logins_per_user_count AS
(
    SELECT userID,
        LoginDate,
        count(*) AS count_logins
    FROM user_logins
    GROUP BY 1, 2
)
```

After producing the login histogram, we measure the following metrics in order to measure the level of density/velocity in user logins:

- Rate of normal volume days out of total number of active days for this user
- Rate of abnormal volume days out of total number of active days for this user

- Rate of abnormal volume days out of sum of logins, allowing a focus on users who consistently show abnormal figures versus users who spiked for only a short period of time

- Average login rate: simple division of logins out of all active days

```
SELECT userID,
  sum(CASE
      WHEN count_logins = 1 THEN 1
      ELSE 0
    END)/count(*) AS perc_of_1_logins_in_perc,
  sum(CASE
      WHEN count_logins >1 THEN 1
      ELSE 0 END)/count(*) AS perc_of_above_1_logins_in_perc,
  sum(CASE
      WHEN count_logins >1 THEN count_logins
      ELSE 0
    END)/sum(count_logins) AS perc_of_above_1_logins_sum(count_logins)
  sum(count_logins) total_login
FROM daily_logins_per_user_count
GROUP BY 1;
```

It's quite easy to add IP/cookie/device aggregations to this standard query in order to measure different aspects of abnormality and gain further analytics insights from this basic practice. Playing with the threshold of what's considered normal is also simple and effective, if we wish to look both for fraud-related abnormalities and for possible legitimate scenarios of highly engaged users.

Crises: Planning and Response

We wrote this book in 2021, during the COVID-19 pandemic, so the topic of what to do in preparation for and during a crisis was an issue on everyone's minds. Of course, part of the nature of crises is that they tend to require you to "expect the unexpected"; if you'd known it was coming, you'd have been well prepared and your team likely wouldn't have been in crisis mode.

However, there are certain lessons you can draw from the pandemic to help prepare your team and your business for future crises. This exercise, while outside the normal run of daily duties, is well worth engaging in at least once a year because whatever else might vary from crisis to crisis, there is one thing you can be sure about: it will put new pressure on your fraud prevention team.

Eighty percent of Certified Fraud Examiners say fraud levels rise in times of economic distress, a trend many fraud analysts saw firsthand during the pandemic.[5] At the same

---

5 Bruce Dorris, "Coronavirus Pandemic Is a Perfect Storm for Fraud" (*https://oreil.ly/0skvr*), Association of Certified Fraud Examiners, press release, March 31, 2020.

time, the Ponemon Institute found that organizations' ability to protect themselves against fraud fell during the pandemic. Prior to COVID-19, according to one report, 45% of respondents rated their fraud prevention effectiveness as high or very high, whereas just over a year later, only 34% rated themselves that way.[6] Crisis planning will help your fraud team stay on top of things when it happens, so think of it (and explain the very real need for it to management) as similar to penetration testing or business continuity planning. If the worst happens, the impact on the business can be just as bad.

Economic Stress Affects Consumers' Situations—and Decisions

Whatever kind of crisis you're facing, it's likely that it places new financial stress on some or most of your users. This inevitably impacts the landscape in which fraud prevention professionals are working.

When more people are unemployed, the pool of potential mules on which fraudsters can draw widens. People who are frightened about remaining unemployed are less likely to look into the fine print of their job and more likely to close their eyes to anything that ought to alert them that they're being used as part of a criminal enterprise. During the COVID-19 crisis, this was notable: criminal organizations started scaling up their muling operations, expanding into new areas and even new countries. It wasn't even restricted to drop shipping. Mules became a way to outsource elements of social engineering, as fraudsters mined their local knowledge. It meant easy tailoring for geographies, cultures, and languages. Even countries that previously had low levels of online fraud were affected now that mules could be found almost everywhere.

Of course, some people were responding to the COVID-19 crisis by setting up legitimate businesses, which sometimes involved ordering items in bulk that they would repackage with other items and sell as packs: survival packs, hygiene packs, crafts activities, care packages, and so on. Fraud teams needed to avoid banning this activity despite its similarity to mule operations.

Additionally, phishing attempts spiked dramatically. Consumers were online more than ever, trying out new sites, and were rushed and stressed, making them easier targets than usual for phishing schemes of all kinds. For fraud prevention, the key consequence is the abundance of stolen information newly available to fraudsters, especially for ATO attempts. Unsurprisingly, the frequency of ATO attempts jumped in response.

---

6 Rahul Pangam, "Is Your Business Prepared for The Rise in Online Fraud? New Research Shows the Real Cost of Fraud" (*https://oreil.ly/ty7Hi*), PayPal, press release, April 12, 2021.

Each challenge requires adjustment by itself. When they all happened together, fraud prevention teams were faced with risk from all sides. As Alon Shemesh, cofounder of Difftone, cofounder of Forter, and veteran analytics leader at Fraud Sciences and PayPal, commented:

> In a situation like this, it's like a perfect storm. There's the social engineering side—it's much easier to trick people into giving their data. On top of that, there's the technical [side]—home infrastructure is less secure, but that's what people were using. And then you need to think about the working experience of fraud prevention teams, who are usually used to working closely together, flagging changes and checking in with one another to verify identities, details, or trends. Suddenly, that practiced collaboration is much harder.

Long-Term Planning

This is a good place to mention the long-term planning needed in a crisis. In the case of the COVID-19 pandemic, ATO jumped, certainly—but not to the same extent as phishing. That's a clue that farsighted fraudsters were storing up details to use more slowly, at times when fraud teams would be less suspicious and at especially busy times of the year when ATO is more likely to go unnoticed.

In a crisis, much of your resources will go into keeping track of the immediate moment and dealing with immediate challenges. But it's equally important to track the trends that are likely to mean trouble down the road—and put measures in place to at least address them later if you can't do that right away.

In the same way, if you're struggling to adjust to a new working situation, such as one in which analysts are mostly working from home, finding short-term solutions is important. But analyzing what's really putting pressure on the team and what longer-term changes are needed in order to adapt is vital for longer-term success.

Prepare for Shifts in User Behaviors

All fraud prevention teams rely on analyzing the typical behavior of users on their site, and teams that rely heavily on machine learning do so even more. How can you identify a fraudster acting like a thief if you don't know what normal ought to look like?

During a crisis, user behavior changes dramatically and quickly. During the COVID-19 pandemic, of course, there was a sudden shift to working from home, which meant new users and addresses were in play. Different times of the day became the most popular shopping times because parents with children at home had to work around their schedules. New delivery times were in demand now that people were home most of the time. Ordering online and getting the goods from a convenient pickup location was suddenly the rage. Teenagers were shopping with their parents' cards.

Those particular changes were specific to the situation, but similar changes may follow in any other crisis. A shift in the hot products of the day is almost certain, and fraudsters will be on top of this as it happens. It's their business; they'll be watching as avidly as any warehouse logistics manager.

Depending on the nature of your business and of the crisis, you may experience a flood of orders, or a sudden drought. In either case, there's a consequence for fraud prevention. Uri Arad, vice president of product at Identiq, notes that in this circumstance, you need to change your focus on decline rates, chargeback rates, attack rates, and false positive rates.Uri Arad, "Preparing for the Online Fraud Challenges of the Coronavirus Crisis" (*https://oreil.ly/Co24L*), Digital Commerce 360, March 16, 2020. If your business is experiencing less traffic than usual but fraudsters are hitting as often as usual, a spike in decline rate means you're doing well.

If you have a lot of new accounts being set up or dormant accounts coming to life, that's positive; but there's likely to be a higher level of fraudulent attempts mixed in among the legitimate activity than you would usually expect. Take this into account when you're analyzing your work, and make sure your KPIs are adjusted accordingly to reflect the new position you and your business are in.

You need to be prepared for analysis that doesn't rely on typical patterns since, as Arad puts it, "In this situation, everything looks like an anomaly."[7] Think of tools and other trends you can analyze that aren't affected by this crisis. If your machine learning models are struggling, be ready to retrain on the new data, and have processes in place to get through the time of shifting sands.

Regardless of what's hitting your particular business, you may see more new users than usual. That's something many companies (and their fraud analysts) saw right from the start of the COVID-19 crisis, when so many consumers began shopping online far more than they had previously, including older generations who were fairly new to online shopping as a whole. Fraudsters love to hide in waves like these, knowing you're busy and may be paying less attention than usual, so have steps in place to analyze new accounts before they become problematic.

Interdepartmental Communication and Collaboration

Users are going to be under added stress, just like you are. This means it's not a good time to add extra friction unnecessarily. Users who feel that a brand failed them at a time of crisis may never return. On the other hand, with fraud on the rise you need to

---

7 Joan Goodchild, "How Merchants Can Defend Against Coronavirus Fraud" (*https://oreil.ly/TI3rb*), Card Not Present, March 26, 2020.

step cautiously. It's valuable to place emphasis on interdepartmental communications. It won't feel like a priority, but when you're caught between a rock and a hard place when it comes to fraud and friction, having the input and support of your marketing and customer support teams can be essential in finding a solution that represents the best balance for your customers and is easy to justify to your management.

It's vital to be transparent about your challenges, solutions, and decisions. Keep records of these as much as possible. Present them regularly (if not frequently) to management so that they understand your needs and difficulties. This will mean you are well positioned to deal with any questions or new developments and to make a persuasive case for new resources should you need them.

If there are external organizations you ordinarily work closely with, take into account that your relationships may be changing while you're both under new stresses. Teams that are in regular contact with law enforcement, for example, may discover that there are fewer resources available to deal with fraud carried out against online banking when different kinds of crime are suddenly growing beyond expectations. Prioritize issues, be clear about which things can wait, and be sensitive to the wider impact of the crisis on society and your partners.

Friendly Fraud

Some changes in user behavior aren't so innocent.

As Karisse Hendrick, founder and principal consultant at Chargelytics Consulting and host of the *Fraudology* podcast (*https://oreil.ly/INacE*), said in drawing on her experience from the economic crisis of 2008–2009 and the recent pandemic:

> Before the 2008 financial crisis, the term *friendly fraud* was unknown in ecommerce. That changed fast once economic uncertainty started to bite. We saw first-party fraud (friendly fraud) rise quickly as consumers sought to find ways to still receive the items they wanted, essentially without paying for them. But a lot of companies didn't learn a lesson from that change of customer behavior for the next economic crisis. In 2020, the new face of friendly fraud was refunding fraud, and most retailers weren't ready for that either. It took many merchants a long time to even realize that was what was happening to them. Friendly fraud is a hugely underestimated factor in times of great economic stress. The fact is, when that situation comes, there's likely to be a massive uptick, and merchants need to be proactive about it rather than wait to get hit. You have to be on top of the data and willing to be flexible. And you need to be very aware of all the context, from people's living situations to the changing rules of card networks or processors.

Unfortunately, consumers won't always be willing to restrain their buying habits just because their income has decreased. Friendly fraud (*first-party fraud* in the UK) is an easy answer: either directly, by buying goods and then reporting a chargeback, or by using professional refund fraudsters. During the pandemic, this trend, which was previously more the province of physical goods, was exacerbated by the popularity of digital goods (gift cards, bitcoin) and the ease with which these can also be charged back. The need to cancel events also encouraged chargebacks for tickets, another digital good.

For the fraud prevention team, it's something to track carefully, but it's also worth warning management of the likelihood of the problem before it starts. Ultimately, there's a policy decision to be made here, and it's not generally the province of the fraud team to make it. Flagging the issue early on, based on experience of past crises, shows your expertise.

It also means you'll have a clear policy to work from once the trend does start to rear its head, which in turn means you'll know from the start what you need to be tracking (e.g., number of purchases involved, price of purchases, comparison to past legitimate purchases, etc.). You'll also know whether it's your job to combat this, or whether it will be passed on to Customer Service, in which case you'll likely have to provide a certain amount of information when required.

Prioritizing New Projects

This is something your team should start doing as a matter of course, rather than in reaction to a crisis. Something many teams learned during the pandemic was that new projects, even ones they were truly excited about, had to be postponed or canceled due to the onslaught of new challenges they were facing.

For certain projects, such as the adaptations needed to prepare for PSD 2, which was about to become a legal requirement in the EU, this wasn't possible. Some UK companies had to prioritize Brexit strategies for the same reason: whatever else was happening in the world, that deadline was still going to be there, and the business was still going to need to be ready. Other companies found themselves prioritizing other projects because they believed they were essential to keeping up with trends or issues such as data privacy or inclusion, even without a deadline to meet.

When you're planning a new collaborative activity, a new project, or a new partnership, work out where it fits on this scale. If a crisis hits and normal functioning is suspended, is this something you would instantly postpone? Prioritize no matter what? Prioritize depending on circumstances?

This will help you understand the position of the project in your company and your team, and it will also be valuable in the event of a crisis. Teams that let PSD 2 preparation slide, hoping for another extension, fell into full-fledged panic mode when it became clear that an extension would not be forthcoming. Don't put yourself in that position; plan against it.

Summary

This chapter explored some of the fundamentals of fraud analysis: the things a good fraud analyst or manager needs to bear in mind all the time. These factors should inform or be reflected in the strategy you build for your fraud-fighting team and the tactics you use to achieve it. They're also essential in understanding the rest of the book. Think about them as we move to the next chapter, where we'll look at building, investing in, and evaluating your fraud team and the tools and systems that are right for you and your company.

## CHAPTER 4

Fraud Prevention Evaluation and Investment

Money makes the world go round...
—John Kander and Fred Ebb[1]

The bread and butter of fraud prevention is in research identification (through fraud analysis, modeling, reverse engineering, etc.) and mitigation—and balancing that process with avoiding friction for good customers as much as possible. But a whole framework of systems, tools, and departmental investment is needed to support those efforts, and that's what this chapter focuses on.

The more care you take to ensure that your framework is the right fit for your team's needs and your company's structure, the more effectively it will support your fraud prevention work.

Moreover, it's important to position the fraud prevention department appropriately within the wider organization. Your team will work best if it has close collaborative relationships with various other departments, and you're more likely to get the resources you need if management understands your work and what you do for the company. Even though it's only tangentially related to the crux of the job, it's far more important than many teams realize, and it's as important to invest in these relationships and educational efforts as it is in analysis and research.

---

1 John Kander and Fred Ebb, "Money," in *Cabaret*, music by John Kander, lyrics by Fred Ebb, book by Joe Masteroff (1966).

Types of Fraud Prevention Solutions

Fraud prevention solutions are not a one-size-fits-all kind of discussion. There's little point in arguing about which is the "best" fraud prevention solution or tool. All the options have different advantages and disadvantages. The question is: What's best for your situation and goals?

This section looks at the main categories of solutions and tools you can use as the technical basis for your system. Bear in mind, though, that this technical basis must be guided by the experience and expertise of fraud prevention experts and by the research and insights of fraud analysts. Fraud prevention is not a "buy off the shelf, then set and forget" kind of profession.

Rules Engines

Rules engines are the traditional standby of fraud prevention. The principle of how rules engines work is simple; your transactions or online activity flows through a system, which can pick out certain characteristics. You can create a rule to say that any transaction above $200 should always go to manual review, or that logins from a specific geographical area should always be reviewed, or even reject activity from one country in particular (something that would result in an unfortunate number of false positives!).

You can set rules leveraging a huge range of factors, including type of item, price of item, time zone, geographical location, address details, phone information, email details, time of day, device information, browser information, and so on. There is also a wide range of consequences: you can automatically approve or reject, send to manual review, automatically require two-factor authentication (2FA), and so forth.

The downside is that rules tend to be a rather blanket approach to fraud: even if you've experienced a lot of fraudulent transactions from Nigeria lately, do you really want to block all transactions coming from there? You should, of course, combine different rules for a more nuanced approach, though it will still have a rather broad brushstroke effect.

Rules are also entirely dependent on the efforts of you and your team. They won't update to reflect changes in customer behavior or fraud tactics unless you're updating them. Existing rules will remain even if they're no longer relevant, unless you remove them—which can result in legacy rules causing confusion down the line.

On the other hand, rules are easy to work with, take effect quickly, and give your team a sense of control. When things are changing fast, it's valuable to have rules to work with so that your team can react quickly and decisively to swiftly moving circumstances. That's something more than one team saw during the COVID-19 pandemic.

Rules engines can be built in-house, which enables you to make them tightly tailored to your needs and means you are entirely in control of how your system is built and the data in it. They can also be sourced from a vendor, meaning they can be spun up quickly and should be kept up to date with the latest technological developments for you without you having to continually invest in the system. Many teams combine aspects of both the in-house and vendor-sourced options.

Machine Learning

We won't say much about how machine learning systems work here, because that's something we cover more fully in Chapter 5, which deals with fraud modeling. Instead, we'll touch on the topic here to place machine learning within the context of fraud fighting systems.

Machine learning systems have been in vogue in fraud prevention since around 2015, and the concept is simple: machines can be trained to recognize transactions or activity as fraudulent or legitimate based on past examples, and they can then accurately predict whether a new example will turn out to be fraud or legit.

One main advantage is that machine learning systems can adapt quickly to big new fraud tricks. Unlike manual reviewers, they see all the data, not just a small slice, and they don't have to wait to confer with colleagues and then laboriously work out the best rule to add. They also notice patterns that humans are likely to overlook, and can be very nuanced in how they evaluate each instance compared to the broad brushstroke approach of a rules engine.

The downsides include that these systems tend to have a *black box* element; it can be hard to know why they're making certain decisions or which factors they're considering. This can be uncomfortable for teams who like to know what's going on, and is a risk when it comes to avoiding bias. It can also make it difficult to correct the machine when it makes mistakes, and it can take time for a model to adapt to changes that are occur of the blue and don't match the variables they've been trained to deal with (e.g., as we saw during the COVID-19 pandemic). Training a new model likewise takes time.

Moreover, some of the challenges machine learning faces when it comes to fraud prevention (which we look at in detail in Chapter 5) mean that in order to offset them, domain expertise is essential—but can be difficult to employ successfully with a pure machine learning model, particularly if the fraud team wants to be able to do this independently.

Hybrid Systems

Hybrid models combine machine learning with rules in some way. This might be starting out with a rules engine approach and adding machine learning for specific purposes such as pattern recognition (a machine can often notice patterns a human might miss). Or it could mean using a machine learning system as a base and being able to add rules to cope when things change quickly or to reflect new research from your team.

A hybrid model has emerged as the most popular with most fraud departments in recent years because of the potential to combine the advantages of both rules and machine learning in one system. When they talk about hybrid, different companies and different vendors mean very different things—and reflect a different balance between rules and machine learning—so it's important to clarify this in discussions whenever that's relevant for you.

Data Enrichment Tools

When your site sees a transaction or account activity, you have a certain set of data to work with. You'll receive some information straight from the customer: name, email, perhaps phone number or address, and credit card number or other means of payment. You'll also likely have some information you collect, such as IP address, device information, browser information, and so on.

Data enrichment tools let you enter any of those data points into their system, and receive whatever additional information they have from third-party sources or simply from having seen this information before. Many of these tools can be integrated directly into your own system, making enriching the data easy and, in some cases, automated.

There are a huge number of data enrichment tools out there. Some focus on specific data points, which are the only ones your team can send them for enrichment—email, device, IP, address, behavior—while others take a more holistic approach. Some provide certain sorts of data, meaning that regardless of whether you send email, phone, or device, you'll expect them to send you further information on an associated social profile, or credit score, or whatever their specialty is. Others provide a range of types of data in response.

These can be extremely valuable in supplementing your own information, particularly with a new customer or with a customer adding or using new information. However, not every tool will be right for you.

You need to consider the return on investment (ROI): how much does any particular tool add to your accuracy? Many will allow you a trial period to determine this, or will accept a short-term contract initially so that you can test it out. Different companies have different needs. The fact that behavioral data was absolutely essential to fighting fraud when you were working at a bank doesn't mean it'll be as valuable once you're working at an apparel retailer. You need to decide whether what you're getting is worth the price you're paying.

Similarly, some tools are stronger in certain regions than others, and you need to explore this before you sign. One particular tool might be great for North America but has virtually no coverage in Japan or Brazil. Depending on your audience, that may or may not matter.

There's also the question of freshness. Since much of this kind of data comes from third parties, notably data brokers, ensuring that it's fresh can be difficult. People move around, get new phone numbers, change companies, and update credit cards. Talking to others in the fraud prevention industry can be essential here: the community has knowledge to share and is usually very willing to do so. We encourage you to leverage this as a resource.

Consortium Model

Fraud fighters are unusually willing to collaborate with one another, including across companies and industries. This is in some ways a function of the nature of the job. Other departments, such as Marketing, Sales, Finance, Product, Logistics, and so on, are competing with other companies and their equivalent departments in those companies. Often, their success can spell annoyance or frustration for the equivalent departments in other organizations. In fraud prevention, this is not the case. Fraud fighters have a shared enemy: fraudsters. They're competing, not against one another but against the common enemy.

As part of that ongoing battle, fraud fighters pool knowledge, sharing information about current trends, new fraudster techniques, and data points known to be associated with fraud. Much of this collaborative effort happens at conferences and industry events, and in regularly scheduled merchant calls. Direct data sharing sometimes happens very informally—via a group email with spreadsheets attached, for example—and sometimes indirectly, as when merchants in an industry prefer to all use the same fraud prevention vendor so that they can benefit indirectly from one another's experiences.

Using a consortium model is a way to make the data sharing more formalized and direct. Various fraud prevention teams upload their fraud records to a centralized location, which all the teams can access and integrate as part of their own systems. You could think of it as a shared decline list, but on a large scale.

Some consortiums are run by third parties or a group of merchants purely in order to establish and maintain the consortium. Others evolve as a by-product of a fraud prevention solution; as a solution becomes used by many merchants, marketplaces, or banks, the solution sees and stores data and analysis from many different sources.

Each company using the solution effectively benefits from that accidental consortium. Many fraud prevention services can testify that the network effect brought them to greatness, thanks to being able to see a single attacker moving between banks, retailers, advertisers, exchanges, and so on. DoubleVerify in adtech fraud prevention; Forter and Riskified in ecommerce protection; and Cyota (acquired by RSA and now spun off as Outseer), IBM Trusteer, and Biocatch in banking protection are just a few examples.

Cyota is a good example of the network effect in action. Uri Rivner, cofounder of AML innovation startup Regutize (and a cofounder of BioCatch), helped Cyota (in his role as vice president of international marketing) make the ideas behind risk-based authentication and the eFraud Network not just a reality but an accepted industry practice. Uri noted:

> Cyota paved the way, and companies like BioCatch brought new fields of science into play right when the industry most needed them. BioCatch started by collecting behavioral biometric data such as mouse motion, typing patterns, and the way one holds and operates a mobile device. Initially the focus was on building behavioral profiles and flagging anomalies which might indicate someone else was operating inside the user's online account, but after going live with the tech we discovered something amazing. Looking at the way cybercriminals were operating gave us a huge amount of data no one had ever seen before—and by working with large banks we had just enough examples of fraudulent behaviors to really understand fraudster interactions and behavioral patterns. This allowed us to model the typical behavior of fraudsters and the tools they operate, such as remote access, which, coupled with what we knew about the user behavior history, was 20 times more accurate in detecting fraud than just looking at the user profiles.

Uri gave the example of identifying remote access attacks: "When you control someone else's device remotely over the internet, your hand–eye coordination gets awkward and delayed due to latency; given sufficiently sensitive behavioral analytics, it can be immediately detected." Uri added that sharing criminal behavioral patterns across the industry was a huge boost to detection.

In the world of ecommerce, consortium models are equally helpful, since fraudsters like to reuse email accounts, phone numbers, and so forth across sites. This fraudulent practice is aimed at maximizing their ROI (because setting up accounts takes time), thus a consortium model can be an effective way for companies to protect their systems against data points that have already become burnt on other sites.

In a way, buying into a consortium is like having a special kind of data enrichment particularly targeted to what you're looking for and want to guard against.

Using consortium data

Consortium data can be powerful, especially when companies within a single industry all use the same consortium, as fraudsters often specialize in particular industries. However, there are some caveats that come with this model.

First, decline list data has a lag built in: you don't discover that an email address is problematic until a chargeback comes in, which may be days, weeks, or months after the address was used. As fraud fighters say, "A decline list is a great way to catch last month's fraudsters." It's potentially valuable, since one site's fraudsters from last month may be yours today, but it's potentially too late to be useful. You need to be aware of this, and not treat the consortium as a silver bullet.

Second, the consortium model can encourage teams to think about email addresses, phone numbers, and so on as "good" or "bad," which is inaccurate and misleading. An email address is just an email address. It's how it's used that matters. Emails that end up compromised through account takeover (ATO), for instance, are not problematic in themselves. They just went through a "bad patch," so to speak. Similarly with physical addresses, the fact that a place was used by fraudsters for a little while says nothing about the place itself. Maybe it's an office or large apartment building with a concierge—most people in the building are legitimate customers, and you don't want to tar them with the fraudsters' brush. Maybe it was a *drop house* for a while (a place used by criminals as a delivery point or storage location for stolen or illegal goods), but now the fraudsters have moved on and legitimate customers live there. Perhaps the phone number used to belong to a criminal (*https://oreil.ly/ S3awX*). It's even possible that a credit card that has been compromised is still being used by the real customer, whose orders should be accepted. And so on.

In general, you can risk-score email addresses and phone numbers to help detect obvious risk issues (e.g., the email address is only one day old, or the phone number is a nonfixed Voice over IP [VoIP] number—i.e., just a free internet number).

Data points are not bad. Users can be bad. Identities can be bad. It's those you need to watch out for and identify. Consortium data can help you do that, as long as you don't get confused about what it's giving you. See more on this topic in Chapter 15.

There is also a third point regarding the consortium model that is more of a limitation than a caveat. Consortiums are useful for sharing decline list data: the fraud records associated with fraudulent activity. In terms of privacy considerations and legal or regulatory restrictions, this falls comfortably into the category of prevention of illegal activity, but not always. These same considerations, however, prevent most companies from sharing information relating to good customers in a similar fashion, even if they were willing to do so, which for competitive reasons most would not be.

The difference between the consortium model and the more standard data enrichment model is that with data enrichment, when companies share their users' data in order to learn more in connection with it, the data is being shared with a trusted third party: the data broker or third-party provider. In a consortium, it is shared more directly with other online businesses, some of which may be competitors. It is a nice thing about the fraud industry that competing companies are willing to share fraud data with one another in order to collaborate against the fraudsters, who are their common enemy, but of course it does limit the nature of the collaborative effort, since it's also important not to give a competitor an advantage through sharing data not directly related to fraudsters.

Providerless consortiums

An interesting alternative has been developed very recently as part of what technology research and consulting company Gartner calls the privacy-enhancing computation trend, so called because it draws on privacy-enhancing technology (PET). In this model, the consortium can pool all kinds of knowledge—regarding both good and bad users—because none of the personal user data is actually shared with other companies or any third party. For this reason, the trend is sometimes referred to as *providerless* since the third-party provider is removed from the equation. The sensitive user data does not leave the possession of the company trying to verify it.

This form of consortium relies on some form of privacy-enhancing technique such as homomorphic encryption, multiparty computation, zero knowledge proofs, and so on. An interesting paper from the World Economic Forum (*https://oreil.ly/uzTnk*) goes into the details of how each of those techniques works and gives examples of the uses in financial services, so you can check that out for more information. But the basic idea is not hard to grasp.

Imagine that you and a friend wanted to see whether your bank cards had the same CVV number (the three-digit security code on the back). There's something like a 1:1,000 chance that you do, so it's by no means impossible. You don't want to tell each other what your number is, since you are fraud analysts and know how risky this would be. You could tell a trusted third party—but you really would have to trust them, and being fraud analysts, you err on the side of caution when it comes to trust and safety.

One idea would be for you to roll dice together a number of times, and add or multiply the rolls to come up with a huge random number. You use a calculator to add that huge number to your CVV, resulting in an even larger number. You can now both tell that very large number to a third party, who can tell you whether you have a match.

The third party gets no information beyond match/no match; they cannot learn your CVV numbers, because they do not know the random number you and your friend got from the dice rolls. You and your friend cannot learn each other's CVVs (unless it is a match, of course), because you don't tell each other your final number. This is an admittedly much simplified version of the kinds of privacy-enhancing technologies that can enable companies to see whether user data they're seeing is trusted by—or conversely, considered fraudulent by—the other companies in the consortium.

The providerless consortium model is still new, but it has already found real-life expression in Identiq (*https://www.identiq.com*), an identity validation network that enables companies to leverage one another's data to validate identities without sharing any personal user data at all. Other companies are also considering the ways PETs may be used within identity validation or fraud prevention. (Full disclosure: Shoshana Maraney, one of the authors of this book, currently works at Identiq and is intrigued by the collaborative possibilities the providerless trend represents for the fraud prevention community.)

The providerless approach is an interesting refinement on the data enrichment and consortium tools, particularly in the context of increasing data privacy regulation around the world. It also offers interesting possibilities with regard to pooling knowledge about which customers *can* be trusted rather than just which can't.

Building a Research Analytics Team

To make the most of the solutions and tools you choose, you'll need a capable research analytics team to make sure you're always tailoring to the specific needs of your business and the behaviors of your customers. Even for a fairly small team, you need to start off with a couple of real domain experts: people who have been fighting fraud for some time and have a good, broad understanding of both the *granular* level—what to look for when reviewing individual transactions—and the *macro* level—seeing which trends have wide impact and putting that knowledge to use to protect the business. With fraud research and analytics, two is always better than one; fraud analysts benefit enormously from being able to check intuitions against each other, brainstorm, and work through challenges together.

As long as your team is guided by experienced professionals, you can recruit other team members for junior positions. Experience working with data is a plus, but statistical expertise isn't necessary as long as candidates show aptitude and are willing to learn. Over time, you can train them to spot anomalies in the data your company sees and develop an intuition for when something isn't right with a transaction.

It's a good idea to start new employees off with manual reviews so that they build up an understanding of typical transactions and interactions with the site, as well as get to know the profile of your customers—in addition, of course, to getting a sense for the fraud attacks and fraudsters your team faces. However, it's equally important to train them in gap analysis—that is, comparing true results with predictions, and sampling and then reviewing to find a root cause for any blind spots that caused gaps in performance. Encourage the team to think about what could be changed in your models to improve the system's ability to both catch fraud and avoid friction. Fraud analysis is not rote work; you want to train analysts to look for patterns outside individual transactions, seek out ways to corroborate and leverage that knowledge, and build the insights gained into your system.

In terms of team culture, encouraging creativity is as important as the more obvious virtues of data analysis and careful investigation. You want your team to think about different kinds of data sources they could use to confirm or reject hypotheses, brainstorm new ways to put existing data or tools to use, and be able to balance diverse possibilities in their minds at once.

For this reason, it's important not to insist that fraud analysts be consistently conservative. It's true that chargebacks must be kept low, but there's always a small amount of maneuvering room to try out new tools or techniques that could, if successful, improve your results, even if sometimes you're unlucky and they backfire. Equally, if you consistently make analysts focus on the transactions they miss—the chargebacks they didn't stop—they'll become very conservative and your approval rate will go down. (Fraud managers, you can experiment to see whether this holds true for your team, if you like. Anecdotally, the results seem pretty consistent. An exclusive focus on chargebacks for your team is not good for a company's sales.) Teams must focus on preventing false positives as well as chargebacks to keep the balance.

In the same way, team structure should be kept as flat as possible; stringent hierarchies limit employees' willingness to experiment and suggest new ways of doing things. It's also important to remind team members of the positive side of the job (helping smooth customer journeys, protecting the business from loss, solving tough problems) if the negative side of seeing so much criminal activity seems to get them down. This is most relevant in companies that are more likely to hear from victims of fraud, including banks, cryptocurrency companies, and gift card companies, but can be a challenge in other industries as well.

Within this context, it's important to mention the value of bottom-up analysis, as explained in Ohad Samet's book *Introduction to Online Payments Risk Management* (O'Reilly). The world of online payments has evolved considerably since that book was published, but the key tenets of training and approach described for fraud teams are just as relevant today as they were when the book was written. Samet lays out the importance of inductive research and reasoning, with fraud analysts being taught to sample many case studies (of transactions, logins, account creations, etc.—whatever is relevant for your business) and then to tease out both the legitimate and the fraudulent stories for each one, matching the data that can be seen. Finding more sources to support or refuse each possibility is the natural next step. From there, fraud analysts can draw on their case study experience to suggest large-scale heuristics that can be checked against the company's database.

It's particularly important to draw attention to this bottom-up kind of analysis because the top-down model, using a regression-based approach, is in many ways more instinctively obvious within the fraud-fighting use case. Companies, after all, have so much data—so what does it tell you? What does it lead you to deduce or plan? The top-down approach is necessary, of course, and we'll mention it in Chapter 5. But the fact is that often, fraud happens in small volumes, and fraudsters are always trying to mimic the behavior of good customers.

You need to balance out both of those challenges, and the best way to do it is by using your human resources most effectively, including their creative abilities. As vice president of product at Identiq, Uri Arad, puts it in his interview on the *Fraudology* podcast, drawing on nearly a decade of fighting fraud at PayPal:[2]

> The data-based approach, with machine learning and statistics, is great at giving you the big picture. And the story-based approach, with people digging into individual cases, is great at giving you the insight into the details that we need to really understand what's going on. When you put the two together, that's extremely powerful.

Collaborating with Customer Support

Working in sync with and supporting other departments is important, generally speaking, in your organization, but in many cases the fraud prevention team has a special relationship with customer support, and where they don't, it's possible they should.

Customer support is on the front lines of consumer interaction with your business. That also means they're the most likely to be in direct contact with the fraudsters trying to steal from your business. Customer support training is more likely to focus on company policy and customer enablement, ensuring customers get a good experience, than it is on identifying and blocking fraudsters. Fraud departments should ensure that this important element is covered as well, and updated regularly in line with developing fraud trends.

There are two parts to this collaboration. First, fraud fighters can help customer support representatives understand the tricks fraudsters are likely to play on them, from calling up to change an address after a transaction has been approved, to professional refund fraud, to ATO attempts. Representatives who aren't trained not to give away sensitive user information or even company information, such as which systems are

---

2 Karisse Hendrick, "A 21st Century Approach to Enabling Merchant Collaboration (w/ Uri Arad at Identiq)" (*https://oreil.ly/KMMFV*), June 10, 2021, in *Fraudology*, produced by Rolled Up Podcast Network, podcast.

used internally, may become a weak link in the security and fraud prevention chain. Hardening against attacks at the customer support level protects the whole business from fraud and from security attacks more generally.

Second, if a tight feedback loop is set up, customer support experiences can feed into fraud teams' knowledge of customers and trends. Companies that are not set up to make the connections in this way may go for months or even years without realizing that they're suffering a serious refund fraud attack, for example, because the information that shows it (which may include representatives being able to recognize certain fraudsters' voices on the phone and the scripts they use) stays within customer support and isn't integrated into the systems of knowledge belonging to the fraud prevention team.

Measuring Loss and Impact

As we said in Chapter 3, once upon a time, fraud prevention teams were measured on how low they could keep the company's fraud chargebacks. The only relevant key performance indicator (KPI) was the number of fraud chargebacks received—usually measured in dollars, though sometimes by percentage of transactions. There's a compelling logic to it. These chargebacks are the most obvious fraud cost to an ecommerce business in particular. The rules from the card networks support this approach as well; companies that see their chargebacks rise above 1% are, in ordinary circumstances, likely to see consequences leading to probationary terms, fines, or even an inability to process certain card brands.

In fact, though, measuring the company's true fraud losses and the impact of the fraud-fighting team is more complex, as many companies have come to realize in recent years. This has made setting KPIs, measuring loss, and measuring the fraud prevention team's impact all the more difficult—not least because part of doing this effectively involves ensuring that upper management decision-makers understand fraud, fraud prevention, and the relevant context.

Companies nowadays usually *don't* want to keep chargebacks to an absolute minimum. Of course, it's crucial to stay well below the chargeback thresholds (*https://oreil.ly/l4B1d*) set by the card companies, with a comfortable margin of error in case you're suddenly hit by an unexpected fraud ring or something similar, but there's still a wide gap between this and trying to aim for absolute zero when it comes to chargebacks. Overly focusing on minimizing chargebacks implies stringent policies that are likely causing high false positives, which are, after all, another form of loss to the business and one that is widely agreed to often be larger than fraud chargebacks, sometimes by quite some margin. False positives are, unfortunately, notoriously difficult to calculate, and doing so requires continual research into declined transactions and the willingness to let some "gray area" test cases through to see whether they are fraudulent or not.

It's crucial that upper management understand the trade-off involved between chargebacks and false positives, and that this is part of the process of setting reasonable KPIs and measuring the impact of the team. Some education may be necessary here, and fraud prevention leaders should consider this an intrinsic part of their job. If avoiding false positives is to be a KPI for your team, it must be clear what calculation is involved here.

Regarding choosing which metrics the department should focus on, bear in mind that you can't set KPIs in a vacuum. Does your company value precision or speed more highly? That will impact your policy for manual reviews. What balance should you seek to strike in terms of chargebacks versus false positives? That's intimately connected to the level of focus on customer experience, as well as the nature of your product. What level of friction is acceptable? That depends on your market and your vertical. Setting realistic targets that will match the priorities of the company as a whole requires educating upper management about how fraud and fraud prevention fit into the wider business, as well as discussions about how they see the role of your team in supporting wider priorities.

Benchmarking against industry averages is also important. The fraud rates, challenges, and even chargebacks seen by a gift card marketplace will be very different from those seen by an apparel retailer. A bank would have an entirely different profile again—and *neobanks* (aka internet-only banks) versus traditional banks may have different norms and expectations. Anti–money laundering (AML) is another story altogether (and has a different kind of calculation regarding mistakes, relating to the regulatory requirements involved). You can't realistically measure your own loss unless you understand it in the context of the wider industry of which you're a part. If you have 0.6% fraud chargebacks in an industry that typically sees 0.3%, you're in a very different position than a team with 0.6% chargebacks in an industry that typically sees 0.8% to 0.9%.

Unfortunately, benchmarks are often difficult to assess, since much of this information is the kind companies prefer to keep private. Surveys such as the Merchant Risk Council's Global Fraud Survey (often carried out in conjunction with CyberSource) or the LexisNexis True Cost of Fraud report can give you reasonable insight into metrics across different industries, though there is a limit to how granular these surveys can be. Informal discussions with fraud fighters from other companies will also give you a useful sense of where you stand. This type of information is equally important when talking to and educating upper management.

Measuring impact is tricky as well. The value of a prevented fraudulent transaction is not the only amount involved here. Here are some other factors to consider:

- The actual amount of fraud you're seeing—your *fraud rate*—is lower than it would be if you were not protecting the business effectively. If your entire team went on holiday (or became worse at their jobs), fraudsters would discover this quickly and the fraud rate would be a lot higher. Think about how quickly fraud rings jump on a vulnerability once it's been discovered; it would be like that on a larger scale and without correction. So, you're actually saving the business far more than the amount of fraud you're stopping. There's a lot of potential fraud that never comes your way because you're making the business a hard target to attack. This is difficult to measure, but using examples of fraud rings and extrapolating can provide an illustration of the point. You may also sometimes see chatter in fraudster forums sharing news about companies that are trying to fill a number of fraud prevention positions; fraudsters like it when that happens because they know the department is overstretched. They're likely to attack. These sorts of discussions also illustrate the point.

- There are additional costs associated with most transactions, particularly physical goods, including logistical efforts, the cost of replacing the item, and the item's unavailability for other customers. This sort of thing is included in what Lexis-Nexis calls its *multiplier*, which the company uses to calculate how much each dollar of fraud (or prevented fraud) actually represents to the business. It's usually at least three times the amount connected to direct loss through chargebacks. This same analogy applies to the opening of online accounts for banks. It can be far more costly to close bogus bank accounts (due to operational losses) than the dollar amount of relevant actual fraud losses.

- If your team protects against account-level fraud, such as account takeover, fake reviews, or collusion in a marketplace, you're protecting the business's reputation in meaningful and valuable ways and are undoubtedly having an impact, even if it's one that's hard to measure with a number. You can, however, provide numbers relating to fake reviews prevented, accounts protected from being hacked, and so on, and it is crucial that you *do* present these figures to upper management. When your impact extends well beyond checkout, it's important that this is visible. There may be related KPIs you want to consider that are based on these sorts of metrics.

Justifying the Cost of Fraud Prevention Investment

It can be frustrating, but the reality is that you're always going to have to justify your team's head count, budget, and investment in new tools or technologies. Even if you know you're doing a great job and compare favorably to the rest of your industry, your upper managers likely don't know that. And even if they do, they'll need to be able to defend that to board members, shareholders, and other stakeholders.

First and foremost, you need numbers. Here are just some of the essential figures:

- Your fraud rate, or the number of attacks you're seeing as a percentage of overall transactions or activities. You may want to break this down into types of attack.

- The number of fraudulent attempts you stop, both as a percentage of the total number of attacks and in dollar value.

- The exposure dollar amount versus the actual losses (e.g., you have $5 million in potential transaction losses, but as a function of your fraud team and your tools the actual losses were only $75,000).

- Your chargeback rate.

- Your successful chargeback dispute rate.

- Your manual review rate, or how many transactions or activities you manually review, as a percentage of total transactions or activities.

- The percentage of manually reviewed cases that are approved.

- The average speed of manual review.

- If relevant, figures relating to account-level abuses such as coupon abuse, wire fraud losses, peer-to-peer (P2P) fraud losses, fake reviews, and more that harm the business's bottom line and/or reputation.

What you want to do is convey how much you're saving the business every year (or quarter, as the case may be). You need your execs to see your work in the context of the bigger picture. Get them to imagine what life would be like without a fraud team—because it wouldn't be pretty.

Once you've set that scene, you can tie it back to your tools and head count. If your manual review team is working quickly and furiously (and accurately), present numbers for how it would be if that team were smaller or, if you're angling for increasing the head count, larger. If your hybrid system enabled you to support the company's entering a new market with low chargebacks, low friction, and low false positives, make sure credit is given to that system (and to your team for choosing it). If you want a new tool, measure what you estimate the results would be in the relevant area if you did have it.

Some of this is an annual, biannual, or quarterly exercise. But to lay the groundwork for success, you need to make sure there's an ongoing educational effort reaching out to the whole company, and especially to upper management. You can't afford to let that slip.

Interdepartmental Relations

Fraud prevention departments often operate in something of a silo within their organization. The approach and the kind of work that's integral to the job can seem very foreign to other parts of the company. The exceptions may be the Trust and Safety department and the Cybersecurity department, and it may be worth investing in close relationships with these teams, which face similar opponents, concerns, and attacks. As Uri Lapidot, senior product manager of risk at Intuit, said:

> Fraud teams may well have valuable context to share which can help cybersecurity and trust and safety teams, and vice versa. More than that, the teams often have overlapping interests and priorities, and working together can make [the] best use of each department's resources and knowledge. Keeping in close contact, with regularly scheduled syncs, is important for everyone involved.

The distance between fraud prevention and departments outside the cybersecurity or trust and safety realms is a problem, though. You can't stay in your comfort zone. Fraud fighters should not underestimate the importance of interdepartmental relations.

If others in your organization don't understand your work, what you do, or how you do it, that's an opportunity for education. You can run lunch and learn sessions, or teach Fraud 101 in company onboarding classes for new employees. Fraud is fascinating, and not just to fraud analysts, as long as you relate the topic to your audience and the company and use some real-life stories to illustrate your points effectively.

As we've said, much of fraud prevention involves finding the right balance (or the right compromise) between customer experience and aversion to risk. There are a lot of other departments that are affected by that decision, including marketing, sales, product, and customer support. If you ignore them, they'll continue to grumble and think you're a bunch of naysayers. If you involve them in the challenges and trade-offs and ensure over time that they understand the bigger picture from your perspective, they'll join you in finding workable solutions. They'll also start remembering to loop the Fraud Prevention department into discussions like entering a new market, or let you know in advance about a coupon program they're rolling out or a flash sale they're contemplating.

We've heard from a lot of fraud analysts that they're often the last to know about this sort of thing, and that sometimes they learn about it too late—when false positives (or new fraud) have already spiked. To tweak Hanlon's Razor, never attribute to malice that which is adequately explained by ignorance. They didn't let you know, because they didn't realize you needed to know. And it *is* part of your job to make sure they do realize that going forward.

Other departments don't know much about fraud prevention. You need to educate them so that they can understand how their work relates to yours, believe that you're working toward the same ultimate goal as they are, and want to work together to achieve success for the company.

As an illustration of why it's so vital to develop rich, collaborative interdepartmental partnerships, Tal Yeshanov, head of risk and financial operations at Plastiq, talked about her experiences of how working with marketing teams has been so valuable to her fraud team's success:

> At the end of the day, your marketing and fraud teams are both trying to answer the question, "Who is this user?" The end goal is different, and the KPIs are different, which can obscure this important truth, but the fact is that sharing some data around the users such as IP, device, time zone, language settings, email, phone, account age, transaction volume, transaction velocity, etc., can help both teams excel at what they do. Once teams come to see that their work, and goals, are really not so different, they're often eager to see what they can achieve together.

> Fraud and marketing teams just have to work together. Marketing's job is to bring awareness of product and feature offerings to users. When marketing teams launch campaigns, especially successful ones, it'll mean users will come and transact. The marketing team will decide on the message/discount/promotion to offer, the timing of when to launch (around holidays usually), and the scope/size of the campaign (how often, how long, and to whom). All of these things will affect risk teams, and they should plan to work together to have a strategy in place to handle the increased transaction volume.

Tal also offered a few things to watch out for, to show how interlaced the marketing and fraud concerns really are:

The overall count of transactions will increase
This means more users will place orders. Make sure fraud teams are staffed and trained appropriately.

The dollar value of each transaction may increase
This means users may choose to spend more money to take advantage of/qualify for a promotion. Make sure to adapt rules, models, and workflows to account for this so that false positives are kept to a minimum.

The behavior of users will change
Maybe instead of buying one item they'll buy three, instead of shipping to their own home they'll ship to a friend, or instead of placing the order from their home, they might be doing it from the airport or a hotel (especially if it's around the holidays at a time when folks are traveling). As we mentioned, fraud teams need to look at past trends and speak to marketing to make sure they account for these changes so that legitimate users don't fall prey to the systems meant to catch the fraudsters.

The type of transaction may be different

Perhaps a user has only ever bought one sort of item, but now with an incentive the user may choose to branch out and buy different types of things. Make sure your fraud team and marketing team are both aware of what the other is doing.

Data Analysis Strategy

Data analysis makes or breaks fraud prevention efforts. It's easy to focus on the immediate analysis needs: the transactions, logins, and so on flowing through the system now. There's a vital place for that, and in many cases it's what most members of the team will spend the most time on. But if you never look beyond that, it will take over your horizon, leaving you continually fighting fires. Strategy is important so that you understand the structure of how your team is approaching the challenges they face, and how to improve it for better results. It's something you need to take time for, even when things are busy, because it might not be urgent, but it's very important.

Depending on your priorities as a department and a company, you may take a different approach to data analysis strategy. But there are two points we want to highlight that are broadly relevant. The first is that you need to build into your quarterly plans the right connections between your automation and your human expertise.

These should not be run separately; you'll get the best results if each one guides the other. For example, you will get the most out of your machine learning models if you have a domain expert regularly review the features that come from it. Many of those features will be meaningful, but sometimes it will be either random or related to a trend you understand within a relevant cultural or social context that the machine lacks. In these cases, you need to have the machine either ignore the features or modify them appropriately, if they're going to stop fraud without adding false positives.

Similarly, teams should schedule regular brainstorming sessions to explore, generate, and then test complex features related to cases too rare or too complicated for the model to notice. Too rare is obvious, and the material for noticing such cases may come from your own random sampling of cases or from collaboration with customer service teams. For example, take internet cafes in developing nations. Flights booked from these are usually more likely to be fraudulent. But what if the person at the keyboard matches the persona you've built up of an international traveler? Then it's actually a good sign. People are complicated. A model that is confused by receiving too many mixed signals (both good and bad) will simply balance this out as nonindicative one way or the other. But a human expert can understand the information in context and make sure it's used appropriately.

The second point we want to highlight is the importance of working with customer support teams as a part of your data analysis strategy specifically. With the right trusting relationship and regular contact, these teams can give you the best direction possible when you want to look for developing fraud trends. If you hear that customer support had a spate of customers who are supposed to be 80-year-old females but their phones are always answered by a young male, you can feed that knowledge back into your system and flag those transactions.

Work with the customer support team to agree on a list of suspicious occurrences and the fraud indicators they hear or see. Then add a button to their system that lets them report in real time whenever something like this happens by choosing the appropriate indicator from a simple drop-down menu. The easier you make it for them to help you, the more help you'll get and the more data you'll get. Your team can then look for patterns. It won't be a huge amount of data and it won't be the kind you could plug in to an automated model, but it will be enough and it will be chosen carefully enough to be worth your fraud team's time. A domain expert will be able to work out whether it's just a coincidence or the tip of a fraud iceberg.

 Make sure you notify the customer support team when their contributions have helped you. It's great for building up a good relationship and makes it more likely they'll want to help in the future. Plus, you never know: it might inspire one or two of them to become fraud analysts in time.

Fraud Tech Strategy

Your fraud tech strategy will vary enormously depending on your budget and the resources available to you for onboarding new tools. As with data analysis strategy, there are a few broadly relevant points we want to highlight.

First, your fraud tech strategy should *be* strategic. Don't integrate it with something just because it sounds fun and shiny and clever. It may be all of those things, but if it's going to do something your business doesn't really need, you're just making your system more complicated for no reason. Even if your organization is willing to simply test out new tech to see what's out there, you should analyze the real weaknesses of your current situation and try to find solutions for those, rather than looking for whatever sounds most exciting.

By contrast, teams who struggle to find the budget or resources for new technologies shouldn't let that limitation stop them from being equally focused on where their weaknesses lie and investing time and research in tools that could have a measurable impact on them. Even if it takes well over a year to get the tool you knew you needed months ago, if it's the right one for you, having to wait doesn't make it less relevant once you've got it. And you do need to keep an eye on what's out there so that once you have the opportunity, you can get what you need.

Second, make sure that when you're designing your tech strategy you cover all the bases in your system. You need to be able to engage in rule-based tactical work so that you can stop specific fraudsters or rings right away or adapt on the fly to fast-changing circumstances. You may also want to have machine learning–powered tech, in which case you should make sure you also plan for the maintenance that goes with it, identifying new trends and related attributes. Within this context, remain agile. For instance, if you've invested heavily in your machine learning team and technology, and it's working really well and your data science partners are helping you solve problems you've been worrying about for years, that's great. But don't forget that you also need the ability to use rules to adapt in the short term (as, for example, at the beginning of the COVID-19 pandemic, when things changed so quickly in so many ways). It's better to write a simple rule to tide you over until your model can be trained than to rely entirely on your normally excellent machine learning system and be blindsided.

Make sure you have a variety of tools and approaches available to you so that you can use whichever tool is most appropriate for the task at hand. You may love your hammer, but that doesn't mean every problem is a nail.

Third, when you're considering your tech needs, remember to think about the whole customer journey, from account creation to login to transaction or action and more. If necessary, prioritize which elements are most crucial for extra support or tooling and address them first (but don't forget the rest of them).

This is just as relevant for the parts of a payment that your company doesn't control; make sure you understand the situation with your authentication flows, and if you're losing out there, explore solutions that can help. As usual, there's often a trade-off in terms of user friction, with greater friction being added to reduce false positives, and that should be a part of your wider understanding of company priorities regarding customer experience. Relatedly, if you're interested in frustrating fraudsters by forcing them to provide (and thus burn) more data through authentication processes, that may be relevant to your tech strategy too.

Data Privacy Considerations

Fraud prevention and other work designed to detect and block criminal activity are exempted from many of the data privacy considerations that constrain other industries and departments. For example, Recital 47 (*https://oreil.ly/VxT63*) of the EU's General Data Protection Regulation (GDPR) notes, "The processing of personal data strictly necessary for the purposes of preventing fraud also constitutes a legitimate interest of the data controller concerned." In a similar vein, the California

Privacy Rights Act (CPRA) (*https://oreil.ly/clS8F*) maintains that fraud prevention is an exception to the right to delete "to the extent the use of the consumer's personal information is reasonably necessary and proportionate for those purposes."

The lawmakers are, of course, following a compelling logic; failing to exempt fraud prevention from restrictions on sharing data would play into fraudsters' hands by making it far harder to identify thieves at work, since each company would only be able to work with their own data, plus whatever additional information or clarification they could gain by working collaboratively with other groups using privacy enhancing technology of some form. Data enrichment tools, and in many cases, even third-party solution providers, would no longer be of use, crippling fraud detection efforts. In the same way, the right to insist that a company holding your data deletes it, as introduced by legislation like GDPR, is reasonably mitigated by fraud prevention needs, since if fraudsters could successfully demand the deletion of their data, they would be much harder to catch on their next attempt. Regulators are not in the business of making life easier for fraudsters (at least not intentionally).

For all these reasons, it seems likely that future data privacy legislation, including legislation governing data transfers between jurisdictions, will follow similar patterns in exempting fraud prevention from many of their demands. However, this does not mean fraud prevention departments are unaffected. As teams preparing for GDPR will recall, the structure and searchable nature of the databases used must be amenable to right-to-access requests, right-to-delete requests when appropriate, and so on. Procedures must also be put in place to enable fraud teams to determine when the right-to-delete requests may safely be complied with. Moreover, identity verification processes, necessary to ensure that the person requesting their data really is the person in question, may fall to the lot of the fraud prevention team.

Beyond this, you'll note the words *strictly necessary* and *reasonably necessary and proportionate* used in the regulations quoted earlier. The interpretation of these words, and others like them elsewhere in the regulations, is hugely important in marking out what fraud fighters can and can't do with and about users' data. That's a field day for lawyers, but as part of that discussion, fraud prevention teams need to be able to explain what data they use, why they need it, and what they do with it. This is also worth bearing in mind when considering new tools for data enrichment.

It is important that fraud-fighting teams work together with their company's legal team to ensure that everything is being done not only in compliance with the relevant local laws, but also in ways that are likely to be future-proofed against coming changes. A thorough audit of which data is sent to which vendors and a shrewd analysis of the necessity of various relationships with data brokers may also be valuable. It's important to know how your team stands with regard to data sharing and legislation in order to make your case convincingly should it be necessary to defend your data-sharing practices.

Identifying and Combating New Threats Without Undue Friction

Much of a fraud team's day-to-day work is focused on the immediate moment: which activities or transactions are fraudulent, what patterns or fraud trends or techniques are showing up this week, and how to find the balance between friction and fraud prevention for the customers you have now.

However, research into new threats remains essential. First, if left undetected for long, a new trick can be enormously costly for the business. Second, panicked reactions to surprise threats when they are eventually discovered often result in high friction and lost business. Third, remembering the importance of demonstrating expertise to upper management, it's important to show that you are on top of developments and not learning about a new threat months after the rest of the community has begun talking about it.

Research is often all very good in theory, but it can fall by the wayside under the pressures of more urgent problems. To avoid this, it's worth choosing specific individuals whose job is to investigate certain areas of your own data a specified number of times per month or quarter, and nominate other team members to keep track of forums, articles, and newsletters in the fraud-fighting community. Regular weekly meetings for those who engage in manual reviews are also valuable to enable discussion that can bring new patterns to light. Making these activities set events on the team's calendar will prevent their accidental disappearance.

When new threats are identified, of course, it is important to remember that detection and prevention should be carried out with as little friction as possible for good users. It is always tempting in these situations to overreact and go too far on the risk-averse side of the spectrum, so establishing a procedure for dealing with new threats, which includes the consideration of friction, may be worthwhile.

Keeping Up with New Fraud-Fighting Tools

Just as new fraud techniques evolve over time, vendors are continually developing new fraud-fighting tools to combat them. As with new threats, it's worth having one or more people on your team whose job includes regularly researching new tools so that your team doesn't miss out on the latest option that precisely matches the need you've recently discovered. Some particularly large fraud teams have one person dedicated to this role.

It's important, of course, to assess each tool carefully both alone and in comparison to your existing tools and systems. How much will this new tool improve your accuracy in either increasing fraud detection or reducing friction? Always test the results against your current setup. No matter how good a tool is, even if it comes highly recommended by trusted comrades in the industry, it might not be a good fit for your needs and risk profile.

Summary

This chapter outlined aspects of the framework that underlie a successful fraud prevention team. The system you use, the structure of your team, your relationships with other departments, data privacy considerations, and keeping up with new developments in both fraud and fraud prevention are important elements of creating and running effective fraud-fighting efforts in your company. The next chapter is, in a sense, a companion chapter to this one, exploring fraud prevention modeling options, challenges, and solutions. For many teams, this will be an equally essential fraud-fighting necessity, though the kind of model you use will depend on the challenges you face and the industry in which you're operating.

## CHAPTER 5

Machine Learning and Fraud Modeling

You keep using that word. I do not think it means what you think it means.
—Inigo Montoya, *The Princess Bride*[1]

Before *machine learning* became a buzzword, there were rules. Most fraud analysts still remember using rules exclusively in their fraud automation, and rules continue to be important. But nowadays, they're often used in combination with machine learning. The dominance of machine learning can make it feel like it has been in place for years, but it's actually a relatively new development.

Up until the early 2010s, virtually no fraud team was using machine learning, though many organizations boasted about their early experiments in the field. One of the true pioneers—Fraud Sciences, acquired by PayPal in 2008—made it a habit to hold routine brainstorms to promote a steady stream of "creative juices" as its teams were building the first fraud classifiers. Each and every manually investigated fraud transaction would be inspected by a fraud analyst, who needed to suggest ideas for a model feature (or at the very least, select the most prominent "reasons for analyst decisions" so that those reasons would be turned into features in the model; a list of guesstimated options would then be presented on the in-house fraud investigation UI). Such practices boosted the art and science of fraud detection and helped it scale up rapidly.

Even five years ago, machine learning still felt new, and not every company was willing to take the plunge (although for marketing purposes, many companies claimed to use AI and machine learning on a daily basis). Now it's everywhere. That ubiquity means it's worth taking a step back to remember the advantages of machine learning compared to those of rules engines. It's important not to take the benefits for granted,

---

1 William Goldman, *The Princess Bride*, directed by Rob Reiner (20th Century Fox, 1987).

particularly since we're going to spend some of this chapter talking about the challenges machine learning faces when it comes to fraud prevention.

 Bear in mind as you read this chapter that we're not suggesting machine learning is better than human intelligence. This is not a binary question. Fraud detection and prevention work best in layers. Aside from the automation question, there are things no system can give, such as human research, context, and the ability to make deductions, draw further conclusions, and make strategic plans based on them. Domain expertise, as we noted before and will continue to point out, is essential and irreplaceable. Used appropriately, it can greatly increase the effectiveness and success of a machine learning system. As will become clear later in the chapter, domain expertise is particularly vital when combating some of the challenges machine learning faces within fraud prevention.

The aim of this chapter is not to enable you to create a machine learning model from scratch. For that, you need software engineers or data scientists or, probably, both. The purpose of this chapter is to help you understand the context in which machine learning is used within fraud prevention, what it can do, what it struggles with, and in a general sense, how it works. If you do want to dive into the details of machine learning from the mathematical perspective, there are wonderful courses by Andrew Ng (*https://oreil.ly/Oj4Wi*) and Yaser Abu-Mostafa (*https://oreil.ly/WCLR2*) you could try.

Instead of being presumptuous enough to claim that we can teach modeling in this book, we'll aim to demystify the concept of machine learning in fraud prevention. As Noam Naveh puts it:[2]

> Machine learning is an umbrella term for the process of developing and using statistical models to make predictions based on past data. As an example, this may entail training a model on a large number of past transactions, each labeled "fraudulent" or "legit," then asking the model to predict whether a new transaction is fraudulent or legit. The term "machine learning" is so sexy that it has become synonymous with a cure-all solution to fraud (and many other problems).

We will do our best in this chapter to highlight the types of diseases that machine learning can cure, and the possible side effects.

---

2 Noam Naveh, "Machine Learning: Is It Your Best Bet for Online Fraud Prevention?" (*https://oreil.ly/fCTVs*) *Fraud Strategy* (blog), May 18, 2015.

Advantages of Machine Learning

Machine learning offers a number of advantages:

Scale

Ecommerce, online banking, and online payments more generally have grown astronomically in recent years, and this was before the digital transformation resulting from the COVID-19 pandemic. Organizations are simply dealing with far greater numbers of users, orders, and interactions now. Machines have no difficulty with that. Moreover, the more data you can include in your data sets, the more accurate you'll be in your decisions, and machines find it much easier to deal with the sheer scale of data now involved in any single decision. Since rules rely on humans keeping up with what's going on, their evolution is far more likely to lag behind.

Subtlety

Rules make large, sweeping strokes. Models can be far more subtle, which is more appropriate for the fraud-fighting use case. For instance, you don't want a rule that a virtual private network (VPN) + reshipper combination should either be declined or be sent to manual review. You want a system to be able to recognize automatically when this is a sign of fraud and when it's a sign of a Chinese shopper acting in a completely normal and legitimate manner.

Diversity

Increasingly, businesses work on a global basis. There are simply too many variables to build into reasonable rule sets; you'd need different sets of rules for every country, age group, and so on. Machines have no trouble adapting to different groups, as long as they have enough data (more on that point later in this chapter).

Adaptability

Rules engines quickly become obsolete; it's hard to escape a "set and forget" mentality. Once you've put a rule in place, it will keep doing its job(s). But it might not be relevant for long. Once it's stopped being a useful rule, it may remain in place for quite a while, as few teams have the time or flexibility to review their entire rules set often, even if they do it regularly. Irrelevant rules can cause false positives, let fraud through, and even clash with one another. Machine learning won't have this problem—though you do need to ensure that you're retraining your models on a regular basis so that your system stays up to date with current trends.

Load variance

Holiday periods, flash sales, and so on flood your system and your team with data and users. For your team, that's stressful. For a machine learning system, it just means more machines need to be on the job. This also makes life easier for your team, as it can reduce the number of extra analysts you need for these periods. (Of course, there's still an increase in manual reviews, but machine learning can reduce the amount of manual review you need to do, and it takes the pressure off the need to continually adapt the rules on top of manual review.) Just make sure to train your model separately on data sets that focus on the holiday/flash-sale time frame. Otherwise, your model might classify the typical "holiday shopper" as fraud (more on dealing with transaction load variance can be found in an RSA lecture titled "We're Trending!! When Traffic Is Spiking, How Do You Know It's Legit?" (*https://oreil.ly/nmlcH*)).

Pattern recognition

Machines are great at this, because again, they see all the data. No single analyst can do this, and although fraud teams can do it very effectively with good communication, continual research, and regular collaboration, they can't match the speed at which fraudsters work. Moreover, there are some patterns fraud analysts are less likely to see by themselves, because they hide within data points that typically get less human attention. Machines can help draw attention to these, as well as enable reaction to them. Beyond reacting to specific threats, fraud analysts, seeing the patterns in context, can then draw deductions and make decisions about where to go next to protect the business.

The Challenges of Machine Learning in Fraud Prevention

Fraud prevention is perhaps one of the most compelling examples of the value of machine learning in action. Analyst firms Gartner and Forrester were talking about the in-depth details of machine learning in this context well before they were giving much time to exploring its possibilities in other fields. In many ways, it's a great fit, and the results have been impressive.

Nonetheless, there are certain characteristics of the fraud prevention use case that actually stand out as particularly *inappropriate* for machine learning. Though these can be managed and their effect mitigated, it is crucial that you understand what they are and their impact on your systems, and also to appreciate that although impactful, machine learning is not magic.

Most of these aspects cause difficulties with rules engines as well, though in that context they tend to be overlooked. They're reflective of the nature of fraud prevention in general. Don't think of them as problems. They're…challenges.

Relative Paucity of Data

It seems strange to talk about this in the era of big data, but when it comes to fraud prevention, there's a relative paucity of data. You might have lots of orders and lots of users, but you probably don't have *that* many fraudulent ones.

We're speaking relatively here. We know it can feel like a lot, and that it can represent substantial risk and loss to the business. But in machine learning terms, it's really not that much, especially when you factor in the number of parameters you want to include. For instance, to give a very simplified case, you'll want to give the machine examples of your different product categories and the range of devices and browsers used by customers. Think how many variables there are just in those basic parameters. So many product categories, so many devices, so many browsers. But the machine needs a good number of examples of *all* of them, plus all the different ways they combine.

This is even more notable when you take into account the different kinds of fraud. Stolen credit card fraud is not the same as account takeover (ATO), but it's probable your team needs to guard against both. This means the machine needs enough examples of all the kinds of fraud you're up against. You might not have that many instances of fraud of certain types, or certain techniques.

Plus, fraudsters adapt like lightning, and you don't want to wait months before your system has enough data to identify and prevent a new technique accurately.

Moreover, many businesses operate within more than one vertical, or even industry. The patterns of fraud against your laptops may be different from those attacking your headphones. Or they might not. But they might. That's even more challenging when it comes to marketplaces, which typically have greater diversity.

And think about geography. Maybe you sell primarily in the United States, so you have enough data from there. But you also sell in Europe, and a little in the Asia-Pacific region. Each country you sell to has slightly different norms, and that's just considering legitimate buyers! Fraudsters sometimes show trends depending on the country as well. Do you have enough data for the machine to learn accurately about all of them?

Again, bear in mind that you really don't want the machine making the wrong deductions and labeling incorrectly, where it can be avoided. That can be expensive to the business and difficult to track down and fix.

Delayed Feedback and Overfitting

With fraud prevention, much of the feedback you get about whether a decision was correct or not comes with a delay. Chargebacks, for instance, may come one to three months after a transaction was processed. Sometimes consumers won't notice a fraudulent transaction on their card, or that their account has been hacked and misused, until much later. For instance, they may not notice their loyalty points have been stolen until the holidays, when they planned to use them, even if the theft occurred nearly a year earlier. They might not notice at all.

All of this means that the feedback your system is getting—which is what tells it whether its predictions were accurate or not—is often delayed, sometimes significantly so. But fraudsters move quickly. If you're really unlucky, an especially sneaky trick might go unnoticed for over a month, until the chargebacks start coming in.

One of the reasons this delay is so problematic is the danger of *overfitting*, or training a model to deal with a set of data so precisely that it becomes too tightly tailored, making it unreliable when making predictions about new data.

In other words, it's not hard to train a machine to pick out fraudulent and legitimate instances with absolute precision—when it comes to training data. But the more precise it is, the more likely that learning won't adapt well to the real world. For instance, it may have learned to pick out some edge cases as fraudulent because they combined a specific browser, device, and product. Those were the things that linked those cases, in the machine's "eyes," based only on the training data. But in reality, when you give it new data you want to be able to accept some transactions that match that pattern.

Of course, with the delayed feedback you might not notice this problem for some time, which means you'd be rejecting those transactions for the wrong reasons. If you don't conduct regular research, you may not notice false positive problems at all.

That's overfitting, and it applies as much to fraud cases as to false positives. And overfitting is more concerning when you remember that, in the case of fraud prevention, it's combined with relative paucity of data.

The Labeled Data Difficulty

The labeled data difficulty is a particularly interesting challenge. *Labeled data* is often thought of as a model training problem, which it is, but it's also pertinent as your model becomes increasingly better tailored to your needs.

The core concept of how a supervised machine learning system works is simple: you give the machine lots of data and make sure it's labeled. (Unsupervised machine learning is even simpler: you just give it a lot of data. More on this distinction in "Classification Versus Clustering" on page 96.) So, if you want to teach a supervised machine learning system to recognize photos of cats successfully, you give it lots of photos labeled "cats" and lots labeled "not cats." The machine learns to recognize "cats" and can then do so with new, unlabeled photos in the future.

So, to train a machine learning algorithm in the first place, you need to feed it many examples of transactions or actions from the past labeled as either legitimate or fraudulent. It is crucial that these labels be as accurate as possible; otherwise, you'll be training the machine to recognize the wrong things, and then it'll make mistakes with the new cases you give it and you'll end up with either chargebacks or false declines.

There are some obvious challenges here. First, there's the delayed feedback issue just discussed. If a transaction is only a couple of weeks old and the chargeback hasn't come through, you'll treat it as legitimate and the machine will learn from a mistaken label. But if you ignore everything from the past three months, the machine won't have access to the latest patterns and trends.

Second, you've got false positives to worry about. We all have them. But you don't want the machine to learn from them. A risk-averse mentality can be really problematic here because the fact is, if you reject a transaction outright, you never get the data at all. So, you're not given the chance to learn to avoid false positives.

An additional problem, often overlooked, is the price of success. Say your machine learning system is doing really well. You trained it effectively, it adapted and tailored admirably to your particular needs and trends, and you're stopping fraudsters left and right and letting good users in smoothly. You end up with much less data about fraud, fraudsters, and fraud attacks. You're blocking the fraudsters, so your model isn't getting new information about fraudulent transactions or actions on your site. When a fraudster or a fraud ring tries something really new, you'll be blindsided.

Additionally, if your successful attack rate is really low, it's likely at the cost of false positives. You're preventing people from buying, or you're blocking them from entering or using their account. It's for this reason that some sophisticated fraud teams prefer to purposely allow a small number of dubious transactions to go through in order to learn whether they are indeed fraudulent or not. This way, they avoid high false positives—they're not being overly cautious—and they give the machine new data to learn from so that it continues to learn about new tricks and techniques fraudsters are evolving.

The extent to which this policy is possible depends on your business and risk appetite, but as long as you have clear limitations on the risk you're willing to run, the overall results can be very much in your favor compared to the costs of false positives.

Intelligent Adversary

Fraudsters fight back! Infuriating, absorbing, and intriguing, this is the aspect of the profession that keeps many fraud analysts coming back for more. Fraud prevention would not be endlessly absorbing if you weren't up against intelligent adversaries.

Fraudsters were, and are, highly skilled at scoping out rules meant to guard against them. If a retailer sends every order over $200 to manual review, fraudsters will work that out and make orders of $199. If bill-ship mismatch is caught by your address verification service (AVS) and declined by a particular site, they'll cheat AVS by matching numbers but not road names, or they'll use customer service to change the address only *after* the order has been approved. And so on.

A similar approach works against machine learning. From the fraudster point of view, the result of the machine learning systems is another kind of web of rules (admittedly, a more complex one), which nevertheless is essentially a framework they can work out and work around.

There are also tricks that are more likely to work against machines than humans, such as intentionally throwing a lot of fraudulent attacks at a particular time of day to oversensitize the machine to that time through overfitting, and then purposely attacking at a different time. Fraudsters love playing these sorts of games.

You never have to worry about this sort of thing when you're teaching a machine to recognize cat photos.

Explainability, Ethics, and Bias

To emphasize the difference between an algorithm trained to identify cat photos and an algorithm designed to support fraud decisions, consider the challenge of racial discrimination in face recognition technology (*https://oreil.ly/QiH4f*). Many of the data scientists we interviewed for this book openly argued that it's much better to train a model that would show mediocre performance for the entire population than to create a model that shows 100% accuracy in facial recognition for white males only, while discriminating against minorities. (Google certainly learned the importance of this truth with its Pixel 6 Camera (*https://oreil.ly/mK5jl*).)

The importance of creating an ethical model, unbiased by racial and socioeconomic factors, goes far beyond the potential impact on the brand in the public view. Auditors may rightfully demand to know that when Bob or Alice applies for a loan they will not be declined based on their gender, sexuality, or race. However, how does the question of socioeconomic class play into the credit decision? Can, and should, a model be unbiased toward this metric, which is highly correlative with Bob's or Alice's likelihood of repaying their debt?

Most data scientists when faced with this type of dilemma will opt for training a model on features that are easy to expose and explain in case of an audit, but are not too obviously derived from a person's origin. For example, both zip codes and number of bedrooms make good features, since a person's living conditions reveal something about their financial situation.

Of course, this type of political strategy of model design has its flaws. Is it possible that Alice, who lives in a fairly nice neighborhood in a one-bedroom apartment, deserves a loan because her last name would teach us that she came from a family of recent immigrants who had to build themselves from scratch, so she knows the value of money? Is it possible that Bob, who lives in the same nice neighborhood in a one-bedroom apartment, is really a member of the wealthy Walton family, but his living conditions indicate that he's the least responsible member of his clan? And how will gentrification affect the models' performance? We can't fully trust the automated algorithms to make the best conscientious decision, so the current tendency in the field is to restrict models with blindfolds.

Fraud decisioning models suffer from the same ethical dilemma as the algorithms that make headlines for racial and gender bias in health care (*https://oreil.ly/F0Tnx*), or those that feed our future fears of autonomous cars (try the Moral Machine (*https://www.moralmachine.net*) to understand how unnerving it must be to design the models that decide between crashing into one young pedestrian or two elderly ones). The ethical considerations may easily slow down technology, as data scientists who work in heavily regulated industries, such as consumer credit, may give up neural networks modeling to avoid these issues.

For similar reasons, many data scientists may be discouraged from going too deep (forgive the pun) into deep learning. The lure of using deep learning tech is obvious, partly because it should save the manual steps of feature extraction, as several "machine learning as a service" operations promise to do. Figure 5-1 emphasizes the "magic" of generating features out of the data automatically.

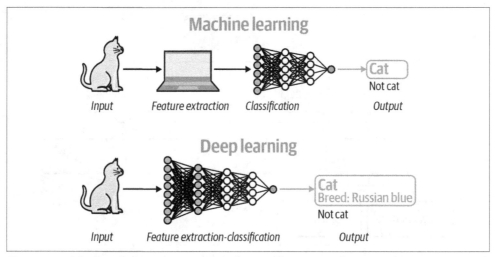

Figure 5-1. Machine learning versus deep learning[3]

However, due to the numerous reasons mentioned so far, the vast majority of organizations will still opt for the more "controlled" flavors of machine learning. Banks, retailers, and everything in between all fear the risk of insulting a customer with a decision to decline their transaction, plus the risk of having to explain the decision to

---

3 Adapted from Aaron Edell, "Understand These Four Advanced Concepts to Sound like a Machine Learning Master" (*https://oreil.ly/Hau5S*), *Towards Data Science* (blog), November 20, 2018.

an auditor, especially when the industry is painfully aware of the correlation (if not causation) between socioeconomic status and fraud.

Thus, as long as biased models are considered worse than poor-performance models, we'll need to double down on making the models as explainable as possible. Auditors, senior management, and the press may understand in theory that correlation is not the same as causality. But in practice they want to know *why* Alice's loan application was denied and will be unforgiving if they come to believe that the model discriminates against females.

Over the second half of the past decade, many data scientists have turned to tree models, partly because the process of their training allows some visibility and explainability for product, business, and compliance purposes. A tree model (see Figure 5-2) is usually considered less of a black box than many other forms of machine learning, because it's fairly easy to follow its path of a specific decision. It's not easy to change a tree model once it's trained (you cannot control the route that the model has chosen), but at least now you'll be able to demonstrate that it wasn't "just" Alice's gender that played into the decision.

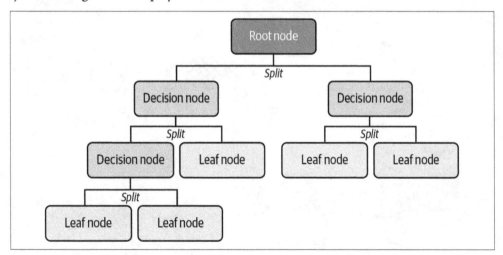

Figure 5-2. Example of a simple decision tree template

Dynamic Policies and the Merits of Story-Based Models

Even if we were to set aside ethical complexities, the best fraud prediction classifier is still seldom trusted to make the final call. Model outputs are rarely used directly to make decisions, because at best they can provide a probability score or a likelihood that a certain payment is fraudulent. It takes policy considerations, often backed with a set of policy rules, to set the threshold.

In the vast majority of cases, organizations will not aim to reach 0% fraud, since that would require impossibly high decline rates (some would say that only a 0% approval rate can lead to 0% fraud). When a business tries to expand into a new region or audience, or when sales are spiking during the holidays, you may want to penetrate the market and accept more fraud.

On the negative side, data scientists often feel that their work is being cast aside too easily with any new business opportunity. On the positive side, dynamic business can yield control groups. It also encourages data scientists to push the envelope and develop models for use cases of higher resolution.

Story-based models—often from the family of clustering—are a good way to bridge the gap between data scientists and policy teams. For example, a model that aims to find only tourists in your buying population (sending things to hotels or hostels, using hotel/hostel WiFi or airport WiFi, etc.) is sometimes far more practical than a huge model that predicts overall fraud. Opting for this type of higher-resolution model can benefit both model performance and model explainability by breaking down the modeling problem into smaller questions.

So, instead of a model that needs to identify all fraud, how about aiming for a model that only spots cases of teenage fraudsters who are using stolen identities of people they know to pay for gaming goods? Yes, you'll need to work harder to reach a reasonable training set—and you risk overfitting—but you'll be able to bring more delicacy into the modeling work in addition to higher clarity for your auditors and your product and business colleagues.

Using "smaller" models will give product/policy/business folks a stronger sense of control, since they'll be able to ask you to shut down only the model that's affecting one specific story (not that we're trying to minimize the impact this can have, but at least it's less intimidating than shutting down a model with even wider impact). Neural networks are probably less suitable for this purpose, as they are much less transparent and intuitive than tree models or regression.

For an even higher level of transparency, visualizations can be helpful. Many types of models can be explained with a what-if visualization tool (such as GitHub's What-If Tool (*https://oreil.ly/4J0LF*); see Figure 5-3). The life of your data scientists becomes much easier once your product team can show that the model would make the same decision for (for instance) a bald person and a person with hair by simply clicking the button and changing the value from "bald" to "not bald" on the drop-down list.

Figure 5-3. Example of what easy-to-read output from a model might look like

Moreover, story-based classifiers are a great way to promote the collaboration between data scientists and in-domain experts. The following section details our view on how to create an effective data science and domain expert "squad."

Data Scientists and Domain Experts: Best Practices for a Fruitful Collaboration

We have seen, in practice, tremendous value from working with data scientists and have great respect for their contribution to the fraud prevention effort, especially in the context of machine learning. There's nothing like having someone with a PhD in statistics to help you navigate what is always essentially a probabilistic exercise.

That said, we strongly believe that trying to apply data science to fraud prevention without the benefit of strong domain expertise in this field is futile. This was one area where we experienced an astonishing amount of unanimity from the experts we consulted, both fraud analysts and data scientists. It's a collaborative effort.

The two main reasons this collaboration is so crucial reflect topics we've covered already in this chapter:

Labeling
    As we said, most fields of fraud prevention suffer from training sets of chronically insubstantial quality. Fraud cases are relatively rare, they are naturally diverse because fraudsters change their behavior frequently, and friendly fraud causes terrible noise. Because of all this, a fraud analyst is often needed to do some clever cherry-picking; that is, decide which fraud cases represent a behavior

---

that is likely to repeat itself in the future and that should be considered as candidates for a separate training set for another model. For example, imagine a classifier aiming to predict fraud but trained on a mix of ATO and account-opening fraud; the results would be far from optimal. On the other hand, too much cherry-picking will result in a highly overfitted model. Getting it right requires both data science knowledge and fraud domain expertise.

Featuring

Features can be extracted from a data set automatically, but due to the aforementioned limited nature of training sets, many of these may be ineffective. Think of a fraud trend in which a single fraudster generates thousands of incidents using a set of stolen credit cards. If the set of cards the fraudster happened to purchase were sorted alphabetically by cardholder name, a large number of incidents would have the same first letter to their name. Software that automatically generates features would then suggest the letter *A* as a feature. A domain expert is needed at least to sanity-check the features, predict significant codependencies, and uncover complex features (such as IP types) that can represent significant informational gain for the model.

That said, some areas more naturally will be the domain of a data science/machine learning expert and others more naturally will belong to fraud fighters. In the first category, you'd find cases such as spam and social media abuse scenarios, where offensive behavior happens en masse and often with automated or cookie-cutter behavior (think of social media bots and trolls; even the human ones are fairly consistent in behavior).

Adtech fraud, at least in its basic form, is also heavily automated and therefore is a good candidate for using machine learning to tackle anomaly detection and building effective models. (For more on this use case, see Chapter 23.) Catching distributed denial-of-service (DDoS) attacks and brute-force scenarios (such as password guessing and credential stuffing) may also be good candidates for this category.

In these realms of anomaly detection, when your analysis is aimed at finding mostly bots, a top-down analysis is probably the most efficient approach. You'll be able to start with high-level breakdowns of your traffic, such as mobile versus desktop or Android versus iOS, then gradually drill down toward spotting the problem area that is infected by the bot.

On the other hand, when it comes to the more human forms of manipulation, such as impersonation in its various forms as well as social engineering and mules, you're likely to want the human touch. Trying to apply models and/or top-down regressions will be like finding a needle in a haystack for these scenarios. In some contexts, artificial intelligence is just not that intelligent.

Working Well Together

Despite all the reasons data scientists and fraud experts have to collaborate, it can sometimes be difficult to meld their different perspectives and, sometimes, priorities. Here are some tips to make the process of generating new models work well in your team.

Be clear about who is responsible for which elements

For instance, who codes the features? Many of the veterans we consulted remember fondly the collaborative process of a developer and an analyst working together, aiming for an elaborate, complex feature that is able to separate fraud from not-fraud with great precision. This might be a good methodology for building a holistic model, such as one that covers all the ATO cases in your business. But it's probably less relevant when you need a quick solution for a more local problem—and that's often what you'll be working on. Don't stick to a division of work you're used to just because it's familiar; consider whether it makes sense in the context of the challenge you're dealing with.

Establish a goal

Do you want to teach the system what to look for? Create a model that can take actions? Help your team with research? If you want the model to take actions, do you want it to be able to block transactions or actions? Be clear about the goal from the start, because it impacts everything else. Your model and its input should depend on what you want the outcome to be. Don't just throw money or code or models at the problem.

Establish your focus

This relies on what you want to do with the information from the model. If you're focusing on avoiding false positives and want to send uncertain cases to manual review, you'll want the model to be looking at the "gray area" examples. It doesn't need many instances of clear fraud. On the other hand, if you're focusing on blocking fraud, instances of clear fraud are your main interest.

Know what main features the model should be looking at

You might want the model itself to come up with some of these, but even then it's recommended that you at least have a working theory to estimate what the key features should be. A good place to start could be a checklist of potential features your manual review teams can tick as they go through cases. If a certain feature gets selected often as a key reason code, it should be a strong feature in the model as well.

Determine your risk appetite

Is this a "one strike and you're out" sort of situation, or do you want to limit the number of times a user can take a certain action? If the latter, do you need to do research to work out how many times would be optimal in this case? Many data scientists will attest that model output can never be used directly to make decisions, because a policy decision will always be needed to adjust the threshold to reality. For instance, if the organization wants to go into a new region and penetrate the market, more fraud should be tolerated. In a similar manner, some policies are only set in order to create a control group, such as deciding that transactions below a certain amount should pass/fail/go to review regardless of the model's decision.

Determine what prior knowledge can be introduced into the model

There are ample ways for domain experts to introduce their knowledge into the modeling process. An open dialogue with data science teams should emphasize that a "knowledgeable" model will enjoy fewer weights, which traditionally is a recommended way to control overfitting (*https://oreil.ly/TBGzA*). As a domain expert, you should be there, side by side with the data scientist, to assess feature importance and conduct thorough gap analyses on cases that contradict your intuition. Don't ignore cases in the test set that received a high fraud probability by the classifier, despite showing a "legit" key feature, such as a governmental IP. Some of the best fraud stories, if not some of the strongest improvements to the model, are revealed this way.

Determine which model best suits the problem

Consult your data science team openly (and patiently) about the many possible options. Classifiers and regressions may work well traditionally, when a domain expert is available to "clean" and exclude outliers in order to reduce the noise that could "confuse" the model. For example, it used to be popular to decide that IP geolocation features need to be tuned in order to exclude satellite connections, whose geolocation is nonindicative for the users' location. Nowadays, tree-based models are often used in a manner that should overcome this need for exclusion, but a fairly long process of random forest training may be needed in order to validate that the features selected by most trees still make sense (e.g., if your data scientists work several weeks and train 100 trees showing that the most indicative feature in 99 of the trees turned out to be "Buyer's first name starts with the letter A," you'll know something went wrong, probably in the training set).

Find out what the process is for fine tuning, retraining, and gap analysis

This is possibly the most important question to bring up with the data scientists when trying to decide on the right type of model to train. Explainability is a huge issue in data science today, as some algorithms make it easier than others. More on this in just a moment.

If you don't understand, ask

Data scientists sometimes use technical terminology in normal conversations. That's customary for a data scientist, and it's also customary for someone to interrupt them politely and ask for an explanation of the term. If you need to ask more than once, that's OK too. This isn't your field, and the right thing to do is ask for more information. Luckily, you have an expert to help you. In the same way, encourage data scientists to ask about fraud terms and techniques so that they have valuable context in which to work.

Be kind to one another

No, this isn't a self-help book, but just giving one another the benefit of the doubt really can go a long way. Start with the default assumption that everyone wants the best outcome for the company. It's almost always the truth. They just have different perspectives on the nature of the best outcome and how to get there. Data scientists might feel that exploring fun new techniques or technologies is worthwhile because when they work they can bring huge benefits to the team and the company. Fraud analysts might be desperate for an immediate solution to an urgent problem, even if it's not elegant. Everyone is doing their best. Try to bear that in mind, especially when you head into a meeting where you suspect the people in the room aren't going to agree or have quite the same approach or priorities in mind.

Popular Machine Learning Approaches

The shared factor with the approaches we'll discuss is that (take a deep breath, machine learning lovers) fraud analysts cannot live by machine learning alone. Machine learning is a hugely powerful tool in the fraud analyst's kit, but it's just a tool and not a silver bullet. The good news is that fraud analysts can't be replaced by machine learning either. They can't even be replaced by data scientists. If anything, fraud domain expertise is even more vital than ever.

We'll talk in just a moment about the most popular machine learning types of models and how they adapt to the most common challenges we discussed. But what's common to all of them is that they rely on fraud teams engaging in research and review, and feeding intelligence back into the model.

Let's take an extreme case to illustrate this point. Think of what happened when the COVID-19 pandemic hit. Machine learning systems struggled to catch up with the wildly different patterns they were suddenly seeing. Teams that understood the context it was happening in and could step in to make the necessary adjustments had the most success in adapting quickly to the new situation. They could, where relevant, add rules to deal with the pressing problems and then work on adapting their machine learning system after that.

In a less dramatic sense, this happens all the time. Fine-tuning requires context. Analysis of the big picture requires both context and domain expertise. Machine learning systems need fraud analysts working with them to prune, trim, water, and graft in new data where relevant (to take a gardening analogy possibly slightly too far).

The more a shift to machine learning can remove the stresses of manual review of transactions and actions taking place right now, the more time your team can spend on bigger-picture analysis and research that will teach your team and your company more about your users, the fraudsters attacking you, and how to improve your system overall.

Accuracy Versus Explainability and Predictability

Like everything else in fraud prevention, machine learning is about trade-offs. When choosing types of models, one of the most striking trade-offs is the one between accuracy and explainability/interpretability. Accuracy is, of course, vital—but how important is it that you are able to understand *why* the machine made the decision that it did? In the case of cat photos, you might not care. But with fraud prevention, patterns in user behavior, products, fraud tactics, and so on are constantly shifting. You do need to have a reasonable level of explainability in order to know when you need to change things, and predict how the model will behave after the change. You can't just think about where you are now. You need to plan ahead for what will happen next month, or next quarter, or next year. Wherever possible, it's really essential to build a feedback loop that allows analytics/operations to improve labeling of real data toward the next model.

For this reason, it's the three model types trending toward the righthand side of the graph in Figure 5-4 that are most popular in fraud prevention, with random forests—which you can see strike more of a balance between accuracy and interpretability—probably the most popular in the industry at the moment. Some of the "cooler" technology, such as neural networks, may promise great results, but would it be easy enough to deep-dive into a neural network model in three to four months when the fraud pattern shifts? Probably not.

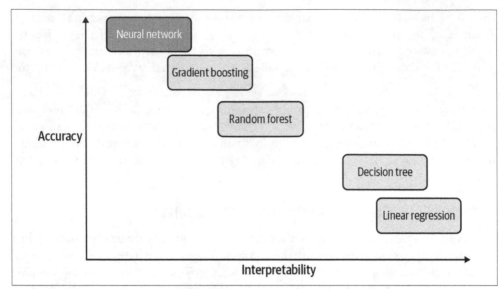

Figure 5-4. Accuracy versus interpretability in machine learning model types

Classification Versus Clustering

Both classification and clustering have their place in fraud prevention machine learning discussions. Both are used to categorize transactions, actions, and so on into one of a number of classes based on the features each transaction or action demonstrates. With classification you give predefined labels, whereas with clustering you don't label the data and instead see what the machine finds by itself. That's why classification is supervised learning and clustering is unsupervised learning. If you want to know more about the technical distinction between classification and clustering, "Classification vs Clustering" (*https://oreil.ly/TPlZr*) is a good place to start. Each has advantages and disadvantages. Table 5-1 shows some of these.

Table 5-1. Characteristics of classification versus clustering models

Parameter	Classification	Clustering
Type	Used for supervised learning	Used for unsupervised learning
Basic	Process of classifying the input instances based on their corresponding class labels	Grouping the instances based on their similarity without the help of class labels
Need	It has labels, so the data set needs to be trained and tested to verify the model that was created	There is no need to train or test the data set
Complexity	More complex than clustering	Less complex than classification
Example algorithms	Logistic regression; Naive Bayes	K-means clustering algorithm; Fuzzy C-means clustering algorithm; Gaussian (EM) clustering algorithm; etc.

Generally speaking, classifiers are the natural go-to for designing a predictive algorithm that separates fraud from not-fraud. Clustering is used for clarity, when researchers want to understand what's going on in the ocean of data that usually accompanies any online operation. Clustering is also sometimes a good way to bring data scientists into the loop of fraud discussions earlier in the process. Instead of waiting for the analysts to come up with features, data scientists can identify clusters of similar cases that will help fraud fighters brainstorm for feature ideas.

For example, clustering models are wonderful for similarity detection in cases that require some cultural delicacy. Models that aim to cluster together users from the same community can be an alternative to "origin" or "ethnicity" features. Will the results be 100% free of bias? Probably not. Can they nonetheless help provide credit to users who would be missed by a more conservative model? Probably.

Precision versus recall

Once a classifier is on its way to completion, it's time to have a serious talk about setting the right threshold. The most accurate model in the world could show catastrophic results if it is not utilized properly. A classic example for this statement would be the question of setting a threshold for your predictive model.

Looking at the results of your classifier will suggest a separation between the fraud and not-fraud cases that probably looks something like Figure 5-5.

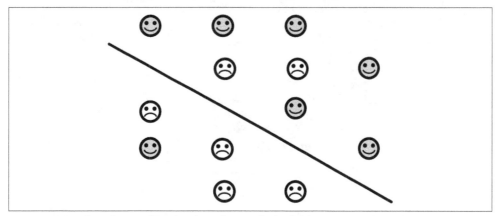

Figure 5-5. What the results of a classifier might look like

Yes, it would be nice if all the smiley faces were on one side and all the frowns were on the other, but that's not realistic in the complex, messy, real world of fraud and fraud prevention. Machine learning isn't magic. Everything we've said in previous chapters about the balance between stopping fraud and encouraging sales is just as true here. You'll have to decide, internally, where you want to fall on the fraud versus false positive scale. Is it more important to stop fraud, or to avoid insulting customers by wrongful rejection?

In this context, it's worth saying a word about precision and recall, terms you'll likely hear a lot if you're hanging around data scientists. While fraud fighters tend to talk about *accuracy*—how precise the model was at predicting fraud, ideally with low chargebacks and low false positives—you'll likely find that data scientists talk about precision and recall.

For the purposes of most fraud detection discussions, *precision* refers to how often the transactions you reject are in fact true positives; that is, they really are fraud. In the same way, *recall* is telling you how much of the fraud attacking your business your team manages to catch. You can get an impression of how these terms play out in relation to one another in Figure 5-6. In terms of an illustrative example, in Figure 5-5, four out of five of the cases you stopped really were true fraud, so your precision rate is 4/5, or 80%. In terms of recall, you caught four out of six fraud attacks, so your recall rate is 4/6, or 66.6%.

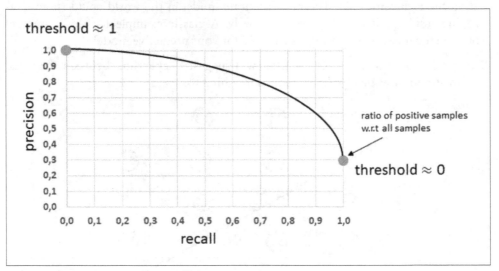

Figure 5-6. Precision versus recall[4]

It's important to remember, as we've mentioned before, that the desired recall versus precision (also known as sensitivity versus accuracy or true fraud versus insult) is not a data science question, but rather, a business question. Is your business financially stable enough to endure a few fraud cases slipping through the cracks? Can your business grow with decline rates that allow for catching enough fraud? Check your

---

4 Thomas Kurbiel, "Gaining an Intuitive Understanding of Precision, Recall and Area Under Curve" (*https://oreil.ly/lKtLL*), *Towards Data Science* (blog), April 28, 2018.

fraud/insult graph to make the best decision possible. For more about the precision versus recall question, see Thomas Kurbiel's blog post, "Gaining an Intuitive Understanding of Precision, Recall and Area Under Curve" (*https://oreil.ly/lKtLL*).

In the real world, you're not going to catch 100% of the fraud and at the same time avoid 100% of the false positives. When you start thinking about where you want to put your thresholds, it's crucial to understand what the trade-offs are for the model. If you can improve precision by 10% at the cost of recall going down by 15%, is that worth it? Depending on your priorities, it might be. The important thing is that the decision is a conscious one.

Success criteria

Clear key performance indicators (KPIs) are needed for any type of work, but in modeling they are even more crucial, since both the training set and the validation/gap analysis to be performed on the test set need to be sampled and reviewed, preferably manually. If your model yields a probability score, aim to sample both the lowest and highest scores, plus some that are nearing your expected threshold and a few that present extremely high rates of features that you expected to be effective. You'll also want to look at a few that do not present any of the expected key features but still had high probability scores. "Surprises" in the test set are usually a gold mine that should be used to generate features for the next model.

When you're conducting your gap analysis review, take into account these questions:

- Do the key features present themselves in the incident?
- Is the incident fraudulent?
- Does the incident match the major fraud type that appeared on the training set?

Summary

This chapter looked at why machine learning has been such a huge leap for fraud detection and prevention, and also why it's not a silver bullet. We explored the challenges machine learning faces when dealing with fraud prevention specifically, and looked at some important terms and types of models used. We learned—to quote Zach Moshe, an experienced leading data scientist who contributed greatly in inspiration and guidance to this chapter—that "models are a bit like kids. Give them a playground of data to play with and they'll do wonderful things, but don't forget to give them a couple of boundaries so that your prior knowledge of the world can steer them, or at least nudge them, in the right direction."

We now have all the context we need to move on to talking about specific types of fraud and fraud analysis, which is what the rest of the book is about. So, bring with you the knowledge you've gained so far as we dive into a range of fraudster MOs and what fraud fighters can do to identify and stop them.

 We want to thank Zach Moshe and Gali Ellenblum, whose inspiring insights were generously shared with us in a series of (fun!) interviews and correspondences. These experts hold vast experience and deep understanding, accumulated over years of research for giants such as Google, Apple, and PayPal, as well as through their significant contributions as engineers, data scientists, and/or consultants to several successful startups, including Forter, Signifyd, Wonga, Simplex, Klarna, FriendlyCredit, and more. Please note that both Zach and Gali, as well as the writers of this book, come mainly from the fields of ecommerce and so the evolution of machine learning and the best practices that we've recommended apply mostly to use cases from these areas, notably the use cases of credit, payments, and consumer account protection.

Ecommerce Fraud Analytics

The preceding chapters covered the wider trends and frameworks we consider relevant to fraud analysts in almost any industry. In many ways, of course, fraudsters are agnostics; the same fraudster or fraud organization may attack more than one industry. Fraudsters do not think in terms of clear categories for our convenience. They look for vulnerabilities everywhere, and they exploit them when they find them.

Fraud analysts who have worked across industries such as retail, banking, and online marketplaces will likely relate to this. Elena Michaeli, who has worked in banking, peer-to-peer (P2P) payments, and an online chat platform and is now at Shutterstock, said: "Each industry is different and there's a lot to learn, but really what struck me most about the fraudsters we were blocking, as I moved between industries, was the similarities I saw. The same sorts of techniques, the same types of attacks. Sometimes even the same fraud rings!"

However, as fraud fighters we need to be sensitive to the differences between industries. Certain attacks tend to be far more common in certain industries, which makes particular identification processes and mitigation strategies more appropriate in those industries.

Part II focuses on attacks that are typically carried out against ecommerce companies. While these attacks are especially relevant to fraud prevention professionals working in ecommerce, some are also relevant to fraud fighters working in the online and banking arenas and to anti–money laundering (AML) professionals.

Most chapters in the rest of the book include both a theoretical description of the fraud attack and an example for a datapoint that can be used during investigation. For instance, Chapter 6 uses only IPs as the chosen datapoint, when in reality, IPs, emails, phones, and many more pieces of data will play into your analysis; Chapter 7 focuses on physical address analysis, when in fact, addresses are always analyzed in the context of IPs, identities, and so on.

The Preface provides a breakdown of which data point is discussed in which chapter.

Stolen Credit Card Fraud

He deals the cards... and those he plays never suspect...
—Sting[1]

The first fraud victim Gilit ever met was her father. A careful man, he checked his credit card statements regularly. One fine day he was surprised to see that he had bought goods in Ukraine and had run up charges with various online gaming vendors. Initially he was surprised: he couldn't understand how the theft was possible, since the card was still in his wallet and he had never used it online. But then he was amused: the bank that issued the card reassured him he would not be footing the bill for any of this activity, and he enjoyed imagining himself roaming Kyiv.

This kind of introduction to fraud isn't unusual, and Shoshana has similar stories to tell from the experiences of her family and friends. Stolen credit card fraud is the form of fraud that regular consumers are most likely to be aware of, through personal experience or that of a friend or family member. Unfortunately, even fairly basic attacks such as this one still manage to go unnoticed from time to time.

Attacks more carefully matched to the victim's buying habits also fall into this fraud category and are more difficult to stop. In both cases, it can take time for a consumer to notice there's a problem, because the credit card statement is so unclear that the consumer misses the first few instances of theft when they're glancing through it. This delay (as discussed in Chapter 5) adds to the challenge, since fraud prevention teams won't be alerted to a fraudulent transaction through a chargeback until the customer notices the problem and initiates the chargeback process.

---

1 Sting, "Shape of My Heart," written by Sting and Dominic Miller, track 10 on *Ten Summoner's Tales*, A&M, 1993.

It's true that fraudsters using this MO tend to have a "done is better than perfect" approach. This can lull companies into a false sense of security, assuming they'll easily be able to stop such attacks. That in itself is a risk. We should remain vigilant against this prevalent form of attack, keeping in mind that our system is sometimes vulnerable to even the simplest attacks and that fraud doesn't have to be elegant in order to be effective. There are many blind spots impairing the fraud-fighting abilities of retailers and banks.

Stolen Credit Card Fraud Is Supported by Silos

Part of the challenge of combating stolen credit card fraud comes not from the fraudsters, but from a weakness in our own systems. Fraud teams are currently forced to work in silos, withholding key information from one another.

On the one hand, retailers have no access to a user's credit card history, so they have to do what they can with the information available to them about the user or their previous transactions. On the other hand, banks and card networks (Visa, American Express, MasterCard, Discover), which have granular visibility into the customer's history, lack full resolution on the purchased items of each specific order and on the profile of the person making it. (You can learn more about how card networks and banks tackle credit card fraud in this part of the book, and by reading about the work of leaders such as Visa's Carolina Barcenas (*https://oreil.ly/sd0jm*).)

A combination of privacy regulations and market evolution has led to poor collaboration between financial institutions and ecommerce retailers. PSD 2 and open banking reforms, along with various fintech operations, aim to change that. The evolution of privacy-enhancing technologies (PET), which enable different organizations to leverage one another's data without sharing it, and the providerless options they are beginning to generate, also offer interesting possibilities. (For more on providerless options in fraud prevention, see Chapter 4.)

We don't cover these trends in this book, because it will be some time before we know whether our defenses against stolen credit card fraud truly become more resilient. Nonetheless, these developments are strategically important for fraud leaders to stay on top of. Real strides in what is possible through collaboration and a greater ability to leverage wider data sets could make a significant difference in how effective a fraud team can be against stolen credit card fraud.

Defining Stolen Credit Card Fraud

Stolen credit card fraud is often the "gateway MO" for fraudsters who are making the transition from physical theft and/or card skimming. Many remain amateurs, through either lack of ability or lack of investment in the techniques and knowledge required for proficiency. While they typically learn from one another's experiences on dark web forums or channels, the information shared on the relatively open (and not invitation-only) channels tends to be fairly basic. This can lead fraud teams to discount this form of fraud as essentially amateur, but this would be a mistake; some fraudsters become masters of this domain, making them a serious threat.

For the purposes of our discussion, which aims to identify and stop this kind of fraud, we'll define stolen credit card fraud as the checkpoint where an attacker already has the compromised credentials (credit card number, expiration date, name on card, CVV) and they are attempting to purchase goods or sign up to a service in order to monetize those stolen details.

Monetization is typically achievable by reselling the goods that were purchased; this could mean selling sneakers from the back of a van, trading cryptocurrency, conducting a dropshipping scheme, and so on. For this discussion, we're excluding the various phishing/hacking actions that are a necessary first step in obtaining the stolen credit card details. We're also excluding the vast ecosystem of trading stolen credit card information on the dark web, which is both too large to cover in any detail and not directly relevant to stopping this form of fraud; what matters when you're trying to identify and prevent stolen credit card fraud is that the fraudster has these details and is trying to use them. How they got the information is interesting but won't help you stop them once they're on your site.

It's true that the market for stolen credit cards has become so advanced that "fraud end-to-end services" are available (e.g., fraudsters can purchase a bundle of stolen credit card + matching virtual private network [VPN] + matching aged/spoofed email). However, here we'll focus on the scenario of a fraudster who managed to get only the credit card details of their victim. The more complex "bundle" scenario will be covered in Chapter 15.

Definitions of Common Terms in Email Analysis

Aged email
> This is an email created by a fraudster, often including a username to match a specific victim's identity, which is then left alone to "age" for a period of time before the attack. The email thus circumvents checks put in place to identify emails created minutes or seconds before an attack.

Spoofed/hacked email
> This is the true email of the victim that has been hacked/breached by the fraudster. Many fraudsters purchase access to a spoofed email belonging to another victim as well (preferably a victim with a username that resembles the name on the stolen credit card), resulting in a synthetic identity that can be more difficult to identify as a false one.

> *Email mismatch*
>
> Fraudsters may use their own email or a disposable email address for the purpose of an attack. In these cases, there would be clear mismatches between the username and/or email domain and the identity of the victim (e.g., a stolen card belonging to a 70-year-old female who lives in Seoul is clearly a mismatch for the hypothetical email address *dude2009@mail.ru*).

Modus Operandi

Our situation: this fraudster is looking at an ecommerce retailer's website, preparing to add their desired items to the cart and hoping to breeze through the checkout and payment page without being denied by the retailer/payment processor.

This is Impersonation 101. The fraudster is hoping to pass as the true owner of the credit card, so they are trying to think of everything that would make them resemble their victim.

A smart fraudster would start this process of impersonation long before they ever land on their target's website or app, making them much harder to catch. They would need to prepare the following resources:

- A clean device that has no cookies to tie it to previous attacks, nor any fraud-related software/apps/plug-ins installed
- Device settings to match the profile of the cardholder (e.g., if you're an EU-based fraudster who wishes to monetize a stolen credit card from Japan, you'd want to emulate a mobile device that is commonly used in Tokyo)
- An IP provider + geolocation to match the victim's alleged lifestyle
- Browsing and behavioral patterns tailored to match the victim's alleged lifestyle (this includes time zone, language, browser history, referral URL, and browsing speed)

Once prepared, the fraudster can go shopping, hoping that:

- Their target retailer won't be too much of an anomaly from the victim's purchase history.
- The victim does not already have an existing account with this retailer.
- The stolen credit card has not been used by another fraudster on this retailer's system.
- The velocity in amount/number of items that the fraudster plans to purchase won't ring any bells on the retailer's side.
- The credit card won't hit its credit limit.

The smart fraudster will provide the following details on the checkout page:

- Cardholder name and billing/shipping address. This should be properly spelled and cased, not be copied/pasted, and be typed in at a reasonable pace. (In the case of physical goods, things get tricky regarding the shipping address, and we'll discuss that in Chapter 7.)

- Contact email. Sometimes fraudsters provide the true email of the victim, hoping the retailer won't attempt contact. However, access to email is usually required or desired by the fraudster, so most fraudsters would go for a recently generated email (or a spoofed email of another victim), preferably one with a handle name similar to the cardholder's name. It's rare to see fraudsters who have access to the true email of the cardholder in this kind of attack, though fraud fighters can never say never with these sorts of things, and certainly this does occur as part of account takeover (ATO)-type attacks.

- Contact phone. What the fraudster puts here depends on the type of goods involved. Some services require access to the relevant phone and/or demand two-factor authentication (2FA). Fraudsters can bypass this, which we'll discuss in Chapter 13. In the stolen credit card MO, it's more common to see fraudsters providing bogus info and/or Voice over IP (VoIP)/disposable/public phone numbers that would match the geography of the cardholder. Some fraudsters also provide the true phone number of the victim. In either case, their hope is that the retailer won't attempt to contact the customer by phone.

- Additional personal identifiable information (PII) is sometimes required (e.g., ID docs). This form of identification is mentioned in Chapter 13.

Finally, the fraudster hits the "complete order" button and hopes their stolen goods are on the way.

Identification

There are, of course, a number of factors that contribute to the identification of stolen credit card fraud. We will be focusing on IP fraud identification, since the ecommerce vertical is key for defining what should qualify as suspicious IP behavior. As we explained in the Preface, the other factors are discussed in other chapters. We will also leave IP consistency, which is a related issue, to the banking chapters, where it is more relevant.

It's worth noting that this chapter is one of the longest in the book. This is for two reasons. First, over the course of our careers in fraud prevention, we've noticed frequent confusion regarding differences and distinctions between types of IPs, what deductions can be drawn from them, and what further research this should impel. We hope this chapter helps. Second, in the series of roundtable discussions run by Identiq in 2021 and 2022, the subject of IPs came up in almost every discussion and over a wide range of topics—far more than any other data point that was raised for debate. It's obviously a subject of great interest to many fraud teams and fraud fighters, so we've given it some breathing room here.

 This chapter assumes previous knowledge about IP connection types. If you would like to learn more about this subject, more detailed information about the following topics can help: IP addresses and IP headers (*https://oreil.ly/R4W2R*), how computer networks work (*https://oreil.ly/bf2m5*), web bots and proxy servers (*https://oreil.ly/ryYl7*), internet core protocols (*https://oreil.ly/BSAR9*), and network security (*https://oreil.ly/cba2d*).

In a nutshell, the identification of impersonation through IP masking is based on looking for one or more of the following:

Mismatched IP
Geolocation/profiling mismatches between the IP connection and the cardholder's alleged location/profile

Repeat offender IP
Significant evidence of the IP being linked to previous attacks

Nonunique IP
Significant evidence of attempts to cover the tracks of IPs by using public IPs

Masked IP
Significant evidence of attempts to cover the tracks of IPs by using proxies or VPNs of all sorts

In the next several sections, we'll elaborate on each type of malicious IP we're trying to identify.

Mismatched IP

Profiling mismatches is based on identifying the organization to which the IP is registered. For example, IP 168.169.96.2 is registered to a New York–based educational organization (*https://oreil.ly/sEMAb*). If we find this IP in a context that does not match the expected activity of this organization, we should suspect that it is being used as a proxy.

Unfortunately, nonprofit organizations, which are frequently understaffed or run on a largely volunteer basis, often suffer from poor cybersecurity hygiene, which can make them popular components in a fraudster's IP attack arsenal. This technique has a psychological aspect, as fraud analysts may be predisposed to have positive feelings about a nonprofit due to the good work they do, and therefore may be less suspicious or more likely to give actions apparently coming from there the benefit of the doubt. Fraud teams should guard against this natural but dangerous prejudice.

Geographical mismatches can be calculated by comparing IP geos (obtainable through many third-party tools and services). We won't go into how this is derived; what is important to note is that while it can be useful, geolocation information should be taken with a huge spoonful of salt, for these reasons:

- Absolute distance is too simplistic to be a fraud metric. Substantial distance can be explained by the low density of IPs in a region (e.g., there are simply not that many IPs in Siberia, nor in parts of the rural United States). Satellite connections will also show large distances (e.g., Saudi Arabia, or marine connections).

- Country/city comparisons are often too simplistic. People often travel between Switzerland and Italy/Germany/France, for example. Also, though less common, there may be historical/social/economic reasons for distance; for example, a French Antilles IP might be registered in Paris if the service provider is French.

- Controlled organization IPs (corporate, military, etc.) would also impact a simple analysis of distance mismatch.

- Last but not least, there are lots of connection types whose geolocation reflects a company server and not the end user. Companies using hosting services by Amazon could show a single US geolocation for all their employees. Mobile connection types can be terribly aggregated as well, reaching city/state resolution at best.

If you need further convincing about why pure IP geolocation should not be treated as a wholly reliable indicator of location, never mind guilt or legitimacy, read the story of the unfortunate Kansas farm (*https://oreil.ly/kw5B6*) that was mistakenly associated with all kinds of nefarious activity (and suffered numerous unpleasant consequences) simply because its IP was close to the center of the country, which was the default used by IP geolocation identifying service MaxMind for cases where it didn't have an accurate IP.

As discussed earlier, avoiding false positives and unnecessary friction is nowadays as important to most fraud teams as preventing successful fraud; the challenge and fascination of fraud prevention lies in finding the right balance between the two. If you rely too much on IP geolocation without combining other factors or considering possible nuance, you'll fall too far on the side of stopping fraud and reject or frustrate too many good customers.

 Interestingly, there is no specific geography as such attached to an IP. The IP is a number of octets that are assigned and then reassigned (and then re-reassigned...) to an organization. All the other data regarding the IP is statistical and inherited from actions done online. However, since the statistical data and the deductions derived from it are generally reliable and do relate to geography, and since that's one of the main uses of IPs in fraud fighting, we will refer loosely to the idea of IP geolocation even though it is not technically precise.

Repeat Offender IP

As with geolocation distance, linking repeat offenders by IP alone, without additional incriminating evidence, should not be treated as a smoking gun. IPs are often aggregated in a way that means they represent many users (home connections can be recycled by the ISP, mobile IPs are aggregated to a cell tower level, network address translation [NAT] routers will translate many employees of a corporation into a single IP, etc.).

The same is true of IP reputation lists and databases. For instance, IPs that were placed on a block list for spreading spam might be completely clean in every other aspect, and certainly safe from the perspective of preventing credit card fraud.

Nonunique IPs

This is where a fraudster uses public WiFi networks in order to mask the perpetrator's identity. It could involve (among others) taking over your neighbors' open WiFi, squatting on a local coffee shop's WiFi, or using the network of a university or high school.

At times it appears that this method of using nonunique IPs as obfuscation is becoming less popular, but since fraudster fashions often come in waves, we have included this method not only for completeness but also because it may once again become a technique of choice, especially if some new refinement is also developed.

An example of a nonunique IP type that used to be favored by fraudsters is Tor (*https://www.torproject.org*). Tor proxies, originally designed for privacy, quickly became a fraudster's heaven, so sometimes Googling an IP string with the word "Tor" or looking for the Tor regular expression on the reverse DNS of the IP is worthwhile. Keep in mind that Tor IPs may end up on multiple computers (any computer that permits Tor), so fraudsters who are a bit more savvy may prefer an open HTTP. Figure 6-1 shows a Tor example.

Figure 6-1. What your browser will show when you browse to 103.208.220.226, which is currently used as a Tor proxy

Masked IP

Masked IPs are more challenging, and therefore, more fun to research! There are so many hosting and VPN services out there for various personal and business uses. Fraudsters use all of them, although generally speaking, business connections are usually safer. The first thing to bear in mind is that not every proxy/VPN/hosting IP is necessarily fraud. There are plenty of legitimate uses for these technologies. Once again, overreliance on this factor will result in high false positives. The likelihood of it being a fraud indicator depends, in part, on the type of retailer and the tech savviness of its audience (e.g., gaming versus apparel).

Here are two examples of masked IPs using traceroute checks. Traceroute is a fairly old practice and it doesn't scale well (there are more scalable ways to ping the IP), but it is great as a manual research tool when you're looking at individual transactions or users. In most cases where scale is an issue, teams will generally rely on IP mapping vendors to do the job, so we decided not to focus on scale as a major factor for this section.

In the first example, 40.89.186.56 is a French IP, registered as a Microsoft Azure data center. Running a traceroute check (Figure 6-2) shows a flow from London to Paris, using MSN servers. This is a reasonable flow for a packet of this IP, which demonstrates that even if the IP has been used as a proxy in the past, it is probably not being used to mask traffic from another server at this moment. We might predict that connection speed should be OK as well (though we won't go into patent-protected connection speed measurements here).

GeoIP2 City Results

IP Address	Country Code	Location	Network	Postal Code	Approximate Coordinates*	Accuracy Radius (km)	ISP	Organization	Domain	Metro Code
40.89.186.56	FR	Paris, Paris, lle-de-France, France, Europe	40.89.184.0/22	75001	48.8607, 2.3281	500	Microsoft Corporation	Microsoft Azure		

```
C:\Users\gilits>tracert 40.89.186.56

Tracing route to 40.89.186.56 over a maximum of 30 hops

  1     4 ms    <1 ms    <1 ms  192.168.1.1
  2    28 ms    19 ms     12 ms  10.20.64.1
  3     *         *         *    Request timed out.
  4    19 ms    14 ms     20 ms  172.17.3.65
  5    17 ms     *         *     172.17.3.74
  6     *         *         *    Request timed out.
 12   120 ms    97 ms     84 ms  ae55.edge3.London1.Level3.net [212.113.15.77]
 13     *       92 ms      *     ae1.ae1.ear5.London2.level3.net [4.69.201.114]
 14    71 ms    71 ms     68 ms  ae60-0.lts-96cbe-1a.ntwk.msn.net [104.44.37.11]
 15    69 ms    68 ms     75 ms  ae26-0.icr01.lon24.ntwk.msn.net [104.44.239.105]
 16    73 ms    69 ms     72 ms  be-120-0.ibr02.lon24.ntwk.msn.net [104.44.21.115]
 17    68 ms    72 ms     69 ms  104.44.17.82
 18    70 ms    70 ms     77 ms  ae122-0.icr02.par21.ntwk.msn.net [104.44.11.242]
 19     *         *         *    Request timed out.
```

Figure 6-2. MaxMind geoIP check and traceroute check for IP 40.89.186.56

In the second example, 168.169.96.2 is the alleged New York IP from the educational organization we mentioned earlier. The traceroute (Figure 6-3) shows a French server belonging to an EU organization (Seabone.net, probably in charge of the optic sub-Atlantic fiber); then the packet continues to global servers (probably in the Asia-Pacific region) of CogentCo. Looking at the legit scenario, it's just a poor level of service from the hosting provider. Looking at the fraud scenario, the server is used to relay malicious HTTP requests from far, far away.

Looking at these two examples, you can see how we're effectively following the geographic and IP routes of a packet of data. It's a trail, which should show a route that makes sense within the context of the story. If it doesn't make sense—if it jumps wildly from one country to another one that's far away—it may be a sign that the hosting is located somewhere else and that what you're seeing is obfuscation. For example, Figure 6-3 shows that the location isn't really New York, but rather, somewhere in the EU. Crucially, here and in almost every situation, you need to remember that there's a good story for this—bad connections happen to even the best users—so you'll want to investigate further to see what the other data points are telling you and build up an understanding of whether it's a good story or a fraudulent one.

GeoIP2 City Plus Database Results

IP Address	Country Code	Location	Network	Postal Code	Approximate Coordinates*	Accuracy Radius (km)	ISP
40.89.186.56	FR	Paris, Paris, Île-de-France, France, Europe	40.89.128.0/18	75001	48.8323, 2.4075	1000	Microsoft Corporation

```
Tracing route to 40.89.186.56 over a maximum of 30 hops
 1     4 ms    <1 ms    <1 ms  192.168.1.1
 2    28 ms    19 ms    12 ms  10.20.64.1
 3     *        *        *     Request timed out.
 4    19 ms    14 ms    20 ms  172.17.3.65
 5    17 ms     *        *     172.17.3.74
 6     *        *        *     Request timed out.
12   120 ms    97 ms    84 ms  ae55.edge3.London1.Level3.net [212.113.15.77]
13     *       92 ms     *     ae1.ae1.ear5.London2.level3.net [4.69.201.114]
14    71 ms    71 ms    68 ms  ae60-0.lts-96cbe-1a.ntwk.msn.net [104.44.37.11]
15    69 ms    68 ms    75 ms  ae26-0.icr01.lon24.ntwk.msn.net [104.44.239.105]
16    73 ms    69 ms    72 ms  be-120-0.ibr02.lon24.ntwk.msn.net [104.44.21.115]
17    68 ms    72 ms    69 ms  104.44.17.82
18    70 ms    70 ms    77 ms  ae122-0.icr02.par21.ntwk.msn.net [104.44.11.242]
19     *        *        *     Request timed out.
```

Figure 6-3. MaxMind geoIP check and traceroute check for IP 168.169.96.2

Warning: The Reliability of IP Analysis May Vary Depending on Locale

Since dissecting IP data is crucial for proper fraud detection (stolen credit card fraud and virtually all other types of fraud), almost every risk department seeks help from digital mapping services, which translate IPs into geography and Whois/ASN (autonomous system number) data (i.e., registration data). The information you can get from these services is very often valuable in helping you find out more about the user and work out whether their story is legitimate or not. However, the data from digital mapping services is not gospel truth, so it's important to take it with a grain of salt. Fraud analysts sometimes learn to rely too heavily on them, and this can lead to false declines that really should have been avoided. (Think of the Kansas example we cited earlier!) It's something fraud managers need to ensure their team understands so that they can use these useful tools appropriately, but not blindly.

In this section, we'll explain why the reliability you experience from these services may also depend on the markets your traffic typically comes from globally. This is also something to bear in mind if your company plans to enter new markets, as it may impact your accuracy (whether positively or negatively).

To clarify, let's dive a bit deeper than usual into what one of the major players in this field has to offer. Following are some interesting parts of the reader to the GeoIP2 service by MaxMind, a digital mapping service that is a good example of these types of services. MaxMind (and similar services, such as Digital Envoy) typically updates its records on a monthly or quarterly basis, unless prompted by its customers on a specific inquiry. It bases its telemetry on the ASN records that can be scrapped or downloaded from regional internet registry services (*https://oreil.ly/wa4dv*) around the globe, as shown in Figure 6-4. Naturally, not all registrars keep their data equally up to date. As explained by AFRINIC's website (*https://oreil.ly/SilU6*): "We often reduce Africa to a single country or economy but we tend to forget that it is made up of 54 different nations, more than in any other continent of the world. Africa is therefore a complex set of countries having different levels of connectivity." As a result, some users in Africa will opt for services in a neighboring country. Many service providers enter the game every year, while others go out of business. This makes it difficult for any data service to keep up with the ongoing changes. Moreover, data services will not be dividing their resources equally among the different regions, since most customers of MaxMind care about the data of ARIN and RIPE more than they do about the data of AFRINIC or and parts of APNIC/LACNIC. At the end of the day, data accuracy "follows the money," so it favors the northern hemisphere.

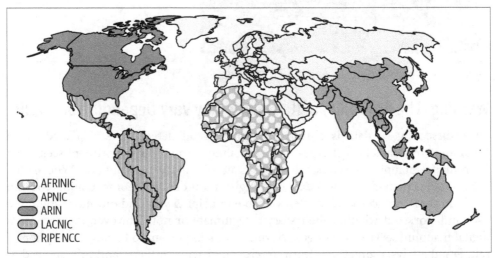

Figure 6-4. Map of regional internet registries[2]

The following subsections offer pointers to keep in mind when inspecting this type of service.

Response to the latest technology

IPv4 and IPv6 are both supported equally by MaxMind (and by most of the larger vendors in the industry). However, at the time of this writing, IPv6 is still only partially adopted by the industry. With emerging markets such as India and Malaysia among the top countries in IPv6 adoption, we should probably expect lower levels of geographic precision for IPv6 data. Would services like MaxMind be able to tailor specific types of parameters that would generate better clarity for IPv6?

---

2 Image originally created by user Sémhur, *Regional Internet Registries World Map* (*https://oreil.ly/ckQph*), Wikimedia Commons, last updated February 8, 2020.

What about string manipulations to translate IPv6 into IPv4, when it's possible? How about Apple's 2021 Private Relay release (*https://oreil.ly/QPi6B*)? MaxMind, like most services, quickly claimed to update (*https://oreil.ly/a6kvR*) its records to reflect this new feature, but only time will tell how well its accuracy measures against a giant like Apple, which promises increased anonymity to its users.

Resolution of supported locales

Locale codes can hint at the level of coverage the services offer globally. For example, MaxMind promises impressive resolution into regions such as Devon in England (population: nearly 800,000 in 2019), but some tests are necessary to determine whether it can promise the same for the non-Western world. Can MaxMind spot regions such as the "small" city of Thane, near Mumbai (population: nearly 2 million in 2019)? Could we expect connection speeds in Africa to be thoroughly tested in cases where connection speed plays a part in determining connection type? Table 6-1 shows how MaxMind's impressive documentation (*https://oreil.ly/hu9wA*) refers to the detailed resolution available for subdivision in some regions.

Table 6-1. Excerpt from MaxMind's GeoIP2 database dictionary

Name	Type	Description
country_name	string	The country name for this location in the file's locale.
subdivision_1_iso_code	string (1–3)	A string of up to three characters containing the region portion of the ISO 3166-2 code for the first-level region associated with the IP address. Some countries have two levels of subdivisions, in which case this is the least specific. For example, in the UK this will be a country like "England," not a county like "Devon."
subdivision_1_name	string	The subdivision name for this location in the file's locale. As with the subdivision code, this is the least specific subdivision for the location.
subdivision_2_iso_code	string (1–3)	A string of up to three characters containing the region portion of the ISO 3166-2 code for the second-level region associated with the IP address. For countries with two levels of subdivision, this will be the most specific. For example, in the UK this will be a county like "Devon," not a country like "England."

Default locales

The excellent documentation offered by MaxMind reveals that when no specific locale is identified, the system will fall back to "en". It seems that only seven non–English-speaking locales are supported. You'll need to check your data and verify that this default is acceptable for your purposes. Here's the snippet of code to look out for in services of this sort:

```
:param locales: ... The default value is ['en'].The order of the locales is
significant. When a record class has multiple names (country, city, etc.), its
name property will return the name in the first locale...
        Currently, the valid locale codes are:
```

```
        * de – German
        * es – Spanish
        * fr – French
        * ja – Japanese
        * pt-BR -- Brazilian Portuguese
        * ru – Russian
        * zh-CN -- Simplified Chinese.
    if locales is None:
        locales = ["en"]
```

As with so many things, half the battle with IP accuracy is knowing you need to question it. Using this information, you can assess how reliable IP analysis of this kind is likely to be for the different global markets you serve, and you can weigh the information accordingly within your fraud prevention system.

Mitigation

Having explored the question of identification of problematic IP addresses and the limitations involved, we will now focus on how to mitigate the problem. Regarding IPs, our working assumption here is that the end goal should be to design an automated system to decline payments from IPs that have been detected as operated by attackers. We have established that relying blindly on external digital mapping services will not do the trick. Therefore, it's imperative that we learn how to utilize data from external vendors in the unique context of the MO demonstrated by the fraudsters we hope to catch.

Note that the same considerations come into play during manual review, and can be used as such, but at the least it is preferable to have a sensible automated scoring system in place to provide a score for manual reviewers to use for IPs, rather than have to measure every element every time, which would be very time-consuming. Of course, in cases where in-depth research is required, and for sampling and analysis to improve the system, drilling down into the details will also be necessary. But this is not the standard for day-to-day use.

Here are important considerations to bear in mind when employing IP geolocation in your fraud system:

- You need recovery of this data point to be fast, and if possible, in real time. Even if you have a huge amount of computing power to play with, you'll still almost certainly depend on external IP geolocation data sources, which have their own service-level agreement (SLA). Calling them costs time and money. You can mitigate this issue by leveraging denylist-based checkpoints and/or batch downloads from the data sources, as opposed to real-time calls.

- Don't get complacent. Data sources should be frequently challenged and refreshed. Manual sampling will show you that simple regex lookup can teach you a lot (e.g., look for IPs registered under organizations with "hotel" in their names).

- If possible, query more than one service for Whois/ASN data. Cross-reference different services against each other, plus do reverse DNS. Along these lines, it's worth learning about the gethostbyaddr function, for instance, in the DNS/ Reverse DNS Lookups (*https://oreil.ly/WsYhg*) section of *PHP 5 Unleashed* by John Coggeshall (SAMS). For example:

```
import socket

ipAddress = "8.8.8.8"
hostName = socket.gethostbyaddr(ipAddress)
print("Host Name for the IP address {} is {}".format(
    ipAddress, hostName))
```

would have the output:

```
Host Name for the IP address 8.8.8.8 is ('dns.google',
['8.8.8.8.in-addr.arpa'], ['8.8.8.8'])
```

- Accumulated metrics (e.g., how frequently this IP has been recorded on your system) can help you avoid false positives, but of course, unless you're working in a consortium or using a consortium tool, you'll miss fraudsters who are known to other merchants.

- It's a great idea to explore other interesting metrics within your system to see whether they can improve your accuracy when it comes to detecting bad IPs. You might consider metrics such as country/language breakdown, operating system breakdown, number of devices, weekend/night activity, and so on. Some may be valuable in your company, others may not; this varies substantially from business to business, even within the same industry. Regardless, bear in mind that they will only work reliably if you have enough data; check this before you invest time in an analysis! Insufficient data gives unreliable results.

Having outlined these general considerations when using IP addresses, we'll now look at a couple of examples.

Example 1: Using IP Geolocation to Identify Legitimate Hotel IPs

For the purposes of this example, we'll assume we are a travel retailer focusing on selling flight tickets. Our purpose is to identify orders placed by buyers who were browsing from hotel WiFi/landline connections. The rationale behind this is that hotel IPs tend to cause false positives simply because their geolocation doesn't match the country of the tourist's billing address, and we want to avoid these false positives. We'll use the following (very simple) database table, called ORDERS, which holds the following data points to identify potentially fraudulent IPs:

ORDERS.orderID	ORDERS.Order date	ORDERS.IP	ORDERS.IP country (from third-party vendor)	Whois query result: ORDERS.Hostname (from third-party vendor, etc.)	Billing address country
1111	January 1	1.1.1.1	Slovakia	Metronet.sk	US
1122	January 1	2.2.2.2	US	Hilton.com	US
2233	January 2	3.3.3.3	Ireland	Hilton.com	US
3333	January 4	1.1.1.1	Slovakia	Metronet.sk	France
5555	January 30	1.1.1.1	Slovakia	Metronet.sk	Germany
6666	January 30	4.4.4.4	Slovakia	Metronet.sk	Slovakia

The following simple query will return IPs that should be considered to be hotels by our fraud detection system. First, we'll fetch the list of IPs whose domain name clearly indicates they are owned by a well-known hotel:

```
WITH hotel_ip_based_on_domain AS
(
    SELECT    orders.ip
    FROM      orders
    WHERE     orders.hostname LIKE '%Hilton%'
    GROUP BY 1)
/* Second, we'll fetch the list of IPs who show buyers coming from more than
2 countries per month */
WITH hotel_ip_based_on_billing_country_distribution AS
(
    SELECT orders.ip,
        month(orders.order_date) AS month,
        count(DISTINCT orders.billing_country)
    FROM orders
    GROUP BY 1, 2
    HAVING count(DISTINCT orders.billing_country)>2)
/* We'll unify the lists using union-all to remove duplicates */
SELECT ip
FROM   hotel_ip_based_on_domain
UNION ALL
SELECT ip
FROM   hotel_ip_based_on_billing_country_distribution;
```

This query returns the following results (an explanation of the results follows):

IP
1.1.1.1
2.2.2.2
3.3.3.3

- IPs 1.1.1.1 and 2.2.2.2 were both returned thanks to their Hilton hostname.

- IP 3.3.3.3 was returned because it showed users visiting from three billing countries, which according to our logic indicates a hotel. One might note that Metronet is not a hostname associated with the travel industry, nor even with business connections. It is a popular ISP in Slovakia, so it is quite possible that the "hotel" behind the data is in fact a small B & B/couch-surfing establishment. Alternatively, it could even be a mobile cellular tower that happens to be in an area where many tourists are placing orders (e.g., an airport).

- IP 4.4.4.4 was not returned, because it only showed orders from Slovakia. The fact that IP 4.4.4.4 is registered to Metronet, just like IP 3.3.3.3, can be used if we wish to reach an alternative hotel detection heuristic, one based on country distribution per hostname. For example:

```
WITH hotel_ip_based_on_billing_country_distribution AS
(
        SELECT TOP(10) PERCENT hostname
        FROM /* top 10% most likely hotel IPs */
            (
            SELECT    orders.hostname,
                      month (orders.order_date) AS month, (
                      CASE
                          WHEN orders.billing_country<>orders.ipcountry
                            THEN 1
                            ELSE 0
                      END)                        /* crossborder orders */
                      /count(orders.orderid)*100 /* divided by all orders */
                      AS percentage_of_crossborder
            FROM      orders
            GROUP BY 1,2
            ORDER BY percentage_of_crossborder DESC ));
```

Obviously, there are many cool tricks and fun considerations we could build on this simple example, and we'll suggest a few here to refine the hostname method and the country distribution method.

Regarding the hostname method, you'll need to consider that maintenance will be required. If you go by the method of domain names, for example, you'll need to update the list of hotels regularly as this is a fairly dynamic list. You may also run into trouble with heavy queries, since using the LIKE clause might soon become too heavy. For this reason, using more generic terms may be preferable. For example, look for the regex "hotel" in various languages, which should show up in the orgName field, if you have that available. Importantly, the hostname method is somewhat prone to false positives. To balance this, you could use the billing_country_distri bution method as a precautionary measurement. For instance, if the domain name "hilton.com" shows up for IPs in Ireland, without any significant non-Irish billing countries, perhaps this is not truly the IP of a hotel.

Regarding the country distribution method, bear in mind that distribution heuristics require statistical know-how. That may or may not be problematic, depending on your use case; while the simple examples described here can work well for individual ecommerce retailers, they will not be accurate enough to take on big data challenges, such as those usually encountered by payment giants. In those cases, one might consider more delicate approaches for calculating a distribution score, such as calculating a variance score.

Also, bear in mind that distribution heuristics require threshold adjustments. Picking an arbitrary threshold of two billing countries per IP per month is obviously naive; one could easily think of nonhotel scenarios that could explain why visitors from two or three different countries would show up from a single IP (e.g., an office of an international corporation, where employees from different countries often visit). Using percentiles instead of a numeric threshold can help to some extent. Still, even for teams using a percentile-based threshold, it's highly recommended that the threshold be revisited, with the following considerations in mind:

- The vertical of the retailer (since, for example, travel retailers expect to find many hotel IPs in their data).

- The billing countries. Does the country breakdown match our expectations about the breakdown of incoming tourism to this country?

- The transaction status. Can we be sure that all the orders coming from allegedly detected hotels were legit? Perhaps some of them ended up in fraud charge-backs, and therefore they should be excluded from the metrics that impact hotel detection.

- The risk of fraud rings. Were there suspicious similarities between the orders from a certain IP? Perhaps there's a specific fraudster operating from this alleged hotel.

- IP connection type. Is it likely for a respectable hotel to be operating from a residential broadband connection (one that doesn't show the hotel's name on the domainName field)?

- Travel trends. Are there many tourists to this country in this season/year? For example, in countries that only get significant international tourism during the summer, you may decide to limit hotel identification to July/August traffic alone.

Example 2: Using IP Traffic Trends to Identify Fake-Hotel IPs

While the previous example focused on enabling legit traffic via identification of legit hotel IPs, there will always be cases of alleged hotel IPs that are actually operated by fraudsters. A rather fancy way of finding alleged hotel IPs whose behavior indicates foul play is to break down the yearly login activity of each IP by month. The following example assumes that July and August are the high season of tourism for the IP in question:[3]

```python
ts_info['is_high_season'] = ts_info['login_month'].apply(
    lambda t: int(t.month in [7, 8]))
```

Figure 6-5 shows the graph generated by the following code. As you can see, traffic drops during the two months of the high season. Clearly, this IP should not be considered to be a hotel in our risk system! It's highly unlikely that traffic would take a nosedive in a hotel during the time of year that should be busiest (we're assuming non–COVID-19 pandemic conditions for this example). To generate this chart, you would need a CSV file of IPs and their month of login. We used July and August as "high season" for simplicity, but this may vary based on the IP geolocation.

```python
import pandas as pd
import matplotlib.pyplot as plt
from matplotlib.lines import Line2D

ts_legend_elements = [
    Line2D([0], [0], color='green', label='High season'),
    Line2D([0], [0], color='blue', label='Low season')]

ts_info = pd.read_csv('ts_info.csv', index_col='ip')
ts_info['login_month'] = pd.to_datetime(ts_info['login_month'])
ts_info['is_high_season'] = ts_info['login_month'].apply(
    lambda t: int(t.month in [7, 8]))

for ip in ts_info.index.unique():
    fig, ax = plt.subplots()
    plt.bar(ts_info.loc[ip]['login_month'],
            ts_info.loc[ip]['logins'],
            color=ts_info.loc[ip]['is_high_season'].
            map({0: 'blue', 1: 'green'}))
    ax.legend(handles=ts_legend_elements, loc='upper right')
    plt.title('logins per month and tourism season={}'.format(ip))
    plt.show()
```

---

3 (Find out more about useful lambda timestamp functions in Matias Eiletz's post, "Mastering Dates and Timestamps in Pandas (and Python in General)" (*https://oreil.ly/7Mmvc*).)

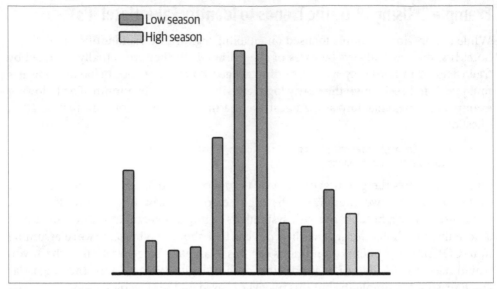

Figure 6-5. Volumes of activity from a hotel IP, showing that traffic during the months of the high season is lower than expected

Figure 6-5 shows that what we have here is not likely to be a functioning hotel. Crucially, though, you need to remember that there is also a good version of the story here. It might not be fraudulent just because it's supposed to be a hotel IP and almost certainly is not. For example, it could easily be a corporate headquarters for a hotel chain; that would be a legitimate use of the hotel designation and would also explain the quiet summer months; the corporate employees are away on vacation. In the same way, it could be a separate network maintained for the hotel's IT department, many of whom also go away in the summer. So, you wouldn't want to automatically penalize the traffic. This is just one data point. You need more information to build up the story of the identity and what's going on.

However, even if it is a good story, you won't want to give it the special hotel status in your system. Real hotels usually get special dispensations because they're an unusual case—it's common for hotels to have many people staying in them from all over the world. So, they'll be using credit cards and customer behaviors and devices from all over the world, and only staying there for short periods of time. This means a lot of factors that might be red flags in other situations, such as multiple cards from multiple countries using the same IP, shouldn't be considered that way for hotels. That's why it's so important to be precise about whether an alleged hotel IP really is one or not.

Example 3: Using Hierarchy in Variable Design

In this section, we'll move from inspecting a single IP to considering multiple inputs.

To expand on our hotel IP example, we could face a follow-up question of what to do if there are several IPs involved with a single order. For example, if a customer logs into their account from a "Hilton" IP in Ireland, then three days later places an order from an unknown IP in Slovakia, would we say this person is likely to be traveling, or that their account was hacked?

Here we're talking about the concept of using hierarchy, which we can manifest using an SQL CASE clause. The example will demonstrate how multiple pieces of IP data can be combined into a unified observation about an account and/or user.

For this example, let's imagine again that we are an ecommerce retailer in the field of travel services. We wish to identify users who are likely to be frequent hotel visitors. For simplicity, we'll use only two IPs for each account in our database:

- IP of account sign-up
- IP of last login to the account

Table 6-2 shows a sample of IPs from our ACCOUNTS table.

Table 6-2. IPs from the ACCOUNTS table

ACCOUNTS.accountID	ACCOUNTS.IP_action	ACCOUNTS.IP	ACCOUNTS.IP_connection_type
1111	SignUp	1.1.1.1	Hotel
1111	LastLogin	2.2.2.2	Anonymous proxy
2222	SignUp	3.3.3.3	Hotel
2222	LastLogin	1.1.1.1	Hotel

How should we decide which of these users is a typical traveler? It depends on whether you suspect ATO or not. (See Chapter 13 for an in-depth look at ATO. For now, we'll just state that although ATO is a different attack method than stolen card fraud, you sometimes need to bear in mind the former when considering the latter.)

If you don't suspect ATO, it's fine to use both the LastLogin IP and the SignUp IP as indicators for travelers. Your query would look a bit like this:

```
SELECT accounts.accountid,
    SUM (CASE
            WHEN accounts.ip_connection_type = 'Hotel'
            THEN 0.5
            ELSE 0
        END)
    AS Hotel_IPs_rate
GROUP BY 1;
```

If you do suspect ATO, you would prefer to ignore the LastLogin IP and trust only the SignUp IP as an indicator for travelers. Your query would look a bit like this:

```
SELECT accounts.accountid,
    SUM (CASE
            WHEN accounts.ip_connection_type = 'Hotel'
                AND accounts.ip_action = 'SignUp'
            THEN 0.5
            ELSE 0
        END)
    AS Hotel_IPs_rate
FROM accounts
GROUP BY 1;
```

Since neither option is perfect, you may wish to go for a model to take into account other metrics. ATO analysis in general is a challenge suited for machine learning–powered models. We'll go into more detail on this in Chapter 13, which focuses on ATO.

Using Hierarchy in IP Typology Variable Design

So far we have argued that hierarchy can be useful for selecting the most suitable IP type for your use case when you want to aggregate several IPs that are logged into a single account. Similarly, the concept of hierarchy can be used for selecting the most indicative IP type when faced with contradicting evidence on a single IP. For example, when using more than one digital mapping service (e.g., using MaxMind and IP2Location, or any other competitor), you're bound to encounter cases of contradictions (i.e., one service claiming that a certain IP belongs to a hotel and another service claiming that the IP represents an anonymous proxy).

The implementation of hierarchy should then be based on your use case. The default should usually aim to enable good users so that positive categories would win over fraudulent categories. Good factors to emphasize here are how monitored the IPs are likely to be, as well as how reliably they can be pinpointed geographically. A military network, for example, is heavily monitored and can be pinpointed geographically with precision. A proposed hierarchy list of IP categories in this case would be as follows, in order from most to least monitored (i.e., the user of this IP believes they could be traced by their connection):

- Military/corporate/government connections (monitored network)
- Hotel/airport connections
- Universities/educational establishment connections
- Broadband home connections
- Broadband business connections
- Mobile connections

- Satellite connections
- Public WiFis at a local institution/business
- Security/VPN service connections/small business
- Data center/cloud/hosting service connections
- Anonymous proxy connections

Naturally, if your company is dealing with a fraud ring, you might consider reversing this hierarchy in an attempt to hunt down all the proxies in your system. Another option is to sort your priorities based on the level of specificity; that is, which type of IP can teach you the most about the identity of the person using it. Here's an example of a hierarchy of choosing the best type of IP to learn about your user's identity, in order from REVEALING to ANONYMOUS (i.e., analytics may gain intelligence about this user from their IP):

- Military/corporate/government connections
- Small-business IP
- Broadband home connections
- Universities/educational establishment connections
- Hotel/airport connections
- Data center/cloud/hosting service connections
- Public WiFis at a local institution/business
- Hosting service connections
- Satellite connections
- Mobile connections
- Anonymous proxy connections

 There are additional methods for gaining IP intelligence beyond the ones discussed here. Obviously, many fraud-fighting organizations and services rely on network diagnostics heuristics (open port scan, latency or packet relay diagnostics, and more). Alternatively, some mobile SDKs (and to a more limited extent, web SDKs) gain insight on mobile and WiFi connections by tapping into device data (e.g., Service Set Identifier [SSID]/WiFi name). It might be worth asking yourself whether your use case deserves the tech and/or legal effort of gaining this level of quality data on your IPs. For inspiration, see an old yet reliable patent in this domain (*https://oreil.ly/l0T2S*), focusing on detecting relayed communications.

Summary

In this chapter, we looked at stolen credit card fraud, which to ecommerce is perhaps the most basic "building block" in fraud, one which other techniques build on and is often the gateway new fraudsters use as they hone their criminal skills. We also looked at IP identification and mitigation, which is similarly fundamental, as it's a form of analysis that's necessary regardless of industry or the kind of fraud you're aiming to prevent. Detailed IP information is also enormously valuable when you're piecing together the story of an action or transaction and deciding whether it's a fraudulent story or a legitimate one. It's one of the crucial abilities you'll need to use in combination with the analysis we'll discuss in the forthcoming chapters, such as address analysis, which we'll look at next.

## CHAPTER 7

Address Manipulation and Mules

Here, there and everywhere…
—The Beatles[1]

If your job includes protecting a retailer that deals in tangible shipping items, this chapter is for you. If you work purely in digital goods or financial services, this chapter may be less relevant—however, fraud analysts in banking should take note that some of these tricks are used against your customers occasionally, targeting new credit or debit cards. Essentially, if there's something physical being shipped, fraudsters are interested in targeting it.

So Many Different Ways to Steal

Even the most amateur fraudsters know that dealing with the shipping address is a fraud challenge. Unlike cookies, IP manipulation, device information, and other, more subtle signs of identity, physical address is a problem that stares the fraudster in the face when they try to place an order. They want to steal an object or objects. That means they need to get their hands on it. What are their options? They can send it directly to their own address, but that would be far too obvious a sign that the shipping and billing addresses have no connection and that fraud is in play, and would give their real address to people who might try to send law enforcement there. And besides, often the fraudster lives in a different country from the victim.

The problem boils down to this: the fraudster needs to look like the cardholder, or at least like someone the cardholder would plausibly be sending the item to (e.g., a relative). To deal with this problem, fraudsters engage in *address manipulation*.

---

1 The Beatles, "Here, There and Everywhere," written by John Lennon and Paul McCartney, track 5 on *Revolver*, Parlophone, 1966.

That is, they find some way to circumvent or cheat the address challenge, concealing the address mismatch. There are a number of different approaches to address manipulation, and because fraudsters of all abilities engage in it, these approaches vary considerably in complexity and sophistication.

It's important to bear in mind that an attempt to conceal an address mismatch doesn't unerringly point to fraud. There are plenty of legitimate reasons why a good consumer might accidentally trigger a red flag in your system: they could be using reshippers to ensure a reliable delivery company on their home turf, or using a workaround to avoid taxes or reduce delivery costs, or sending various items for an event to someone who will repack them into branded individual gift packages, and so on. This means that uncovering address manipulation is not enough to prove fraud. It's a valuable signal, but as with the other things we discuss in this book, it must be viewed in the context of the rest of the story about the user and the transaction. The address, in itself, is neither good nor bad. It's the identity behind the purchase that you need to worry about.

Most legitimate travelers, expats, and others don't make any attempt to conceal a discrepancy between shipping and billing addresses. If there is an obvious, glaring geographic mismatch—a billing address in Los Angeles with a shipping address in Timbuktu, for example—it's actually quite likely to be legitimate. Although more investigation should be done, it's important to make sure your system doesn't automatically treat such mismatches as fraud. If it does, you'll end up with a lot of false positives. After all, if there wasn't a legitimate demand for shipping to a place other than your billing address, retailers wouldn't be offering this option.

Physical Interception of Package: Porch Piracy

Porch piracy is when fraudsters physically intercept the package at the cardholder's true address. When they place the order they'll use the billing address of the card for a perfect match, making it more likely the order will go through, but they'll use their own phone number so that they are updated about delivery progress. The same process works with account takeover (ATO), with sites that show the tracking of the item in the account; fraudsters can see when the real owner of the account has placed an order and can sign in to check on its progress. In either case, as scary as it sounds, the fraudster can then simply lurk in the bushes near the house, waiting for the courier to arrive with the goods.

Porch piracy is more common than it used to be, including for simple cases of theft in which a criminal tours a neighborhood looking for packages on porches and walks off with them. (We don't look at that form of criminal activity here, because it's not in scope for most online fraud prevention teams.) A 2020 study found that 43% of survey respondents had had a package stolen, and of those, 64% said they'd been a victim of package theft more than once.[2] The 64% figure isn't surprising, since fraudsters are most likely to bother with porch piracy when fairly high-value items are involved, and some households are more likely to order more high-value items online than others. Moreover, where ATO is involved, it's common for the fraudster to strike multiple times.

Physical Interception of Package: Convince the Courier

A variant on porch piracy that doesn't involve suspiciously lurking in the bushes, the convince-the-courier method has the fraudster in contact with the courier (usually because the fraudster placed the order with their own phone number).

The fraudster will convince the courier to modify the shipping address ever so slightly—to meet them at the corner of the street because they've been out and are just heading back, or at the door to the large apartment building, for example. It's the kind of thing couriers experience all the time in perfectly legitimate situations, and they like to accommodate as part of good customer relations, making it very hard for them to detect the difference between normal and fraudulent use cases.

Send Package to a Convenient Location: Open House for Fraud

Using this method, fraudsters aim to make the delivery address one with easy public access, where they can hang around waiting for packages without looking suspicious. Open houses held for real estate being offered for sale are very popular for this one, and so are small businesses such as corner shops, hair and nail salons, and stores in local malls. In these cases, the location gives the appearance of legitimacy, both when being searched as part of a fraud review at the time of transaction, and for the courier when they arrive at the destination.

However, from time to time, other public, though less legitimate-looking, addresses will be used, such as a parking lot or even a cemetery, because of the ease of access. If chosen carefully, such addresses look reasonable from a distance when reviewed by an automated system or reviewer, and of course can be used over and over again, simplifying the process from the fraudster's perspective. Couriers are likely to deliver the package even if they have their doubts about the address. Alternatively, this method can also be combined with the convince-the-courier method so that the courier never quite reaches the parking lot or cemetery but is met close by.

This method does require research on the part of the fraudster, and sometimes an arrangement with a local business, so perhaps for this reason it is most commonly

---

2 C+R Research, *2020 Package Theft Statistics Report* (*https://oreil.ly/bM9jR*), accessed March 4, 2022.

seen in use when high-end goods are being stolen. Within that context, it's a very popular method.

Send Package to a Convenient Location: Reshippers

Cross-border reshipping or freight forwarding services gained enormous popularity during the 2010s, and were at one point the fraudster's first choice when stealing physical goods. It's easy to see the appeal; it seemed like such a simple solution to the physical goods shipping problem.

Back in the day, the retailer never saw the final address of the shopper. They only had visibility into the address of the reshipping company itself, which was where the retailer was supposed to be sending the package. So, a fraudster could use a reshipper to both conceal their true location and make sure the package reached them. Since there are plenty of legitimate consumers who use reshipping services, it wasn't an automatic sign of fraud, and fraud teams learned to be cautious but not overly paranoid about these services.

However, many reshipping services nowadays make an effort to be more transparent, if not about the identity of the customer at the final destination then at least about the country and region of delivery. This makes reshippers far less attractive for fraudsters, since it means most retailers will have the ability to identify heavy abusers of reshippers by tracing the patterns in the addresses involved in the scams. On the other hand, some do still employ this method, using a number of convenient addresses in their own country to make it more difficult to see these patterns.

Given the growth of the online criminal ecosystem into its current intricate system of organized criminal groups, as discussed in the Preface and Chapter 2, it's not surprising that some of these large groups have a number of addresses they can use where relevant. In addition, since reshippers have become more respectable and less associated with fraud attempts in recent years, fraud teams are less primed to be suspicious, which aids those fraud groups who can employ them effectively. The cat-and-mouse game, as always, continues.

Remote Interception of Package: Convince Customer Support

Fraudsters know that orders are examined for fraud at the time of transaction, but they also know that many businesses do not have measures in place to prevent suspicious activity later in the process. They take advantage of that vulnerability to try to solve the shipping challenge. They'll match the billing and shipping addresses initially, and only after the order has been approved will they call customer support and request that the address be changed to something more convenient for the fraudster.

They're usually careful about this; they won't be changing the address to a different country, or even a different city, which might set off alarm bells for the support representative. Instead, they'll make a small change within the same city or area—perhaps using one of the locations described earlier in the section on open houses. The request seems like a small change to the support representative, but it's significant enough, in fraud terms, that it might have been able to tip the scales in favor of a decline had that address been included in the original order in place of a perfect address match.

Remote Interception of Package: AVS Manipulation

Manipulation of the address using an address verification service (AVS) can be done both before and after the point of transaction. In both cases, fraudsters take advantage of the fact that (as discussed in Chapter 1) the AVS system only checks the numbers of an address, not the words. Fraudsters using it at checkout will use AVS manipulation to make sure the building number and zip code of the billing address match the building number and zip code of the shipping address. That will be enough to pass an automated AVS check, though it may be a red flag for any reviewer who casts an eye over the order. Unfortunately, an AVS match makes it less likely that a review will take place.

More subtle is the fraudster who places an order with only a number match, using the street name of the address they intend to use. Then they call customer support to request a small—such a small!—change to the address, simply shifting the building and/or apartment number but keeping the same street. It's hard to blame a support agent for being taken in.

Mule Interception of Package

Fraudsters like to use mules to do their heavy lifting for them (that's why they're referred to as mules, after all). A *mule* is similar to a patsy or a cat's-paw: it's someone the fraudster employs to perform tasks that are either repetitive or simply require them to live in a particular location. Our focus here is on shipping mules; money mules, a related but slightly different flavor, are discussed in Chapter 20.

With shipping mules, fraudsters will typically advertise for people to receive and repackage goods for them and then send the goods to whichever address the fraudster gives them. Mules are a part of the dark economy that has been around for many years, but which grew considerably during the COVID-19 pandemic when more people were out of work and looking for jobs they could do from home. Desperation may have also made some people willing to ignore signs that the work might not be entirely legitimate. This situation is now beginning to be called *the gig economy of fraud* (more on this in Chapter 2, and in Chapter 17 on marketplace attacks). Mules are usually paid, at least for a while, though a fraudster will sometimes end the relationship by simply disappearing, leaving the mule unpaid for the month and possibly out of pocket for expenses they had laid out, expecting to be reimbursed.

Fraudsters know that retailers are more tolerant of billing/shipping mismatches when the shipping address is in the same area as the billing address. Many legitimate customers send packages to friends, family, and workplaces nearby. Moreover, updating a billing address when a customer moves can take a long time, leading to mismatches even when the packages are coming to the cardholder.

So, if the fraudster can buy stolen card information for a number of cards, all connected to the same geographic area, and they can find a mule who lives in the right area, they can place plenty of fraudulent purchases that look legitimate, have them all sent to the mule, and then have the mule send them on to wherever is convenient for the fraudster. Due to the growth of available mules as a result of the pandemic, it's now easy for fraudsters to find mules almost anywhere they need, via social media, Craigslist, and so on. Often, they'll add the cardholder's last name to the mule's name in the address so that it looks like the purchase is being sent to a family member.

 Mules can also be used to support most of the other interception methods. For example, a mule can meet a courier and take a package from them, or pick packages up from an accommodating local business.

More Advanced: Adding an Address to the Card

This method is more advanced, requiring considerably more effort on the fraudster's part, and as such is typically employed with high-value goods to make it worth the work involved. Here, the fraudster targets the customer support representatives of the credit card's issuer and persuades them to add their (the fraudster's) own shipping address to the credit card on file. This way, there's no need to come up with methods to get around the lack of a match; there will be a match with the address on file.

To convince the support agent, fraudsters need to do quite a bit of research into the cardholder so that they can answer questions about them convincingly and also provide a convincing reason for the new address. Social engineering attacks are the most likely way for a fraudster to get this information, using scams such as romance scams, catfishing, and IT tech support scams. This method also requires an intimate knowledge of the processes of the issuer involved so that the fraudster will know what they'll be asked and what to say to make it convincing. All of this is entirely possible for the fraudster to achieve, but does represent a considerable investment of time and effort. For that reason, only a small percentage of fraudsters use this method, but those who do can be very dangerous with their knowledge.

More Advanced: Adding an Address to Data Enrichment Services

This attack method is similar to adding an address to the credit card. Here, the fraudster aims to build up a convincing picture online that connects the cardholder to the fraudster's address. To do this, they'll target data enrichment services (see Chapter 4), getting customer support representatives of those services to add their own address to the information they have on file for the cardholder. Like adding an address to a card, this method takes time and requires knowing the processes of the data enrichment services. Therefore, like that method, this one is usually used when targeting high-value items that make the investment worthwhile.

More Advanced: Dropshipping Direct/Triangulation

In this scenario, the fraudster essentially runs a retail operation of their own and gets the goods sent directly to their customers from another supplier. It's generally called triangulation (*https://oreil.ly/YqfZu*), and it's very similar to dropshipping. However, instead of running a legitimate business, the fraudster collects real payments from their own customers (and in the process, gains their payment information for future fraud) and uses stolen information to place the order with the merchant.

This fraudulent transaction is, of course, carried out using the shipping address of the fraudster's customer, so it doesn't look suspicious. The fraudster is usually careful to match it with stolen payment information that has a billing address that looks convincingly close. This is easier than it might sound, when you remember that much of this stolen information will come from previous customers and that fraudsters target ads for their "business" using the same location targeting abilities that are available to legitimate businesses. It's a fraud scam that practically runs by itself after a little while.

 As with reshippers, merely identifying a dropshipper is not enough for a fraud team. Plenty of dropshippers, and plenty of reshippers, are legitimate businesses providing a useful service for their customers. Fraud analysts need to be able to identify those that are using this business model as a cover for fraudulent activities. This is unlikely to be something a single fraud analyst would do as part of a transaction review; rather, such a project should be agreed on by the team as a priority and given its own time for research, results analysis, and implementation of confirmed results.

Now that we've explored a number of the most common ways to manipulate an address or reroute a package to the fraudster's desired destination, let's take a look at how you can identify those attacks when they're being used against your business. For this chapter, we'll be focusing on the types of attacks that are tied to address spoofing.

Identification and Mitigation

There are a number of standard identification methods most fraud departments use which, as discussed earlier, fraudsters are adept at circumventing: notably, AVS and other forms of matching billing and shipping addresses. We don't discuss those here, partly because they are so standard and partly because they are as well known to fraudsters as to fraud fighters. Similarly, we don't discuss the vulnerabilities of not having uniform formats for addresses in your system so that fraudsters can pretend to have a new address simply by adding dots or dashes or similar symbols. The need for uniformity is well known and is not complex from the fraud analysis perspective. If your system lacks it, fraudsters will take advantage.

Instead, this section looks at other ways to identify shipping manipulation, in the context of open houses, mules, and reshippers. We won't be discussing dropshipping or the advanced card/data enrichment techniques individually, except to say that if you are concerned that these methods are being employed against you, the linking logics discussed in Chapter 5 are probably the best way to approach an analysis and mitigation effort.

First, we'll say a few words about the physical interception models and the customer support trick. In these cases, there really isn't a lot that a fraud team can do to identify a problem (at least from the address angle) at the point of transaction. At that point, the address checks out. That's the point of these methods.

What you can do is make sure the systems that track the next steps (e.g., the courier or delivery service delivering the package, the customer support department that takes the calls, or the department that handles complaints and/or refunds) are giving your fraud prevention system the data it needs to track the story as it unfolds. You need to know when a package was picked up "near the destination" but not at the given shipping address. You need to know when a customer complains that they never received their package. You need to know that a customer support representative changed the address—or, if you've alerted them to the trick and trained them on a response, that the representative was asked to change the address and refused.

Your system needs all that information because otherwise, it will have the wrong information when the chargeback comes in and you'll take the wrong lessons from that. In the case of porch piracy, you'll probably never even know that fraud occurred. You need to be able to track these fraud methods in your system so that you can work out how serious a problem they're posing for your business and act accordingly. You can't do that by yourself. You need to work with other departments.

If you don't have proper address tracking of this nature set up already, it may sound daunting, but it's often quite simple as long as you take it slow and approach it as an exercise in education and appreciation: your job is to teach your colleagues about the problems and the damage they do to the business, and how collaboration between your departments could make a big difference. Remember that you're asking for something that's outside their normal working responsibilities, so make sure to express your gratitude for their help and to share the credit when that data helps you make things safer for the company.

These sorts of changes don't come with SQL or Python scripts you can plug in to work magic. Yet, improving your company's processes in these sorts of ways is just as important as finding the right fraud tools or digging into some good analytical research. When it's done right, the impact can be just as big.

Open House

The advantage your fraud team has with the open house scenario is that by its very nature, it has the fraudster reusing the same address multiple times. If this happens with many packages, especially using different names and especially in a fairly short period of time, that's a red flag and your system needs to be set up to recognize it. It's not a definite sign of fraud—there are legitimate locker or PO box–style arrangements for exactly this sort of setup, for example—but it means you'll want your system, and likely a human analyst, taking a look to see more.

Because of this weakness, fraudsters often use the location to hit multiple businesses, ensuring that each company only sees the address a few times. If you suspect you're being targeted by a ring using this model, it may be worthwhile exploring the possibility of collaborating with other companies to help protect all of your businesses.

Mules

To identify manipulated shipping addresses, one needs to research the qualities of the addresses. If you think about it, your database has a lot of information about how ordinary, legitimate people typically type addresses in different countries. If you can draw out and leverage that knowledge, you can then pinpoint anomalies to that standard usage. Those anomalies do not provide ironclad certainty of fraud (it could be a legitimate foreigner to the city using nonstandard capitalization or shortening), but they are a good indication that more investigation may be worthwhile.

The following hypothetical query syntax is effective for detecting abnormalities in addresses on your system:

```
WITH table_of_how_many_times_each_combination_of_zip_and_city_appeared AS
    (
        SELECT
            zipcode,
            city,
            COUNT(*) AS count_orders
        FROM
            shipping_addresses
        GROUP BY 1, 2
```

```
      )
SELECT
    city,
    PERCENT_RANK() OVER (PARTITION BY zipcode
ORDER BY
    count_orders) AS pctrank
ORDER BY
    pctrank ASC;
```

This query would yield the rarest combinations of zip codes and city names, providing that your data holds the city as typed in by the end user (and not normalized). You would see a table that looks something like Table 7-1.

Table 7-1. Example shipping address details

shipping_addresses_zipcode	shipping_addresses_city (as entered by the user)	count(order_id)
10025	New York	13490
10025	NYC	9832
10025	newyork	12
10025	New york	31
60198	Tel Aviv	2846
60198	TLV	712
60198	Telaviv	4

With this logic, you will find, for example, that most Israelis would write "Tel Aviv" or "Tel-Aviv" or even "TLV", but not "telaviv" as a single word. Therefore, this query would reveal nonlocals using a Tel Aviv shipping address. For New York, you can see that both "New York" and "NY" are commonly used, but that "newyork" is not. Nonlocals may be worth looking into—unless, of course, they're sending goods to a hotel, which can be seen as a good sign supporting a legitimate travel story. Looking at this specific example, the system should probably decline the four orders with "Telaviv" and the 12 orders with "newyork" as the shipping city. The 31 orders with "New york" as the shipping city might be worth manual review or extra authentication flows.

Using this query, you'll also be able to detect cases when nonlocal fraudsters have tried to enter the shipping addresses of their mules. Bear in mind that there will be some legit scenarios of nonlocals shipping goods to Israeli/New York addresses, but they will probably be negligible—it's rare for a mistake to happen in this context, because usually the friend or family member will be using the address provided by the recipient—and that will include standard usage. For whatever reason, the same does not hold true with fraudsters and their mules. Perhaps, psychologically speaking, the fraudster feels they've already done all the hard work arranging the mule and matching the card and shipping address, so they are sloppier when it comes to actually entering in the address.

That said, you may find that some cases of misspelling are more common than others. New York, for example, is more likely to see legitimate variety than Lafayette, Louisiana, simply because of its popularity as a shipping destination, so your model should be more or less forgiving accordingly. A model can work through these examples alone, if you have a large enough training set, but the common sense search method described here can allow you to use advanced logic, even if you don't have enough data/capacity to train a model.

You can use queries like the previous one we gave (and we encourage you to get creative about finding similar queries) to distinguish between common mistakes even locals make—adding an extra "0" at the end of a zip code that already has two or three, for example—versus unusual mistakes, which are signs that more investigation might be worthwhile.

Reshippers

Unlike mules, most businesses do want to allow reshippers; as mentioned, there are plenty of legitimate uses for them. However, there are certain reshippers you'll want to either ban or mark as "gray" if they're repeatedly associated with fraud attacks.

Monitoring reshippers is often a matter of ongoing surveillance for excessive users. If you're lucky, the reshipper address will include indicators for the specific customer behind it. For example, in the following address, the suffix -CN6372 would indicate the customer and probably would also hint that the destination is in China:

95-CN6372 Mayhill St Unit H Saddle Brook, NJ 07663

However, there will be many cases where the shipping address doesn't indicate the end user. It's wise to keep track of the frequency of orders coming in from reshipper addresses so that you can spot that a specific reshipper is suddenly gaining momentum in a suspicious manner. A useful Pandas data frame for this would be `data_pivot_nunique`. By using it (along with its simpler variation, `data_pivot_count`), you would be able to spot both cases when a repeating user is placing many orders using a reshipper service, whether or not they repeat the same email address in all their orders:

```
data_pivot_nunique=data.pivot_table(index=['hour'], columns='reshipper',
values='user-emails', aggfunc='nunique').reset_index()
```

In Figure 7-1, we follow a fraudster who was hitting the system with multiple orders to a reshipper twice a day. You can see how the number of orders per hour spiked from the usual benchmark (which was about 10 to 20 per hour) to more than 150 on two specific hours of the day.

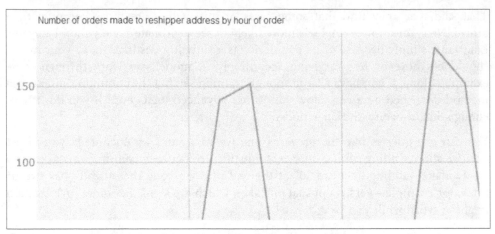

Figure 7-1. An abnormal spike in the number of orders made to one specific reshipper, suggesting that one (or two) fraudsters are placing their orders at this time

Here's the code to generate the chart:

```
fig = px.line(data_pivot_count, x="hour", y="number of orders",  title="Number of
orders made to reshipper address by hour of order") fig.show()
```

You might want to search for a promotion that would have encouraged and would explain these spikes, or perhaps there's a legitimate link between the orders (e.g., businesses coordinating an event together). An anomalous result like this is not conclusive on its own. But it is a very strong signal, and is definitely a sign that more investigation is needed.

 When measuring abnormality by hours for reshippers, it's important to look into the market that they serve. A reshipper that caters to Australia, New Zealand, and Singapore will obviously have more traffic during nighttime hours in the United States. Finding out the region that each reshipper caters to is achievable manually (e.g., via a web search) or statistically, given enough historical data.

The example given here is by no means the only way to identify and prevent reshipping abuse. However, it's a good way to illustrate the sorts of analyses you can run that will help your business. With this case, as with mules, it's important to think around the problem, exploring different ways you can identify abnormalities with addresses and their use, rather than relying solely on tools or techniques like AVS, which, although useful to an extent, are both limited and known to fraudsters who have therefore developed ways to get around them. As always, the cat-and-mouse game continues. To get ahead, fraud prevention teams need to get creative and find different ways to see what the data is telling them.

Summary

In this chapter, we explored different ways fraudsters work around the challenge of billing/shipping mismatch so that they can make an order look convincing, but also benefit from the theft. We also looked at ways that fraud departments can identify and mitigate these tricks. In the next chapter, we'll look at another way of getting around the shipping challenge: leveraging click-and-collect.

## CHAPTER 8

BORIS and BOPIS Fraud

I went down to the sacred store...
  —Don McLean[1]

This chapter looks at the fraud associated with Buy Online, Pick up In Store (BOPIS) and Buy Online, Return In Store (BORIS) programs. Within these definitions, we're including the curbside options made popular due to the COVID-19 pandemic, looking specifically at the additional risks that came with pandemic practices. This is because they're relevant at the time of publication, and because, given the convenience of the option, we suspect a lot of BOPIS/BORIS programs will become permanent features of the retail landscape.

The great advantage of BOPIS, from the fraudster perspective, is that it circumvents the shipping challenges discussed in the previous chapter. If you're picking up an order in a store or a distribution/fulfillment center, you don't need to provide a shipping address, which means fraudsters don't need to work out a way to use an address that matches the billing address of the payment method they've stolen. They just go pick it up at the store.

Some companies will accept a credit card with any billing address without further checks, as long as it's from the right country. They know good customers often order goods to pick up near their work, which may be far from their home address; and sometimes use BOPIS to send items to family members or friends, or alternatively, have family or friends pick up the parcel for them so that it will be there when they visit. They may do this because they will want an item during their stay, or because it's not available in their own area, or to avoid tax. All of these are perfectly legitimate activities. Not performing checks, though, does make things easier for fraudsters.

---

1 Don McLean, "American Pie," track 1 on *American Pie*, United Artists, 1971.

For those companies that *do* perform checks when there's a substantial billing/pickup disparity (and fraudsters know and share the identities of these companies), fraudsters use the tried-and-tested mule pickup method (mules being people the fraudster employs to perform tasks that are either repetitive or simply require them to live in a particular location; see Chapters 2, 7, and 20 for more on mules). Mules are also the answer for BOPIS fraud carried out by fraudsters who are not based in the local area. They are a great way for fraudsters to expand their reach and scale up.

Mules are also often used in attacking BORIS programs—that is, returning items, typically in exchange for cash. If this is done shortly after the initial purchase, it can be a great way to monetize a purchase made with stolen payment information. Some fraudsters do this on their own account, attacking the stores in their own local area (using a fairly wide definition of "local"). But the really problematic ones are those who use mules to expand their scale—the potential loss is simply far higher. In a sense, this type of fraud is a subset of the mule-based schemes covered in the previous chapter.

BOPIS and BORIS programs share two additional extra elements that make fraud prevention particularly challenging. First, they are promoted by companies as convenient for customers, which means they have to be smooth and speedy. That doesn't leave much time for identification processes. And second, the people interacting with the customer (and thus making the call on the ground about whether to allow the pickup or return) are not fraud prevention professionals. In many companies, they don't have access to any information regarding fraud scores or risk factors for customers who are picking up or returning goods.

BOPIS and BORIS fraud has been around since these programs began. As we hope should be clear by now, once there's an opportunity, fraudsters will exploit it. For a number of years, BOPIS and BORIS fraud remained relatively uncommon. Perhaps fraudsters were simply leery of risking being caught twice: online at checkout, and then again in real life at pickup. The risk of being caught on CCTV, and the fact that local law enforcement is willing and able to act on crime in stores (compared to the complex jurisdictional elements that deter action from law enforcement with online cases), all added up to making this kind of fraud less appealing to fraudsters.

However, fraudsters have slowly begun migrating to fraud in this channel, perhaps because it's more common than it used to be, as far more stores rolled out BOPIS and BORIS programs during the pandemic. These usually have included an option for curbside pickup, to give customers an alternative to in-store shopping, which had become unattractive.

At the same time, stores dialed down their requests for identification to minimize face-to-face contact to acknowledge the fact that customers were wearing masks, and to speed up the process whose sudden popularity put so much pressure on their in-store teams. BOPIS and BORIS, usually at curbside, then became much easier for a fraudster to exploit, and fraud in these areas has grown accordingly.

The growth in popularity has also led to a new twist on the traditional theme: combined with account takeover (ATO), fraudsters check accounts they've taken over to see when orders are placed as BOPIS orders, and then either go themselves or send a mule to pick up the order before the customer can get there.

Despite the pandemic pressures, these are still relatively rare forms of fraud (compared to simple stolen credit card use online, or ATO, for example), but they are now substantial enough that many stores that once felt safe ignoring them have put measures in place to protect their businesses, particularly those selling relatively high-ticket items.

Identification and Mitigation

Identifying and mitigating BOPIS and BORIS fraud comes in two parts. The online part (before, during, or slightly after the transaction) is the clear domain of the fraud team, and we will spend time discussing it. Before that, though, we'll look at the policies related to mitigation, and to the second part of the problem: the point of pickup or return. These parts are often overlooked by fraud prevention teams, and we would like to emphasize their importance in addition to the importance of the online identification and mitigation process with which fraud teams may be more familiar.

Pickup and Return: Educating Employees Outside Your Department

The pickup or return part of the process is not handled by fraud teams, but by in-store employees or sometimes employees from the warehouse part of the business. It is easy to dismiss this part of the process on the basis that it's not the fraud team's responsibility. But when it comes down to it, it *is* on the fraud team to make these employees aware of the risks and to train them in how to handle them. It's fraud, after all. Other departments don't know about fraud. The fraud department is, ultimately, responsible for it.

Often, this means fraud prevention leaders need to make management aware of the issues and explain why further training, and perhaps process alterations, are needed on the logistical or customer-facing side of the business. Prioritizing employee safety as part of this training is crucial. Few stores want their employees to get involved in an altercation, and this is something that should be highlighted as well.

This kind of training, involving educating employees outside your own department, might sound like a lot of work, but it's worthwhile; it's a great way to show management that your team is thinking strategically about how to protect the business, it shows you're on top of current trends, and ultimately it gets you more data. That's because you can train employees to feed valuable information back into your own detection systems, and make sure the structure is in place for this to happen. As in other areas, collaboration with other departments is crucial in order to develop really effective fraud mitigation strategies.

Policy Decisions: Part of Fraud Prevention

Part of BORIS mitigation is a policy decision. The easiest way to stop BORIS fraud is to have a store policy that identification at pickup is required, and that when a card is used to make the purchase, returns will be credited to that card and that card only. This policy stops the majority of BORIS fraud right away.

On the other hand, it causes a less ideal experience for good customers, who are, after all, the vast majority. Legitimate customers might prefer cash back or store credit; they might need the money urgently, or they've canceled that card already, or they're sending friends or family to make the return, and so forth. The same card policy may seriously inconvenience and annoy these sorts of customers.

Working out whether it's worth it is partly a numbers game. How many BORIS fraudulent returns did you have over the past month/quarter/year? How much was lost? How often do customers not want to have a refund put on the card they used for the purchase? It's also partly a question of business philosophy; some companies put customer experience so high up in their list of priorities that this option wouldn't even be considered.

Policy decisions like these are not ones a fraud team should make on their own, but it is an important discussion to have with the relevant parts of the business if BORIS fraud starts to be a serious problem. Fraud managers need to ensure that their voice is heard as part of the policy discussion.

Online Identification and Mitigation

To prevent BOPIS and BORIS fraud before they become a problem, at the point of transaction when the order is being attempted, fraud teams rely on similar techniques to those they use against other forms of fraud at the point of transaction. The BOPIS-ATO method mentioned earlier, where fraudsters ghost an account and then dive in to pick up a legitimately ordered package before the customer can do so, can be prevented in the same way standard ATO can be prevented; the challenge here is one of ATO, rather than being specific to BOPIS/BORIS. It is an important signal, though, for teams to take ATO seriously for the purpose of protecting the account, even when no transaction is being made. ATO should not be flagged only at the point of transaction; if you take that approach, you will miss this fraud trend every time it attacks your site.

The danger of BOPIS/BORIS fraud attacks is greatest when they're done well and at scale—when they become effective enough to become a serious, serial offense. Bear in mind that since physical goods are always involved, when BOPIS/BORIS fraud is successful the store loses out twice: once in repaying the victim whose payment method was used, and again in the form of the goods themselves (BOPIS) or the cash refund (BORIS). This can add up, and it's when it adds up that it becomes a problem.

Retailers with branches in port cities may see these stores particularly targeted, with losses really mounting—it's so easy to move goods from the store to be shipped. Once a fraudster realizes this, it's natural for them to try to repeat the scam. For this reason, the rest of this chapter focuses on identifying and mitigating repetition; i.e., spotting links between seemingly unrelated users or orders in your system. This is often associated with fraud rings—multiple actors attacking your system multiple times—though it may also be a sign of a single, particularly determined actor who appears to be many different actors.

Here, as is so often the case, what you really want to know is the identity behind the attack. What do you know about this identity, or this account? Does this order match previous legitimate ones or not? Is it a new account?

A fraudster carrying out BOPIS/BORIS attacks at scale will ensure that their orders present a variety of different profiles. They'll be for varied items, at different prices (though often within a rough price range), and for delivery to different stores. If the fraudster is using mules, they may choose stores spread out all over the country to confuse the picture as much as they can. However, there will be similarities or shared characteristics which a dedicated fraud team can uncover and use to identify, and therefore block, this type of fraud. For instance, it may be a certain behavioral pattern, a particular device type, or certain email addresses which share a certain format.

Table 8-1 shows orders that share similar IPs (sharing the same C-class—the first three octets of an IPv4 dot-decimal form, such as 1.1.1.1 and 1.1.1.2). This kind of linking is fairly common among fraudsters who are obscuring their true IP. They may be using a proxy that shifts to new IPs according to a list that is generally ordered in this way rather than randomized, or they may be using an ISP/VPN (virtual private network) service, which typically assigns users a range of similar IPs.

In the data set shown in Table 8-1, repetition of similar IPs reveals probable BOPIS fraud:

- Orders 1122 and 2233 probably represent a fraudster (or a mule placing the orders as per the fraudster's instructions) who is located in Montana and plans to have the stolen goods picked up at the Montana store. There are two stolen cards/accounts being monetized, one from California and one from Hawaii. Obviously, there could always be a legitimate explanation for this pattern (and two orders per day could just be a coincidence), so analyzing the volume is critical.

- Orders 3333, 5555, and 6666 probably represent a fraudster who is not based in the United States, but rather, uses a proxy/VPN that "places" them in New Hampshire. It seems like the fraudster selected this proxy because they wanted to match the billing state of the first victim, but then on January 30 they got lazy and continued to use the same VPN for stolen credentials for other states. (Fraudsters are human, and laziness like this is enormously valuable for a fraud team, so it's worth watching out for.) This fraudster also has a mule to pick up the stolen goods in Arizona. Order 1111 is probably unrelated to this fraudster.

Table 8-1. Showing repetition of similar IP addresses, indicating probable BOPIS fraud

Order ID	Order date	IP	IP geolocation (state)	Selected pickup location (state)	Billing address (state)
1111	January 3	1.1.1.1	New Hampshire	New York	New Hampshire
1122	January 28	2.2.2.2	Montana	Montana	California
2233	January 28	2.2.2.4	Montana	Montana	Hawaii
3333	January 29	1.1.1.2	New Hampshire	Arizona	New Hampshire
5555	January 30	1.1.1.2	New Hampshire	Arizona	Ohio
6666	January 30	1.1.1.3	New Hampshire	Arizona	Nebraska

You could query for the most significant attacks based on a moving average of a three-day window:

```
SELECT
    c_class_ip,
    order_date,
    AVG(daily_count) OVER(
ORDER BY
    order_date ROWS BETWEEN 2 PRECEDING AND CURRENT ROW) AS moving_average
FROM
    (
        SELECT
            substr(ip, 1, instr(ip, '.', 1, 3) - 1) AS c_class_ip,
            order_date,
            COUNT(orderid) AS daily_count
        FROM
            orders
        GROUP BY 1, 2
    )
    AS daily_count_nested_table;
```

Note that moving averages will not function well if you have missing data for some of the dates. Consider using date offset if your database supports it, or opt for something more naive such as grouping by ISOweek. If your data set includes periods of high seasonality, consider using weighted moving averages (which is easier to do in Python than in SQL).

You can clearly see the suspicious pattern here, showing links between the orders that should not be there if they were really entirely separate orders placed by different people, but equally showing too much difference to look like orders made legitimately by the same person. Of course, this by itself is not a sure sign of fraud: you would want to look for as many linking factors as possible to confirm that you're seeing a fraud ring. The more links you identify between orders performed within a short time of one another, the more caution you should practice with regard to this order.

You can do further research and decline outright, at least above a certain order value, or you can add friction: call the customer; or request that the teams handling item pickup or return use strong customer identification; or don't allow anyone other than the cardholder bearing an ID to pick up or return the item; or allow pickup or return only at a store near the AVS-approved billing address; and so on. No authentication process is bulletproof, of course, but each one makes the fraudster's life harder. If you make your store too much hassle to attack, they'll simply move elsewhere; as we've said, fraudsters are sensitively tuned in to their own return on investment (ROI). In this case, unfortunately, it's like the joke about running away from a bear: you don't need to be the fastest, you just need not to be the slowest. In this case, you don't need to be impregnable, you just need to be more difficult to attack than other stores.

At the same time, bear in mind the need to maintain the right balance between fraud prevention and customer experience. Adding friction may help stop fraud, but it may also stop good customers from ordering from your store. Make sure you keep an eye on the numbers so that you know how much of a problem BOPIS/BORIS is in your company, as well as customer reactions to additional friction.

Summary

This chapter looked at the BOPIS/BORIS attack method, in which fraudsters leverage the vulnerabilities in this pickup/return method to commit fraud. We looked at the additional vulnerabilities introduced into the process by the growth of curbside pickup and other practices that became common during the COVID-19 pandemic. We also looked at the methods fraud teams should use to identify and stop this kind of fraud: both in terms of interdepartmental collaboration and training, and in terms of linking orders and accounts to one another to identify patterns of bad behavior. Interestingly, although digital goods fraud is almost the opposite of the BOPIS challenge (since the physical address and delivery aspect is removed from the equation entirely), the work of linking remains relevant there as well—something worth bearing in mind when reading the next chapter.

## CHAPTER 9

Digital Goods and Cryptocurrency Fraud

Living in a material world...
　　—Madonna[1]

The term *digital goods* covers a wide range of items, from streaming or software sub-scriptions and services to ticketing, gaming, gambling, gift cards, and more. Although cryptocurrency is a separate phenomenon with its own rules and regulations, we are addressing all of these diverse industries in this chapter because, from the perspective of fraudsters and fraud fighters, the similarities are far greater than the differences.

A fraudster looks at both digital goods and cryptocurrency in the same way, exploit-ing the vulnerabilities common to each. The idea is to translate a stolen payment account or card into goods or cash (gift cards and cryptocurrency essentially being forms of cash), maximizing the amount spent, and flipping the goods as quickly as possible. With digital goods, that's very fast indeed.

To do this, fraudsters focusing on digital goods and/or cryptocurrency tend to uti-lize the methods we talked about so far, such as IP masking and mules. Mules in particular are popular in cryptocurrency fraud because they can provide their true IDs or, if they're aware that something illegitimate is going on and they don't mind, they can use stolen IDs provided for them by the fraudster but with their own headshot. This is important because cryptocurrency is now regulated, so many of the Know Your Customer (KYC) types of considerations apply here just as they do with other currencies. In fact, this is the main difference between digital goods and cryptocurrencies—with the exception of certain products such as open loop cards, which are similar to prepaid cards and do require basic KYC.

---

1 Madonna, "Material Girl," written by Peter Brown and Robert Rans, track 1 on *Like a Virgin*, Sire Records, 1984.

This makes sense, since a necessary function of a successful form of cryptocurrency is its ability to function as cash, so it needs to be regulated just like other forms of currency conversion do. We'll cover this in more detail later in this chapter and in Chapter 22, but for now it's important to understand that fraudsters like to use cryptocurrency as an anonymizing factor in their operations, breaking the trail between an illicit activity and the money they got from it. They might change stolen funds into cryptocurrency, and move the cryptocurrency around and obfuscate its origin as much as possible before changing it into *fiat* (government-issued currency). Separately, they might sell stolen items for cryptocurrency. In this sense, cryptocurrency fraud is important to fraud analysts who are outside this industry and whose companies do not accept it as a form of payment, because the cryptocurrency system is so embedded in how fraudsters approach so many kinds of fraud and its monetization. As we've said repeatedly in this book, fraudsters don't care about our categories. They'll use any and all tools and tricks available to them.

What's also interesting is that cryptocurrency is being considered by some companies to ameliorate, to some extent, the risky nature of certain purchases—something Identiq cofounder Uri Arad, formerly the head of analytics and research in PayPal's risk department, pointed out is only a logical next step now that cryptocurrencies are entering the mainstream—because, crucially, there are no chargebacks with cryptocurrency. That's a significant reduction in risk if you're an online merchant. On the other hand, as Uri noted, there is an inherent risk in terms of the volatility of the cryptocurrencies themselves and in terms of cryptocurrencies being part of a many-layered fraud scheme.

Definition and Fraudster MO

The greatest similarity between digital goods and cryptocurrency, unfortunately, is that they are ideal for fraud attacks when you consider monetization and anonymity. In both cases, there's no shipping address, which makes all the handstands we discussed in Chapter 7 with mules and shipping address manipulation unnecessary and vastly streamlines the attack considerations.

In addition, the goods arrive almost immediately, making a single attack easy to keep track of and dramatically reducing the danger of the cardholder noticing the attack in time to stop it. Turning the stolen goods into a profitable sale is also very easy, since there's always a ready market for these items, and legitimate "deals" of getting a reduced price or additional services are common enough for consumers not to be suspicious (or at least for consumers to be able to ignore their doubts). The speed at which the goods can be transferred also makes it far less likely that anyone will catch on until it's too late. When it comes to cryptocurrency it's even easier, since it's effectively equivalent to cash; fraudsters can easily convert it to fiat in exchanges, or even pay for things with it directly.

The time factor makes things particularly difficult for the fraud team, who must balance between customer experience and fraud prevention even more than fraud teams in other industries. Customers expect to get their digital goods right away. They might be standing in line waiting to make a purchase with a gift card, or heading to a venue and purchasing a ticket while en route, or buying a subscription so that they can use it right away.

That puts a lot of pressure on the fraud team for both speed and accuracy. Sometimes a fraud team will even be aware of a particular rush, such as in cases in which a venue is intentionally looking to maximize revenue by continuing to sell tickets right through the first half of an event, and so will have to prioritize those orders appropriately. Jordan Harris, a senior director at a major ticket sales company, notes the importance of prioritizing good customers while fighting fraud and the difficulty of maintaining that perspective when you're in the thick of the decisions: "Most consumers are good, but it's easy to forget that, because we live and breathe the fraud. We see the bad; it dominates our perspective. But the lion's share is good customers. And customer experience is absolutely crucial here."

It's especially true in ticketing, since delays can be so painful—customers may not be able to enter the venue with their friends, or they may have to wait until the event has already begun—but the same point holds true for almost every other kind of digital goods as well.

Anonymization can be attractive for good customers for multiple reasons, but it's certainly a huge plus for fraudsters. Many forms of digital subscription, and many digital services, only ask for minimal user information at sign-up. Sometimes just an email address is enough. In gaming and sometimes gambling, aliases are very common as part of the online persona used as part of the game, or to distance the online activity from someone's real life. This is all very reasonable, but it's a great help to fraudsters as well.

Gift cards are often bought as presents (the clue is in the name there) and, once purchased, might belong to anyone. Crucially, they are easily transferable multiple times without any record of that transfer occurring, making them ideal for use as payment or as a way to transfer money to a fraudster. The anonymity aspect affects which cryptocurrencies are most popular with fraudsters as well, with the more anonymous taking first place: among them Zcash and Monero, though it's worth noting that while fraudsters like these cryptocurrencies as post-payment vehicles, it's difficult to purchase them directly with fiat, limiting their use to some extent. Of course, the anonymity is also very attractive to privacy-conscious users and often is a core part of the brand, distinguishing the currency from other similar offerings.

The digital aspect in both cases has another implication, which is that the goods are often potentially unlimited in amount, and it is in fact common to see both fraudsters and real shoppers spending huge amounts of money on digital goods and cryptocurrency. Digital goods sometimes, but not always, see purchases split into multiple orders. This may be due to regulations such as the daily limit on gift card orders mandated by the Financial Crimes Enforcement Network. Or it may be for verisimilitude since subscriptions or gaming purchases are often part of a wider shopping spree that includes multiple items—but again, this is common for both legitimate and fraudulent customers. So, it's easy for fraudsters to commit this kind of fraud, and fraud fighters lack some of the information they usually rely on *and* have to distinguish between legit and fraud in cases where good and bad users behave very similarly.

As if that weren't enough, the scale of the loss involved can be huge if a fraud team doesn't catch an attack in time, especially in the case of cash-equivalent goods like gift cards and cryptocurrencies, which generate nearly 100% loss to the seller. This factor is considerably reduced in the case of digital goods such as subscription services and access to online software, where the seller doesn't incur a loss on the goods themselves, but it may be poor comfort if a fraudulent transaction results in a chargeback that the merchant has to cover.

The scale for digital goods and cryptocurrency is so risky partly because, in many cases, both have an addictive quality to them. This makes some good users more likely to spend larger amounts and make repeat purchases, often in quick succession—just like fraudsters. They are probably a platform's best customers, so adding friction or blocking them is to be avoided wherever possible, as long as their behavior can be distinguished from that of fraudsters. This enthusiasm also sometimes makes these customers less suspicious in their interactions with other people on the platform or connected to the goods in question, because their desire to complete the transaction, continue their gameplay, or buy cryptocurrency while the price is right (to give just a few examples) overwhelms their instincts to be cautious, smoothing the path to exploitation by a fraudster via social engineering.

The addictive aspect also increases the likelihood of family fraud and friendly fraud, which we discussed in Chapter 8. Since family fraud and friendly fraud can affect a fraud team's metrics (including fraud chargeback limits), it's worth keeping an eye on this factor as well (we'll discuss this more in Chapter 10).

The addictive nature of some kinds of digital goods and cryptocurrency can sometimes create a sort of hybrid between family fraud and social engineering, with family members or friends manipulating a cardholder into enabling and subsidizing their addiction. This can be difficult to spot, so it is worth educating customer support representatives about the possibility and teaching them to watch out for signs that it is occurring. For example, if an adult is being coached through the process of buying gaming accessories or cryptocurrency by what appears to be a teenager, it can be worth asking gentle questions about the purchase to test whether the adult really understands what's going on or even knows which platform is being used or the nature of the purchase. If nothing else, it gives your business ammunition to contest a chargeback later should one be made, but in an ideal scenario it gives the cardholder greater context so that they understand what they're being asked to do and can make a more informed decision about whether to proceed.

Subscriptions are an exception to the large amounts often seen in digital goods, but their modest sums work in the fraudsters' favor as well, because cardholders are unlikely to notice the amount coming off their card. This means fraudsters can use many accounts or payment methods to make the same purchase over and over again, reaching scale in a different way. They can even use nearly burnt cards or accounts to maximize the value of the stolen data, since only a small amount is needed each time.

Ticketing fraud and gift card fraud belong to the digital goods categories discussed in this chapter and reflect most of the generalizations we've made. However, each has idiosyncrasies that are worth highlighting, and for clarity we devote the following two subsections on them before we move on to social engineering, which is particularly prevalent in digital goods attacks. (We have not highlighted the unique aspects of gaming in a similar section, because many of the challenges that are specific to gaming relate more to trust and safety concerns than to fraud, and although fraud teams are often drawn into these discussions, they are not as relevant for this book, though they could easily be the subject of a book in their own right.)

Ticketing Fraud

Ticketing fraud, meaning fraud carried out against and leveraging sites and apps that supply tickets for events of various kinds, shares many of the challenges we've discussed so far in this chapter. However, it's a problem that has a couple of unusual possible solutions. Both are speculative at this stage, but they are intriguing enough that we wanted to include them. We're grateful to Jordan Harris for sharing his thoughts on these.

To a great extent, ticketing is an anonymous business, like the rest of digital goods; you can't guarantee who's sitting in that seat (which comes with other trust and safety issues, but that's a problem for another book). Counterfeiting tickets happens all too often, as does friendly fraud, even to the egregious extent of a customer who attends an event and then claims afterward to the merchant that they never bought the ticket. Where ticketing has an edge is the ability to issue new barcodes to tie specific tickets to specific purchases so that individuals can't buy a ticket, resell it, and try to use the original ticket. So, once a ticket has been resold, no one can use the barcode of the original ticket because the ticket's barcode was reissued when it was resold.

In a similar way, Harris noted the intriguing possibilities of blockchain technology as a future solution to some of these challenges. He discussed the idea of a clean ledger of a journey of a ticket, even over many sites if it happened to be resold multiple times. Venues could use the same technology to enhance the experience. For example, they might attach a coupon that corresponds to the identity of the time-of-event ticketholder's favorite concession food. It's not a practical option yet, but we found the possibility intriguing enough to include here. Perhaps if you're reading this and would like to explore the possibility, you could be part of making it happen.

Gift Card Fraud

In the context of digital goods, we'd be remiss not to devote a little time to discussing *gift card fraud*, or fraud leveraging gift cards directly from stores, third-party gift card sellers, or marketplaces. We talked about gift card fraud earlier in this chapter in the context of anonymity, but it's such a significant trend that we're going to devote a little more time to it here as well. About one in four people who tell the Federal Trade Commission (FTC) they lost money to fraud say they paid with a gift card, and gift cards have been one of the top reported fraud payment methods (*https://oreil.ly/MKAx8*) since 2018.

There was also a notable increase in gift card purchases, both legitimate and fraudulent, at the start of the COVID-19 pandemic. Although this has decreased more recently, it has by no means disappeared. Good customers were purchasing gift cards as presents to show they were thinking of people they couldn't see in person, to support local businesses, and even to make charitable donations so that people in immediate need could buy groceries, for example. Fraudsters inevitably took advantage of the flood of gift card purchases to hide among the good customers.

Arielle Caron, now group product manager of Risk at Etsy, and until recently head of Risk Product & Risk Data Science at a large gift card company, explained to us that "COVID offered unique scam opportunities that fraudsters were quick to exploit, including representing themselves as coming from the Centers for Disease Control and Prevention or the World Health Organization; this is in addition to the usual IRS, bail bonds, tech, and romance scams, which also all grew during this period."

Gift cards are popular with fraudsters because there are so many ways to leverage them, meaning there are many avenues available for successful theft. Following are the four main avenues:

Straightforward monetization, with a bit of money laundering thrown in
> Fraudsters can use stolen payment methods to buy gift cards. They then either use the gift card to purchase goods that can be resold or returned for a cash refund, or turn around and resell the gift card, with a discount, to a consumer.

Account takeover (ATO)
> Fraudsters hack into an account and drain whatever gift cards are associated with the account. The accounts in this case are usually either a specific retailer's account or an email account that can be scraped to find gift cards. ATO against a gift card marketplace is also possible, but there the monetization is slightly different, with stored payment methods in those accounts used to buy more gift cards.

Refunding
> In this type of attack, fraudsters purchase something with stolen payment information, and then return it right away in exchange for a gift card. This type of attack is far more anonymous, and unlike a credit card, it's unlikely to be blocked once fraud has been uncovered in the chain of events. The gift card is then monetized as in the first method.

Victim-assisted fraud
> This type of fraud has grown significantly in recent years, particularly since the start of the COVID-19 pandemic, and it presents unique challenges for a fraud fighter because the victims themselves are convinced to purchase the gift cards, which they then send to the fraudster thinking it's a legitimate payment for some service or, at times, as part of an extortion scheme.

The first three kinds of attack are not unique from a fraud prevention perspective. Stolen credit cards, ATO, and refund fraud are approached in the same way across fraud-fighting teams regardless of whether gift cards are involved. However, since gift cards are so high risk and can be monetized by fraudsters so quickly, there is often greater pressure involved where gift cards are concerned.

The particularly unpleasant victim-assisted fraud is rather different, and far more akin to the authorized push payment fraud seen by fraud analysts in banking (see Chapters 11 and 14), except in some ways the challenge is even greater. While banks have vast amounts of information about their customers' typical buying habits, age, and so forth, and so can explore ways to protect customers who are vulnerable from being tricked into sending payments to a fraudster, the same is not true for sites that provide gift cards, who often do a lot of business through guest checkout and in these cases have very little information about their users.

Brute-force gift card theft and physical gift card theft are additional tactics that are popular among fraudsters. With the brute-force method, fraudsters simply enter number after number into a gift card site or marketplace in an attempt to find a number that is tied to a gift card with money on it. With physical gift card fraud, fraudsters leverage the vulnerability of the information available on the physical cards, which are generally easily visible in the store. We did not include these two types in this discussion, because the former has more in common with bots or cookie-cutter brute-force attacks (as discussed in Chapter 14) than it does with anything unique to gift cards (other than the fact that the gift card can be monetized as soon as it has been revealed), and the latter is not a card-not-present problem, which makes it less relevant for inclusion in a book focused on online fraud.

Social Engineering

We talked about the social engineer as a psychological fraudster back in Chapter 2 when we looked at different fraudster archetypes. Psychological fraudsters hit every industry, but they're particularly prevalent in digital goods and cryptocurrency, where they trick vulnerable people into sending them money directly via gift cards or cryptocurrency. That's why it's called victim-assisted fraud: the fraudster is sneaky enough to convince the victim to participate in being defrauded. If the scam involves gift cards, the cards are sometimes converted into cryptocurrency, which is in turn changed into other currencies, ensuring that a complaint to the gift card issuer will come too late to result in the fraudster losing access to the money. Arielle Caron noted that on the basis of her observations, victim-assisted fraud at least doubled as a proportion of total fraud during the COVID-19 pandemic.

Social engineers rely on manipulating strong emotions in their victim, in particular either love or fear. Love can be leveraged through romance scams, in which fraudsters convince a victim over a period of weeks or months that they are romantically interested in them and then send an urgent request for money (via gift cards or cryptocurrency) in order to help them buy flight tickets to come and visit the victim, cure a relative, pay off debts so that they can start fresh, and so on. Love also comes into play when a scammer pretends to be a relative of the victim in immediate need of financial assistance, or even needing to be bailed out of jail.

Fear has a broad range of applications. Some scams involve a sort of catfish setup, typically involving blackmail and extortion as an end goal. Some work by terrifying victims into believing they owe a fine or a debt, usually to an established institution such as a bank or the government, which must be paid at once via, you guessed it, a gift card or cryptocurrency. Sometimes the fraudster will convince the victim that their bank account has been hacked into or their identity has been stolen, and they need to protect what's left of their money by sending it to a safe place such as in a gift card or as cryptocurrency. Or perhaps, most popular at the time of this writing, a similar story will play out with the fraudster pretending to be from technical support, helping the user maintain access to their assets by creating a new account as the old one will soon be deleted or has a technical problem. Sometimes a scammer will convince a victim that they'll lose out on a really fantastic deal for an item they want unless they take advantage of the cheap price today, using—surprise, surprise—gift cards or cryptocurrency.

Explained in black and white like this, the scams sound absurd. But these social engineers are masters of manipulation. They know just what to say and which buttons to push. They have a lot of experience and they can jump on every weakness they find. There's a reason we classified them as psychological fraudsters in Chapter 2.

These fraudsters tend to target vulnerable people wherever possible: people who are lonely and likely to be open to an attempt to develop a relationship, as with romance scams, or young and inexperienced, or elderly and unaware of the dangers of technology, or in a position where they're likely to be especially afraid of the threat of law enforcement. In fact, they share information about people they've managed to steal from successfully. Once someone has been put on one of these "scammers' lists," they might get tens or even hundreds of calls a month from different scammers, all trying to take advantage of the advertised vulnerability.

Psychological fraudsters tailor their approach carefully to target each victim, in terms of their age, gender, background, and so forth—all information that is easy to find online nowadays. They often use the sales tactic of creating a sense of urgency, making it hard for victims to think straight. They'll lie to increase stress, or choose times of the day that are likely to be most hectic. They'll have a story worked out with supporting details and language; instead of gift cards or cryptocurrency, for example, they'll talk about "electronic vouchers." They tell victims exactly what to say in case anyone questions them during a purchase.

Fraudsters like to target vulnerable people because they're easiest to scam. But they'll go after anyone, given half a chance, and they're very skilled. Almost any ordinary, intelligent person might fall for it at one time or another. And when gift cards or cryptocurrency is involved, all the fraudster needs is to rush and bully someone through a purchase. Within seconds, the money is gone. And it's very hard to get back.

It is worth noting at this point that dealing with victim-assisted fraud can be distressing for fraud prevention teams, particularly if it becomes a trend you're seeing in your business. Carmen Honacker, senior manager of Customer and Payment Fraud at Booking.com, who has considerable experience with digital goods, noted:

Fraud fighters often identify strongly with doing the right thing, especially when it comes to fraud prevention and the crimes it is often connected to. It can be very upsetting for fraud fighters to see cases where a victim has been tricked and cheated out of their savings, even if this loss is outside the fraud area they control (like in Trust & Safety). Often, fraud teams will want to do anything in their power to fix the situation by working with other business stakeholders and right that wrong as well.

If this good Samaritan impulse can be accommodated, it's worth seeing that as a legitimate use of your team's time (as long as it doesn't take up more time than is reasonable). It's better for your business's relationship with customers and better for team morale. It is worthwhile involving team members in discussions about how to prevent this kind of fraud from recurring, and in research to find the data to back up prevention hypotheses. Additionally, give those interacting with victims the tools to report the incident themselves on the FTC's fraud reporting website (*https://oreil.ly/MKAx8*), and encourage them to educate themselves. There are great resources to start with at the FTC's Consumer Information page on gift card scams (*http://ftc.gov/giftcards*). Try to have your team feel that if they have to see a lot of the problem, then at least they're part of the solution.

Managers may also need to provide gentle counseling if a team member experiences heightened empathy when working directly with a victim. It may be difficult to set aside your feelings when you are listening to the plight of an elderly person who has been cheated out of their life savings. Beyond this, you may also want to introduce the issue of social engineering fraud to upper management, helping relevant stakeholders understand the problem and facilitating a decision about what company policy should be. Many companies affected by this are willing to make the victims whole where possible, reimbursing what was lost or perhaps offering credit or gift cards in a portion of the total amount lost, purely as a goodwill gesture or as part of a focus on good customer experience. If your company has such a policy, make sure your fraud team knows about it; it can alleviate the distress of analysts who have become involved with particularly upsetting cases.

There's a fraud flavor that has been growing in recent years, which probably fits into the social engineering category here but might also be part of friendly fraud. This is when fraudsters "set up shop," usually somewhere like privacy-conscious messaging app Telegram, though occasionally on regular social media or even a website, purporting to offer great deals on goods of various kinds. Food delivery is increasingly common in this scam, but other industries are affected as well. Customers place an order with the fraudster, sometimes sending a screenshot of their cart (including their shipping address) before payment, so that the fraudster is clear about what they want and where to send it. The fraudster places the order, using stolen payment information. The customer gets their goods, no one pays for them (or rather, payment is made and usually charged back), and the fraudster is paid by the customer using cryptocurrency or sometimes gift cards.

It's not always clear whether the customers are aware of the fraud and don't care, or whether they've turned a willful blind eye to suspicious behavior. Certainly, the fraudsters invest a lot in presenting their services as reliable and safe, even to the extent of facilitating reviews and offering customer service in terms of tracking the order and so on, so there is undoubtedly a social engineering element. Whether they succeed in convincing people that they're legitimate as well as reliable is an open question.

Identification and Mitigation

Identification of digital goods fraud or cryptocurrency fraud involves two main components, both of them crucial. The first is deep analysis of your own data, because there are almost always patterns that show that a particular type of scam is in play, whether it's a certain set of behaviors on a site, a range of IPs, specific products fraudsters target, and so on. You need to drill down into the affected products; perhaps with gift cards, there are too many round numbers or there are specific denominations they target. Or with subscriptions, maybe there's a specific combination purchased together.

As Arielle Caron noted:

> Fraudsters often target specific brands or combinations of brands, and a higher likelihood of larger denominations. These and other similar order characteristics lend themselves to the construction of rules for a quick way to stop the bleeding from emerging fraud patterns. Regarding the strategic rather than tactical perspective, we find the greatest predictive value to come from risk modeling, including custom models for high-risk brands.

Of course, as Arielle pointed out, "Online victim-assisted fraud presents an unusual challenge and can be difficult to detect with traditional methods, because the victim's machine, IP, and information look legitimate and are not associated with prior fraud; however, there are some patterns in their behavior that look unusual, especially around velocity and purchase totals."

This brings us to the second element, which is diving into user account information. Many industries with digital goods possess rich user account information. Gaming sites, for instance, know a lot about their users' typical behaviors. Even in industries where anonymity is higher, if the account is an established one there will at least be a history of purchases and so forth. You can use this history in two ways. First, protect accounts from ATO victim-assisted fraud by flagging when behavior is suddenly not typical. Second, use your data to build rich personas of types of users, based on age, location, interests, typical purchases, velocity of purchases, and so on. Then, even with a new customer, as soon as you can work out which persona they are most like, you can flag whether their behavior is markedly different from what you would expect.

Let's look at a simple example of how this might play out. Using the following query, we can look for users who fit a specific profile in terms of age and behavior:

```
WITH table_of_age_tiers_and_their_operating_systems_and_monthly_stats AS
(
    SELECT
        customer_id,
        CASE
            WHEN age_of_customer_upon_account_opening <= 20
            THEN 'underage - alert compliance'
            WHEN age_of_customer_upon_account_opening <= 35 THEN '20-35'
            WHEN age_of_customer_upon_account_opening <= 50 THEN '35-50'
            WHEN age_of_customer_upon_account_opening <= 70 THEN '50-70'
            WHEN age_of_customer_upon_account_opening <= 120 THEN '70+'
            ELSE 'error - check if the DOB was properly enterted during KYC'
        END
        AS age_tier , operating_system_of_signup_session
    FROM
        account_opening
)
a
INNER JOIN
    (
    SELECT
        customer_id,
        year_id,
        month_id,
        average(checkout_time) AS checkout_time,
        SUM(purchase_amount) AS monthly_spend
    FROM
        customer_transactions
    GROUP BY 1, 2, 3
    )
    b
```

```
        ON (a.customer_id = b.customer_id)
SELECT
    age_tier,
    operating_system_of_signup_session,
    average (checkout_time),
    average (monthly_spend)
FROM
    table_of_age_tiers_and_their_operating_systems_and_monthly_stats
GROUP BY 1, 2;
```

After running the query, we get output in the format shown in Table 9-1.

Table 9-1. Query results: age tiers and their aggregated metrics over operating systems

Age_tier	Operating_sys tem_of_signup_session	Average (checkout_time)	Average (monthly_spend)
50–70	iOS	27 minutes	$3K
70+	Android	26 minutes	$2K
70+	Windows	56 minutes	$0.5K

Using profiling like this, you can look for things that don't add up. For example, you might see an elderly person who has very fast browsing, has a hyped-up browser, and moves around the site with far greater speed and familiarity than you would expect, resulting in a far shorter checkout time than the average for this age group. If their spend is also well out of the normal range for this group, more investigation is surely worthwhile. We focused on an older age group in our example, but of course, using the same technique you might see a young person who appears to have access to a corporate account.

These sorts of trends can be spotted well before checkout and can flag the need to investigate further. This helps mitigate the real-time challenge that is always present with these sorts of goods. You can also automate certain friction flows to kick in if some of these suspicious flags are raised. This'll gather further information about the customer and help you see what's going on.

The same sort of approach to building customer profiles can be applied even in the anonymous atmosphere of the crypto ecosystem, using open ledger intelligence. Given a bitcoin wallet ID that was provided by your customer upon their trans-action, you'll be able to look up their previous interactions on Bitcoin Explorer (*http://blockchain.com/explorer*) and hopefully decipher whether this customer is a newbie to crypto (or perhaps is setting up a new bitcoin address per transaction), and/or whether this person transacts with any known exchange, and/or whether they demonstrate gambling-related activity, and so on.

Admittedly, intelligence in the field of cryptocurrency is delicate and time consum-ing. Resources such as Bitcoin Who's Who (*https://www.bitcoinwhoswho.com*) support both manual research and API integration, though you'll need to tailor their data to your needs. A few dozen vendors in this field have already reached some maturity (we'll touch on examples, such as Chainalysis, in Chapter 22), but not to the extent of full-blown fraud prevention.

At the risk of sounding repetitive, this type of benchmark, which you get from working out averages and norms, needs to be taken with a grain of salt. The signs you get should be cause for investigation and further research, not instant declines, unless of course suspicious profiling signals are joined by other suspicious factors. As soon as crypto prices start to climb, you'll probably find that 80-year-old citizens with outdated operating systems and clunky internet connectivity will be doubling down on their investments and checkout speed.

It might be wise to refresh the benchmarks you're using whenever you predict a volatile uptick is about to emerge. In cryptocurrency, you should be able to stay at least one step ahead of the flood of incoming traffic by following the market (e.g., using price scrapers such as cryptocurrencies-scraper (*https://oreil.ly/07fXi*)). In other types of digital goods, such as gaming, you'll need to carefully monitor the community buzz in order to anticipate an uptick in activity, such as an exciting game release.

It's also worth analyzing which groups are most vulnerable on your particular platform. When speaking to fraud-fighting experts in the industry of cryptocurrency, for instance, one often hears frustration about the impact of fraud attacks against senior citizens. Soups Ranjan, CEO of Sardine (*http://sardine.ai*), a behavior-based fraud prevention platform for fintechs and crypto companies, who previously led the FinCrime risk department at Revolut (2019–2020) and was Director of Data Science and Risk at Coinbase (2015–2019), described the struggle:

> I searched for a way to stop this … you don't want to discriminate against users based on age. Ethically, legally, and also business wise, it wouldn't be the right thing to do. Still, nothing gets my blood boiling more than these remote access scams, where attackers spook victims as IRS agents or appeal to their greed as crypto investment advisors.

> Attacks of this sort cannot be caught by KYC systems, because the identity is valid. When fraudsters manage to convince a victim to install a remote desktop controller, like TeamViewer, on their machine, neither KYC nor liveness checks are able to help. Some clever fraudsters will use remote desktop control to blank out the screen of the victim while they are on the phone "instructing" the victim so that the victim won't notice anything, even if their webcam starts to record their image, in order to pass liveness checks.

Ranjan added that he sees two major types of support scams:

> The first includes a victim who creates an account as per the fraudster's instruction, but then leaves the account in the hands of the fraudster; the second, which is even more risky, is similar to an investment scam. Fraudsters call in, presenting themselves as the support team of a crypto exchange, or even post on social media with links to fake

websites, mimicking real support pages of various cryptocurrency services. This leads the victim to think that they are speaking to a representative of a crypto exchange and they willingly install a remote desktop controller and/or purchase crypto and send it directly to the fraudster's address.

At the end of the day, the only way to fully save a single victim from the claws of social engineering support schemes is to make them painfully aware of what's happening, similar to the methods we suggest in combating authorized push payment fraud in Chapter 14. Even if your support team calls an elderly customer and hears them saying "yes, everything's fine, I made these orders on my own free will," there will still be cases where, 10 minutes into the call, you'll find out that an investment scam is happening in the background. Ponzi schemes of this sort may last for months or even years, while showing false reports of handsome profit to the alleged investors. All this time, funds will be funneled directly to the fraudster. Protection from these schemes is an ethical duty for us all.

 This section focused on what fraud prevention teams can do to identify and mitigate attacks against digital goods and cryptocurrency. In terms of providing advice to victims, it is particularly worthwhile for the consumer to set push alerts for when their money is spent online. Since the delivery is close to instantaneous, it's really the only way for victims to become aware of what's going on (and block further attempts using their financials) in a remotely timely fashion. Of course, this isn't something that will likely help fraud fighters directly, but in the long term, the more consumers can be introduced to this option and persuaded to set it up, the easier it will be to restrict the fraud prevention challenge of digital goods.

Summary

This chapter looked at digital goods fraud and cryptocurrency fraud, and why they are so tightly related. We explored gift card fraud, which to an extent bridges both of these categories; touched on some interesting future solutions in the realm of ticketing fraud; and looked at ways to identify and mitigate different types of fraud associated with digital goods and cryptocurrency. There's a strong connection between many of the tactics discussed in this chapter and those we discuss in Part III of the book. For example, just as gift card victim-assisted fraud is in some ways similar to authorized push payment fraud, digital goods reflect some of the same trends as in banking, because to a fraudster, they're all just ways of moving money around and stealing it. Before we head down that road, however, we'll look at an aspect of fraud that causes pain for every industry: friendly fraud.

## CHAPTER 10

First-Party Fraud (aka Friendly Fraud) and Refund Fraud

You've got a friend in me…
    —Randy Newman[1]

As we mentioned in Chapter 2, friendly fraud is distinctively different from the other types of fraud discussed in this book. Notably, *friendly fraud* is carried out by someone who uses their own identity, credit card, and other identifying details to buy an item and then submits a friendly fraud *chargeback*—they received the item, but file a fraudulent chargeback for it anyway—rather than honestly paying for it. Alternatively, the customer admits to making the purchase but fraudulently claims they never received the item and demands a refund, thus effectively getting the item for free.

In contrast, the other kinds of fraud we explore in this book involve the fraudster *hiding* their own identity and obfuscating all signs that ought to point to it. They usually try to create a fake or synthetic identity to hide behind, or try to steal someone else's to use as a mask. With friendly fraud, it's a completely different scenario. It is the real customer, acting fraudulently, without impersonating anyone else.

Friendly fraud is sometimes also called *first-party fraud* or *first-party misuse*, and these terms and variants of them are catching on. Certainly, there's something uncomfortable about the term *friendly* in this context since what's really happening is that people are trying to steal from a merchant by lying about their actions. Especially considering the potential loss to a business that can result, there's nothing friendly

---

1 Randy Newman, "You've Got a Friend in Me," in *Toy Story*, directed by John Lasseter (Walt Disney Pictures, 1995).

about it, and that's why we titled the chapter the way we did. However, since friendly fraud is still the most commonly used term in the industry to refer to this problem, we are using it in this chapter to avoid confusion.

As noted in Chapter 3, friendly fraud typically increases at times of economic stress or uncertainty. This means having methods and policies in place internally to deal with it is particularly important so that fraud teams are clear about what does and does not fall under their responsibility. When a crisis does occur, it's unlikely you'll have time to prioritize these processes—they need to be clear to everyone all the time. Since interdepartmental collaboration and compromise is usually necessary to reach this point of clarity, they are best carried out during calm periods and reviewed annually to ensure that policies and processes are keeping up with the evolving situation.

On this point, Julie Fergerson, CEO of the Merchant Risk Council, noted:

> From my perspective, based on the broad view I have at the MRC, friendly fraud is the number one problem that fraud professionals are facing today. Some physical goods merchants are seeing as much as 30% of their transactions come back as friendly fraud. It's a problem that represents up to 80% of all fraud for many of our merchant members.

 It's crucial for fraud prevention teams to carry out as accurate an assessment as they can into how much friendly fraud is costing their business so that they can make decisions grounded in a realistic understanding of the situation.

Types of Friendly Fraud

There are a number of different types of friendly fraud, driven by different intentions and motivations on the part of the buyer.

Genuine Mistake

Let's begin with the case of the genuine mistake, in order to set it aside. Its identification and mitigation are different from the other cases and it isn't really the direct responsibility of the fraud team. Sometimes a friendly fraud chargeback is just a mistake. It's most common in cases where a business bills under a different name than the consumer remembers, resulting in the consumer really thinking the charge is fraudulent. For example, a consumer purchases an item from GreatGifts.com, but on their card statement the payment was made to ACME Inc. They won't remember (or, in most cases, check) that they did in fact pay that amount on that date for whatever they bought. They will see ACME and think, *this has nothing to do with me.* Similarly with subscriptions: a customer signs up for a service and doesn't realize they'll be billed every month through auto-renewal.

 Businesses can reduce the likelihood of this kind of friendly fraud by making sure payments, names, and so forth are clear and consistent to the customer. Using customer support representatives to interact with these customers is also often successful, because it is a matter of clearing up confusion rather than accusing someone of fraud. Just note that although billing practices and customer support processes are not a natural part of the fraud prevention team's concerns, *all fraud chargebacks count toward your fraud limits.* That's often the case with internal key performance indicators (KPIs) and is certainly true with regard to the card networks' programs. So, it is in your best interests to work with your company's chargebacks team (if you have one), finance or billing teams, customer service teams, and perhaps others to make sure real mistakes are as unlikely as possible. It is also worth running an analysis from time to time to ensure that this kind of mistake isn't costing you in fraud chargebacks. If it is, it's worthwhile to try to solve it.

Family Fraud

In between the honest mistake and standard friendly fraud falls *family fraud*. This is when someone else from the family uses the card (e.g., a husband uses a wife's card or a teenager uses a parent's card) to make a purchase that the cardholder either doesn't know about or forgets about.

There *can* be a truly fraudulent aspect here—think of the teenager buying games they're not supposed to be playing online and not telling their parents what they're doing—but the bad intent is not that of the cardholder, who is usually unaware of what's really going on. What to do in these cases is, again, a question of policy. Often, customer support can be brought in to help and bring clarity to the situation. From the fraud perspective, it's worth being aware of the distinction, because if the cardholder has an account with your business, you can use behavioral analytics where possible to flag occasions where the identity on your site doesn't match the behavior that the identity behind the card usually displays. For many businesses, this form of friendly fraud is very minor and rarely seen, but it's worth keeping an eye on (including syncing with customer support representatives) to check that it stays that way so that you can take action if it changes. For businesses that routinely suffer from this problem, customer education (or, rather, cardholder education) is key, and some gaming companies have developed impressive educational resources and centers for this purpose.

Buyer's Remorse, Customer Resentment, and Mens Rea

When people in the industry talk about friendly fraud, they usually mean cases where some form of malicious intent is involved—either at the time of the transaction, or later, when the chargeback is filed. Here are the three main types of friendly fraud:

Buyer's remorse

> This occurs when the customer makes the purchase with legitimate intent, but then realizes they don't have the money for it or they don't really want it. They wish they hadn't made the purchase, but instead of returning the goods, they file a chargeback to get their money back. These cases can be as simple as a customer who bought an expensive sweater and then realized it was more than they could afford, or as complex as a customer who was caught up in what turned out to be a romance scam, in which the scammer persuaded them to send money and only too late realized what was going on.

Customer resentment

> Sometimes customers who receive the wrong product or receive their purchase much later than expected (perhaps long after they needed it) become angry with the brand. To "get back at" the company in question, they file a fraud chargeback rather than returning the goods or filing a service chargeback, which is the proper form of action in cases when a customer is dissatisfied for appropriate reasons. It is notable that severe restrictions on returns policies may increase the likelihood of this behavior since, rather than give up, many customers become determined to get their money back, and fraud chargebacks are known to be a more reliable way to do that (for the consumer) than service chargebacks. When it comes to fraud chargebacks, banks tend to take the side of the consumer—and a lot of consumers know this.

Mens rea (guilty mind)

> Sometimes the customer has bad intentions right from the start. They always intended to get the goods for free. One of the easiest ways to do that is through a fraud chargeback. All forms of friendly fraud are problematic, but this deliberate kind is the one that fraud teams generally most want to stop, because if not prevented, it often becomes a serial offense and can get very costly in terms of loss to the business.

Although friendly fraudsters are usually working for themselves, so to speak (except in the more complex case of refund as a service; more on that shortly), some form loose groups in which they share tactics or even videos on how best to carry out friendly fraud. Sometimes the individuals in the group will be linked by shared experiences or characteristics, similar to social media groups of young mothers, or people from a specific school, or like-minded hobbyists. This gives them a strong sense of community and a desire to help others in the group by sharing what they have found works best. It's not a fraud ring, per se, because they're not working in tandem to carry out the fraud, but it means that vulnerabilities in your system, once found, will be shared quickly and widely. It also means the potential scale of the loss increases dramatically; some groups have hundreds or even thousands of members.

Fraud Versus Abuse

As mentioned in Chapter 1, it's not always easy to distinguish between *fraud* (which fraud teams ought to be stopping) and *abuse* (which generally comes down to a policy decision, often not in fraud teams' hands). There's no hard-and-fast, agreed-upon definition for these terms in the fraud prevention industry, but generally *abuse* is used to refer to cases that we might call "cheating"—when customers who are ordinarily good customers cheat to take advantage of a promotion or a vulnerability in the system. For instance, they might set up a number of false email addresses so that they can pretend to have made successful referrals or so that they can use a coupon intended for a single use per person more than once. There are no chargebacks involved here. It's not fraud, exactly. It's…cheating.

The Tendency to Tolerate Abuse

In general, abuse of this kind finds far more tolerance from companies than fraud. For one thing, sometimes it is a brand's most loyal and enthusiastic customers who abuse the system from time to time. You could say they're a little overenthusiastic— too keen to get their hands on the goods—but such customers are usually far more valuable overall than the small loss their abuse results in, so the business doesn't want to put too many obstacles in their path. Another reason abuse is often tolerated is that the loss involved is frequently fairly minor—the sort of amount a marketing department might be willing to lose as part of the cost of a campaign, if that helped make the campaign successful.

Fraud departments tend to have a nuanced reaction toward abuse. On the one hand, it results in loss to the business, and fraud fighters usually have a strong desire to prevent this from happening. On this level, abuse offends their sensibilities. On the other hand, abuse is rarely seen as the responsibility of the fraud team; it doesn't affect their KPIs. And even more than with ordinary fraud, the need to avoid friction for good customers is always a serious consideration, and with abuse the tendency is likely to go more toward free of friction than free of fraud.

In general, it's valuable to cultivate a realistic approach to this problem. You'll never be allowed to stop all abuse, because there are too many good business reasons not to, and there will be times when you won't be allowed to stop much or, perhaps, any. The decision, in this case, will rarely be in the fraud team's hands.

It's also worthwhile having a data-driven understanding of exactly what abuse does to your company. How much loss is involved? How does this differ depending on the type of offer involved, or the market being appealed to with a particular promotion, or the age group being targeted? Crucially, at what point does abuse become *chronic*—meaning, is there evidence to show that a customer who cheats a few times will stop there, but one who successfully cheats six times will go on as long as they can get away with it? And most importantly, at what point does this customer, and this promotion, start representing actual loss overall to the business, as opposed to just less money coming in than might otherwise?

Staying on top of all this information will mean that when someone from another department does come to your team to ask about the phenomenon of abuse, you'll be able to answer intelligently. But more than that, you may be able to take a proactive approach, educating the relevant departments (marketing, product, sales, or whoever it might be) about the risks to your business and the data behind those risks. You can help them make informed decisions.

Once more, this helps show the greater value of your team and its work to upper management, it helps protect the business, and it deepens your collaborative relationships with other departments. With a little effort, this can impel them to eagerly let you know about planned promotions or other ideas so that you can help them think through the risk consequences, information that will affect your actual fraud-fighting work and help you better prepare for coming risks.

Reseller Abuse

Reseller abuse occurs when popular items are targeted by resellers, who aim to purchase the goods on one site so that they can resell them at a higher price elsewhere. Frequently, they'll try to buy up large numbers of the goods being targeted. It's not fraud—the payment will go through legitimately—but it often violates the terms and conditions of the site, and as such falls under abuse. Fashion—in particular, sneakers and luxury items—are especially prone to this form of abuse, though it can also plague special edition electronics and other items.

Reseller abuse can be harder to catch than regular abuse, since resellers are often willing to invest more resources in finding ways to flag when items they're looking for go on sale, to conceal their repeated purchases, and to make the purchases quickly before someone else has a chance to do so and the items run out. Bots are often used as part of this process, so if resellers are a problem for your business, investing in bot detection and blocking is likely to be worthwhile.

Beyond that, the same kinds of linking methods, such as flagging when accounts share addresses, IPs, or other similar data, as we've discussed for other forms of fraud, are as applicable to this kind of abuse—and in fact are even more likely to be valuable, since resellers are often not as good at hiding their tracks as professional fraudsters.

Whether or not your business wants to stop resellers, though, is a policy decision and as such is likely to be out of the hands of your fraud team.

Refund Fraud

Refund fraud, or *returns fraud*, is often not considered the province of the fraud prevention team. In the simplest case, the customer buys an article, files a complaint about it (usually either that it's broken or that it never arrived), and thus aims to keep both the item and the refund.

 Refund fraud is different from refund *abuse*, which falls into the "cheating" category and includes behaviors such as buying multiple colors or sizes and returning the ones that don't fit or find favor, or buying an item, wearing it once, and returning it (common with costly apparel). As with other forms of abuse, different businesses have different policies and levels of tolerance for this kind of behavior, but it is rarely the job of the fraud prevention team to police or prevent it.

There are some methods that can be used to mitigate this kind of fraud, as with other forms of friendly fraud, and we discuss them in the next section. However, what we want to draw attention to in this section is an increasingly popular form of refund fraud that edges disturbingly into the more professional territory associated with forms of fraud that are more commonly the focus of a fraud team's work.

The core of "refund as a service" fraud[2] is very similar to standard refund fraud, but with a professional fraudster inserted into the process to increase the efficiency and scale involved. A number of fraudsters have developed a specialization in refunds and now advertise their services in dealing with the refund process successfully on behalf of a customer, using their in-depth knowledge of the retailer's returns policies and processes. Telegram and Reddit seem to be the most common channels for their promotions, presumably because consumers about to engage in something illegal feel more comfortable in these more anonymous environments, but they can be seen on other social media platforms as well.

The way it works is simple. The customer chooses a "refundster" (to coin a term, since this kind of fraudster is running a different sort of scheme than most fraudsters) who specializes in the industry and usually the specific merchant whose goods they want to "buy." The customer places the order themselves, and is advised by the refundster to avoid signing for the package when it arrives or to use a fake name

---

2 We like this term because it echoes the emphasis on scale associated with the software as a service model, and also the efficiency and professionalism associated with what is often referred to as *crime as a service* (the specialization and selling of specific tools and services now common in the online criminal ecosystem).

if pressed to sign. Once the customer has the package in hand, they update the refundster and send them all the relevant information (order number, price, date, etc.).

The refundster then does all the work of getting the refund, usually calling or using chat to talk to customer service to say the package never arrived, or was broken, or was possibly stolen by porch pirates. Using their knowledge of the process involved, they know exactly what to say that will work with each merchant. Some even know the individual quirks of particular customer service representatives, and know what to say to speed or ease the process along.

If the item must be returned, there are many ways around that, including sending an empty envelope with the right information on it as a label (the label is processed and entered into the system, but the envelope is usually thrown away as junk mail), sending an empty box, sending a box filled with items to make up the right weight (whose label, with the right weight, can be used as part of the refund process), or even sending a box with dry ice which is the right weight at the start but melts in transit so that it looks like the item was stolen en route. There's also the fake tracking ID (fake TID) approach, in which shipping manipulation is used to make it appear that the item has been returned, though in fact a different, but similar, address was used. The refundster takes care of it all.

Once the refund has been processed, the customer gets to keep the goods and most of the money. They pay the refundster a percentage of the value of the item, usually 5% to 25%. It's a bargain.

Often, a consumer will be tempted to hire a refundster more than once, to get goods far more cheaply than would otherwise be possible. They rarely experience negative consequences, and when they do, it's frequently at a significant delay. Frank McKenna (*https://oreil.ly/4kVxQ*) (better known in the industry as Frank on Fraud) points out that sometimes this can really bite consumers if the refundster gets carried away and takes actions such as filing false police reports or using case numbers from old police reports to support the claim with the merchant. In such cases, it often takes time for the paperwork to catch up to the consumer, who may have tried this trick many times before they get burned by it, whether that means trouble over faked police reports or even being stuck with the bill when a refundster doesn't succeed.

This form of fraud has been around for a number of years, but it really took off during the COVID-19 pandemic. As Identiq's cofounder and vice president of Product, Uri Arad, notes in "The New Year Threat: Revamped Refund Fraud," the pandemic not only gave more consumers reason to look for cheats like this (because financial instability made paying full price difficult), it also provided the perfect setting for refund as a service, making it easier to carry out successfully in a number of ways:[3]

- The sheer scale of online shopping at a time when many customers were avoiding in-store shopping was challenging for many businesses to keep up with, and refund fraud is especially hard to catch because uncovering a real problem in this area requires collaboration among departments, none of which is really tasked with identifying the problem.

- Delivery processes were relaxed to respect customers' preferences to reduce face-to-face interactions with couriers. Notably, signing for packages became far less common, meaning no proof of delivery.

- Returns processes were similarly relaxed, with many businesses waiving the need for previously essential elements such as the box or shipping label. Some even preferred to tell customers not to return the items at all.

In "Refunding Fraud: The Industrialization of Friendly Fraud" (*https://oreil.ly/ORcGd*), Karisse Hendrick notes that just as friendly fraud really came into its own during the 2008–2009 financial crisis and then remained a problem for companies, there's a danger that something similar will happen with refund as a service following the COVID-19 pandemic. That being the case, it may be worth retailers' while to spend some time and effort identifying and mitigating this kind of fraud to prevent it from becoming a serious long-term problem. Refund as a service is a form of friendly fraud at scale, and this could spell real financial loss for a company that doesn't take steps to combat it.

Identification and Mitigation

In this section, we'll look primarily at ways that individual fraud departments can respond to the challenge of friendly fraud. Before that, though, we want to note that the nature of the problem means that working with issuers and card networks to change the way friendly fraud is currently dealt with is an equally important part of reaching a better footing.

Notably, the Merchant Risk Council is working to get issuers to treat friendly fraud cases as disputes rather than chargebacks. It is also working to institute a liability shift, moving liability for the cost from merchants to issuers in cases where the merchants can prove it was friendly fraud but for whatever reason the cost will not be borne by the consumer.

---

3 Uri Arad, "The New Year Threat: Revamped Refund Fraud" (*https://oreil.ly/BnXbj*), Card Not Present, January 28, 2021.

We strongly encourage fraud fighters to keep abreast of the developments in this area, and perhaps offer assistance where appropriate. A good place to check regularly is the MRC Advocacy page (*https://oreil.ly/xtbAn*).

Identification

Identifying individual, early cases of friendly fraud is very difficult, and unless the customer has exposed their actions publicly, such as by posting photos of themselves online wearing the clothes or accessories they claimed never arrived or attending the concert they claimed they never bought tickets for, it may be impossible. That's not as problematic as it sounds, though, because individual cases of friendly fraud are rarely that damaging for a business. Friendly fraud becomes dangerous when it becomes serial.

Fortunately, identifying serial offenders is much easier, because friendly fraudsters are, by definition, not professionals; they may know one or two tricks to confuse the trail, but because they're using their own information and rarely making much effort to conceal themselves, you can identify a repeated pattern quite easily as long as you're looking for it, whether they're filing fake fraud chargebacks or making fraudulent returns. Sometimes customer support can even get a beginner friendly fraudster to admit they're faking it on the phone by being friendly and understanding, but firm about company policy—something that can encourage even the most customer-focused ecommerce teams to agree to block a customer.

In the case of suspected "friendly fraud/first customer fraud," it's possible to give a customer the benefit of the doubt for the first chargeback. But it's advisable to put a process in place to prevent anybody from taking advantage a second time. For instance, in gaming, parents who claim they had no idea their child was using their credit card for purchases can be educated on overall parental settings, payments, security settings, and family fraud. If they attempt another chargeback later, there's proof that they did know about the problem and are responsible. Carmen Honacker, head of Customer and Payment Fraud at Booking.com, noted the value of this approach both in appealing chargebacks and in stopping further attempts by the same person. She also flagged another option within gaming: creating a sandbox-style environment where offenders can only play one another, with reduced privileges, for some set period of time.

Blocking/banning offenders for a period is also an option, both in gaming and in other industries; ultimately, the idea is to hold customers accountable and teach them that there are consequences, in order to deter them from making friendly fraud a habit. The more collaboration can be employed with other merchants in this area, the better, since the consequences will be more serious and the ability to stop a friendly fraudster before they attack too many businesses is much increased.

Certain goods are more prone to friendly fraud than others. There's a direct causal relationship between the nonphysical nature of goods and buyer's remorse: if they didn't get something they can hold, they're more likely to cheat about it. In the same way, there's also a direct relationship between long order fulfillment times and buyer's resentment, presumably because the long wait time annoys the customer and gives them too much time to think. So, from the one side, for instance, bitcoin is particularly prone to friendly fraud. And from the other, concert tickets (which might be for an event a year ahead) and furniture (which takes time to make) are particularly common in friendly fraud as well. Bearing this in mind can help identify the sorts of products most likely to be affected in your business.

The caveat here is that you do need to be looking for friendly fraud in order to find it. And it may often be hiding behind "Item Not Delivered" claims, or suspicious patterns within refund processes such as consistent time periods between an order being delivered and a refund being ordered, or customer support representatives who are sure they have heard that voice before this week asking about a completely different order from a completely different customer. (In terms of voice identification and recognizing repeated callers, automated solutions such as Nuance can be a valuable addition to fraud prevention efforts.) In the same way, listening to customer support representatives can help you identify when a group of friendly fraudsters start using the same tactics—often, tips that one of them has shared on a social media group of like-minded individuals.

There are interesting possibilities opening up through the evolution of privacy-enhancing technology (PET; discussed in Chapter 4) which retailers may be able to use to compare information about customers' returns or chargeback habits without sharing any personal customer data. Using this technology, it may be possible for one retailer to discover that the new customer on their site is a customer with a habit of friendly fraud with other merchants. This would also give valuable extra data to use in discussions with those in the company who make policies regarding friendly fraud—though such knowledge should be used cautiously, since customer behavior varies depending on the site; a user who regularly defrauds apparel retailers may not demonstrate similar behavior with food delivery companies, for example.

Mitigation

What you can do about friendly fraudsters, once identified, may depend on your company and its attitude toward good customers. Some businesses put so much emphasis on customer experience that they are unwilling to take any steps against friendly fraud, except in the most egregious examples. As with abuse, though, the more data you have about the problem, the more likely you are to be able to influence those policies to take friendly fraud more seriously.

You may also be able to find solutions that find a middle ground between blocking a customer and allowing them free rein: adding delay to a refund process, for example, or only permitting refunds to be given as store credit. You may be able to institute different policies for different risk levels of customers; someone you're fairly sure is a frequent friendly fraudster might not be allowed refunds at all, but only be offered a second item to be sent to them for the full price, should they claim "Item Not Received."

Fraud teams also usually have more leverage when it comes to friendly fraud as opposed to abuse, because fraud chargebacks are one of the primary metrics used to judge fraud departments' success. If friendly fraud is causing fraud chargebacks to skyrocket, that's clearly a problem the fraud team can press to have solved.

Some forms of mitigation for friendly fraud must be collaborative efforts with other departments, notably product and customer support. The psychological approach—which aims to reduce fraudulent behavior by making customers more aware of what they are doing—has some proponents. To understand this approach, think of the famous experiment (*https://oreil.ly/9zHNV*) that found that people who had been encouraged to remember the Ten Commandments before taking a test were less likely to cheat on the test than those who had been asked to remember 10 books they had read at school. Similar results have been achieved by getting people to sign an honor pledge. It is possible to use checkboxes against declarations of good faith, or digital signatures, as a friction step for customers you suspect may habitually cheat or carry out friendly fraud. Anecdotally, results from this sort of approach are mixed, with some reporting good results and others not seeing much impact. If you can target only those you think may commit friendly fraud, though, it may be worth a shot in your business.

Equally, if your business is being repeatedly hit by the same refundsters or rings, your customer support team may be able to tell you they're seeing or hearing suspicious patterns, or even repeated voices. Similarly, they'll be able to flag that they think a teenager may be taking advantage of a parent's credit card, or that when someone calls on behalf of an elderly relative, that's often a warning sign. If you work together closely, you'll be able to turn this information into a good understanding of the kind of friendly fraud you're facing, and perhaps find ways to teach customer support to handle different sorts of situations. You can also have support reps feed their experiences back into your model in real time, which can sometimes help hold a dubious order, or at least make it less likely that future ones will go through. It's worth saying here that Gilit has worked closely with customer support more than once, in different contexts, and always found them eager to collaborate and helpful in catching and stopping fraud.

Because friendly fraud is really only a problem when a business is hit by it at scale, most methods for mitigating it revolve around finding patterns behind attacks. We won't focus here on drawing the lines directly between different accounts or fraudulent orders, because as previously mentioned, finding the similarities here is typically relatively easy, since friendly fraudsters are not usually taking many steps to hide. What we will look at are a couple of examples of how you can approach the problem from a slightly different direction.

As we've tried to emphasize, an important and often overlooked aspect of the friendly-fraud conundrum is the importance of customer support representatives in the chain of these transactions. Within the context of chats or calls, customer service representatives are often targeted and turned into vulnerabilities for your business. These calls (if you have transcripts) or chats can equally be sources of information about how these attacks are being carried out.

For example, consider the following SQL query. Here, we're looking for patterns in a chat to see whether we can identify weaknesses that specific customer support representatives may have. For instance, perhaps some are more likely to grant a refund to a female, or to agree that returning an item isn't necessary if the person on the call comes from their hometown or supports the same baseball team.

For these queries, it's easier if your internal database already includes information such as the gender, hometown, place of birth, and so forth of your support reps. You can then draw on this information to narrow down queries fairly easily. If you don't have that kind of data, though, you can use code to fill in some of the blanks, such as determining gender using name analysis (*https://oreil.ly/2E9sl*) or publicly available information from social networks:

```
SELECT
    customer_support_rep_id,
    customer_support_rep_name,
    (
        CASE
            customer_gender SUM(
            CASE
                WHEN 'female' THEN 1 ELSE 0
            END
    ) / COUNT(refund_id)*100 AS female_pct    -- % of refund approvals for females
    FROM
        approved_refunds
    WHERE
        refund_status = 'approved'
    )
GROUP BY 1, 2
ORDER BY 3 DESC;
```

In the output example shown in Table 10-1, we see that John is far more lenient toward requests from females in comparison to George—maybe George is still fretting over Eric and Pattie. But jokes aside, only a consistent trend that lasts more than a few weeks (and more than a few dozen individual cases) is worth addressing. So many human-element factors can play into the representative's decision that analysts should be extra careful before jumping to conclusions.

Table 10-1. Sample output for the customer support weaknesses query

customer_support_rep_id	customer_support_rep_name	female_%
1	John Lennon	80
2	Yoko Ono	70
3	Paul McCartney	60
4	George Harrison	7

 If anything, it's worth giving representatives access to this data, along with the department's benchmarks, so that they'll be able to decide for themselves if there's a chance they have significant biases toward certain genders, origins, orientations, and so forth.

If you find patterns of this sort, you can use them to identify and mitigate friendly fraud. You can alert the representative in question that they're being manipulated in this way, and advise them to watch out for this "tell" in the future. If they hear it again, they can raise a flag about the interaction. Beyond that, you can also use this information to tie the transactions together, to see whether you can find other similarities or linking factors between them. This is something that can be especially relevant when you're considering the problem of refundsters, who are otherwise so difficult to catch because the initial orders are, of course, placed by the many different real customers and so can't be identified by looking for the ordinary suspicious signals or linking signs.

Let's look at another piece of code that generates a word cloud example of refund request repetitions. This feature is supported by many business intelligence (BI) tools, including Tableau (*https://oreil.ly/hR2Lj*), and even some free web tools for small, one-time data sets, such as the word cloud generator from Wordclouds.com (*https://www.wordclouds.com*). Using Python to create word clouds is preferred if you plan to have a daily/weekly/monthly report that would alert customer support reps of the most recent trends in customer complaints. This type of approach can empower support teams to identify fraud long before any artificial intelligence–powered model can pick up on them.

To generate a word cloud using Python, download pillow and word cloud packages (in addition to numpy, pandas, and matplotlib). There are also excellent tutorials and resources for troubleshooting online, such as this one at DataCamp (*https://oreil.ly/sTw1E*).

Example 10-1 shows the code; the result is shown in Figure 10-1.

Example 10-1. Generating a word cloud to find frequent words used on customer complaints

```python
# Start with loading all necessary libraries
import numpy as np
import pandas as pd
from os import path
from PIL import Image
import matplotlib.pyplot as plt
from wordcloud import WordCloud, STOPWORDS, ImageColorGenerator
stopwords = set(STOPWORDS)

# Load data
df = pd.read_csv("data/chats_or_emails_or_transcripts_of_customer_complaints.csv",
    index_col=0)

print(
    "There are {} countries mentioned by customers such as {}... \n".format(
        len(df.country.unique()), ", ".join(df.country.unique()[:5])
    )
)

# Generate and show word cloud
def show_wordcloud(data, title = None):
    wordcloud = WordCloud(
        background_color='white',
        stopwords=stopwords,
        max_words=200,
        max_font_size=40,
        scale=3,
        random_state=1
    ).generate(str(data))

    fig = plt.figure(1, figsize=(12, 12))
    plt.axis('off')
    if title:
        fig.suptitle(title, fontsize=20)
        fig.subplots_adjust(top=2.3)

    plt.imshow(wordcloud)
    plt.show()

show_wordcloud(df, "Complaints Wordcloud")
```

Figure 10-1. The word cloud resulting from the code in Example 10-1

Using the script in Example 10-1 will show you that this agent, or perhaps this team of agents, is being targeted using specific language or approaches, presumably ones that the ring behind them has discovered are especially effective in this case. In this example, you can see that hard-luck stories—requests for help and charity—are being used against this customer support team (unfortunately, this really does happen). But it might be lots of things. For instance, perhaps being especially polite is what works against this team or a member of the team. Or perhaps the team or a team member might be easily intimidated by threats of lawsuits. Maybe this agent has a weak spot when it comes to tales of family mishaps and mistakes. Once you know it's happening and can tell the team or the relevant agent to watch out for it, you can identify and prevent friendly fraud associated with the trend.

It's worth noting with this example that catching repeated behavior like this is useful not only against professional refundsters, but also against the groups of friendly fraudsters who share their tips and tricks with one another. This is valuable because, as mentioned earlier, these groups can turn a vulnerability into a real problem through their reach and the resultant scale.

Summary

This chapter looked at the different types of friendly fraud, how friendly fraud differs from abuse, and how to identify and mitigate it. We noted the importance of interdepartmental collaboration in both catching this kind of fraud and dealing with it—something that is equally relevant, if not even more so, within the field of banking, which will be the focus of the next part of the book.

## PART III

Consumer Banking Fraud Analytics

This part of the book concentrates on fraud as it relates to banking and financial institutions.

The fact that we're shifting our focus from ecommerce to banking is not to say that this section is irrelevant to fraud fighters working in ecommerce businesses or online marketplaces. Many of the fraud techniques that receive attention in the banking industry are also used against ecommerce sites.

As we have said before in this book, fraudsters don't confine themselves to categories. A fraud prevention professional might spend their entire career in banking, but a fraudster will look for opportunities everywhere and exploit whatever vulnerabilities they can find. Fraudsters might specialize in one area or industry, but they rarely confine their activities to it. Doing so would limit their ability to monetize theft: stolen data that failed to be useful in attacking a bank might be put to work to attack an online marketplace; conversely, the wrong kind of data for attacking an ecommerce site could be the right kind of data to begin applying for credit and building up a credit profile for a fake identity. And so on.

This part of the book includes a chapter on opening fraudulent online accounts and a chapter on account takeover (ATO). And while we give extra attention to the banking use case in terms of language and examples, much of the material is just as relevant to ecommerce sites, which also suffer from these forms of fraud. In the same way, the chapters in Part II, which focus on challenges like dealing with stolen credit cards, are relevant to fraud fighters working in financial institutions.

Moreover, an awareness of the main challenges fraud fighters in different industries face is valuable in preparing for whatever direction fraud moves in the future. For instance, sites that are seeing a reduction in fraud since applying a form of 3-D Secure (3DS) (*https://oreil.ly/Lq3kV*) in accordance with the PSD 2 regulation (*https://oreil.ly/GVKnO*) may see ATO attempts increase. Knowing about ATO and how banks (which have faced this challenge head-on for many years) fight it gives a fraud prevention team a head start in protecting their own business, if ATO becomes a serious threat there.

 Fraudsters don't give up when the fraud-fighting industry blocks them in one place. They flow to another place to find fresh vulnerabilities. The more a fraud fighter knows about the big picture of fraud and fraud prevention, the better prepared they are to guard against whatever the fraudsters come up with next.

## CHAPTER 11

Banking Fraud Prevention: Wider Context

You know I work all day to get you money to buy you things...
—The Beatles[1]

This chapter sets the scene for a focus on banking, laying the foundation for the chapters ahead and highlighting some features, such as social engineering and deepfakes, which are relevant contexts for all the banking chapters rather than being especially relevant to any particular chapter.

Differences Between Banking and Ecommerce

There are two main differences between the experience of fraud prevention at a bank or other financial institution and the experience of fraud prevention at an ecommerce company or online marketplace. We want to highlight these distinctions here as important context for the remainder of the book.

The first difference is that, compared to ecommerce businesses, banks are relatively data poor when it comes to individual transactions or in-session data. An ecommerce fraud team, analyzing a transaction to decide whether to approve or decline it, can look at the details of the product being purchased, the journey the customer took on the website, the journeys other customers took on previous visits to the site, and a wealth of metadata relating to the device, IP, and so on. Banks have none of that. They have, more or less, the information the customer enters at checkout, together with what they see when the customer is in session at their bank. It's not nothing, but it's thin indeed compared to what ecommerce fraud fighters see.

---

1 The Beatles, "A Hard Day's Night," written by John Lennon and Paul McCartney, track 1 on *A Hard Day's Night*, Parlophone, 1964.

Of course, banks do have rich historical account information and metadata from visits to an account. In fact, their insight into the lifetime identity and behavior of the bank customer is extremely rich—more so than many ecommerce stores—because although visits to a bank may not be very frequent, they are probably regular and are often carried out over a long period of time (customers frequently stay with the same bank for many years). Moreover, banks' fraud teams have access to credit scores and history, which are excellent sources of information about a customer's financial situation and can help them make sense of purchases and patterns. That's a lot of information, and Chapter 13 discusses its value in the context of ATO. But it's of limited help when deciding whether a particular transaction is legitimate or not, and so those decisions are harder for a bank's fraud prevention team to make with confidence.

On the other hand, fraud-fighting teams in financial institutions also tend to be resource rich—far more so than the average ecommerce team. This is partly the nature of the business; a fraud team at a bank isn't going to have to fight and educate extensively in order to have their importance to the business recognized. It's obvious that banks need to fight fraud, both on their own behalf and on that of their customers. It's their job to look after money. For this reason, banks have been fighting fraud for longer than most online businesses. Moreover, banks and other financial institutions have legal obligations in the form of compliance that are far more extensive than those seen in ecommerce, because their industry is highly regulated. Fraud fighting is an important part of that, and of being able to show that the business is taking its anticrime responsibilities seriously. Banks that fail to do so can suffer crippling penalties.

In practice, this means fraud prevention departments in financial institutions are likely to have larger teams, making manual review at scale more feasible. They are also likely to have access to more tools, meaning that banks can protect themselves with a sort of patchwork effect, trying out different solutions to protect different potential vulnerabilities. It also means, generally, that they receive a bigger budget with which to give a far deeper level of protection to customers than an ecommerce business would likely receive.

This is a great advantage, and it means fraud fighters can balance the relatively staid and slow-moving nature of most financial institutions (which might otherwise be a weakness when compared to agile and fast-moving fraudsters) by trying out innovative new fraud prevention solutions and tools. Of course, keeping an eye out for these tools and investing effort into assessing which ones are effective for your particular challenges takes resources; but then, as we said, banks are relatively resource rich.

The Context of Cybercrime

As we shift to a greater focus on fraud prevention within financial institutions, we want to add some clarity as to where the scenarios in this book, which fraud fighters face daily, fit in the chain of cybercrime. We covered this briefly in the Preface, but it's worth expanding on it a little here, because the large criminal organizations that invest so much time and money into cybercrime often focus specifically on financial institutions. It's about return on investment (ROI); the potential payoff is greater. Fraudsters rob banks because, as the infamous bank robber Willie Sutton may have said when asked why he robbed banks, "that's where the money is." The effort involved for fraudsters to carry out fraud against a bank successfully is greater compared to that required for most other online businesses. If the fraudsters have a large and organized network, however, the extra effort is well within their capabilities and can be well worth it, as long as the payoff is good enough.

Fraud attacks against financial institutions are more likely to show signs of sophisticated cybercrime beyond the world of fraud. Highly developed, and at times targeted, modular malware built and tailored by experts to attack a specific bank would be a good example. Phishing schemes also are likely to have more effort invested in them when they're targeting bank accounts.

These elements and others like them are not inherently fraud techniques and fall more naturally into the cybercrime category, though they will be familiar to fraud fighters as an integral part of tactics, techniques, and procedures (TTPs) because they're the tools used for the crime. Because they are used so often as part of a fraud attack, we will include them in our discussions where relevant. However, as discussed in the Preface, we will not venture further into the cybercrime jungle. Threats like ransomware, data breach attacks, hacking for nonfraud purposes, and even nation state activity, albeit pressing concerns for financial institutions today, are all beyond the scope of this book.

Social Engineering in Banking

Social engineering has come up many times already in this book, in a variety of contexts. As discussed in Chapter 2 and Chapter 9, fraudsters use it to persuade customers to hand over their information or to unwittingly give them access to their accounts. Social engineering gives fraudsters the psychological edge they need to drive successful phishing attacks, persuade their victims to transfer their money to them, and so on.

While social engineering is used by fraudsters across industries, it's especially pivotal in banking. In a sense, social engineering is the human complement to malware. If you want to encourage a customer to download a password sniffer onto their computer, the easiest way to do that is to contact them, claim you're from their bank or from a cybersecurity company, and persuade them to download an "antivirus" program that is being rolled out to protect all the bank's customers. Or, just as effectively, the fraudster could purport to be from technical support, helping a customer "set up a new account and move their money to it" because "their account has been compromised"—and then use remote access software to access the customer's account through the customer's own machine. For this reason, Chapter 14 discusses social engineering and malware in depth.

Even more than ecommerce sites, banks need to be on the lookout for signs of social engineering, and in particular, they need to be alert to the possibility that psychological attacks of this kind may be attempted at scale. Reputation and trust are even more important to financial institutions than they are to online businesses. Additionally, the damage a fraudster can inflict by tricking a customer is even greater if they've tricked the customer to give them access to their funds. Fraud prevention teams at financial institutions need to be constantly aware of this danger.

Within this context, it is worth calling out authorized push payment fraud, the banking equivalent of victim-assisted fraud, which we discussed in Chapter 9. If a customer's account is hacked in to and their money is sent to the fraudster's account, that's one thing. But if the customer is tricked into logging in to their account and voluntarily moving the money to what they thought was a safe destination…that's much more complicated. With careful social engineering, unfortunately, it's all too possible. And it's a more pressing problem than ever. In 2021, UK Finance, a trade association for the UK banking and financial services sector, reported that for the first time, authorized push payment fraud losses had overtaken card crime in the UK.[2]

When corporate bank accounts are targeted by social engineering fraudsters, the direct financial impact of fraud can become massive, as can the peripheral damage to the public's trust, given that banks are required to report large-scale incidents of fraud. The riskier monetization of ATO is business email compromise (BEC) fraud, sometimes defined separately (*https://oreil.ly/YFptO*) from email accounts compromise (EAC) fraud. BEC/EAC attacks are a combination of email ATO and social engineering. In 2016, this notorious form of fraud reportedly caused almost $50 million worth of damage (*https://oreil.ly/O3fJy*) in a single blow.

Fraud prevention departments may need to be responsible for training customer support departments to recognize signs that indicate social engineering may be at play, either with a fraudster trying to trick them into giving up information or through a customer story that shows they're acting under someone else's malicious guidance. In such cases, it may be wisest to transfer calls to members of the fraud prevention team, or to create an automated process that flags an account and its activities. In general, asking for further details to add color to the story can be very valuable, particularly

---

2 "APP Fraud Losses Overtake Card Crime in H1 2021" (*https://oreil.ly/mXkfb*), Finextra, September 22, 2021.

over a phone call; it's the small details that can give a clue as to whether fraud is present or not. This is true for many of the types of fraud addressed in the remainder of the book.

A Note on Perspective

Before we dive into banking fraud and fraud prevention, we want to issue a word of warning. Fraudsters are willing to invest considerable time and effort into attacks against banks and financial institutions because the potential payoff is so great. It's easy to get caught up in the importance of different aspects of attacks, or potential attacks, and of course it is important to spend time understanding the threats involved and how you can protect your business from them. That importance is reflected in this book. For example, malware is so frequently a part of fraud attacks against financial institutions that it gets its own chapter devoted to discussing the most common malware types and how they play into fraud schemes. Beyond that, because malware is also an important component of many types of fraud attacks, notably opening fake accounts and ATO, further discussions of malware being used in these cases appears within the relevant chapters.

Despite the emphasis on malware in fraud departments, in industry discussions, and in this book, maintaining perspective is important. Malware is only an instrument that plays a role in larger schemes. Fraudsters keep their eyes on the prize. Fraud teams need to as well, even when certain fraud techniques or tools are particularly fascinating and it would be easy to be distracted by them. They're important because of the role they play in the bigger picture.

Deepfakes: A Word of Warning

A deepfake is any audio or visual representation of an individual that looks or sounds like them but does not originate from them. It could be a recording that sounds like a person's voice but was actually created by a computer program based on recordings of the person's voice. Similarly, photos and videos can be created based on real footage, and they can be so convincing it's hard to tell the difference between the fake content and the real content. For example, the way someone's mouth moves in a video could be altered so that they appear to be saying something they didn't actually say. You could think of it as Photoshop gone completely wild.

As with malware, deepfakes can be used at a number of points in the customer journey, and so we discuss them here as a technique, rather than attaching a discussion to any one type of attack. Unlike malware, deepfakes are a fairly new attack method and are, so far, a relatively rare component of fraud attacks. They're intriguing, though, which is why so much digital ink is spilled discussing them.

Of course, faked photos and recordings aren't new, but the sophistication involved in deepfakes takes the results to a whole new level. The word deepfake itself is a combination of deep learning and fake because the development of deep learning machine learning enabled this leap forward.

At the time of this writing, deepfakes have largely been used for humor, entertainment, or political purposes, with a nasty sideline in pornographic attacks. The financial fraud use case has, perhaps surprisingly, been slow to develop. Nonetheless, there are already examples of deepfakes getting into the fraud action, the most famous case being the CEO who was tricked into transferring $243,000 (*https://oreil.ly/SzmKG*) on what he thought were the instructions of the head of his firm's parent company. More recently, a complex heist (*https://oreil.ly/xxMPv*) used deepfake voice tech as part of a scheme to steal $400,000; you can see the power of deepfake technology from the fact that the bank manager in this case had spoken to the company director in the past and was convinced that it was that director who was now ordering him to transfer the money. In a case in China, tax scammers using deepfake facial recognition tech created fake tax invoices (*https://oreil.ly/G1qHe*) valued at $76.2 million. We won't be mentioning deepfakes much in this book, because on a daily basis, fraud fighters don't need to worry about them…yet. Because it seems like such an obvious future direction for the criminal ecosystem, however, we're mentioning deepfakes here to flag the risk and encourage businesses to prepare actively for it rather than be caught out and have to be reactive when the attacks have already begun.

It seems likely that as biometrics, and in particular facial recognition, become more common in the identity validation process, especially for financial institutions, fraudsters will start investing more in deepfake technology to create fakes to use as part of their fraud attacks. A natural way to trick facial recognition systems is to create a convincing deepfake of the face you need to log in with—one that is good enough to pass a liveness test. In the same way, fake faces can be used for synthetic identities—something we discuss in Chapter 15. The shift to biometrics has been slow so far, with many organizations and consumers holding tight to the category of things people know (passwords) rather than things they are (fingerprints). However, there are signs that this is changing and, inevitably, fraudsters will see this as a new opportunity.

Identity verification solutions have protected against easy scamming when it comes to logging in by building liveness checks into the process. A static image won't cut it: the person needs to move as directed at the right times. However, deepfakes hold out the possibility that this will not be sufficient protection for long. As with every antifraud technology, this will become an ongoing arms race between fraudsters and fraud fighters. It's important to keep an eye on how the race ebbs and flows, as it almost certainly will, to ensure that your business is not relying on an outdated approach or version. For now, though, deepfakes are more of a theoretical (if fascinating) danger than a present one. But given their potential as a criminal tool, they're worth investigating to ensure that your institution is protected against the danger they may present.

Summary

This chapter laid the groundwork for the chapters ahead, which dive into different attacks used against banks and other financial institutions. With the right context established, we can now move on to looking more deeply at different types of attacks.

## CHAPTER 12

Online Account Opening Fraud

I'm about to give you all of my money...
—Otis Redding[1]

It makes sense to start the section on banking and the fraud challenges banks and financial institutions face with a look at online account opening fraud. In part, of course, this is because an account is necessary for a fraudster to commit many forms of banking-related fraud. But we're also starting with this topic because it was the cornerstone of many banks' fraud-fighting efforts before things moved online, and it remains a crucial step in protecting the entire financial ecosystem from malicious actors. It's stopping fraud at the door, so to speak.

False Accounts: Context

Perhaps the primary risk associated with online account opening fraud is that of money mules setting up an account for the purpose of moving money around as part of a fraudulent scheme. It's certainly one of the most memorable risks: people still talk about the 37 money mules (*https://oreil.ly/an0VE*) acting in concert who moved more than $3 million in stolen funds back when the Zeus Trojan was taking banking by storm.

Money muling was once associated only with young people. But during the COVID-19 pandemic in particular, the age range widened considerably, and now you can find money mules ranging in age from 18 to about 50. Online security specialist Ken Palla, who has many years of experience in the banking space, pointed out to us that there are unlikely to be negative consequences for someone moving into money

---

1 Otis Redding, "Respect," track 2 on *Otis Blue*, Volt, 1965 (covered by Aretha Franklin in 1967).

muling for the first time: if they get caught, they can always claim ignorance. Even if they get caught a second time, prosecution is unlikely, even though money mules are complicit in the illegal transfer of funds they've enabled. Without prosecution, money mules often return to the attack, increasing the scale of the problem and unaware that they're likely heading for a fall in the future. (Unlike fraudsters, money mules often use their own real identities, so their crimes may well come back to haunt them, especially if they keep it up.) Keep money mules in mind as you read this chapter, since they're a typical use case. Chapter 20 covers money mules in more detail, but for now we'll just note that they're often an element in money laundering, taking the funds from a fraudulent enterprise and moving them around in ways that ultimately make it look like they were gained legitimately.

There are other issues with fake accounts, or accounts set up for a problematic purpose. They may be designed for credit or lending fraud (more on that in Chapter 16), including loan stacking using multiple accounts; they may be intended for stimulus fraud as has been the case during the COVID-19 pandemic; they may be part of a synthetic identity attack; and so on. If setting up an account is particularly easy, a customer might set up many of them in order to receive small amounts from businesses that deposit 50 cents or a dollar into an account to check that the account is legitimate—a fraudster who sets up thousands of such accounts can rake in more money than you'd think. In some cases, more commonly within ecommerce, account opening is used by fraudsters simply to check whether an account with that email address already exists. If it does, they know it's a good target for account takeover (ATO) fraud (covered in Chapter 13).

Sometimes the data being used to set up the account will be fake, or *synthetic*, with documents stolen or faked to look plausible. Sometimes a real customer's identity will be stolen and used to set up an account of which they are unaware. The fraudster may even have gotten the information directly from the customer, under a pretext such as pretending to help them apply for an account. With mules, of course, sometimes their real identities are used to set up a fresh account for their work as a fraud accomplice. A fraudster or ring may have many mules working for them in this capacity. Sometimes the mules are aware of what they're doing, and other times they've been convinced by a specious story on the part of the fraudster or are willfully blind to what's going on. Fraud prevention teams need to be able to catch all of these possible cases.

Before we start to look at ways to prevent fraudulent accounts from being set up, it's worth noting that there are lots of good reasons for legitimate customers to set up multiple accounts. A customer may have an account of their own and one shared with a spouse or partner, a business partner, or a child, or they may also have a family account. They may have an account that exists only for direct deposit of their paychecks, or only for holiday funds. It's easy to get overexcited about the risk of multiple accounts, since fraudsters often attempt to set up and use multiple accounts. But it's important not to confuse that trend with a suspicion of multiple accounts in themselves.

It's important to bear in mind the positive impact of preventing account opening fraud. Stopping malicious actors from opening fraudulent accounts doesn't just protect a bank from money laundering concerns (although of course, compliance in that area is vital) or future loss. It also guards the rest of the financial ecosystem from a variety of risks, including protecting customers from identity theft, which can result in victims having their credit score ruined, reputation damaged by insurance fraud, money stolen through stimulus fraud, and so on. Synthetic identities have similar dangers and can affect the real people involved if much of their data is used (e.g., think of the damage that can be done with a Social Security number). Chapter 15 has more on identity theft and synthetic identities.

Beyond the damage done to individuals, there are also the risks to insurance companies, credit card companies, and mortgage companies if malicious actors are able to set up bank accounts that they can leverage into creating a plausible identity that can be mined for credit, loans, and so forth. The knock-on effect of this kind of fraud, left unchecked, would be truly alarming, especially when you realize that it's highly repeatable. A fraudster who has found a reliable way to use synthetic identities to set up accounts could apply for hundreds of accounts a day with different credit and loan companies, using a range of different bank accounts to do so. Moreover, such deep frauds are often left to mature over years, until the fraudster feels they have effectively maxed out the potential of the account and "busts out," stealing as much as they can as quickly as possible in as many ways as possible and making the fraudulent nature of the account obvious once it's too late.

The core of preventing online account opening fraud is analyzing the identity presented, and determining first whether it is a real identity and second whether the person currently using it is the person to whom that identity belongs (if a business account is being set up, the same applies for the business). Banks have an advantage here over the ecommerce businesses we discussed in the previous section because with banks, some friction is expected when confirming identities during the onboarding process; it's actually something customers usually find reassuring. Because of the importance of banks as institutions—they hold people's money and financial security—customers have a much higher level of tolerance for jumping through hoops that are clearly designed to protect users and their money. This makes document verification, age checks, and even demands for utility bills or similar documents as proof of address acceptable parts of the process. The increased popularity of online banking is helpful here as well; when Chase Bank surveyed customers and noncustomers age 18 to 65, they found that 80% prefer to manage their finances digitally as opposed to in person.[2] Customers have an incentive to jump through the hoops that are put in front of them, within reason.

This acceptance of friction applies less in the case of *neobanks*, also called *challenger banks* or *online-only banks*, which have an interesting challenge in that they have all the regulatory responsibilities of any bank but have some of the agility and smooth experience—and expectations—of an online site or app. The best solution in this case seems to be a judicious staggering of friction, allowing customers to set up an account with minimal information, and only a small check as required by Know Your Customer (KYC) policies and common sense, but adding further authentication processes as the customer becomes more engaged and wants to use their bank account in more varied ways. An advantage that neobanks have—which perhaps balances out the extra pressure to avoid friction, at least to some extent—is that their users tend to be more tech aware. Thus, methods such as liveness checks, which may confuse older customers, are appropriate for this audience.

 Although the focus here is on banks and financial institutions, preventing fraud at sign-up has value for ecommerce sites and marketplaces as well, if only because failing to do so makes the account look legitimate when it is activated, perhaps months later, to be leveraged for fraud. There's also the confusion that fake accounts cause in an ecosystem and analyses of that ecosystem, and the connection to promotion abuse of various kinds, which can scale up to be a serious problem if left unhindered.

Identification and Mitigation

A variety of methods and tools are available to help protect an institution from fraudulent account sign-ups. Which ones are most relevant for your organization depends on a variety of factors, including how much emphasis the business places on low customer friction at the start, the audience you serve, and the types of fraud you commonly see. As we'll see in Chapter 13, it's important to take a layered approach. It's unlikely that any single method will solve the problem for you, and if it did,

---

2 Brett Holzhauer, "Digital Banking As The New Normal In 2021: What To Expect From Banks" (*https://oreil.ly/JRq23*), *Forbes*, last updated January 11, 2021.

fraudsters would soon identify it and work around it. Layering your defenses is the best way to stop fraud at the door.

That said, all organizations should take steps to identify bots, which are often used by fraudsters to attempt to set up many fake accounts very quickly, preparing the ground for future fraudulent activity. We talk about bots in depth in Chapter 23, but it's important to note that they're very relevant in the context of account creation. If steps are not in place to catch bots and prevent them from initiating account creation, the damage later on can be considerable. Bear in mind that bots may be used to automate any of the steps in account creation if your organization breaks the flow into more than one step, and so analyzing only one part of the flow will leave your organization vulnerable. Fraudsters test your processes and will exploit any weaknesses they find.

Protecting against account opening fraud is just one part of the protection of the business and the customer journey for which fraud prevention teams are responsible. Account opening should be treated as an important milestone for both the customer and fraud prevention teams, but it should not be viewed in isolation from future account activity. Security and cybersecurity professionals often complain that the fact that someone is inside a building doesn't mean they have the right to be there—there's a human tendency to assume that once someone is there, they must be allowed to be there. Criminals of all kinds exploit this assumption.

The same is true with account opening: even if your organization carries out rigorous checks before allowing someone to open an account, it's not wise to let this turn into an assumption that everyone with an account is legitimate. Perhaps there were orange flags, but not enough to prevent account opening, and the fraud analyst decided on balance to allow it. Put measures in place to analyze the account regularly to make sure things continue to look legitimate. As Chapter 15 discusses, this is especially relevant with synthetic identities, but it's important with other types of account opening fraud as well.

In this context, you can put in place policies to limit the agency given to new accounts, making them less valuable to mules. For example, perhaps accounts that are less than three months old and lack a certain minimum amount of activity should not be able to receive or transfer cryptocurrency, or be able to receive a loan or credit over a certain minimum amount, or be allowed to receive money above a certain amount.

Even before that point, there are steps that would normally be expected to happen in conjunction with account opening that become suspicious if they are missing. Perhaps the account was allowed to proceed, but the credit or debit card sent to the customer as a result was never activated. Or perhaps the account was opened but then lay dormant for six months. Each bank has its own norms for how long it takes customers to begin to use their accounts, and the fraud prevention team should use that norm as a baseline. But generally speaking, although it may take time for a customer to move over—they may move paychecks or bills over piecemeal—there is activity within the first few months. If there isn't, it might be time to review the account opening information again.

The information gained at account opening is valuable in determining whether the consumer's behavior continues to match what would be expected of someone of that persona (more on customer personas later in this chapter). If it doesn't, your team needs to know. Don't treat account opening as a siloed problem when it ought to be simply the first step in the journey of protection.

Asking Questions, Mapping the Story

As we said elsewhere in this book with regard to IP addresses, emails, and other data points, what's important is to look for the whole story behind the details that come with the account opening. Does this look plausible? Does it match what's known about this customer already?

Of course, it's important to have automated checks in place to validate individual data points as much as possible—phone numbers, email addresses, device fingerprinting, physical addresses, and so forth—and we'll discuss document verification soon as well. Each data point may have a risk score associated with it; a phone risk score would take into account the risk of SIM swaps and porting and the age of the phone record with the mobile company, while an email risk score would include the age of the email, whether it's from a reputable provider, and whether the pattern of the email looks legitimate or is similar to patterns seen in previous fraudulent cases. (On the subject of emails, a word of caution: companies such as Apple are now providing consumers with the ability to use burner email addresses to protect their privacy and avoid spam. Customers are probably less likely to use such burner addresses for a bank account, but nonetheless, it's a factor that needs to be taken into account.) It's also important to be able to identify throwaway details, which legitimate customers rarely give to banks, and to be able to identify suspicious *velocity*; if the same device keeps returning with different apparent details, that's not a good sign. But overall, what you need to know is: does the story presented here make sense?

To analyze whether the story makes sense, it's valuable to ask questions, something a bank is able to do without feeling intrusive, and something ecommerce sites typically have to do without. Details such as tax status, primary citizenship, marital status, current employment, current income, and the purpose of the account provide a rich picture of the customer. If there are details that don't seem to match up—for example, if their primary residence is in a different state or country and they give no reason for setting up an additional account, or if their income vastly exceeds what you would expect for their stated profession—the system can flag this for review.

As always, it's important to bear both a legitimate and a fraudulent story in mind during review. Perhaps the customer works for a company with offices in the state or country you're in and they are planning to relocate. Perhaps when they gave "cleaning company" as their profession they meant they run a large cleaning business, rather than working as a cleaner. This sort of research may be done best by a human analyst, rather than trusting an automated process, though again, parts of it, particularly the data gathering side, may be automated. Using as many data sources as possible for corroborating evidence, including credit bureaus, will smooth the process both before and during review, and it's worth encouraging your team to get creative about which data sources might be valuable.

For instance, say you need to solve the problem of how to approach customers whose primary citizenship and place of residence is outside the United States and who are applying for a US account. Perhaps you could match to databases that reflect students coming to study in the United States from abroad (Figure 12-1). In that case, you would want to try to incorporate these types of census data sets into your methodology so that applications of foreign students will be treated more forgivingly.

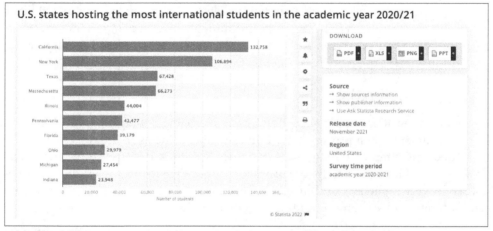

Figure 12-1. Ranking of US states hosting international students[3]

Alternatively, you could use more granular data sets, like the one shown in Figure 12-2, to evaluate the likelihood that someone from Utah will move to Hawaii and apply for a student account there versus the (much higher) likelihood that someone from Washington would do the same.

---

3 Erin Duffin, "US States Hosting the Most International Students in the Academic Year 2020/21" (*https:// oreil.ly/EAQYK*), Statista, November 17, 2021.

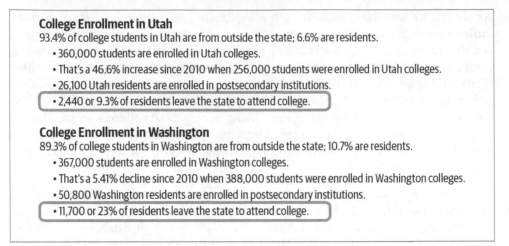

College Enrollment in Utah
93.4% of college students in Utah are from outside the state; 6.6% are residents.
- 360,000 students are enrolled in Utah colleges.
- That's a 46.6% increase since 2010 when 256,000 students were enrolled in Utah colleges.
- 26,100 Utah residents are enrolled in postsecondary institutions.
- 2,440 or 9.3% of residents leave the state to attend college.

College Enrollment in Washington
89.3% of college students in Washington are from outside the state; 10.7% are residents.
- 367,000 students are enrolled in Washington colleges.
- That's a 5.41% decline since 2010 when 388,000 students were enrolled in Washington colleges.
- 50,800 Washington residents are enrolled in postsecondary institutions.
- 11,700 or 23% of residents leave the state to attend college.

Figure 12-2. College enrollment comparison[4]

The more data available to your fraud prevention team, the more accurate their decisions will be. With open banking (*https://oreil.ly/RYZoZ*) bringing new possibilities of all kinds to customers and financial institutions alike, it's important to remain open-minded about what data you might be able to use to make fighting fraud easier, and the customer experience even smoother.

Document Verification

All banks, even those that can rely on customers being willing to invest time and effort in authentication processes, try to make onboarding as frictionless as possible. The time you're most likely to lose a customer is right at the start, when they don't know you and have nothing to lose by walking away. One report found that requiring a user to visit a physical branch or post documents in the mail resulted in a 23% drop-off rate, with customers heading to a competitor.[5]

Financial institutions have invested considerable resources into testing different approaches over the past decade. They have been helped by the development of a more standardized identification document process in the United States known as REAL ID (*https://oreil.ly/tRVWX*), and by a number of excellent document verification systems that try to minimize friction as much as possible. Scans that can be done via phone and that use AI to keep up with fraudster tricks can often catch fraudulent documentation even when the forgery is excellent. Moreover, as we discussed in

---

4 Melanie Hanson, "College Enrollment & Student Demographic Statistics" (*https://oreil.ly/T4EOk*), Education Data Initiative, last updated January 22, 2021.

5 Alex Rolfe, "Bank Identity Checks Push One in Four Consumers to a Competitor" (*https://oreil.ly/v3tFX*), Payments Cards & Mobile, June 11, 2021.

Chapter 5, image recognition is a particularly well-developed use case for machine learning. Ensuring that a person performing a selfie check matches the image on the documentation is a natural fit. *Liveness checks*, which ensure that the individual involved is really there and not merely an image or hologram, have become equally effective. Different solutions have different strengths and features, so it is important for every fraud team to carefully analyze their needs and what would best fit their requirements.

It's also important to determine where it makes sense for your business to use document verification; younger consumers tend to be particularly sensitive to the friction of document verification, so if your institution works with a large number of millennials and Gen Z consumers, it may be worth postponing document verification until after they've already set up and perhaps begun to use the account.

In addition to checking whether a specific document seems to be real, it's also important to check that the document hasn't been seen before in your own accounts in order to prevent a customer from setting up multiple accounts using their own identification, perhaps using a variation on their name each time. In the same way, if a customer has been rejected once, it's important to catch a second attempt to use the same identification.

Fraudsters sometimes go to creative lengths to pass selfie checks attached to an ID, employing hats, scarves, glasses, masks, and even makeup (*https://oreil.ly/HsHWI*). One of our wonderful tech reviewers, Brett Holleman, commented that when two of his children were 8 and 12 years old, respectively, they used to have fun passing for each other on the iPhone face recognition program. With fraudsters, if they do find a vulnerability in the solution you're using, they'll leverage it again and again. Some organizations flag known "fraudster faces" so that the system can identify a bad actor when they come back, regardless of how they're dressed or what color their hair is.

All document verification solutions will need to keep evolving, of course; the highly sophisticated deepfake technology already available, discussed in Chapter 11, indicates that this is a field that will keep developing. Like most aspects of fraud prevention, it's a continual arms race between the forces of fraud and the fraud fighters who oppose them.

Customer Personas

In addition to document verification, even at the early stage of account opening the concept of customer *personas* can come into play. Essentially, you're analyzing whether the customer looks like the sort of customer they appear to be, because groups of customers tend to act in similar ways: an elderly customer will act differently than a millennial customer will; likewise, there are certain characteristics that many young millennial professionals will share. If you can identify the typical range of behaviors for the young millennial professionals group, you can flag when someone who ought to fit that group isn't acting like it.

The onboarding process typically involves the user sharing a certain amount of information about themselves and interacting with the site even if in only a limited way. Beyond that, of course, there is the usual data that can be collected about a customer online, such as IP address and useragent information. There are also a number of highly effective solutions for banks based on behavioral biometrics[6] that can assist teams in this area and will flag, for instance, when someone is copying and pasting details that are rarely copied or pasted or is entering a Social Security number slowly when most customers type it in seconds. All the information you have should form a coherent picture of the customer.

Fraud teams should have a clear sense of how different personas usually behave. For example, an 80-year-old female opening an online account for the first time, probably with the same bank she's banked with all her life, will have a different online persona than a young professional who may have two or three accounts at different banks for different reasons and has likely only decided to open this account for a specific benefit, such as a card known to have good loyalty rewards or on the recommendation of a friend.

If the information the customer is giving about themselves doesn't match the way they're behaving or the device, browser, extensions, or versions they're using, further friction can be inserted into the process as extra authentication. Again, with banks, unlike with ecommerce, extra friction is not ideal, but it's not disastrous either from the perspective of customer experience. Customers expect banks to be extra careful. Customer support representatives, calling customers for extra checks, can even play into this expectation on the call, emphasizing their duty to take care of their customers. Fraudsters rarely like to interact as part of an account opening process, so a customer who runs off scared at the sign of any kind of interaction, even a reasonable level such as a phone call, is worth flagging so that a repeat attempt can be more easily identified.

Personas is another area where it's important to remember that account opening is only the first step in the fraud prevention process. If the account was allowed originally based on the persona of an 80-year-old, but appears to be used to purchase a gym membership, protein shakes, and energy bars—well, you might need to do some more digging there. Perhaps a family member is taking advantage. Neither account opening behavior nor purchases are necessarily problematic alone, but taken together, they warrant some caution.

---

6 We discuss behavioral biometrics in Chapter 13, but if you're curious about it now, you can read Shoshanna Solomon's article, "BioCatch Tracks Memory Use to Catch Cybercrooks" (*https://oreil.ly/74cwQ*), which we like because it includes a couple of nicely illustrative images.

Data Retention

Banks and other financial institutions stand in an interesting position when it comes to data retention, and this is something that many fraud teams within such organizations have to face on a regular basis—in particular, when considering the nature of the third-party solutions they want to use. Banks have to keep a large amount of sensitive information about their customers for at least five years. This makes sense when one considers anti–money laundering (AML) responsibilities, the need to be able to follow a paper or money trail, and the sheer importance of financial information to legitimate consumers. For this reason, many banks and financial institutions tend to err on the side of caution and keep even more than what is strictly required by law.

In our privacy-conscious era, however, this kind of retention can also become a liability, particularly in countries affected by the EU's General Data Protection Regulation (GDPR) but increasingly elsewhere in the world as well. Fraud teams may want to protect themselves from having to retain what may feel like an excess amount of information, not least because it can all be requested by a Freedom of Information Act request. Close consultation with the company's legal team is recommended before onboarding new vendor solutions in order to establish the best parameters in each case. Additionally, legal counsel will be able to offer advice about which information would and would not be relevant in the event of a data request. Fortunately, many vendors are able to offer at least some solutions that send verification answers without saving any information, streamlining this process significantly. For instance, a lot goes into document verification, a selfie check, and a liveness scan, but it may be that all you want to save is the response that said it was approved.

Summary

This chapter outlined people's motivations for opening problematic accounts, explored challenges with identifying and preventing these accounts, and discussed elements that fraud teams can use in creating a layered protection system. This leads naturally into a discussion of how to protect good accounts, once established, from being compromised—a practice known as account takeover and the focus of the next chapter.

## CHAPTER 13

Account Takeover

All of me, why not take all of me...
  —Gerald Marks and Seymour Simons[1]

We've mentioned account takeover (ATO) so many times already in this book that it's a relief to arrive at the chapter where we can really dive in! We saved it for this part of the book because while ATO is a common attack method against all industries, it's both particularly serious and, via social engineering and malware, particularly common in banking.

The reason ATO has come up so often already, of course, is because it's such a prominent attack tool in the fraudster toolbox. Gaining access to a victim's account opens up a huge range of possibilities for a creative fraudster. For this reason, though it's often an end in itself—meaning ATO is carried out solely to facilitate fraudulent transactions—it's also sometimes simply one step in a more complex plan that may involve many different fraudster tactics. This is especially true with ATO attacks against banks, but it can happen in ecommerce stores and marketplaces as well.

---

1 Gerald Marks and Seymour Simons, "All of Me," Irving Berlin, Inc., 1931.

This chapter is about *account takeover*, which occurs when a fraudster hacks into an account and starts to leverage it; it's not about *account handover*, which occurs when a previously respectable account is handed over voluntarily to a fraudster, usually either after a period of account aging or as a way to cash out a little before declaring bankruptcy. Account handover can cause considerable chaos, particularly in terms of money laundering but also on online marketplaces. For more on account handover, see Chapters 16 and 20.

In addition, this chapter focuses on ATO carried out against customers, not against employees. Therefore, the technologies and approaches used to protect employee accounts, while fascinating, are not covered here.

ATO: Fueled by Stolen Data

In order to break into someone's account, fraudsters need the person's account information. And following the norms of supply and demand, an efficient slice of the criminal ecosystem is dedicated to providing just that. The data is usually stolen in one of two ways:

Data breaches
> Occur when a hacker steals data—often including usernames, email addresses, and passwords, and sometimes more sensitive information such as Social Security numbers (SSNs) and credit card numbers—from an organization by breaking into the organization's databases and copying the data to a database the hacker owns

Phishing attacks
> Occur when a criminal tricks victims into handing over their information, usually via social engineering attacks, such as malicious emails purporting to be from a trusted source, overlay attacks (discussed later in this chapter), or IT repair scams, etc.

Ecommerce and marketplace sites tend to see more phishing, whereas banks are usually closer to 50:50. We'll treat phishing and *vishing* (stealing personal data via phone calls) as one phenomenon here, because we're not going to be diving into the details of how each type of data theft works. For fraud prevention professionals, what matters is the consequence of both: the wealth of stolen data available to fraudsters which is then employed as part of fraud attacks.

Data breaches have become such a fact of modern life that cybersecurity professionals talk about *breach fatigue*. Consumers are so used to hearing about millions of users having their data stolen from one large company or another that they have become inured to it. In 2020, for example, 37 billion data breach records were leaked, and based on the previous several years, one expects numbers in the tens of billions to feature in this context.[2] The dark market is so flooded with stolen data that account information often changes hands for amounts that seem laughably small: a full set of stolen credentials, including SSN, might cost only $8, while a stolen credit card including name and CVV might go for less than $1.[3]

Another kind of breach is possible as well, when criminals are able to access (and then share information from) the kinds of data enrichment sources that fraud teams usually rely on for identity corroboration. In early 2022, Vice reported on a criminal using—or rather, abusing—TransUnion's TLO investigation tools (*https://www.tlo.com*).[4] If this kind of attack becomes more common, it risks muddying the waters further, in an uncomfortable and dangerous way. It impacts all forms of fraud attack, of course, but is undoubtedly worrying when it comes to ATO.

Phishing attacks have been a problem for many years as well, but they ramped up considerably during the COVID-19 pandemic, which incentivized consumers to set up many new accounts online and offered attackers new opportunities to deluge potential victims. These victims were already under stress and thus were likely to be less wary than usual. A variety of timely scams were also seen: false information purporting to come from the World Health Organization or national or local medical authorities, emails apparently from large companies alerting customers to changes due to the fast-shifting situation, stimulus news, and so on. In addition, new variants on the phishing theme continue to develop, including phishing via QR codes (*https://oreil.ly/ZfYV8*) and fake postings on jobs sites.

The sheer scale of the stolen data that is easily and cheaply available fuels the industrialization of fraud attacks, both through bots and through cookie-cutter fraudsters carrying out what might be called *human automation*. It's simple to run through a long list of stolen credentials, seeing which can be used to break into an email account, retailer account, or even bank account. Consumers, despite widely publicized advice and guidelines on password hygiene and free password management tools, still reuse their passwords. One report found that 91% of consumers use the same passwords on multiple accounts, and 53% haven't changed their passwords in 12 months.[5] This means stolen data remains valuable for a long time after the theft, and can frequently be used to hack into multiple accounts on different sites.

---

2 Risk Based Security, *2020 Year End Report: Data Breach QuickView* (*https://oreil.ly/PFgPM*).

3 "A Look into the Pricing of Stolen Identities for Sale on Dark Web" (*https://oreil.ly/l5s2J*), *Security*, January 22, 2021.

4 Joseph Cox, "Crook Sells Access to Data Tool Used by Private Investigators" (*https://oreil.ly/VCqFz*), *Vice*, January 7, 2022.

5 LastPass, *Psychology of Passwords: The Online Behavior That's Putting You at Risk* (*https://oreil.ly/T5ifM*), LogMeIn, Inc., April 14, 2020.

Interestingly, the nature of the available stolen data means the typical victim of an ATO attack varies slightly depending on whether a bank or a retailer is under attack. Banking fraud teams are more likely to see higher levels of attacks against male victims of a higher median age, whereas ecommerce fraud teams are slightly more likely to see higher levels of attacks against female victims of a slightly younger age. These trends may be changing in the wake of the COVID-19 pandemic, which drew so many more people online and changed shopping and banking habits so substantially. Fraud teams who rely on these norms should be revisiting them regularly to adjust as necessary.

The Attack Stages of ATO

It's often not fully appreciated that an ATO attack may occur in several stages, partially because fraud prevention teams have traditionally been focused on preventing fraudulent actions carried out by leveraging the account (transferring money, making a fraudulent transaction, etc.) and thus have been less interested in the beginning of the attack, which may have occurred months earlier.

Banks are increasingly active in protecting every aspect of an account's history and access, but ecommerce merchants are perhaps not as attuned to the wider risks yet. Raj Khare, former product lead in User Experience and Account Security; Fraud and Risk Management at online shopping marketplace Wish, said this may be a mistake:

> It's not just a matter of financial loss, although that's obviously important to a business. When it comes to ATO you need to consider the reputation damage a business can suffer when customers discover you've allowed a criminal to access their account and details. That customer will likely take a break before buying from you again, or may never return. More than that, they'll probably tell friends and family, who will be less likely to try your site. When you think about the huge effort a company puts into encouraging customers to refer a friend, promote their brand online, and so on, you'd think it would make sense to put a fraction of that effort into preventing ATO, which will undo all that good work.

Raj also pointed out that data can be valuable in persuading managers or upper management that more effort is required in this field:

> I have found putting numbers to the risk to be very effective. Your company measures churn; you can do that for churn related to ATO. You can track, over time, what happens to accounts that suffered from ATO. Was there a delay before the customer used the account again? Did they stop using it altogether? Can you measure the loss associated with each stage of ATO? Many fraud prevention teams don't think of this sort of work as part of the job, but it has to be. It gives important context and gives you invaluable leverage when you're discussing account protection with management. All at once your team presents itself as looking out for the bottom line, and customer

growth, and concentrating on lifetime customer value. It can be excellent positioning for the fraud team, as well as helpful in stopping fraud and bad actors.

Here are the stages of a typical ATO attack carried out against a bank:

- The fraudster gains access to the account. Malware may be used to skim account information when real users access their accounts (this is more typical in banking than in ecommerce), or the stolen data may come from breaches or from phishing. Bots may be used to try multiple sets of details until they find one that works, or cookie-cutter fraudsters may be employed for a similar purpose: they're slower, but many can be employed simultaneously and their mouse and keyboard patterns won't raise flags from systems put in place to recognize bots.

- The fraudster logs in to the account and reviews what's there. This may include the amount of money in the account, any accounts connected to the hacked one, information about past purchases, and cards associated with the account. (In an ecommerce example, this could include loyalty points or gift cards associated with the account.) The fraudster then decides whether or not they want to leverage this account themselves. Sometimes they will, if it happens to match exactly the kind of account they are best set up to exploit. But often they will sell it to someone else, including various details about what it contains (and therefore, how valuable it could be). There are fraudsters who specialize in exactly this: simply finding live account details, assessing the accounts, and selling them for as much as they can get.

- Once the account information has been sold, the new buyer will usually take a peek as well. Depending on whether it matches what they're looking for, this resale process may happen a number of times. During this period, many different IPs may be accessing the account, quite possibly over weeks or months. Each will likely only access the account once or twice, and during this time, no fraudulent activity will be associated with any of these addresses.

- The final buyer of the account details will validate the information they have received, logging in and reviewing the account themselves.

- There will then be a watching period during which the fraudster will log in a number of times, often from the same IP address and device, and review recent activity. Sometimes this will be done on a regular schedule, mimicking the behavior of a user who routinely checks their account. During this period, extra information (tied to the fraudster) may be added to the account, such as a phone number or address.

- The fraud is executed. This is usually an attempt to transfer money in a way that echoes past transfers as much as possible. The flow of an ATO attack against an ecommerce site or marketplace is similar, but usually more condensed in terms of time.

- Finally, as collateral damage, the fraudster will try the stolen password and/or access to email/SIM card in order to change passwords and take over many more accounts. Email ATO can easily lead to leaks of many additional sensitive credentials, images, documents, crypto address keys, and more.

What is notable here is the amount of time involved, which may often represent months elapsed between stages 1 and 6. This is partly due to the reselling process, but a large part of it comes during the watching period, when the time spent doing nothing more harmful than peeking is used to establish the good reputation of the IP address, device, and behavior used on these occasions. This is particularly challenging for fraud prevention models, because models are trained over time. When the attack is gradual enough, it becomes difficult to know when legitimate behavior ends and attack behavior begins. Is that login from three months ago part of the attack, or part of the legitimate identity still using the account? What should the current login be compared against?

 It's also worth noting that there are often three types of fraudster involved in an ATO attack. Raj Khare called these types the *sniffer* type, the *wanderer* type, and the *financial impact* type. The sniffers gain the initial access, the wanderers explore and analyze the account, and the financial impactors make use of it. It's a distinction many nonfraud fighters won't find intuitive, so it's worth explaining explicitly to colleagues from other departments. Giving them names like "sniffer" and "wanderer" might help add a splash of personality, to make the threat seem more real.

The Advantages of ATO

Why go to all this effort? Once again, it comes back to return on investment (ROI): access to a legitimate account gives a fraudster a huge number of avenues that can be exploited for gain. A legitimate account comes with a good reputation, giving anyone using it a substantial advantage in convincing fraud models that their current activities are legitimate, especially since they can confuse the model further by mirroring past behaviors associated with the account *which can be viewed by anyone with access to the account*. A fraudster leveraging a legitimate account, having taken time to intertwine their behavior and profile with the legitimate one, can transfer more money or spend more money faster and far more easily than they could by setting up a new account with fake or stolen details.

To illustrate the scale of activities possible with ATO—and to emphasize the point that ATO is a threat that should be blocked, not only caught and stopped at transfer or checkout—here is a small selection of possible use cases for successful ATO:

- Steal money (bank or payment instrument ATO)
- Gain access to and exploit a saved payment instrument
- Gain access to and exploit saved personal data
- Add additional personal data to an account, such as a phone number or address, which can then be used in future scams
- Launder money
- Gain access to and exploit past purchase history
- Gain access to and monetize saved loyalty points or gift cards attached to the account
- Take advantage of softer risk limits
- Take advantage of softer policy limits
- Leverage marketplace reputation (both buyer and seller)

Overlay Attacks

Overlay attacks are just what they sound like. You can almost think of them as similar to phishing, but with the human element replaced by malware. A fraudster harvests customer data using a legitimate-looking sign-in form that appears to be on your business's website; it *overlays* the real site, to make the trick hard to spot. In some cases this kind of attack is carried out by attacking the company's real website, but that involves a complex cyberattack against the business. More commonly, the attack is carried out through vulnerability on the consumer's end. The consumer will be tricked into downloading malware onto their device, usually as an invisible passenger alongside content the consumer actually wants. This malware is primed to lay low unless the consumer navigates to one of a limited number of bank websites (the sites the fraudster has prepared an overlay for). If the consumer does navigate to the bank website, it will look just the same as usual, but in reality, when they enter their credentials, they'll be sending them to the fraudster. There may be a delay of a few seconds while the malware uses their details to log in to the real site and send them to their account, or they might see an error screen and have to go through the process again, but it is generally virtually unnoticeable to an unsuspicious eye. And why should the consumer be suspicious? They were just logging in to their bank account, as they have done hundreds of times. Everything looked normal.

The reason we're discussing this in a chapter on ATO is that the information can then be easily used to illegitimately access the consumer's account. The fraudster even has information about the IP and device the consumer was using when they were on the overlay, so they can create a convincing match for normal customer behavior when they do take over the account.

Identification and Mitigation

Identification and mitigation of ATO is not a simple process and, as banks know all too well by now, must come from the layering of fraud tools and prevention techniques. No single method can rule them all; you need a fellowship of fraud-fighting methods to defeat the enemy.

Generally speaking, the identification of anomalies in both transactions and account activity is crucial. Refer back to Chapter 3 for a broader focus on anomaly detection. When it comes to ATO specifically, a number of different techniques may be of value in building the layers that will protect your users' accounts.

Biometrics

Biometrics includes both *physical* biometrics data (fingerprints, retina scan, voice recognition, facial recognition, etc.) and *behavioral* biometrics data (typical mouse movements and speed, typing speed and patterns, etc.). In both cases, the idea is that you can use this profile of a person to uniquely identify them, and thus flag when anyone with other physical or behavioral characteristics appears in their account.

Fingerprint access is an option for most sites and apps able to support the technology nowadays, as consumers have become so used to using their fingerprint to access their devices that there is a low level of suspicion or resistance to this method, which is often welcomed as being easy for the consumer. But the more places that use and store fingerprint information, the more likely it is to become an object for data theft itself (this has happened already, though not yet at scale). That means fingerprints should not be relied on as a silver bullet either, because if they fail, fraudsters have the keys to the entire castle.

Beyond this, fingerprint analysis famously requires *fuzzy matching*, since consumers tend to become irritated if the scan doesn't recognize them if they're holding the device slightly differently or they've cut their finger. Fraudsters, of course, are eager (and sometimes manage) to exploit this fuzziness. Additionally, it is worth noting that although fingerprints feel virtually frictionless on a touchscreen device, many people access banks and other sites on their desktops or laptops, which often do not have a fingerprint scanning capability. Using two devices in a two-factor authentication (2FA) way is perfectly possible, but adds friction.

Banks can employ other forms of physical biometrics that consumers may consider too heavy in terms of friction or, probably, too intrusive for online stores or marketplaces. Customers expect banks to have more rigorous identity verification methods in place. In an era of frequent data breaches, most customers are not sanguine about allowing their retina scan or even facial scan to be saved by an online site. Even banks need to be cautious about what they use when allowing a simple account login;

consumers experiencing facial or voice recognition every time they just want to check their bank balance are unlikely to be satisfied with their online experience.

And therein lies the challenge of ATO prevention, because until the fraudster starts to leverage the account, all they're doing is logging in and looking around. By the time they act, the account may be accustomed to their profile.

Behavioral biometrics is different, in that there is no associated friction for the consumer; collecting the relevant data is invisible to the end user. However, data collection does require the addition of some JavaScript code, which is something that has begun to raise privacy flags in certain contexts. JavaScript snippets that catch fraudsters obviously have only the best intentions, but they still require collecting a lot of customer data. Storing this data cannot be taken lightly.

Beyond the privacy concern, there are two other issues with behavioral biometrics. First, there's a learning curve while the system learns what normal behavior is. Second, user behavior varies far more than a perfect model would hope. For example, one of your authors broke her shoulder while writing this book. We promise you that this impacted all of the normal signals connected to typing style and mouse usage. (We worked around it; the book was a really fun project and we loved writing it for you.) In fact, the injury affected physical biometrics as well, particularly during the initial stage.

Less dramatically, user behavior is altered when they log in while inebriated, hung over, or even just extremely relaxed. Equally, times of stress change speed and accuracy. Even how cramped a space the user may be in (on public transport versus sprawled out on a sofa) or how well-lit their environment is may make a difference. Many users log in from different devices, and their behavior may be different on each one. Think about how differently you hold and tap on a phone versus a tablet, or how differently you may be set up on a laptop while traveling versus when you're using the same laptop connected to a screen, keyboard, and mouse. The behavioral model has to deal with all of those variations. That means it must include diversity and flexibility. However, if it includes *too much* diversity and flexibility, it is no longer fit for purpose; it won't catch a fraudster who is a close match for legitimate behavior.

Despite those caveats, biometrics are a powerful indicator of good behavior, and provide a helpful way to identify when a good user has returned using typical behavior, device, and characteristics. This alone can help limit successful ATO. The range of behaviors that biometrics must accommodate, as well as the difficulty of avoiding friction for good users, mean biometrics cannot be relied on alone, but they are a genuinely valuable component of an identity validation process.

Behavioral patterning analytics are slightly separate from behavioral analytics, which are designed to define and pick out a specific individual. Using very similar techniques, companies can build archetypes of behavioral patterns. Consider the way (or, rather, the range of ways) in which a 20-something student typically behaves, compared to a traveling professional in their 30s or an elderly person in their 80s or 90s. Using these archetype profiles won't tell you when a fraudster has hacked into a specific account, necessarily—it could be that the account's behavior is very similar to the relevant archetype. Bots are increasingly designed to mimic human behavior, including human hesitation and slower responses. And where bots are detectable, humans from the gig economy or cookie-cutter fraudsters are sometimes brought in, so ATO attempts are often subtle in wider behavioral terms. But behavioral profiles will certainly help flag when an 80-year-old is suddenly whizzing around the account like a millennial.

Multifactor Authentication

Multifactor authentication (MFA) is a mechanism that checks that a user has two or more pieces of information, typically corresponding to different types of information, before letting the user access an account or a function within an account. When a merchant texts you a code that you have to enter online in order to continue, that's MFA. The types of information considered acceptable are usually as follows:

- Something you know (a password, a PIN code, security questions, etc.)
- Something you have (a credit card, a physical token sent by the bank for that purpose that generates a one-time password, a USB security key, etc.)
- Something you are (back to biometrics)
- Somewhere you are (in certain cases, simply being connected to a particular intranet or virtual private network [VPN], or even being physically in a specific location that is easily checked, especially with mobile apps, can be relevant)

A certain amount of friction is involved here, but it's of a kind that consumers have become used to and are comfortable with. This makes MFA useful as a friction step if your system catches possible ATO, even during user activity in the account. A brief pause requesting, for instance, that a user enter a code that has been sent to them is irritating but only mildly so. (Again, this kind of friction may be more expected within a banking context, but as long as it is used judiciously, it is often considered normal elsewhere as well.)

MFA greatly strengthens authentication processes because, as mentioned, layering is, in essence, built in. You have to have at least two data points that correspond to confirm the identity. Having two elements is harder for a fraudster. MFA is by no means fraudster proof; if they can fool one factor, they can probably fool two. It just requires a little more work.

In practice, MFA is usually a combination of username/email, password, and phone number, with a code being sent to a phone via SMS or email, or through a dedicated authenticator app. Fraudsters, as you should know by now, don't find passwords much of a challenge. Answers to security questions can often be found through online searches and social media. Email addresses are vulnerable through ATO, of course. Within the context of ATO, it's quite probable that successful ATO against a bank means an email is already compromised, and there's a reasonable chance of the same being the case with ecommerce sites or marketplaces.

There are an increasing number of ways around Short Message Service (SMS) verification, namely Time-based One-Time Passwords (TOTP) (*https://oreil.ly/3L02Y*). Fraudsters can try to corrupt an employee of a cell phone network to copy or reroute messages—the human factor is always one of the hardest vulnerabilities to protect against adequately, and unfortunately there have been cases where this occurred. There's also SIM *jacking*, in which fraudsters use social engineering or research to find personal details about a victim and use those to convince a phone carrier they're the victim and they need a new SIM card. The new SIM card is sent to the fraudster, and the victim loses access to their messages entirely, since they're sent to the fraudster instead. This is usually a short-lived success for the fraudster since the victim will start to notice the problem and take steps to fix it, except in cases where fraudsters specifically target recently deceased individuals, in which case the attack can continue far longer. Of course, even a short period of time can be enough for a fraudster to do a lot of damage, since they're poised ready to leverage the opportunity. There's also *SS7 exploitation*, in which attackers tap into the telecom industry's backbone to intercept messages by creating a duplicate number. And of course, a number of SIM swapping stories (*https://oreil.ly/H01MT*) have come to light in recent years, together with other methods also being developed cheaply and easily for fraudsters. The weaknesses are so glaring that well-known cybersecurity expert and blogger Brian Krebs has suggested that we "stop pretending SMS is secure now" (*https://oreil.ly/MIu9h*).

Fraudsters can also combine one or more of these tricks with a little social engineering. For instance, a fraudster who hacks into an account using stolen credentials may be stopped by MFA. They can have an email ready to go to send to the victim to tell them to log in to their account in order to protect or update it, using the information they've just been sent. In reality, they'll send the customer to a fake version of the site or app, one run by the fraudster themselves. It won't always work, but it often will, and fraudsters have a host of variants on this technique. (While writing this book, one of Shoshana's colleagues had a fraudster reach out, supposedly as part of a sale of a washing machine on an online marketplace, asking as part of the process that the colleague "confirm his identity" by sharing the code he was about to receive.) An alternative version of this trick is for the fraudster to call the customer pretending to be the bank, giving them a plausible reason to expect a code to arrive at their email or device shortly. They stay on the phone, and when the code comes through the victim is tricked into reading it out to the "bank representative" on the line. Some of these techniques can now be carried out at considerable scale, with elements like chat or phone calls handed over to one-time password (OTP) bots that automate much of the process (*https://oreil.ly/VFyia*), meaning that fraudsters can carry out more attacks with ease.

As mentioned in Chapter 11, the most notorious combination of ATO with social engineering is business email compromise (BEC) fraud. BEC involves the impersonation of high-level executives by sending phishing emails from seemingly legitimate sources and requesting wire transfers to alternate, fraudulent accounts. Fraudsters can achieve this form of social engineering without access to the true email of the business executive (they can email you from *Bill.Gates@mikrosotf.com* and hope you won't notice the deliberate typos). However, the fraud is much more effective if the attacker sends the phishing email/phone call from the compromised asset of the real CEO, which is why the ATO version of BEC is so dangerous.

Dedicated authenticator apps are less vulnerable, although they can be passed by a sufficiently determined criminal, particularly via social engineering (*https://oreil.ly/ToxEt*). But here the ROI calculation kicks in, and many fraudsters are only willing to invest up to a point. The more common, and the more sophisticated, that overlay malware becomes, however, and the easier it is for criminals to carry out phishing and other forms of social engineering at scale, the greater the vulnerability for this form of authentication as well.

In fact, an executive order (EO 14028) from President Biden instructed all agencies: "For routine self-service access by agency staff, contractors and partners, agency systems must discontinue support for authentication methods that fail to resist phishing, such as protocols that register phone numbers for SMS or voice calls, supply one-time codes, or receive push notifications." That covers the majority of commonly used MFA mechanisms, and is a clear sign that as an industry, we need to both exercise caution and encourage creative solutions for the next, more effective generation of MFA.

Passwordless approaches, such as those based on FIDO2, the open authentication standard hosted by the Fast Identity Online (FIDO) Alliance, offer a secure way to add an authentication layer without adding as much friction as MFA variants, which depend on the user entering passwords or codes. Essentially, the user credentials are decentralized, isolated, and encrypted on users' personal devices, making them less vulnerable to some of the MFA weaknesses we've discussed, since the information stays on the device and isn't shared with servers. As far as we know, these have not had wide uptake yet within the context of protecting consumer accounts (as opposed to employee accounts), but it's an interesting possibility for the future that may help mitigate some of the issues discussed here. FIDO2 and WebAuthn can be used to eliminate passwords for both customers and employees. In mobile, for instance, it's possible to device-bind the mobile phone with a public/private set of keys and use a biometric or a Yubico key as the authenticator. WebAuthn also works with the browser on a PC.

Device Fingerprinting

Device fingerprinting is a technique we've discussed as being useful in multiple fraud prevention scenarios. There's no friction for the user; it's a data-gathering exercise, using as many sources as possible to find out as much information about the device as possible in order to be able to identify it later on. Even when a user changes some of the appearances of their device, as discussed when we talked about user agents back in Chapter 1, patterns can often be picked out that show connections between devices in reality. Much of the information can be collected by the company directly, while additional confirmation can be obtained by using third-party solutions that specialize in device intelligence.

Device fingerprinting is another valuable layer, but given the prevalence of emulators, burner devices, and so on, it is yet another layer to be added to the identification and authentication process rather than a solution in itself. Genesis Market (*https://oreil.ly/oeglT*), on the dark web, is famous for supplying not just the digital fingerprint details of the listed victims, but even a handy app that fraudsters can use to automatically browse the web using the fingerprint they've just purchased, with no effort required on the fraudster's side. The fraudster will appear to be using the same device type, version, and browsers with the same extensions, languages, and time zones as the victim. The profile can achieve a surprising (and problematic) level of detail. There are no silver bullets; fraud prevention teams need a layered, intelligent approach.

 Looking at the problem from the other side, organizations do need to be sensitive to the fact that real users change devices legitimately, so device ambiguity is often a sign that it may be time to apply friction rather than a sign that rejection or ejection from an account is appropriate.

Network Context

As with every other kind of fraud attack, a fraud prevention team should use their own data and knowledge of their own systems and customers to identify ATO. Different attacks or methods are more or less popular at different times in the fraudster community. A fraud ring may be trying a particular set of steps against you over and over again. Your systems should look for patterns of this kind within account usage just as it does with account creation or transfer/transaction points.

Customer Knowledge

Fraud prevention teams working within a bank, as we said earlier, have a limited set of information when it comes to a customer's individual transactions. This can be frustrating, and certainly makes it more difficult to make accurate decisions—including for ATO, since it would be helpful to know which types of product or service a customer usually purchases. However, this built-in paucity of transaction data can encourage the assumption that the system lacks deep customer knowledge more generally, and this is far from true.

A long-term customer relationship, or a relationship with a newer but active customer, provides you with a huge amount of rich data about their behavior and priorities. Fraud prevention teams are good at remembering to use specific data points associated with purchases, payments, or money transfers (amount involved, geographies involved, etc.), but the depth of data goes beyond this, and all of it can be valuable. Think about all the interaction points your customers have with your organization. How often do they contact customer support? Do they open emails you send them? Do they reply? Do they use chat? How engaged are they with their account: are they likely to notice an ongoing ATO attack? What are their contact preferences? If your organization follows Know Your Customer (KYC) practices, what do you know about them from that process?

There are also the profiling aspects: the user's age, gender, professional life, and so on. You can build models that reflect typical behaviors of this sort of profile. When they don't match them, that might be a flag.

Identifying Overlay Attacks

As we explained earlier, overlay attacks are ideal as part of an ATO attack. For the fraudster, they're an easy way to harvest data, and very hard for the bank to spot.

It's so hard to spot these attacks, in fact, that in many cases you will first hear about them from customers, and working out what malware is being used and how to stop it are both likely to involve customer interaction. There is a cybersecurity component to the challenge that overlay attacks represent, and fraud prevention teams can work closely with cybersecurity departments in these matters. Some banks even have cross-departmental strike teams for exactly this sort of case. But because the vulnerability is on the customers' devices, it's very hard to catch unless you're working with your customers.

The first warning that an overlay attack is being used against your business will probably come from affected customers, who may be willing to collaborate with your business to help you investigate where the malware came from, how it works, and what you can learn from it. It's then up to you to decide how, or whether, to notify other customers of the risk. This will typically involve discussions with customer

---

success and account management teams, since it touches directly on the relationship between the business and its customers.

Fraud prevention teams will need to work out where friction can be added in the customer journey to protect against this threat, and what parameters can be used to limit the accounts where friction may be necessary. Certain geographies, types of account, or age ranges of customers may, for example, be particularly affected, depending on where the malware came from originally.

Dynamic Friction

We'd like to close this section by highlighting something we described a number of times in this chapter but haven't yet named or explained as a technique, and that's the importance of dynamic friction when combating ATO. Finding the right balance between being overly permissive about allowing access to an account and adding an unreasonable amount of friction at every step is very difficult. The time involved, which can normalize a fraudster's behavior and access to the account, presents a particular challenge, as does the wealth of stolen data available to fraudsters. Most of the activities a fraudster carries out as part of an ATO attack won't be actively problematic (except for their access to a user's personal data, of course). It isn't a problem…until it is. At that point, your system might not notice them anymore.

When discussing account opening, or protecting the point of transaction or money transfer, what's at stake is an event. You have a specific challenge before you, a particular moment in time, when your team has to decide whether this user is fraudulent or legitimate. ATO isn't like that. It's not an event, it's a process. You may not catch ATO the first time the fraudster logs on to the account, but you'll likely have multiple touchpoints where you *can* do so. That means the concept of dynamic friction is exceptionally relevant here.

You can add different kinds of checks depending on how suspicious the behavior is, and also depending on the action the user is attempting to carry out. If you want to confirm that you don't have a peeking situation, you can require a password reset. If you want to validate identity before allowing the user to add an address to the account, you can use MFA. If the biometrics look strange, you can call the customer. If there are a number of small flags over a period of days or weeks, you can treat them cumulatively and introduce friction when it's appropriate. Finding the balance between protection and friction is hard, but in the case of ATO, you have time on your side, and that means you have more options and the leisure to use them. Your team can evaluate typical ATO patterns in your organization and decide which points, and which kinds of friction, are most appropriate in each case.

Example: Identifying a Trusted Session

The richness of data that can be accumulated over the lifetime of an account often makes it easier to flag trusted sessions rather than "hunt down" suspicious sessions.

A typical approach to what makes a session trustworthy is relying solely on the time factor. For example, if a login event occurred three to six months ago and there has been no complaint or proof of foul play since, in retrospect that login was legitimate.

This typical approach is somewhat limited for two main reasons. The first reason is the risk of falsely trusting a fraudulent login that was not noticed by the account holder. As mentioned earlier, a login event could be a fraudster who's only peeking into the compromised account. Therefore, in theory, a login should be trusted only if it was shortly followed by a payment order or any other activity that is significant enough to be noticed by the true account holder.

The second reason is far more common: most login events are legit, but your system can't afford the leisure of waiting for several months until they're cleared of suspicion. Imagine a person who logs in to their bank account to check their balance because they plan to make a large transfer, such as making a down payment on a home. It's crucial that the login event be quickly identified as trustworthy so that the money transfer is frictionless.

How should trustworthy sessions be identified within the context of an account? As always, it depends on how much effort you're willing to put into it. If you have the dev resources to build your own network analysis from scratch, you'll need to map every IP, cookie, device attribute, and so on into a network of arches and nodes, which involves a considerable amount of effort. Consider services such as TigerGraph, GraphQL, Neo4j, Neptune, and others to help. More on graph databases and network analysis can be found in *Graph Databases* by Ian Robinson, Jim Webber, and Emil Eifrem (O'Reilly), and in various tutorials and case studies online, such as "Dealing with Big Data and Network Analysis Using Neo4j" (*https://oreil.ly/SuNee*).

A lighter approach, probably suitable for smaller databases or for the research phase, would be to use SQL case statements and score trustworthy sessions based on the strongest evidence that ties them to the account history. Example 13-1 is used mostly for the fun of using a table named "old cookies."

Example 13-1. Determining the level of trust for a current login by using an IP or cookie that is more than one year old

```
WITH old_cookies AS
(
    SELECT DISTINCT
        cookie
    FROM
```

```
        account_logins
    WHERE
        login_date > getdate() - 365
)
WITH old_ips AS
(
    SELECT DISTINCT
        ip,
        ip_geolocation,
        ip_isp
    FROM
        account_logins
    WHERE
        login_date > getdate() - 365
)


/* using the old_cookies table and the old_ips tables to score the trust
level on the new login: */
SELECT
    current_login.login_id AS current_login_id,
    CASE
        WHEN
            current_login.cookie = old_cookies.cookie
        THEN
            1
        WHEN
            current_login.ip = old_ips.ip
        THEN
            0.8
        WHEN
            current_login.ip_geolocation = old_ips.ip_geolocation
            AND current_login.ip_isp = old_ips.ip_isp
        THEN
            0.8
        WHEN
            current_login.ip_geolocation = old_ips.ip_geolocation
            OR current_login.ip_geolocation = old_ips.ip_g
            ELSE
                0
    END
    AS current_login_trust_score
FROM
    account_logins AS current_login
    LEFT JOIN
        old_cookies USING (cookie)
    LEFT JOIN
        old_ip USING (ip);
```

Table 13-1 shows the results of Example 13-1.

Table 13-1. Results of Example 13-1

current_login_id	current_login_trust_score
1111	0.8
2222	0.5
3333	1

Using this simple type of methodology should help you decide whether your system needs a more robust session consistency score mechanism. There are a few extra steps you may want to consider as a way to refine this methodology:

- Boost scores in direct correlation to the age of the "old cookie" (or old IP, IP geolocation, etc.). For example, multiply the naive trust score by the age of the oldest matching cookie. Then normalize the scores.

- Adjust scores when the "old cookie" might be a public asset. This is especially relevant for the more common indicators, where the current session's match to the account history might be coincidental (the fraudster happens to be using an IP of the same broadband provider as the victim), or deliberate (the fraudster uses a proxy in New York, since they know the compromised account belongs to a New Yorker). This is when you may want to use the popularity of the old attributes to balance out the trust score.

- Adjust scores based on the activity within the session. A trust score could be lower if it included a suspicious password change or an excessive series of money transfers, but should that really be an immediate cause for nullifying it? Even if the session came from an "old cookie"? Or even if the account performed similar actions frequently in the past? Consider whether your system is better suited for trust scores that reflect only the consistency of the session (i.e., their resemblance to the account history) or whether they should combine consistency with risk.

Once you find a way to identify a steady base of accounts showing high rates of sessions with high trust scores, you will be able to generate smooth checkout flows for the vast majority of your users, saving your energy and/or authentication flows for those few cases that really need the extra attention.

Summary

This chapter explored the complexities of ATO and discussed different strategies that can be used to identify and mitigate it. We discussed the importance of using a layered strategy; because no solution provides surefire protection on its own, a combination can be very powerful in protecting accounts and their real users. The next chapter looks at common malware attacks: another way fraudsters attempt to steal user account data and gain access to and leverage user accounts, particularly in the context of online banking, although also against other online sites.

## CHAPTER 14

Common Malware Attacks

Every step you take, I'll be watching you...
—The Police[1]

Malware, software designed to damage, illegally access, or control computers, networks, servers, and so on, has been a problem in banking for years. That's not surprising, given the large potential payoff of an attack against a bank. Even five years ago malware was still probably one of the main challenges facing banking fraud prevention teams. In the past couple of years, though, fraudsters have prioritized other methods of attack, or combined malware with other forms of attack.

We're still devoting a (shortish) chapter to malware for two reasons. First, there are fashions in fraud, just like in anything else, and chances are good that malware will be back, albeit probably in an altered form (fraudsters can't afford to stand still). In fact, some time after this chapter was written and just before the book was sent to print, a report was published indicating that malware attacking mobile devices specifically is on the rise (*https://oreil.ly/XksJy*), so watch that space to see whether it develops into a longer-term trend. Second, even when malware is less prominent it isn't gone; it's just much less likely to be a problem in isolation. Instead, it works in conjunction with social engineering.

Types of Malware Attacks

There are many different types of malware. For example, with *ransomware*, which has been making international headlines lately, the attackers lock down and hold for ransom crucial company data and processes in a wide variety of industries, such

---

1 The Police, "Every Breath You Take," written by Sting, track 7 on *Synchronicity*, A&M, 1983.

as vital infrastructure, hospitals, educational institutions, and commercial entities. *Remote access tools* (RATs) give hackers access to the victim's machine. Then there are the more traditional Trojan horses, worms, and spyware—programs that add malicious libraries or overwrite legitimate libraries with malicious ones to trick trusted apps into drawing from them. And the list goes on. The names "Zeus," "Kronos," "GozNym," and "Panda" are practically household names and are familiar to anyone with an interest in cybersecurity, hacking, or finance.

Over the past decade, sophisticated malware attacks have gradually moved toward targets that are more lucrative than the average private consumer bank account. The appetite for higher payouts has grown, so cybercriminals have moved into terrorizing health systems (*https://oreil.ly/2IFav*) and/or hacking into cryptocurrency storage companies. According to May Michelson of GK8, attackers have developed the patience and resources needed to break into hot—and even into cold (*https://oreil.ly/EeUYc*)—wallets. Giving the example of an attacker targeting your crypto wallet and managing to infect your PC with malware, May said: "He has all the time in the world to quietly follow your movements and learn about your network. It can be done by malicious code running in the background of your compromised device, doing nothing but waiting for the command to attack."[2] Tens of millions of stolen dollars (*https://oreil.ly/5pGRU*) are worth the wait.

The aforementioned attack methods are a step up from what used to be the "average" cyberattack of the early 2000s. Most of them belong more to the world of cybersecurity than to fraud prevention so we will not be going into the details of exactly what they can do. It's normally the duty of the fraud fighter to identify the moment when a malware attack reaches its monetization phase (e.g., when ransomware attackers attempt to collect their loot via a bank transfer). Still, knowing the cyber "origin story" of the fintech fraud attack gives the fraud fighter more context and improves collaboration with the chief information security officer (CISO) function of the organization. Plus, it's super interesting and worth a chat with your cyber experts, even if it's unlikely to be a problem that your fraud-fighting team will be expected to deal with.

In a perfect world, cyberattackers would be kept at bay by the blessed work of government response teams. Indeed, in many Organisation for Economic Co-operation and Development (OECD) countries, such agencies have been hard at work since the middle of the preceding decade (an example is the formation of CERT-UK (*https://oreil.ly/49Dmv*) in 2014). Computer emergency response teams (CERTs) protect the financial ecosystem from collapse in case of severe cyberattacks, but they would usually arrive at the scene only when an attack becomes massive enough to bring down

---

2 "5 Myths on Cold Wallets (Or: Why There's No Real Cold Wallet Out There)" (*https://oreil.ly/EeUYc*), GK8, July 14, 2020.

at least a bank or two. Rahav Shalom Revivo is the founder of the Fintech-Cyber Innovation lab program for the Israeli Ministry of Finance, the first initiative in the world that leverages government assets and data in order to promote fintech and cyber startups in an open innovation platform. She noted: "the goal is to promote new financial-cyber international relationships, sharing threat intelligence and our intellectual property of protection to the financial ecosystem in order to strengthen the entire financial ecosystem, locally and internationally."

Meanwhile, as it will take a while for the impact of government collaborations to trickle down the industry, it is up to cybersecurity and fraud prevention teams in individual organizations to identify both the larger attacks (which should be reported to the local CERT when applicable) and the smaller ones (which should be handled within the bank, merchant, exchange, etc.).

As Part of Phishing Attacks

Within the fraud prevention context, malware is most likely to be found as part of either phishing attacks or attempts to directly gain entry to an account through remote access. Phishing attacks come in a variety of flavors. There are business email compromise (BEC) (*https://oreil.ly/wQQiX*) scams (where the email appears to come from a known legitimate sender) that lead to an overlay or entirely fake site (see Chapters 12 and 13). There is password-identifying malware, or *sniffers*, which customers are persuaded or tricked into downloading onto their device, sometimes delivered through an ad that pops up on a legitimate website. There's straightforward social engineering, in which someone pretending to be from the bank or in IT repair manages to get the victim to hand over their login details. There's the trick in which fraudsters deliver malware through legitimate app stores by creating a version of a legitimate app and repackaging it with malware for users to download unwittingly. These are more common on third-party app stores but can also be found from time to time even on stores such as Google's or Apple's. The malicious apps are taken down when the issue is flagged, but that can take time, and the damage may be done before that happens.

There's also the brute-force approach of *credential stuffing*, in which fraudsters simply try different username- and password-guessing attempts (often based on information exposed in a breach) using an automated process: if the account doesn't exist, the details are trashed, but if the response is "wrong password," phishing is often used to try to get the right password. That's much easier to do when the fraudster already knows the name and username of the victim and which bank they would expect to hear from. Credential stuffing is easier to catch when it's carried out at great speed, because you can simply have the system flag the unusual velocity, but it can be more difficult to detect when a "low and slow" approach is taken in which fraudsters attempt only a few matches per IP address per hour. A specialized bot detection solution such as F5 Shape Security is more likely to catch these kinds of attacks.

Solutions that identify compromised passwords and usernames (either because they have been offered for sale on the dark web or because they've been used in other attacks) can be helpful in protecting accounts that may be affected as well.

With phishing, some options are more passive, collecting and transmitting data; others are more active, sending the customer to a spurious site or otherwise interfering with the login or checkout process.

 We're talking about this in the context of banking, but readers from the ecommerce space will note the similarities between the malware attacks discussed here and the Magecart-style attacks (*https://oreil.ly/EL5Kl*) that have been a problem in ecommerce for some time.

Standalone phishing has become relatively rare thanks to consumers' greater understanding of cybersecurity, which has led to antivirus software use becoming more ubiquitous. Some of this success is due to substantive efforts from banks to educate consumers about this issue, including about possible signs indicating that some sort of compromise might have occurred, such as websites loading very slowly, devices opening apps on their own or closing certain programs repeatedly, and so on.

Malware with Social Engineering

Also relevant in this context is the increasingly widespread adoption of multifactor authentication (MFA), in which login details aren't enough; an extra factor, such as entering a code sent to a device, is required. (See Chapter 13 for more on MFA.) That's an extra hurdle for the fraudster to overcome, making malware insufficient. Unfortunately, social engineering provides workarounds. The most common is for the fraudster to talk the victim through the sign-in process and have them provide the relevant code over the phone or through chat, enabling the fraudster to gain access smoothly. Or the fraudster uses a RAT-style attack, persuading the victim to let them take over control remotely so that they can "fix" whatever the fictitious problem is. The victim is left with the malware on their machine, which the fraudster can then leverage.

The problem is particularly acute when it comes to authorized push payment scams, in which the victim is tricked into transferring the money themselves, usually by a social engineer on the other end of a phone line. The same scam works through the peer-to-peer (P2P) apps that are becoming increasingly popular. It's similar to the victim-assisted fraud scams described in Chapter 9, and as in that case, there's a question of who ought to take responsibility. The attack used the bank's payment platforms and infrastructure, and wasn't prevented by the bank, but it was the real account owner carrying out the transfer.

This type of attack has become so problematic that the UK campaigning group Which? has begun a campaign to try to get banks to cover the losses in these cases (*https://oreil.ly/tB97y*). Successful pressure from Which? and other consumer groups and UK newspapers has already led to the contingent reimbursement model code going into effect in the UK, which strongly suggests that banks reimburse many victims for these socially engineered scams. It's not clear how many of the scams are being reimbursed, since it varies from bank to bank, but Barclays Bank announced in 2021 that it was reimbursing up to 74% of them, a sign of significant movement on this issue.[3] In November 2021, new UK regulation (*https://oreil.ly/iu1ej*) was announced that will mean banks have to publish information about their performance in relation to authorized push payment scams, which is likely to encourage more banks to take this issue seriously and perform better in terms of protecting customers and reimbursing them when appropriate.

As with victim-assisted fraud, it's easy to imagine that this kind of scam would prey solely on elderly or infirm victims, and try to put in place processes to protect the older age group particularly rather than treating it as a widespread issue. In reality, it's far more complicated. According to the Federal Trade Commission, imposter scams were the top fraud type reported by consumers in 2020, and in total, US consumers lost nearly $30 billion from imposter scams.[4] And the individual amounts are often substantial: as noted by Uri Rivner, BioCatch found that 36% of all reported account takeover (ATO) fraud in 2020 came from social engineering scams; 35% of impersonation scams involved amounts greater than $1,000.

The fraudsters involved are skilled at persuasion, great at building rapport quickly, practiced at choosing plausible stories for their audience, and know when to call to add pressure and plausibility. Perfectly normal, intelligent adults, able to deal with tricks and crises in their daily lives, are manipulated by these malicious actors into sending money to an unknown account, or into letting the bad actor access their device and account. Online security specialist Ken Palla suggested to us that anyone interested in better understanding the psychology involved should refer to books by Robert Cialdini, such as *Influence: Science and Practice*.

It's not yet clear which way regulators will choose to handle the growing problem, but it is clear that one way or another, greater clarity and effort to prevent it is required. Until a better solution is found, the fraudsters will keep on coming—and that isn't good for any of the legitimate players in the ecosystem. Fraud prevention

---

3 Karl Flinders, "Barclays First Bank to Publish Online Scam Refund Details" (*https://oreil.ly/C2jyi*), *Computer Weekly*, May 19, 2021.

4 Federal Trade Commision "New Data Shows FTC Received 2.2 Million Fraud Reports from Consumers in 2020" (*https://oreil.ly/0W6AK*), press release, February 4, 2021.

teams need to work with cybersecurity teams to devise creative ways to block not just the malware part of the attack, but also the social engineering aspect.

 Customer education is very important in this context, and in malware more generally. As mentioned, greater awareness of malware and viruses, and the need to install protection and be more careful about downloads, is one factor that has led to the malware threat being reduced—for now. Unfortunately, social engineering attacks the "human factor," which is not amenable to solution via an antivirus program. Education is an important defensive mechanism and worth investing in, even if it seems like a longer-term solution than fraud fighters usually like.

Identification and Mitigation

Attacks that include malware (even if the attack owes its success largely due to social engineering) likely reflect the involvement of the wider online criminal underground. Creating effective malware is a skill that is usually possessed by criminals who specialize in it. The fraudster employing it is rarely the creator. Either they're a cog in a large criminal organization, as discussed in Chapter 2, or they purchased the malware from an online forum or store.

In either case, it's probable that the same malware is hitting many other targets at around the same time. This is yet another example of why it's so crucial for fraud prevention professionals to develop relationships within the network of fraud fighters, especially within the same industry.

Collaboration Is Key

The more fraud fighters keep in touch with one another, across organizations and across the industry, the more likely it is that malware of this type will be flagged sooner rather than later and good tactics against it will be shared before it can become a serious plague. Identification and mitigation are, in this case, partly a matter of collaboration. That's true in other forms of fraud as well, of course, but it's especially pertinent with malware.

There have been trends for banks to try to collaborate with customers as well, such as by getting them to install specific antivirus software on their computers that protects their visits to the bank's website. If done successfully, these can be very helpful. The trouble with these solutions is that they add to the confusion for the consumer; how are they supposed to know when it's really the bank telling them to put something on their computer, or a fraudster mimicking the program to get malware installed in the first place? In recent years, third-party solutions such as IBM's Trusteer Rapport (*https://oreil.ly/bALpJ*) have become more popular.

Banks can use third parties to protect their own sites, both through JavaScript on the site and through downloaded protective programs. In this way, they can ensure that no overlay or similar attack is present, and they can look for instances of mimic sites pretending to be the bank, to which customers are sent by fraudsters looking to steal their information and device profile. Ken Palla noted that this likely won't be a solution forever: when you consider the SolarWinds cyberattack (*https://oreil.ly/iUQup*) or the Kaseya ransomware attack (*https://oreil.ly/oIcdE*) it's clear that poisoning the ecosystem through the software supplier is a viable attack premise. (Indeed, the SolarWinds attackers are still trying (*https://oreil.ly/WXVnF*).)

Bank fraud teams need to consult with their own cybersecurity teams to discuss the third-party attack problem and how to prevent it, ideally before it happens. For business accounts, working with the company's CISO directly rather than with multiple contact points within the organization is often effective. CISOs are, by nature, cautious about communications, attachments, links, and so on, so they're a sensible contact point when it comes to protective planning against schemes of all kinds. Unfortunately, this solution doesn't work for consumers.

Something that has proven to be effective for consumers is making what they're doing clearer, and what the consequences are. For instance, in the case of authorized push payment fraud, a bank might institute a *transaction nudge*—an in-payment warning window that pops up before a transfer that asks for confirmation from the payee— saying something like "You are about to transfer $X to the FraudFunFund account at Main Bank. Is this what you intend to do? Do you want to proceed?" You can tailor these further by adding an extra step, having the initial message be a targeted drop-down window based on the transaction type, asking the customer to select an option. Based on that response, a more tailored message can then pop up.

In those cases, having to take the extra step, or having the real activity brought to their attention, or seeing additional important information, is sometimes enough to wake the consumer up to what they're really about to do and encourage them to think twice and, hopefully, not take the action. If they thought the money was going to something or someone specific and plausible, this message also alerts them to the fact that there might be something suspicious going on, which means they should take time to look further into the story. Small changes of this kind can be surprisingly effective in countering some of the dangers of social engineering, and add only minimal friction to the customer experience.

Anomaly Detection

The collaborative approaches we've mentioned all focus on trying to identify and block malware and its attendant social engineering factors. The other preventive approach is to focus instead on trying to identify the symptoms of malware, and therefore, by extrapolation, the presence of malware. Once you know you're likely the target of an attack, you can work with your cybersecurity team to find out what's going on, and stop it.

To determine whether malware is at work, you'll need to put in place strong anomaly detection. If possible, involve a cyber research team with reverse engineering capabilities to pinpoint the type of vulnerability that was targeted (e.g., according to Check Point (*https://oreil.ly/TJXhy*), the more commonly manipulated protocols are HTTP, SMTP, POP, and IMAP). When analytics and reverse engineering work together, they can often reach a very deep understanding of the attack, as seen, for example, in the research of Gil Mansharov and Alexey Bukhteyev (*https://oreil.ly/8NHwS*) of Check Point in 2019.

However, before the resources of a reverse engineering expert can be prioritized for investigation, analytics is needed to narrow down the search. Devices that have been infected by malware will often act very excessively, generating volumes that should trigger your anomaly thresholds. For example, websites whose traffic suddenly triples or quadruples should be evaluated for potential ad fraud, powered by malware-infected browsers (see the post "DV Takes Down Zombie Websites" (*https://oreil.ly/ffMY0*) from DoubleVerify, and for further discussion see Chapter 23).

If you believe malware-infected devices are active on your system and you're not able to catch them based on the increase of volume alone, consider looking into models that have tackled malware attacks of recent years. Malware, unlike financial fraud, enjoys a vast background of academic and technological research (just do a web search, for example, for "Magecart detection" and you'll find quite a few open source solutions). There's a lot of helpful research out there, and you may benefit from looking into the data science approach to malware challenges. We recommend the following:

- "Malware Classification Using Convolutional Neural Networks—Step by Step Tutorial" (*https://oreil.ly/myrx4*) by Hugo Mallet
- Malware Classification (*https://oreil.ly/8DCq0*) from Papers With Code
- "Unsupervised Anomaly-Based Malware Detection Using Hardware Features" (*https://oreil.ly/sR6Lc*) by Adrian Tang, Simha Sethumadhavan, and Salvatore Stolfo

It's also worth diving deep into your tried-and-tested fraud prevention approaches, notably biometrics, to see whether these can be valuable in detecting not the malware, but the scam itself in action. For example, Uri Rivner, cofounder of anti–money laundering (AML) innovation startup Regutize (and who previously co-founded BioCatch), noted that when it comes to detecting authorized push payment fraud, behavioral biometrics can be extremely valuable, "uncovering hundreds of micro-behavior patterns that users under deep social engineering often demonstrate, such as hesitation, distraction, duress, and signs of being guided. Combined via machine learning, BioCatch found that those signals were able to flag an active authorized push payment scam against the user."

Summary

Malware has been a fixture of fraud and cybercrime in the banking world for many years, and it's almost certain to continue to be a factor, in ever-evolving form, for years to come. Fraud fighters should continue to keep an eye out for it, and alert one another (and their cybersecurity teams) to new types and tricks. Currently, the greatest challenges from malware typically come in conjunction with social engineering attacks—something that is worth investing considerable effort into blocking, since the resultant losses can otherwise be severe. Another area worth investing time and effort into blocking, for the same reason, is identity fraud and synthetic identity fraud, and that's what we discuss in the next chapter.

We are extremely grateful for the assistance of Ken Palla, whose deep knowledge of banking after five decades in the industry, breadth of experience, and willingness to share that with us made researching and writing this chapter immeasurably easier. His assistance with the entire banking section was invaluable, but this chapter in particular benefited from his help.

## CHAPTER 15

Identity Theft and Synthetic Identities

Do you know who I am?
—Elvis Presley[1]

There's an entertaining sketch by British comedians David Mitchell and Robert Webb in which a consumer is called by their bank and informed that money has been taken from their account by a fraudster who has stolen their identity. The consumer is unimpressed by the term *identity theft*, which he identifies (correctly, in this case) as the bank's attempt to get out of reimbursing the money that has been lost. He still has his identity, he points out. It's the money that's gone.

Most banks, of course, are punctilious about reimbursing customers in cases of successful account takeover (ATO), which is what is really being described here. But the confusion reflected in the sketch about what identity theft really is should be addressed. This chapter focuses on identity theft and the closely related phenomenon of *synthetic identities* as those occasions on which fraudsters use a consumer's identifying details to commit an attack whose success impacts a person's identity rather than just their credit card or bank account. There is no universally accepted definition of identity theft or synthetic identity in this context—a problem that the US Federal Reserve is trying to solve. But there is general agreement about its key features, and we draw on these to form a working definition to use in this book.

---

1 Elvis Presley, "Do You Know Who I Am?", written by Bobby Russell, *From Memphis to Vegas/From Vegas to Memphis*, RCA Records, 1969.

How Identity Fraud Works

The most general description of identity theft is something along the lines of that found on the USAGov website: "Identity (ID) theft happens when someone steals your personal information to commit fraud."[2] While true, this isn't specific enough to describe the difference between identity theft and stolen credit card fraud. If a fraudster comes to an ecommerce website and uses stolen data convincingly enough to make a purchase successfully, they're using someone's stolen personal information to commit fraud. The difference, though, is that here—to go back to the Mitchell and Webb sketch—it's the money that's gone. The cardholder will see the fraudulent purchase on their statement, will complain to the store or the bank, and will get their money back. The ecommerce business loses out financially, but that's not an attack on the business's identity either.

With identity theft the damage is far more wide ranging. As the USAGov website goes on to say, "The identity thief may use your information to apply for credit, file taxes, or get medical services. These acts can damage your credit status, and cost you time and money to restore your good name." Since identity thefts can sometimes be drawn out over years, the potential damage is correspondingly large. In a sense, a fraudster uses stolen personal information to expand the presence and liabilities of an identity for their own (the fraudster's) ultimate benefit.

Synthetic identities have the same effect. Here, a fraudster uses a combination of stolen real identity data and fake data to create a new identity that appears to check out but is far enough away from the reality that the victim is unlikely to find out about it—for example, a real Social Security number (SSN), with perhaps a variant on the real name of the SSN's holder, but with a false email, date of birth, and address. The fraudulent activities attached to the synthetic identity can have the same disastrous impact on the owner of the real identity details. If a real SSN is used, for example, the credit reports of the owner of that SSN may reflect not just the real person's credit history, but that of the synthetic identity as well, a mistake that can take considerable effort to untangle.

The same type of attack works against business identities, using tax ID numbers or other identifying factors, and can be equally or even more disastrous for the real business being leveraged. The real business can end up with a terrible credit history or huge debts, and the resultant confusion can take so long to resolve that the business may go bankrupt in the meantime.

Included in this type of crime, usually as a subset of synthetic identities, are identities made up entirely of fictitious details, without any real personal identifiable information (PII) attached to them. These share many of the same characteristics from the

---

2 USAGov, "Identity Theft" (*https://oreil.ly/cn0l3*), last updated December 14, 2021.

fraud identification and prevention perspective, since they are used in much the same way as other synthetic identities, although they are perhaps less frightening for the general population since no real individual will suffer as a result of them. Even photographs, required as part of an identification process, can nowadays be entirely fake (*https://oreil.ly/mXsuM*).

The very first time a fake or synthetic identity is used, the application will likely be unsuccessful, since there will be no record of the identity in a credit bureau or similar institution. However, the application itself (even though rejected) creates an initial file, and after that, the identity can be used successfully, first in small ways and then expanding over time. It may take time to find an institution willing to accept the identity at first, and sometimes the scam kicks off with a high-risk lender of some sort. But since the fraudster is careful to act like an ideal customer at the start, whoever takes the initial risk will apparently see that their faith is well placed; whatever is borrowed will be paid back with relevant interest either on time or before the due date. After that, the identity is well on its way to building up a good-looking credit score.

In general, fraud using stolen, fake, or synthetic identities is carried out in stages over some period of time. Until recently, that time frame generally ranged from six months to two years, but increasingly fraud teams are seeing cases in which an identity has been built up for three or even five years beforehand. It's likely that this has been done to avoid checks that banks had put in place to catch identities within the known six-month to two-year range. It's probable that fraudsters are keeping some in reserve already, starting to build identities now that perhaps may be used in six or seven years, once the three- to five-year range becomes notorious as well. With so much cheap labor in the criminal gig economy context, it's easy to hire fraudsters to keep checking into the account from time to time to make it look legitimate, set up social profiles, and so on. It's perfectly possible for fraudsters to keep outrunning rules of this kind for a long time to come.

Initially, all of the uses to which the identity is put will be small scale—applying for a credit card with a low limit, perhaps. The fraudster builds up trust in the identity over time, with applications for more cards, perhaps at different banks, making sure that bills are paid promptly and the account is never overdrawn. Drawing on her experience in the credit and loans industry, Arielle Caron, group product manager of Risk at Etsy, noted that at this stage, "the accounts actually look more perfect than average—because normal people miss a payment once in a while." But of course, that's not a fraud sign, exactly—you certainly don't want to start being suspicious of your best real customers.

Once the identity is established, slowly the fraudster will work up to larger and larger loans—for a car, perhaps, or even a mortgage on a house. They may take out a business loan for an entirely fictitious business. That business, in turn, with its legitimate-looking credit report, may sign up with merchant processors to obtain credit card terminals and run up charges on fraudulent cards. There's also *piggybacking* to take into account, in which synthetic identities can be made to support one another in a sort of fake identity network: a new identity could be added as an authorized user to the account belonging to an established one that already has good credit, speeding up the validation process for the new identity. Similarly, identities can be added to a fake business account. Piggybacking also can occur on real accounts belonging to real people who are paid to add the new user. All in all, identity fraud of the kind we're describing here has the potential for theft at an impressive scale, especially when carried out by sophisticated fraud rings or organized crime groups.

Once the fraudster feels the identity has nearly run its course and been maxed out in terms of value, it will usually be put to use in a flurry of activity; all the cards will be used to their maximum levels, which may be quite high at this point after perhaps as many as five years of legitimate-looking behavior. Fast monetization purchases may ensue for items such as gift cards and luxury goods, which can be resold easily. Some fraudsters work with collusive merchants who ring up fictitious purchases in exchange for a cut.

Once the fraudster has gotten all they can reasonably expect to get out of the identity, the identity "busts out" and the fraudster defaults on all its responsibilities. In some cases, they manage to go a second round with the same identity, claiming identity theft after the initial bust-out and then drawing on the lines of credit one more time before giving up on the identity. The cost can be heavy, particularly when you consider how repeatable this form of fraud is; in one case, fraudsters racked up losses for banks of $200 million from 7,000 synthetic identities and 25,000 credit cards, and some experts thought the actual amount was closer to $1 billion—but it was hard to calculate confidently because of the scale and complexity of the scam.[3]

It's also important to bear in mind the often deeply personal nature of this kind of fraud. Maya Har-Noy, a fintech veteran and currently vice president of Financial Strategy at Nuvei, recalled that while she was leading online rent payment and rental communications platform Rentigo in 2014 and 2015 (before it was acquired by Qira), some consumers reported they had made payments for rentals to a scammer, who had stolen the identities of the true owners. The full-blown identity theft was only revealed when the homeowners discovered someone was trying to rent their home—a shocking and emotional experience. Imagine the confusion of having someone knock on your door and introduce themselves as the people who are here to rent your place, followed by the fear surrounding the discovery that your identity has

---

3 US Attorney's Office, District of New Jersey, "Eighteen People Charged In International, $200 Million Credit Card Fraud Scam" (*https://oreil.ly/4S3QU*), press release, February 5, 2013.

been compromised and that there are bank accounts under your name, with all of the devastating risk it represents to your credit score. There's also the loss to the potential renters, who can be scammed out of thousands (*https://oreil.ly/F3pAn*)—often money they can't afford to lose. Businesses need to prevent successful identity theft because it matters—and because their customers may never forgive them if they fail.

Identity Theft and Data Breaches

Similar to the discussion of ATO in Chapter 13, identity theft and synthetic identities are fueled by the massive data breaches of recent years, and by the wealth of data about individuals and businesses now available freely online through social media sites, newspaper articles, and other places. Within the context of identity theft and synthetic identity, it is perhaps worth calling out the data breaches of Experian and Equifax, agencies whose main role is to collect precisely the kind of data used to check identities—or, on the flip side, to impersonate them.

The Equifax breach exposed the personal information of 147 million people in 2017. An attack on an Experian subsidiary in 2014 exposed the SSNs of 200 million Americans, and a further Experian breach in 2015 exposed the data of around 15 million customers. Then, in 2020, another Experian breach exposed the data of 24 million South Africans, while a vulnerability in the company's API in 2021 apparently leaked the credit scores of nearly every American who had one at the time. In 2022, a criminal was found directly abusing access to TransUnion's TLO service. We mention these breaches to illustrate clearly the extent of the challenge facing attempts to prevent identity theft and the creation and exploitation of synthetic identities.

Banks and financial institutions rely on personal, sensitive, private information to validate identities. This data is used precisely because it should tie an identity to an individual with accuracy and reliability. But because this information is so precious, it is of great interest to fraudsters and other criminals—and so, it's always under attack. So much has been stolen or otherwise exposed by now that fraudsters are spoiled with choices when it comes to identity theft.

While this form of fraud is a problem internationally, it is a challenge in the United States especially, partly due to the prevalence of static SSNs, which people generally keep for their whole lives, as a means of identification, and which have been popular targets of breaches. The move to randomization (*https://oreil.ly/zHNI6*) rather than geographically based SSNs also made it more difficult to easily check whether an SSN matched a person's geographical origins.

Identity fraud, whether true-name or synthetic, is a particularly pernicious form of fraud for a number of reasons. The amounts lost can be significant, the industries roped into the fraud can be wide ranging (banks and other financial institutions, medical institutions or insurance companies, retail stores, etc.), and real people can be seriously impacted.

Moreover, vulnerable individuals, particularly children and the elderly, are disproportionately likely to be affected. Stealing a child's identity, or using some of their identifying information as part of a synthetic identity, is ideal for fraudsters because it's so unlikely that anyone will notice what's going on. An adult might run a credit report on their own details out of sensible prudence or in preparation for activity such as applying for a mortgage, and notice that something was wrong. It's far less likely that the same check would be run for a child, and it's also relatively unlikely to be run for an elderly person.

Since identity fraud has the potential to pay off so handsomely, fraudsters engaging in this form of fraud can afford to invest both effort and time in their schemes. And the better it pays off, the more they can invest next time, making the identities even more convincing or expanding the scale of their operation. Within the context of identity fraud, fraudsters can even afford to invest time in thinking ahead about what barriers might be put in their way and work out ways to circumvent them in advance. For example, if banks are likely to use third-party data brokers to corroborate the existence of the data being used to set up a new account, a fraudster can put work into establishing the identity beforehand with those data brokers or with the sources they draw from so that the corroboration will exist. If social media presence is a sign of a real identity, they can create those in advance as well.

Some of the traditional methods that fraud prevention teams rely on to catch other types of fraud won't avail us here, since all the fraudster needs to do is use a clean device and IP to appear beyond reproach. The other signals fraud teams look for to indicate that fraud might be occurring won't be there, because until the identity busts out (or arguably just before), it looks squeaky clean. Behavioral data won't help, because even if someone's identity is being hijacked, their account is not; the behavior on the account will be consistently that of the fraudster, and that behavior will carefully mimic the most innocent of customers—until it's too late.

All things considered, it's easy to understand why the excellent white paper published by the Federal Reserve in July 2019 described this kind of fraud as "the fastest growing type of financial crime in the United States."[4]

Identification and Mitigation

Identity theft and synthetic identities are notoriously difficult to identify. One study suggested that 85% to 95% of applicants identified as potential synthetic identities are not flagged by traditional fraud models.[5] The models that have been trained to catch

---

4 Federal Reserve Banks, *Synthetic Identity Fraud in the US Payment System* (*https://oreil.ly/fLNCS*), July 2019.

short-term fraud (such as the kind that uses a stolen credit card successfully) struggle to identify these kinds of fraud, which are carried out patiently over a far longer period of time with actions that are, for most of that time, almost indistinguishable from legitimate behavior.

There are two key places where identity fraud of this kind can be uncovered before it brings harm to the business: at onboarding, and during the monthly review of accounts that financial institutions often engage in to analyze accounts for a variety of reasons. Onboarding is, of course, preferable, because it stops the problem right at the start, before a false, synthetic, or stolen identity can be misused and add to confusion and risk for the business.

Identifying this kind of fraud often requires considerable research. You don't have any customer activity to draw on at this point, so you're working off the data they're giving you (including data you can gather, such as IP and device fingerprinting). The challenge, of course, is that much of the data that can be checked will be real: names, SSNs, tax IDs, and so on. Credit reports, as discussed, can't be relied on either. So, what's needed here is some digging.

Does the profile of the customer presented through the onboarding process match that shown on a social media profile? Does that profile have history? Is there any corroborating data you can find from property records for relevant demographics? Does that tax ID really belong to that business? Has the business been established for a length of time? In general, the more sources you can bring to bear on this problem, the better, because you're looking for consistency, and consistency over time.

Behavioral data can be particularly useful in this context; fraudsters who get sloppy and resort to copying and pasting details that any normal person would type by default are worth investigating. (Bear in mind that you need to be able to distinguish between copy/paste and password managers, since many legitimate individuals do use the latter, particularly for sensitive accounts such as a bank account.) Similarly with the speed of typing, if an SSN is being entered with laborious care, that's suspicious—most real customers type theirs very quickly, being so familiar with it in so many contexts. All of these kinds of factors can be valuable flags to highlight dubious accounts.

The more you can automate this process, the better, because putting every application through this process manually is clearly impossible. Collaborative efforts, such as consortiums, may be helpful here. As discussed in Chapter 4, some collaborative networks, including Identiq's, now use privacy-enhancing technologies (PETs), meaning organizations can leverage one another's data and trust in customers without needing

---

5 ID Analytics, "Slipping Through the Cracks: How Synthetic Identities Are Beating Your Defenses" (*https://oreil.ly/VKGVL*) (2019), cited in *Synthetic Identity Fraud in the US Payment System*.

to share or exchange any personal customer data or sensitive business information. This consensus effect may have valuable uses, enabling financial institutions to filter applications automatically for identity theft and synthetic fraud. The privacy aspect of the providerless trend may also help reduce the future dangers of large centralized data breaches like those described earlier.

Nonetheless, it's also important to include manual review in the process, for when potential red flags appear and for some random sampling. Sometimes a creative approach to where to look next, or which dots to try to join, is what's needed. Naturally these insights, when repeatable, can sometimes later be included in the automated system.

It's also worth having regular sessions to brainstorm about creative data sources you can use to validate identities as part of this process. Because the potential payoff is considerable, fraudsters are willing to invest more than a modicum of time and effort in establishing these identities and making their application look convincing. The more reputable data sources you're drawing from, the less likely it is that they've covered them all.

Linking

In terms of protection divorced from specific points in time (such as the onboarding event or monthly reviews), this is an area where linking is once again extremely valuable. Often, criminals who excel at identity theft or synthetic identity fraud specialize particularly in linking. They may have many schemes slowly maturing at the same time, each one at a slightly different stage. Although they will typically attack multiple financial institutions, they will often have an affinity for one, or a few, in particular—they'll be familiar with the processes, which makes it easier and faster for them to set up and develop the necessary accounts, and they may have identified specific vulnerabilities that they then leverage over and over again.

All of this means it's especially worth looking for connections between accounts that otherwise seem to be unrelated. Perhaps they use the same IP or device. Perhaps they consistently make payments on the same day of the month, at similar times, to similar stores. (Make sure you're not flagging monthly bills such as utilities, which will give you false positives in this context.) You want to look for any behaviors or data points that demonstrate the same person, or ring, is running the accounts, according to a set schedule rather than the ebb and flow of normal life.

Collaboration

The Federal Reserve notes: "It is imperative that payments industry stakeholders work together to keep up with the evolving threat posed by synthetic identity fraud, which includes anticipating future fraud approaches." The same, surely, is true of the other kinds of identity theft discussed in this chapter.

"Synthetic identity fraud is not a problem that any organization or industry can tackle independently, given its far-reaching effects on the US financial system, healthcare industry, government entities and consumers," the Fed's report says. "Industry collaboration can be a key step toward identifying trends and developing strategies to reduce specific fraud vulnerabilities."[6]

The sheer amount of time and effort that fraudsters are willing and able to invest into these sorts of identity fraud schemes means catching them is especially challenging if a fraud team is working solo. The more that diverse financial organizations and elements of the payments ecosystem can work together to combat identity fraud, the more likely it is that they'll be able to catch frauds before they cause loss or they damage the financial reputation of a real individual.

The Federal Reserve is interested in establishing ways for organizations to work together that, if successful, could possibly act as a model for other countries as well. More contained efforts, such as collaboration between banks specifically, may also be worth exploring. Here again you can see the power of relationships across institutions and even countries. PET and the providerless solutions that leverage it, as mentioned in Chapter 4, may also be a relevant factor in this context, offering interesting possibilities for banks to leverage one another's data without sharing it.

One way or another—given the size of the potential payoff for fraudsters, and the difficulty of identifying these sorts of attacks—it seems likely that collaborative efforts will be required to make it no longer worth fraudsters' time to invest in such attacks. In the meantime, effective firefighting methods for identification and mitigation remain essential.

Cross-sector fraud checks and cross-organizational data sharing: Cifas, SIRA, and credit bureaus

When the Federal Reserve speaks of stronger collaboration between organizations in general and financial institutes in particular, it may be drawing inspiration from the more regulated old continent. The UK leads the game of fraud data sharing, mainly thanks to several national collaborative organizations that have been active for several decades.

Cifas (*https://www.cifas.org.uk*) is a not-for-profit fraud prevention membership organization that was founded in the 1980s (!) to protect against credit-related fraud. Cifas markers are adverse judgments through which one institution, be it a bank, loan company, or an insurer, for example, can warn another about risks associated with a potential customer. The most common filing to the database by members are instances of identity fraud. The most common filing against an individual subject is application fraud or misuse of a facility. As shown in Figure 15-1, it can be helpful to

---

6 *Synthetic Identity Fraud in the US Payment System.*

see different types of fraud checks on a single queue, for cases when a certain stolen or synthetic identity is being used simultaneously by attackers in multiple verticals.

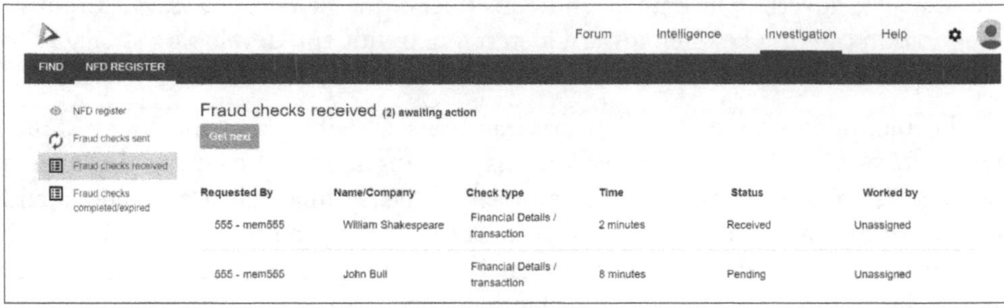

Figure 15-1. Example of a digital fraud check (the Cifas messaging service between members)

Reports of impersonation are filed by lenders for the protection of the identity theft victims. A "Victim of Impersonation" marker will remain visible on the victim's report for 13 months from the date of entry. Of course, most people end up on Cifas records due to the regrettably popular friendly fraud, or first-party fraud. ATO, policy abuse, mortgage and motor fraud, application fraud (such as submitting falsified documents), insurance claims fraud, and even insider employee fraud are neatly separated and stored by Cifas, for up to six years.

Victims can find out about the status of their Cifas records by making a Data Subject Access Request (Data SAR (*https://oreil.ly/QUDty*)). SARs are available to individuals across the EU and UK, as mandated by the General Data Protection Regulation (GDPR (*https://oreil.ly/2ijzn*)).

Many fraud-fighting professionals may be used to seeing GDPR laws as an albatross around their necks, but when it comes to data collaboration it does seem that the United States has something to learn from the progress made by the EU and UK in being able to store and access data (not to mention open banking (*https://oreil.ly/ AwzfV*)). A nice demonstration of the superiority of the UK in Data SARs was carried out by the *New York Times*, checking how much of your personal data can you get (*https://oreil.ly/r1mKg*) in London versus Manhattan. The New York–based reporter was barely able to retain any of her data in this experiment, while the Londoner promptly received all records.

With this level of service, it's no wonder that Cifas also caters to private consumers, offering "Protective Registration" as a paid-for service that individuals can request when they suspect they have been the victim of identity fraud. Consumers actually trust Cifas to protect them from the implications of identity theft after they have given away personal data. If this service goes global, it could be a breakthrough.

When we spoke with Cifas CEO, Mike Haley, his eyes gleamed as he envisioned Cifas activities going global. With 30 years of experience in tackling and preventing fraud across the public, private, and not-for-profit sectors, Mike has led investigative teams in the NHS, Ministry of Defence, Office of Fair Trading, HM Revenue & Customs, and Solicitors Regulation Authority for the UK. He also worked at the National Fraud Authority directing cross-sector fraud prevention strategies, before joining Cifas in 2015. Naturally, he's an advocate for collaboration between sectors.

As Mike told us:

> We already have sister organizations in South Africa and Australia. We're also working to help start operations in Ireland and the Netherlands, where they have a strong chance of getting a grasp on fraud since there aren't that many banks, and if you get four or five of them to collaborate, you have a great start. Singapore also stepped ahead of the game with their announcement of the Cosmic data and information-sharing platform (*https://oreil.ly/eziPa*), which is naturally motivated by their money laundering issues. The US is somewhat behind, and indeed, their loss rates are estimated at about 14% compared to 4% in the UK. If I had to guess, I'd say that within 25 years we'll reach 50 countries who are able to share data efficiently and that will bring us to a completely new world. Fraud fighters will no longer settle for saying "Oh, the offender is in Ukraine, so there's nothing we can do from here."

> Technology is no longer holding us back from reaching effective, real-time data sharing. The popularity of the Cifas fraud check service can attest to this fact. Moreover, data protection laws have matured significantly in many countries over the last few years. Now, it's up to the political climate to shift in the right direction. We're already very close to having a significant fraud discussion in the G7. Once global politics comes to the realization that few rob banks with guns and balaclavas anymore, and that today's crime epidemic is really a digital fraud epidemic, we'll be seeing the collaboration that is already happening on municipal/national levels reaching a global scale.

Cifas may be leading the crusade and doing its best to link between attacks in different verticals (as demonstrated in Figures 15-2 and 15-3), but it is not alone. Systematic integrity risk analysis (SIRA) databases exist in several countries across the Atlantic (to cite the UK again, see SIRA - Digital Marketplace (*https://oreil.ly/goBaY*)), and most credit bureaus (*https://oreil.ly/DipBI*), notably Experian, Equifax, and TransUnion, aim to offer some coverage against identity theft. Fraud data and insight sharing communities continue to flourish wherever fraud exists…meaning everywhere.

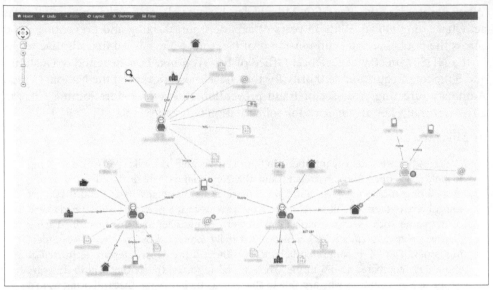

Figure 15-2. Cifas visualization showing how an identity may be linked to several cases of mortgage fraud, internal employee fraud, and insurance fraud

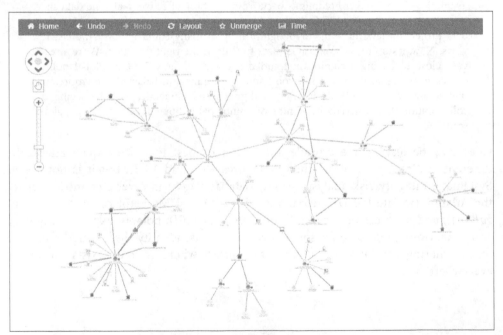

Figure 15-3. Cifas visualization showing how identity assets (such as email, mobile phone number, etc.) can be shared between identities

It certainly seems that the NGO sector of the UK and EU is more established in the field of fraud prevention, with Cifas (and also National Hunter (*https://www.nhunter.co.uk*)) as market leaders, but that doesn't mean the US private sector can't catch up and come up with a one-stop shop shared database for identity theft prevention. Many private sector products cater to the US market in hopes of becoming the one and only platform for case linking (e.g., i2 Platform (*https://i2group.com*) by IBM), but with fierce competition among vendors, it's hard to spot a single source of truth. Perhaps government-backed initiatives such as the Joint Fraud Taskforce (*https://oreil.ly/0HixB*) in the UK, the Financial Fraud Enforcement Task Force (FFETF) (*https://oreil.ly/e1hoH*) in the United States, and InterPol's financial crime units (*https://oreil.ly/MFAMt*) will gradually push toward a unified front, making fraud significantly more challenging for criminals.

Back to Mike Haley's vision, he proudly noted:

> Cifas data already covers 14 different sectors including cryptocurrency and gambling. Organizations today know that fraudsters will not target just one bank, nor will they target just the banking sector. Syndicated data sharing is one of the most important tools for fighting fraudsters who use a single stolen ID to defraud dozens of fintech operations and ecommerce retailers. More and more organizations are realizing that several levels of sharing are needed to keep fraud at bay.

Mike provided, as a striking example, the case of fraud attacks on the 2020 Bounce Back Loan scheme in the UK (*https://oreil.ly/p3a3t*) and its abuse by fraud:

> Fraudsters quickly learned that the 50,000 pounds, which the government had made available to aid businesses during the pandemic, were being administered by 43 lender operations and that you could simply apply for 43 different loans. There was nothing to prevent this excessive double-dipping. Cifas fraud checks immediately became imperative for fighting the types of fraud attacks that leaped during this year: imperso-nation of businesses, account takeovers of businesses, and identity theft of individuals for the purpose of setting up synthetic business accounts. In so many cases, Cifas cross-sector data was able to show that a person was applying several times for a loan, then collecting the illicitly gained funds to put a downpayment on a house, or a Porsche.

Speaking of Porsches, Mike explained that Cifas data is extensive enough to assist in car insurance fraud, a topic that links to ID theft but is beyond the scope of this book:

> Repeating-offender data is often found in cases of ghost brokers (*https://oreil.ly/79Cr6*). These are fraudsters who pretend to be a genuine insurance broker in order to sell fraudulent car insurance. Young drivers sometimes fall for these schemes, in hopes of getting a cheaper quote on their insurance. We're seeing more insurers hitting our fraud checks, mostly when a claim is made, but gradually even when the insurance policy is purchased. There have been incidents of organized crime organizations hiring a bus and crashing into vehicles in order to file whiplash claims for all the bus passengers. Insurers need to be able to not only deny the exaggerated claim, but also turn down this type of bad business in advance.

With fraud schemes becoming more organized, calculated, and abusive, we know of cases where organized crime employees were being placed in banks so that they'll be able to conduct insider fraud many months later. These schemes take forever to prosecute, so in the meantime, fraudster identity data must be shared, via the Cifas Insider Threat DataBase, so that the offender cannot strike again. Cifas makes data available to keep us all safer from fraud.

Last but not least: fraud analysts everywhere, please bear in mind that when a certain piece of identity appears on a fraud-check database, it could still mean you are looking at a true transaction attempt of the innocent victim. If Bob's phone number appears on five mortgage applications this month, Bob might be either the fraudster or the victim. You'll still need to put the data in context in order to make the right decision (or alternatively, choose to decline Bob's application in order to avoid the risk; we won't judge).

Summary

This chapter discussed the complexities of identity theft, synthetic identities, and fake identities. We explored why it can be worthwhile for fraudsters to invest considerable time and effort in developing these elaborate attacks against the financial ecosystem and making the identities (or the use of these identities) look legitimate, and we discussed methods that can be used to identify and prevent these attacks. All of this is worth bearing in mind as we move to the topic of the next chapter: credit and lending.

## CHAPTER 16

Credit and Lending Fraud

Pay me my money down, pay me or go to jail...
—Bruce Springsteen[1]

Lending fraud attracts a slightly different category of fraudsters, compared to the previous genres discussed. The appeal of hard cash at the end of the operation speaks to a population that is less tech savvy than crypto fraudsters, while the relative simplicity means avoiding the logistical complexities connected to shipping scheme cons.

Moreover, the concept of loans will attract people who do not necessarily see themselves as criminals (some of them believe they'll repay the loan, even if they take it under false pretenses). They will often see themselves as victims of the traditional banking system, and for some of them this will be the first and only fraudulent act they will ever perform. Unfortunately, that doesn't make the loss to the bank or fintech any less real, the crime any more legitimate, or the fraudster in question easier to spot.

The MO we're considering in this chapter is of a fraudster who applies for a loan without any intention of ever repaying it, and who does so repeatedly and systematically, through multiple identities. It is this kind of fraud that can result in dangerously mounting losses because, if not prevented, it is so repeatable.

---

1 "Pay Me My Money Down," traditional work song, covered by Bruce Springsteen, track 11 on *We Shall Overcome: The Seeger Sessions*, Columbia, 2006.

Nonprofessional Fraudsters Engaging in Credit and Lending Fraud

There are cases in which individuals in desperate situations will use their own identities and legitimate information to rack up loans (the more, the merrier) either to try to stave off disaster (such as the probable and impending closure of a treasured family business) or in preparation for skipping the country. These cases have a lot in common with friendly fraud, covered in Chapter 10, and are often particularly difficult to spot, though banks do and should look for trends that can indicate that such behavior may be contemplated.

This chapter doesn't focus on those situations, because the qualities and techniques that accompany professional fraud are generally lacking, and all in all it's a different sort of problem. If you look at defaulting on loans, as a pattern, businesses can usually recover some of the lost funds—an average of 30%, or higher in some cases. But with professional fraud, where there's never any intent to return the funds, it's a loss of 100%—or sometimes more, when you take into account loan origination costs sometimes paid as processing fees, fees to partners, and so on.

We don't cover fraud within the peer-to-peer (P2P) lending ecosystem that is carried out through collusion; this form of collusive fraud is very similar to the collusion discussed in Chapter 17, which covers marketplace collusion, so anyone looking for insights into that form of fraud should turn to that chapter.

We'll just mention here the phenomenon of opportunistic actors, such as an accountant who sees an opportunity to set up an extra loan on a client's behalf, and pocket the results. Trusted parties like CPAs have a lot of options for fraud open to them if they start looking for them, though fortunately this is a fairly rare occurrence. In these cases, it's extremely difficult to catch the first occurrence, but smart linking setups should alert the system if it starts to become a pattern. In these cases, the fraudster in question isn't a professional, so it's likely they'll leave a trail of breadcrumbs unintentionally by reusing accounts or other details too often.

Professional Fraudsters and Credit and Lending Fraud

Professional fraudsters attacking lending will often fit the profile of the product-savvy fraudster we discussed in Chapter 2. They will be well versed in your vetting procedures and they will plan their attack on your system for months, often including the setup of a very convincing online business facade.

The fact that synthetic identities are often used, especially those of businesses, makes it seem like lending fraud is a victimless crime. In reality, of course, there's no such thing. Even if they didn't use a stolen identity and didn't tarnish anyone's credit score—and both of these things often are part of the fallout of this sort of scheme—

the fraudsters would still be taking away the money that should've gone to others in need of a lifeline. Even in cases such as the stimulus fraud that ran rampant during the COVID-19 pandemic (*https://oreil.ly/mzlF1*), stealing money from the government is in fact stealing from the taxpayer, who ends up having to pay for the loss in the long run.

When a fraudster needs a convincing cloak of legitimacy in order to get approved for credit, here are their options:

Synthetic identity or stolen identity attack
> Buy it on the dark web or put it together yourself if you have the time. Business identities are preferable, and you'll see a variety of low-cost email domains (it's even easier to keep their Whois data anonymous now, with General Data Protection Regulation [GDPR]). Smarter fraudsters will match the online identity to bookkeeping activity (hacked or manufactured) and even Whitepages or Google Maps records. More on synthetic, fake, and stolen identities can be found in Chapter 15.

Customer extortion
> This is where real consumers or businesses are co-opted so that the fraudster can use their details, effectively making the customer a pawn in the scheme. This method is generally carried out in areas where organized crime is common and a factor in daily life. In many ways, this is similar to the concept of account handover, in which a fraudster purchases a previously legitimate account to trade on its good reputation, but the waters are muddier here because the account often continues to belong to the real owner, who may continue using it for ordinary purposes. This can make the fraud harder to spot, as there won't be a significant change of activity.

Social engineering
> Here, the bad actor pretends to be a tax agent, a potential customer, or some other plausible character. As Gil Rosenthal, risk management consultant and former vice president vice president of Risk Operations at Bluevine, put it: "The common thread is creating an environment of trust with the actual business owner that allows the fraudster to obtain their business and personal information. The criminal might even be able to go back to them for additional pieces of data or documentation if needed."

There is another flavor of social engineering that doesn't require the same level of trust and is similar to the triangulation scheme discussed in Chapter 7. Here, the fraudster creates a site or app that purports to help people to apply for a loan. There may even be a full onboarding and "vetting" flow to make it look convincing. The fraudster will use all of that information to apply for the loan—and if the application is accepted, the loan will be sent to the fraudster's bank account, not the real applicant's. Sometimes the fraudster sets up the process so that their bank account is substituted automatically at the last millisecond before the application is sent. It's more effort to set up that way, but once the scam is running, it barely requires any effort from the fraudster. The victim will be told they were rejected.

Social engineering fraud, unfortunately, is particularly common in the context of schemes, often governmental or charitable schemes, which are set up in order to benefit a disadvantaged group that needs a boost at a particular time. Writing this chapter made Gilit think of her grandmother, who, after the Second World War, spent many hours at her typewriter helping survivors of the Holocaust apply for funds from Germany. She did this out of the kindness of her heart, but you can bet there were others out there working the system as a scam, just as we've described. The same was true during the COVID-19 pandemic, with the stimulus programs; there were community organizations that did all they could to help those who needed assistance get loans to keep their businesses afloat. Unfortunately, it can be very difficult to tell the difference between these setups and fraudsters who are planning to funnel the funds into their own accounts.

Buy Now Pay Later Fraud

Buy Now Pay Later (BNPL) purchases don't really fit into the model we've described here. Although lending is technically involved—if you're effectively giving the customer credit by allowing them to pay later rather than at the point of purchase, you're lending them the money and expecting them to pay it back later—the amounts involved are far smaller, and the process of "requesting the loan" is simply pressing a button at checkout. BNPL payment risks, which are sometimes borne by the BNPL provider, if one is being used, are generally assessed for risk in much the same way any other online transaction is assessed. The same rules or algorithms analyze the details of the user and the purchase to decide whether the transaction should be accepted. Cases in which the customer does not pay for the BNPL purchases are more likely to be akin to friendly fraud than to malicious actors. However, the fact that there is some form of credit assessment involved means the identity theft will likely be somewhat more sophisticated than an average transaction, because the fraudster will know more scrutiny is likely to be involved.

BNPL might be used as a step in many of the types of fraud we've already discussed, such as stolen credit card fraud, account takeover (ATO), and synthetic identity theft. Fraudsters, of course, don't think in terms of the categories that make analysis easier for us, and for them BNPL is just another form of payment they can exploit. Fraud fighters, trained to be suspicious, are not likely to let the charm of a new type of payment stop them from analyzing transactions for all these known kinds of fraud. One thing that is worth noting is that, in contrast to the other kinds of lending discussed in this chapter, customers looking to use BNPL are not amenable to identity checks and delays. Part of the advantage of BNPL is that it's very easy, and fast. The emphasis on avoiding friction is even more important with BNPL purchases than others, though some judicious friction may still be warranted in particularly high-risk transactions. In general, though, identity validation behind the scenes is preferable as much as possible, though since modern fraud teams are already very sensitive to friction and the need to avoid it, this won't represent a particularly new way of doing things.

That said, there is a form of fraud that does leverage the BNPL model: when fraudsters make a small initial purchase or two using BNPL, and then sometime later use the same account to make a higher-dollar purchase, relying on the good reputation of the account and its past purchase(s) to help ease this more expensive transaction through. Except this one, of course, is using a stolen credit card. In some cases, the initial BNPL purchases are never paid for either—but that knowledge comes too late to prevent the larger purchase. In other cases, the initial purchases are actually paid for, generally with a prepaid card, to prepare the ground for a high-value purchase later on. In these cases, the initial purchases may be spaced out for some time before the main theft, building up a profile that looks very reputable. As Karisse Hendrick, founder and principal consultant at Chargelytics Consulting, put it, in this MO, BNPL is being used as a "side door" for fraud. Fraudsters are always looking for new opportunities, but at least in this case, once merchants are aware of it, it should be easy to prevent using normal screening mechanisms.

Drawing on his experiences at PayPal, Identiq vice president of Product Uri Arad said that with BNPL:

> Merchants also need to prepare themselves for the fact that, depending on implementation, the fraud team might lose the input from the issuer, as the card is not charged at the time of payment. Moreover, BNPL credit is not recorded anywhere—not by the bureau, and not by the card issuer—meaning that this type of short-term credit is hard to track and may lead to bust-out scenarios which are hard to detect. It is critical that merchants do not take the credit risk on themselves without understanding it properly. Merchants should also invest extra effort in establishing users' identities, and make sure to track and limit the total credit risk per user and the total exposure for the company.

Identification and Mitigation

Certainly, banks and fintechs that engage in considerable lending activity need to automate a lot of the checks and data enrichment involved in assessing loans for fraud. It wouldn't be practical to do anything else, and machine learning also has a significant role to play in spotting crucial patterns. Most organizations are already using machine learning in this way, or they're moving in that direction, especially the largest ones. One study found that 63% of banks use AI to aid in credit decisions, 56% to help in credit/risk underwriting, and another 56% to identify solutions to potential credit problems.[2] However, the data enrichment, linking, machine learning, and other techniques involved are not distinctively different from those discussed elsewhere in this book, such as in Chapters 6, 7, 9, 10, and 15, and so we will not spend time here outlining specific details of how to do this. Similarly, forged document identification is crucial, but the process is the same as the process discussed in Chapters 12 and 13.

What is distinctive about preventing lending fraud is the emphasis on manual review, which makes sense since investing in manual review to prevent credit and lending fraud is easily justifiable given both the high yield of individual legitimate loans and high losses of individual fraud cases. Robust manual review flows can be exceptionally valuable for cases in which the automated system, be it rules or machine learning or both, has flagged an application for further investigation. (Random sampling is always a good research idea to make sure the automated system is doing its job and to keep on top of developing trends in legitimate as well as fraudulent customer behavior.) This is particularly true given that an emphasis on very smooth onboarding experiences, such as that demonstrated by fintechs like Stripe, Payoneer, and PayPal, can mean that easy onboarding leads to blanket restrictions later on, such as placing holds on a business's balance if the account shows warning signs after onboarding.

Normally, fraud teams go to great lengths to avoid adding friction into the customer experience, so we would not ordinarily advocate steps as standard that by definition are disruptive to a seamless experience. Lending, though, with the exception of BNPL and similar products, can be held to different standards. Customers *expect* to experience some level of friction where a loan is involved; they're asking the bank to give them money, after all. It's only reasonable that checks would be involved. And customers expect a delay. It's very rare to have a loan application instantly approved. Customers expect it to be considered, which takes time. As long as the delay is not too great, it won't conflict with customer expectations because, unusually, in this scenario the expectation is not for a real-time one-click experience. In addition, since it usually involves higher amounts and fewer customers, the value of an accurate decision increases in comparison to the timing and friction costs.

So, phone calls to the customer are not only a good idea, but an obvious and recommended element, to further investigate, check, or question the information you've uncovered from all of the open source and paid data enrichment services used to flesh out the picture of the individual and their financial situation.

In the same way, organizations can push for proof of legitimate activity—not just tax forms, which are regrettably easy to falsify, but something more substantial. Gil Rosenthal noted that during the stimulus loan scams:

---

2 PYMNTS, "Applying AI To Improve Bank Credit Risk" (*https://oreil.ly/FI3i9*), May 3, 2021.

The ease of submitting and being accepted for the loans, and the amount of money potentially on the table, encouraged people to get creative about proving that they had a business which needed a loan...even if it hadn't really existed until thirty seconds ago. There were a number of accounting programs which saw people setting up "businesses" and creating activity, even moving money around from one place to another, so as to set up a legitimate-looking business profile.

Those individuals who saw success with this kind of fakery will often share the knowledge, and so this sort of trick is worth looking for going forward. Think about what would really be convincing as proof of a legitimate existence and activity, and ask for a range of those convincing proofs. You might consider open banking connections to bank accounts that match the identity and show a significant level of activity and age (using a vendor such as Plaid) or perhaps look at assessing similar connections to payroll processors showing individuals receiving payroll over time (using a vendor such as Argyle).

Being able to identify fake customers won't assist you in cases of customers coming from areas where organized crime can threaten people into cooperating, but in those cases typically a local factor is involved, and though you may not catch it the first time, you can and should identify it if it becomes a pattern. Looking for additional signals of potential concern in loan applications coming from high-risk areas can help your organization stay ahead of these attacks and identify them quickly. Making sure to check whether the request for the loan is coming from a user who matches the usual behavioral and biometrics pattern (as discussed in Chapter 13) of the original user will help catch some of these cases. But unfortunately, there are also occasions when the real owners of the account are forced to cooperate to the extent of applying for the loan themselves.

Another thing to note about credit and lending fraudsters is that, as Rosenthal put it, "They're a specialized group. Not that many fraudsters have the patience to invest enough to succeed at this kind of fraud, but for some, the potential payoff is so great that they go for it. Once they've gotten used to what's involved, they'll often try again and again." So, deep research into the patterns of habitual fraudsters in this area is worthwhile; any links you can draw between past cases of fraud and new applications are worth investigating. It might just be the magic link you need to prevent fraud.

In general in this book, we've been careful to note the limitations of badlists or decline lists. They're usually a good tool in the fraud prevention arsenal, but as the saying goes, they're most effective at catching last month's fraudsters, which is sometimes valuable and other times less so. Stopping credit and lending fraud is a context in which they are more valuable. The difference here is the time factor, and it's twofold. First, loans typically play out over a long time, and fraudsters who make a habit of applying for fraudulent loans will often take small loans first to build up the legitimacy of the account. This may occur over a number of different institutions, using the same identity. This builds up a credit report, which can show this activity—

and which can be suspicious, even where the loans are being paid back. Also, in cases where someone is applying for a loan in multiple places, and planning on loan stacking but doesn't want the institutions involved to know what's happening, they'll have to throw all the applications in at the same time. The more closely financial institutions collaborate, the easier it is for them to see when this sort of game is being played. Privacy-enhancing technologies (PETs), and the providerless systems they enable, as mentioned in Chapter 4, may make this kind of collaboration easier and more common in the future.

In the context of credit and lending fraud, badlists need to be maintained for both individual identity parameters and business identifiers. It's not enough to stay vigilant for the next time an offender tries to make their second or third lending attempt; you must stay alert to spot the same offender if they return under the cloak of a newly formed small-business entity.

For example, repeat offenders may be spotted when they try to apply to your system with a previously used private email domain, or a website/subdomain that is provided upon registration, or even a new domain that is being hosted by a previously banned hosting vendor. As an illustrative example, for quite some time many fintech operations reported unpleasant experiences with alleged businesses whose domain was registered on mail.com, a free email domain provider. Individuals who signed up for various types of financial services using emails like "*john@engineer.com*" were basically using the mail.com service to gain some level of "respectability" by presenting themselves as alleged "engineers."

Use your database to find the email domains (or subdomains) that are favored by your attackers, as shown in Example 16-1.

Example 16-1. Email domains with low repayment rates

```
SELECT
    (substring_index(substr(email, instr(email, '@') + 1), '.', 1)) AS domain,
    AVG(loan_repayment_rate),

/* we count loans and not simply emails, because Lenders have a high
 rejection rate and a high abandonment rate,therefore in  many cases an email
will be recorded for an application that was never completed */
    COUNT(loan_id)
GROUP BY 1
ORDER BY 2,3 ASC
LIMIT 2;
```

Table 16-1 shows the results of Example 16-1.

Table 16-1. Results of Example 16-1

DOMAIN	AVG(loan_repayment_rate)	COUNT(loan_id)
engineer.com	0%	5
mail.kz	0%	550

The results show two domains whose history of loan repayment is far from encouraging. The first, engineer.com, should probably be banned from your system. The second, mail.kz, is a different thing altogether. Unlike engineer.com, mail.kz users do not try to pose as alleged high-tech folk. Instead, they are probably just people from Kazakhstan who are using a popular free email provider in their country. Should they all be banned from your system? The answer probably lies in your data (and the extent of financial impact from the defaulted loans).

Summary

This chapter looked at credit and lending fraud, and considered the different approaches fraudsters can use to commit it. We set both the fraud and the preventive measures in the context of how this type of fraud fits into the wider fraud prevention context, and also highlighted the aspects that are more unique to this area. This concludes Part III of the book, and we'll now move on to looking at anti–money laundering (AML), an area that, as we mentioned in this chapter, shares some of the same identification and mitigation techniques needed for preventing credit and lending fraud.

 We want to thank Gil Rosenthal, without whose contributions this chapter would have been far less comprehensive and much less interesting. Gil's in-depth experience and insight into this area have greatly inspired and expanded our understanding of the lending industry and its challenges.

## PART IV

Marketplace Fraud

Online marketplaces are naturally subject to many of the same sorts of attacks as other online businesses: stolen credit cards, phishing, account takeover (ATO), address manipulation, friendly fraud, and so on.

Sometimes slightly different flavors of these sorts of attacks are available on marketplaces specifically, but from the fraud identification and prevention perspective, there's little difference. Readers working within marketplace ecosystems should turn to the earlier chapters for discussion of these fraud attacks, which are as relevant to marketplaces as to other businesses.

However, certain attacks are unique to marketplaces, made possible by their nature and structure. Because of this unique dynamic, we've set marketplace-specific attacks aside in their own part, albeit a short one. There are some vulnerabilities that only exist when you have a buyer and a seller dynamic in play, with users able to play either or both roles. It's these sorts of attacks that we focus on in Chapter 17, where we look at collusion and exit, and in Chapter 18, which deals with seller fraud.

Note that we use the terms *buyer* and *seller* to apply to the appropriate parties in the transaction as catchall terms, regardless of the nature of the marketplace, whether it's ride sharing, apartment rentals, physical goods, digital goods, payments, or other kinds. A driver and rider, renter and landlord, and so on can all fit into the buyer or seller category, and we have used this generic language to include all varieties of the buyer and seller model.

## CHAPTER 17

Marketplace Attacks: Collusion and Exit

'Cause tonight is the night when two become one...
—Spice Girls[1]

Collusion is exactly what it sounds like; it occurs when accounts on a marketplace collude to exploit the platform in order to benefit themselves. In this case, you would say the buyer and the seller are both in on the fraud. The benefit is sometimes directly financial, but it can also be to gain an undeserved reputation boost such as through fake reviews, or it can take the form of money laundering. The accounts involved may in fact be operated by the same fraudster, or by two different fraudsters working together, or by a fraud ring. Gig economy fraudsters may also play a role in the attack.

From the fraudster perspective, marketplaces might as well be made for collusion. There's so much you can do, if you don't care about the marketplace's terms and conditions, mission, or ecosystem. We'll look at the main categories of schemes and then discuss how the fraudster gig economy supports many of these types of fraud.

---

1 Spice Girls, "2 Become 1," written by the Spice Girls, Matt Rowe, and Richard Stannard, track 3 on *Spice*, Virgin, 1996.

Before we start, it's worth distinguishing between collusion and conspiracy, though both are relevant here and you may find both in play in the same fraudulent scenario:

Collusion
> Within the context of fraud prevention, a state of shared credentials between buyer and seller, possibly indicating they are indeed the same person. Collusion may occur both in legitimate and fraudulent scenarios.

Conspiracy
> Within the context of fraud prevention, a state of intended cooperation between two or more parties involved in the transaction, where the buyer and the seller are often the same person and the transaction is performed for fraudulent purposes.

Types of Collusion Attacks

This section covers the different flavors of collusion marketplace attacks.

Money Laundering

It's so simple to understand how fraudsters can use marketplaces for money laundering that it's no wonder fraudsters find this option so attractive. A fraudster who has illicitly gained money that needs to be laundered can simply open two accounts on a marketplace: one buyer's account and one seller's account. As the seller they can post a product or service they're offering, and as the buyer they can purchase the product or service. The payment, whether using a stolen credit card or money gained illegitimately, is then made by the buyer to the seller. The seller then moves the money out of the platform and into an account they own (e.g., a bank or electronic wallet), and voilá—freshly laundered money.

Fraudsters are happy to use well-established marketplaces for their money laundering needs. There are advantages to them in terms of knowing exactly how the system works, being able to rely on a mature ecosystem and payments framework, and so on. They're equally willing, though, to take advantage of marketplace-style setups that have not traditionally had to invest efforts into fighting money laundering. Delivery services are a good example of this, as are crowdfunding platforms; it's so easy to set up a "cause" for funding or for a charitable donation that in reality functions purely as a money laundering operation.

We cover this kind of money laundering in greater detail in Part V, but here we want to highlight a couple of points. First, from the perspective of the marketplace, there may be no active flags that anything problematic has occurred. There will only be a chargeback if a fraudster has used a stolen credit card or other payment method directly on the platform to make the purchase. But if the purpose is straightforward money laundering rather than theft + money laundering, you won't get a chargeback; the theft will have occurred beforehand, on a different site.

Second, and relatedly, the money laundering step that caught your attention may be one part of a more complex fraud scheme—often the final part: laundering the money after the theft has been completed. Sometimes the theft also occurs on the same marketplace (using different accounts, of course), in which case you may be able to trace suspicious similarities among different users, some of whom are associated with chargebacks; but often the theft occurs elsewhere and the marketplace is used purely for money laundering. That makes it harder to catch money laundering, a fact of which fraudsters are well aware.

Feedback Padding and Scams

Feedback padding isn't exactly unheard of in online marketplaces. Even entirely legitimate sellers, setting up their new online storefront, often cheat a little at the start or when launching a new product. They might ask friends and family to leave them good reviews—whether or not they've actually sampled the product or service—or go further and set up fake accounts themselves to make fake purchases and leave positive reviews. It's not usually egregious when it comes to legitimate sellers. In fraud terms, we'd class this as abuse rather than fraud. (For more on the distinction between fraud and abuse, see Chapters 1 and 10.)

Though this kind of activity is not really in the spirit of the marketplace ecosystem, it's understandable, and it's such a common behavior among sellers who are starting up that marketplaces rarely want to clamp down on it too stringently for fear of putting off sellers who could become valuable assets in the ecosystem as they grow. From the fraud-fighting perspective, the trouble is that precisely this behavior is used by fraudsters who are planning to set up shop, put a bit of effort into looking legitimate, and then make some real sales and vanish without ever sending anyone the goods or services on offer. For this reason, feedback padding isn't just a nuisance that puts the integrity of the ecosystem in jeopardy; it's also a fraud problem.

Feedback padding is valuable in conferring respectability on otherwise unconvincing stores, making them far more attractive to customers. The same is true for seller-side scams of other types, including scams that entrap the victim into being a part of the fraud—another form of victim-assisted fraud, as discussed in Chapter 9. Technically, this is collusion, because the fraudster convinces the victim to send them money on a pretext, and it is the victim themselves using the marketplace to send the money, even if they're being guided through every step by the fraudster. If you can't see how feedback padding might be relevant here, imagine a Nigerian prince–style scam in which the scammer looks like they have a legitimate profile and past history, corroborated by what appears to be lots of independent individuals, on a well-known and respectable online marketplace.

Feedback padding can also assist in much smaller-scale scams, like the bizarre Chinese scam attack on Uber (*https://oreil.ly/2H3d6*), where drivers dressed up as zombies to scare people into not taking the ride after all; the drivers earned a small cancellation fee, many times a day, in return for no service. Feedback padding can help this sort of scam continue much longer than would otherwise be possible for a driver. The same is true of scams selling misleadingly described goods, or cheat products like seeds that never sprout but whose instructions tell buyers the flowers won't come until a time after the refund period has elapsed. You would think scams like this would naturally die after a short time, buried under a welter of bad reviews. Feedback padding means they can stretch out far longer.

Incentives and Refund Abuse

In this case, buyers and sellers (who are often, but not always, the same person) conspire to take advantage of the bonus, subsidy, and/or buyer protection policies the platform offers. Buyer and seller protections are offered in different flavors by different marketplaces in order to attract their customer base and build competitive advantage.

For example, a ride-sharing app may offer $10 worth of free rides to new users, provided they take more than one ride in their first month. A user in this case may generate fake rides in order to collect the $10, and then switch to a new disposable phone in order to sign up as a new user and collect another free ride once more. In extreme cases, as told by some fraud-fighting veterans, "drivers" were transporting dozens of mobile phones in order to benefit from this incentive. When we bear in mind that the free rides accumulated in this manner can be resold to a cash-paying customer, we learn that this seemingly minor form of fraud can easily become dangerously popular.

A more lucrative form of abuse via collusion would be defrauding the buyer protection program, by placing a fake order and then issuing a chargeback/refund. For example, consider a fraudster posing as a PayPal seller "selling" something to themselves, then exiting/withdrawing the funds to their bank account and asking for a refund on the buyer's side, claiming a stolen credit card was used, or that the items were never received and/or arrived flawed. Buyer protection programs will usually refund the funds to the buyer's bank account, leaving a handsome profit for the fraudster.

This type of collusion attack has become popular enough to discourage many platforms from offering complete seller protection programs. As a result, innocent users suffer the cost and lose their trust in the marketplace. Disgruntled sellers on these marketplaces often speak up about their experience (an old example can be found on a page called "The Seller Punishment Policy" on PayPalSucks.org). Some cases get more public attention than others; for example, a seller on Upwork shared that Upwork demanded the seller refund $12,500 (*https://oreil.ly/8Pbu8*) due to the use of a stolen credit card by his buyer, several years after the transactions had begun. His story became the talk of the day on HackerNews (*https://oreil.ly/8NBBj*), and his frustration resonated with many other members of the gig economy. It's no wonder that quite a few of these freelancers eventually turn to policy abuse or even fraud. A better path for a marketplace to take would be to invest more in identifying problematic users, protecting both good buyers and good sellers.

When abusive users begin to master the refund flows, they can carry out extremely effective collusion attacks. Fraudsters can create significant losses to the marketplace if they obtain an account that is eligible for seller protection. The platform would reimburse the "seller" for complaints issued by the "buyer," as long as the platform remains blind to the fact that the seller and the buyer are one and the same. This fraud attack is a form of refund fraud that is somewhat similar to carousel fraud (*https://oreil.ly/aFYCn*) (a type of fraud less prevalent in our genre of fintech).

Selling Illegal Goods

This is an interesting form of abuse that is a little different from the others we discuss. In this case, the collusion isn't between a fraudster and themselves, or among a number of fraudsters working together. It's between a fraudster and their market. Let's say a criminal wants to sell drugs. They can do that on a criminal forum, of course, and take payment in bitcoin or directly to an account, but there are three downsides to this approach:

- It's a little more complicated; the mechanism for the payment becomes the responsibility of the criminal.
- The markets and forums of the dark web are notorious for exemplifying the expression, "There's no honor among thieves," and it's not surprising that fraudsters and other criminals often look for legitimate alternatives they can subvert to their own ends. Selling through a legitimate marketplace gives both seller and buyer protection.
- Goods like drugs are appealing to consumers who aren't in any other way a part of the criminal underworld. These customers often feel far more comfortable setting up a false account on a legitimate marketplace to make the purchase than they would transacting exclusively on the dark web. Thus, leveraging legitimate marketplaces increases the audience available to the criminal.

So, the criminal sets up as a seller on an online marketplace. Perhaps they appear to be selling luxury goods. Each item for sale will correspond to a different drug. Different colors could be used to refer to different locations associated with the drugs, or different levels of purity. Customers who want to purchase high-grade heroin can go to the seller on the marketplace and purchase, say, a blue cashmere sweater. The prices on this store will likely not be competitive; they may be rather above what a customer would normally expect to pay, though not so far above that it looks implausible. This deters genuine buyers from making innocent purchases and getting a nasty shock. Perhaps there's a "coupon code" system to make extra sure the seller knows which customers really are his true clients. The purchase is received, the goods are shipped, and the customer leaves a happy review. It's an appalling misuse of the marketplace, but criminals really don't care about that.

For more on this topic, see Chapter 22.

The Gig Economy of Fraud

Chapter 7 talked about the gig economy of fraud, which made sense, because the gig economy of fraud is effectively the traditional fraudster standby of mules, taken to the logical extreme. Money and shipping mules have been around for a long time. These are individuals who are willing to help fraudsters move money around using their real, legitimate accounts or those of their family, or using fake identification and their own physical location, which appears to match the identification; or to help fraudsters by receiving and reshipping stolen goods. Some mules know exactly what they're doing, whereas others are either genuinely innocent or willfully blind to reality. All three kinds proliferated during the COVID-19 pandemic, when many people were unexpectedly out of work and looking for jobs that could be done flexibly and from home. This explosion of options represented a huge opportunity for fraudsters, and as a result, it has become common for fraud fighters to see mules in action doing far more than money and shipping muling.

We mentioned the value of a reputation, for both buyer and seller, when it comes to collusion. Reputation on a marketplace can be built from many small elements: how long the account has existed, how many positive reviews it has received, the level of customer service, and so on. Setting up an account and aging it appropriately, with legitimate-looking behavior and positive reviews, takes time and work. It's not difficult, but it's not something a fraudster could manage convincingly at scale unless they have mules working for them who take care of the reputation-building process. It's worthwhile for a fraudster to pay mules a relatively small amount for this service if it means they get far more legitimate-looking accounts out of it, which can be used more successfully for scams. They can also have more accounts than they could manage alone, increasing the number of times they can play the scam out.

For money laundering, it's even more valuable, as the more reputable the account looks, the more likely a fraudster can use it to move even quite large sums. Your fraud team could catch that more than one person was accessing the account, if you were looking for that—but then, that's not uncommon with real accounts, which are frequently operated by business owners working together, or with employees.

The gig economy of fraud is a problem in the marketplace arena because before this behavior became common, there was a certain limit on the scale at which good reputations could be built. Working with bots was impractical because it was too obvious a sign of fraud. A legitimate-looking account on a marketplace needed plenty of legitimate-looking touchpoints going into it. Fraudsters could do that, of course, but only so often before it became too time consuming. The growth of the gig economy of fraud has dramatically increased the scale available to these operations.

Identification and Mitigation

The advantage a fraud prevention team has when it comes to preventing collusion is the nature of the attack itself: two (or more) accounts are colluding together. This means what you have to look for are common data points that are shared between both buyer and seller. Too many data points in common, or in suspicious combinations, and you start to smell collusion.

As mentioned earlier, it's very difficult to tell the difference between a legitimate seller who is just starting up (and perhaps cheating a little on their reviews) and a fraudulent seller. The same difficulty comes into play when we look at data point similarities. It's worth looking at the unique challenge of marketplaces in this context.

Yanrong Wang, a fraud-fighting veteran with decades of experience in banking and marketplaces (including leading risk management and Trust and Safety groups for Alibaba, PayPal, and Wells Fargo), emphasized the need for high granularity in buyer-seller relation analysis:

> The key is to detect the "abnormal" relationship between the buyer and seller. In order to disguise as a "normal" marketplace transaction, fraudsters will try to spread activities among various buyer and seller accounts, trying to fly under the radar of the fraud screening. Therefore, tools need to be developed to investigate the linkage between the buyers and sellers, and detect distinct patterns. A network visualization review tool for the fraud analysts has proven to be very useful. Such a tool has a seed and its links/its network. A seed is the suspicious account/accounts. A link is defined as two accounts with a "relationship." It could be a marketplace transaction, or some common attributes such as device/IP links, payment instruments, addresses, etc.

> A network is defined as the group of users with links to the seed. Networks can have different levels, just as in normal life your direct friends are your Level 1 network. If the network includes your friends' friends, that is a Level 2 network, etc. Many collusion and exit fraud schemes exhibit a "close" or abnormal concentration network pattern. That is to say, their Level 1 and Level 2 networks seem to be very "exclusive" to a set of accounts, or an abnormally high percentage of detected bad accounts, as opposed to a normal marketplace business whose networks will be more expansive.

Developing such a review tool requires investment into the engineering resources on extensive data processing and visualization, and a close collaboration between the fraud analysts and engineers to test effective "links" and networks. As the fraud evolves, the tool also needs to adapt to incorporate new links and patterns. Discoveries from the network review tool can be fed into machine learning algorithms to detect at a larger scale, finding more suspicious "seeds" and enhancing the review efficiency.

Why Proximity Is Different in Marketplaces

In most online interactions—ecommerce or banking, say—it's unlikely that there will be a random real-life connection between a customer and the site. If it looks like several customers are all signing in one after the other from the same IP or same device, that's usually not a good sign. There may be a predictable physical location that many customers share (e.g., being physically present at a store or bank), but other than that a certain distance is inherent to most online interactions. After all, part of the beauty of the internet is the ability to connect with people far away from you geographically. The same is not true for marketplaces. A seller might be interacting with someone in a different country, but equally, they may be building up a reputation locally and interacting frequently with people physically near them, perhaps even using the same IP addresses. And thus, proximity usually is not fraudulent. Let's look at an example to illustrate this point.

Say you're a graphic designer. You're starting to offer a range of products for businesses and gifts, including printing and shipping items. You set up an account on one or two relevant marketplaces, and dip your toe into the waters of online and social advertising. But at the start, the easiest way to get new business is to target the local market.

You know where the right sort of audience hangs out or visits in your town, so you hand out some flyers and posters to the relevant places, and maybe get your business advertised in a local newsletter and bulletin board. You offer a special hometown discount for the first two months. It's successful, and you get a great local kickoff. You often meet clients face to face, either at a coffee shop or at their place of business, whatever is easiest for them. It adds a personal touch, and they're likely to remember you the next time they need something. You encourage them to order, pay, and review on your online store in the marketplace, helping you build up valuable reputation points.

So far, so normal—and so legitimate. You can imagine similar scenarios for diverse products, fundraising efforts, delivery services, and so on. In the same way, you might have a seller setting up a physical booth at a local market or conference and getting business from the foot traffic, with data and payments entered through a device at the booth. The problem, though, is that in this situation, a particular seller often uses the same IP, and perhaps even the same device, as their customers, and is likely to be online shortly before or just after a customer interaction.

What's more normal than for the local friendly graphic designer to have their store all ready to go on an iPad that they bring with them to the meeting, to make ordering and paying for products as easy as possible for their clients? They might even place the order on behalf of the client, if payment comes on delivery rather than at the point of order. Effectively, they're using the marketplace platform, on their device, as a Point of Sale (POS) system. It's exactly the same behavior you would expect to see from a fraudster acting as both buyer and seller, and it's common enough in legitimate contexts that you can't ignore the use case. You have to try to distinguish between legitimate and fraudulent, even when they look as similar as we've just described.

There's an exercise that might help. Essentially, you use your business's data to work out how risky different combinations of data points really are for your company. You start by thinking through the good and bad stories for each data point you're considering, and end up with something like Table 17-1.

Table 17-1. Exercise for thinking through good and bad stories

Data point	Good story	Bad story
IP	Public WiFi/Family account	Fraudster made sure to work through an appropriate proxy, but then forgot to turn it off when they checked to see whether the money arrived
Same device that belongs to the seller	Using as POS	Lazy/amateurish fraudster
Same device that belongs to the buyer	Using as POS	Stolen device/emulator
Generic device attributes	It's a coincidence. It does happen.	Malware/emulator to mimic victim's device/SIM farm
Email/business email domain	Small business/contractor/gig economy; payment for services	Fraudster sets up a cheap domain to support a fake business; often used in money laundering
Payment instrument	Small business	Money laundering/New user incentive
Buyer's name/phone number	Using as POS	They simply use the buyer's identity to conceal their own; could be a synthetic identity, using a mix of real and fake data
Seller's name/phone number	Using as POS	Money laundering

To work out what's going on in a specific case, you need to look at the whole story. As we've said before, it's not that an IP or an email address "is good" or "is bad"; it's whether it makes sense in the context of a good overall story or a bad overall story. Which is more likely? With this example, let's say we have a set of similarities as in Table 17-1 attached to an account listed as "Gilit and Shoshana's Gift Shop." In that case, the version where the business owners are effectively using the marketplace as a POS is a strong story. On the other hand, if it's just "Shoshana Maraney" with no more plausible business setup attached, it's less plausible. Similarly, say a 1-800 number is being used. That's a fraud sign, of course, but it's also typical for small businesses. So, does this look like a small business? Fraudsters often use the phone number of a random local business that is either defunct or of a type that is relatively unlikely to pick up the phone (e.g., an automated laundrette, or a business that opens only at night or for limited hours), just for the zip code match. If you can find the phone number listed as belonging to that business, does it look like this story belongs to that business? As discussed in Chapter 4, there's the good story and the bad story. You need to find as many data points as possible to confirm one or the other.

Here, you can see that some combinations are particularly fraudulent: if you see the same device, same BIN (*https://www.bincodes.com*) (aka IIN, Bank/Issuer Identification Number), and same IP showing up over and over again, that's very suspicious. It looks like a fraudster with a list of stolen data, moving methodically down their list. The same is true for a combination showing the same device, same IP, and a variety of names starting with the letter *A*, even if the BIN is different. It's just a list again, ordered differently; it's still suspicious, but less so than the first category. You have the same device and the same browsing pattern. It might be a fraudster running through a familiar theft pattern, or it could be the example we gave of a graphic designer or booth operator, making life easier for their customers. If you see the same browsing pattern and the same email address being openly entered every time, that probably *is* the graphic designer, using their own or their business email address rather than demanding that a passerby provide their data.

To work out how fraudulent the similarities are for your business, you'll need SQL that looks something like this:

```
WITH frequency_of_colliding_credit_card AS
    (
        SELECT
            buyer_credit_card_bin,
            COUNT(buyer_credit_card_bin) AS cc_bin_frequency
        FROM
            orders_table
        GROUP BY 1
    )

--the following section of the query includes a CASE statement which gives a
maximal score to cases where the buyer's CC matches the seller's CC, and a
1/bin_frequency if they only share the CC bin. This way, very common BINs aren't
punished too severely. You might want to add a separate, harsher, score for
virtual CC bins:

SELECT
    a.order_id,
    CASE
        WHEN
            a.buyer_credit_card = a.seller_credit_card
```

```
        THEN 1
    WHEN
        a.buyer_credit_card_bin = a.seller_credit_card_bin
    THEN 1 / b.cc_bin_frequency
    ELSE 0
END
AS score_for_cc_collusion_fraud_prob
FROM
    orders_table a
    INNER JOIN
        cc_bin_frequency b USING (buyer_credit_card_bin);
```

Thinking Beyond Immediate Fraud Prevention

As we've said before, it's important to take opportunities to show the rest of the organization, especially upper management, that the fraud department is not only good at fighting fraud but also makes valuable contributions to the business generation side of the company. Challenges like the one we described in the preceding section often represent exactly this sort of opportunity. For example, if you see that your fraud prevention team is having to put effort into distinguishing cases in which customers are effectively using your marketplace as a POS, you can raise this as an interesting customer behavior, which might justify a product to support it. That way, you turn what looks like an abusive pattern into a feature, encouraging customers to "Set up your own POS"—useful for customers, great for the product and marketing suite, and helpful for your team, who can thus easily distinguish between the majority of these confusing but legitimate cases, and fraudsters.

When you discover a customer behavior pattern that's challenging from the fraud prevention perspective, it might be a product opportunity in disguise. This is especially likely to be relevant in the context of marketplaces, because the user base is far more actively engaged in using, exploring, and pushing the boundaries of what your platform makes possible. It's not just a case of the user going through a set flow created by an organization or site; it's interactive, on a number of levels. That can make fraud prevention more difficult, but in turn can lead to solutions that are both good for the business and helpful for fraud fighters too.

For example, one of the sellers on your marketplace may receive 10 payments on a single day, from the allegedly unrelated buyers shown in Table 17-2. The obvious pattern in email usernames and the repetitive IP could indicate a very lazy fraudster, but it could also be a physical event at a public location in Omaha (would it help to know that this IP is registered as a public hotspot of a local sports bar?). If something physical (say, smoothies) is sold at a local event, it makes sense that buyers would not be interested in providing their email address. Instead, the seller (ab)uses your marketplace as a POS solution. The seller's behavior suggests that your marketplace could use an invoicing system for pop-up events of this sort.

Table 17-2. Uniform buyer email pattern, suggesting a pop-up sales event

Buyer email	Buyer IP
Omaha.sale.customer1@gmail.com	402.444.5274
Omaha.sale.customer2@gmail.com	402.444.5274
Omaha.sale.customer3@gmail.com	402.444.5274
Omaha.sale.customer4@gmail.com	402.444.5274

But wait, what if the list of emails looks like Table 17-3? It could be edging toward fraud, but on the other hand it could still be legitimate—just a more personal approach to the same method used in the first example.

Table 17-3. Uniform buyer email pattern, including alleged first names of the shoppers, suggesting a pop-up sales event

Buyer email	Buyer IP
Omaha.sale.Alice@gmail.com	402.444.5274
Omaha.sale.John@gmail.com	402.444.5274
Omaha.sale.George@gmail.com	402.444.5274
Omaha.sale.Paul@gmail.com	402.444.5274

On the other hand, the example in Table 17-4 looks shady, due to the lack of business-related words, plus the extra-lazy usernames selected. In this case, you'd likely want to be doing some further analysis.

Table 17-4. Uniform buyer email pattern without any "hint" of a sales event

Buyer email	Buyer IP
OmahaAAAA@gmail.com	402.444.5274
OmahaBBBB@gmail.com	402.444.5274
OmahaCCCC@gmail.com	402.444.5274
OmahaDDDD@gmail.com	402.444.5274

Each of the three tables presented so far could be fraud. In each scenario, the person who entered the emails is knowingly submitting emails that are most likely unreachable (and if your product requires email confirmation, the payments should fail). However, experience indicates that the first table is far more likely to be driven by legitimate small-business needs.

To classify the repetitive emails in your data set, you could pull up a dump of buyer emails per seller and then vectorize them into lists of typical usernames to see how they correlate with reported fraud cases in your database. You could also match the usernames against lists of frequent ecommerce terms (e.g., *sale*, *store*, and *customer*). Here are a couple of handy lists you can find online:

- Popular Keyword – Ecommerce Keywords (*https://oreil.ly/Jq8Ti*)
- Popular Keyword – Online Stores Keywords (*https://oreil.ly/6hjXb*)

The following Python code can help with turning the dump of emails into tokens:

```
import nltk
import re
import heapq

with open('emails.txt') as f:
    text = f.read()

emails = text.split('\n')

for i in range(len(emails)):
    # use email slicer to omit the generic email domains in our use-case
    # and keep only the username
    emails[i] = emails[i][:emails[i].index('@')]

    # replace non-word characters with spaces so that word_tokenize will
    # treat them as separate words
    emails[i] = re.sub(r'\W', ' ', emails[i])

    # lowercase
    emails[i] = emails[i].lower()

# Creating a Bag of Words model, to identify the frequent email username
# patterns
word2count = {}
for username in emails:
    words = nltk.word_tokenize(username)
    for word in words:
        if word not in word2count.keys():
            word2count[word] = 1
        else:
            word2count[word] += 1

freq_words = heapq.nlargest(10, word2count, key=word2count.get)
```

For more on the Bag of Words model, see "Learning to Classify Text" (*https://oreil.ly/baW3A*) and "Bag of Words (BoW) Model in NLP" (*https://oreil.ly/fCqNb*).

Summary

This chapter explored some of the different ways fraudsters can exploit a marketplace using collusion, either creating multiple accounts as buyers and sellers, working as a ring, using a form of victim-assisted fraud, or collaborating with buyers to misuse the platform. We looked at why distinguishing between legitimate and fraudulent behavior can be particularly challenging on marketplaces, and also at some solutions to that issue. In the next chapter, we'll focus on another example of fraud that exploits the nature of a marketplace: seller fraud.

## CHAPTER 18

Marketplace Attacks: Seller Fraud

Some of them want to use you, some of them want to get used by you…
—Eurythmics[1]

As distinct from the collusion fraud discussed in the previous chapter, here we're considering cases in which only the seller has fraudulent intentions, defrauding legitimate buyers. Unfortunately, there are all too many options for a fraudster looking to misuse an online marketplace by making it a base for criminal operations.

Types of Seller Fraud

We're going to look at three different categories of seller fraud, each of which includes many different types of fraud. The examples we give in each category are by no means exhaustive. If we wanted to try for completeness, we'd need a whole book just on seller fraud, and even then a new form of fraud would undoubtedly pop up a month after the book was published; fraudsters get just as creative about seller fraud as they do about every other kind of fraud. The idea of the categories is to provide a useful framework for thinking about different sorts of seller schemes, because the sorts of solutions you'll want to look at differ depending on the category.

Seller Slipup Segues into Fraud

We're putting seller slipups first because it's often overlooked in fraud discussions, but can represent a more significant portion of a marketplace's seller fraud than many fraud teams expect. Seller slipups are more common than you'd think. They happen

---

1 Eurythmics, "Sweet Dreams (Are Made of This)," written by Annie Lennox and David A. Stewart, track 6 on *Sweet Dreams (Are Made of This)*, RCA, 1983.

when a seller starts out with good intentions, but runs into difficulties so severe they end up having taken orders they can't fulfill. If they can't afford to refund the money, they may simply disappear with money they haven't earned, without providing the customers with the service or product.

It's important to note that there's no initial intent to deceive in a seller slipup. It's akin to a false chargeback filed due to the dreaded buyer's remorse. Additionally, it can happen at any point in a seller's presence on the platform. It may occur early on, with sellers experiencing greater numbers of orders than expected and simply folding under the pressure, but it can also happen to an established seller whose main supplier suddenly fails them, or who lose staff unexpectedly and can't replace them in time, or whose wider business is going bankrupt and their online business goes down with it. Experienced sellers are more likely to be able to handle these sorts of scenarios appropriately (and without cheating their customers) than inexperienced business owners, but major disruptions to their supply chain or staff can crash even a seller who has been going for years. Things can escalate fast, veering wildly out of control within weeks or months, which is especially challenging in industries where there's a long wait time between orders being placed and being fulfilled—think of furniture, for example. Sometimes, when things go wrong, the seller panics and runs off with the cash, leaving angry customers who inevitably turn to the marketplace itself for clarity and recompense. It would be preferable, of course, to catch these slipups before they impact the buyers on the marketplace.

There are certain times when this kind of problem is more likely to occur. The widespread shortages and shipping problems resulting from the COVID-19 pandemic are a good example. Marketplace fraud teams need to be sensitive to the trends in the news that indicate that a period like this might be on its way, or has kicked off. Advice can be given to sellers in advance to try to mitigate these sorts of scenarios. From the fraud prevention side, extra measures can be implemented to monitor sellers and warn the marketplace when something like this might be in the wind.

There is a second variation on this theme, in which a genuine seller gets into financial difficulties and, before they reach the point of bankruptcy, knowingly sells their account (and its good reputation) to a fraudster, who exploits it to the full, attracting as many orders as possible along with the payments for them, never planning to fulfill any of the orders.

Scams

Online marketplaces, where a digital platform enables buyers and sellers to interact and make purchases and payments, are popular places for fraudsters with a scam in mind, so much so that there's a good chance you or a friend or family member has come across a scam on a marketplace in the past, or perhaps even been targeted as a victim.

It's easy to see where this popularity comes from; fraudsters like to leverage the helpful structure and services a marketplace provides for their own illicit ends. It's easier than setting something up themselves; there is less time involved, and so a higher return on investment (ROI) for the fraudster at the end of the day. Storefront design, product or descriptions, payment, and so on are all made easy on a marketplace, especially if a fraudster is part of an organized crime group or working with gig economy fraudsters willing to help set up accounts and age them convincingly. Once a fraudster is used to the marketplace setup, they can rinse and repeat, working at scale.

Marketplaces are popular with fraudsters for triangulation scams (*https://oreil.ly/pWIYA*), as described in Chapter 7. It's an easy way to take in the orders (which are filled by buying items elsewhere with stolen data)—easier than setting up a website from scratch. Additionally, since these scams typically only run for a relatively short period of time (it may be months, but it probably won't be years), marketplaces make it easy to move on to the next fake business, once one fraudulent business has been exposed. Various riffs on this method have been developed, such as the one Tal Yeshanov, head of Risk and Fraud Operations at Plastiq, describes from her time at Uber (*https://oreil.ly/zLdzU*). In this scam, the fraudster inserts themselves into the transaction as a kind of malicious middleman. Organized crime groups, or larger fraud rings, can also run multiple "businesses" of this kind on the platform at once, often creating different seller accounts for slightly different products.

There are also scams working off the gray area surrounding "product not as described" complaints. Some of these are ingenious enough, and brazenly open enough, to garner reluctant respect from the analysts who catch them. Consider the sellers who, when the PS5 was one of the hottest items around, sold "PlayStation console - PS5 - box" for roughly the price of a PS5, but provided only the box. The image and the description were accurate; the fraudsters relied on the fact that many people on the marketplace couldn't read English precisely enough to understand the trickery involved.

Similarly, there are sellers who provide a much cheaper and less attractive version of the product, but one that still matches the description of the product given on the site. Or, again, the sellers who claim to provide seeds that will grow into beautiful flowers…if you wait long enough. In this case, "long enough" is whatever period of time falls after the set limit on time for complaints after purchase. So, by the time the customer can complain, they aren't able to anymore.

However clever these scams are, they frequently end up being the problem of the fraud prevention department; customers are not happy, and they turn to the marketplace for justice. The fraud prevention team needs to be able to stop these schemes to both save the company money (because many marketplaces do refund customers in such situations, if only as a goodwill gesture) and protect its reputation.

There are also sellers who sign up with stolen identities, piggybacking off a genuine, legitimate identity to add respectability to their own account. They may use stolen payment information to pay for whatever expenses are associated with the store, or they may be associated with a synthetic identity attack in which the business itself is a part of the synthetic identity being created and can be used to convince banks to extend a line of credit or a loan for the business, as a step in the monetization of the synthetic identity. These scams can go on for quite a long time before the identity busts out, although the businesses themselves are often fairly lackluster since the fraudster is not primarily interested in monetizing the business itself and doesn't invest a huge amount of effort into it.

Dubious Goods

The dubious goods category is an interesting one, slightly different from most of the types of fraud we discuss in this book, in which the aim is to steal goods or money. Here, it's not straight theft that's involved, but rather, the attempt to extract as much money as possible for goods that are either counterfeit or something the seller ought not to be selling in the first place.

Each different type of dubious good could easily have an entire book devoted to exploring the specific type of fraud involved with it, and the complex legalities and regulatory responsibilities involved. We're not going to dive into those here, not least due to lack of space; instead, we focus on aspects that are typically of most concern to fraud fighters. It is worth mentioning, though, that these sorts of attacks are best combated in concert with your company's legal team, and many marketplaces have an interdepartmental strike force that works specifically on these issues.

Counterfeit items are one of the greatest challenges that fall into this category. In 2021, Amazon reported blocking 10 billion listings (*https://oreil.ly/L6fcI*) for counterfeit items on its third-party marketplace. Depending on their jurisdiction, marketplaces can sometimes be held directly accountable for counterfeit goods being sold through their platform, unless they can prove they have reasonable measures in place to prevent this from happening as much as possible. There are two kinds of counterfeit that may be problematic:

Items pretending to be the real goods
    These are perhaps sold by sellers pretending to be resellers, official or otherwise.

Items that are clearly not genuine
    These are sold for far less money than would be expected for the real brand.

Other kinds of dubious goods include anything that involves copyright infringement: visual, written, audio, and so forth. Sometimes it's clear from the context of the seller that they don't have a legitimate right to the copyright, but sometimes it's not, and many users are not overly concerned about checking.

There are also goods and services that are inherently problematic, such as sellers who offer to provide essays or even dissertations for students—for a price—or even false certificates for degrees and other qualifications. In these cases, there may not be an entity likely to chase these down and cause problems for the marketplace unless they can prove they're taking steps to prevent the abuse (as there are with counterfeiting, where the real brands are often very active in this manner, and with copyright infringement, where the same is true of the owner of the copyright). However, these operations are clearly dubious in nature and represent a risk to the reputation of the marketplace, which means that, once again, a fraud prevention team may be called in to prevent sales of these items where possible.

Identification and Mitigation

This section looks at each seller fraud category we mentioned earlier, and explores the different ways each can be identified and mitigated by fraud prevention teams.

Seller Slipup Segues into Fraud

Seller slipups are an interesting case from the fraud prevention perspective, because they're not amenable to the sorts of methods fraud fighters usually rely on. As with friendly fraud caused by buyer's remorse (discussed in Chapter 10), you can't catch malicious intent at onboarding or early on in the seller lifecycle, because at that point the intent is still legitimate. You don't want to treat them like a fraudster, because they're not one yet.

There are two main things the fraud team can do to help. First, start with analysis. Find the cases that match this description from the past year. How large is the scale of this problem? What linking factors can you find between the cases of seller slipup fraud? Are there any commonalities about their business model, their industry, or the way they're setting up their storefront? Bear in mind that, depending on the size of your data set, there may be a number of overlapping factors in common and that in many cases, individual sellers won't exhibit all of them. Once you have a profile of a seller who might be at risk, you can flag them at onboarding or early on and keep a closer eye on them than you would otherwise. If evidence builds up indicating that a particular flagged seller is showing signs you know to be suspicious, it can be escalated to manual review, and further investigation can be carried out.

The second thing fraud prevention teams can do combines interdepartmental collaboration with an opportunity to show that the team brings extra value to the company. You can use the information you gained through your analysis, and the understanding you will have gained about the seller lifecycle, to work with other departments in your organization to improve (or create) a vetting process for sellers. This can be something that happens only at onboarding, or it can be a process that repeats regularly (usually in reduced form) on a set schedule. A vetting process can include examining their business plan and seeing if it meets certain standards, asking questions to see if they have realistic expectations about how much money will be moving through their hands and how to handle that, whether they have plans in place for dealing with supply problems, and so on. Your marketplace can even start to offer assistance in some of these business planning areas as a feature.

With regard to the sellers who sell their accounts to fraudsters to leverage, the best approach here is to have systems in place to flag significant changes in seller patterns; for example, if the IPs are suddenly coming from a different country or the times of day the seller is most active don't match the previous patterns, you may want to institute manual review to dig deeper and find out what's going on.

Scams

One of the most practical ways to make a marketplace less attractive to a fraudster for a scam is not technically within the province of fraud prevention, but is another example of where fraud fighters can work with other departments for the good of the whole company. Collaborating with product, onboarding, and finance departments can result in policies that protect the business from fraud without harming other business priorities. For example, putting restrictions in place so that sellers can only withdraw funds after a certain period of time can be very effective in slowing things down for fraudsters, and making a marketplace less appealing as a criminal platform.

Where you put this restriction may depend on the sorts of fraud you see most often, so be sure to come to the collaborative process with data on this front. If your marketplace struggles with fraudsters who set up accounts, use them for all they're worth, and then abscond after two or three months, a restriction that prevents sellers from removing any money from the account for the first three months might be helpful. On the other hand, if your marketplace suffers from fraudsters who invest in longer-term scams, having a set three-month period that must elapse after every transaction before the money from that transaction can be removed from the marketplace may be part of the answer. If you're having trouble with "product not as described" scams, only allowing the money for a purchase to be removed from the marketplace once a certain period has passed without complaint may be appropriate. It's crucial to communicate changes to policies of this nature clearly to sellers and internally within your organization; otherwise, you'll end up being blamed for a customer relations disaster. But in general, when policies are explained clearly, the users of a marketplace are willing to adapt.

Policy changes of this type will be of some help against triangulation schemes, since these often run for months rather than years; forcing a fraudulent seller to give up three months of takings every time they feel things are getting too hot for them and move on is a significant loss to the fraudster. That said, it may still be worth the fraudster's time to keep it going as long as possible, and since they can go for some time, the loss to the marketplace may be significant. Triangulation schemes are fairly difficult to identify individually, until chargebacks or complaints mark them out.

One advantage, if it can be so called, that marketplaces have against these scams is that if a fraudster, fraud ring, or organized crime group are attempting this once on a marketplace, they're likely attempting it many times. Finding the connections between the sellers can be very significant, especially if it's clear the seller is trying to make it look as though there is no connection between them.

Legitimate sellers often have more than one virtual shop on a marketplace, particularly if they're selling different types of goods or appealing to different audiences. But they are usually completely open about this connection, sometimes even citing existing stores during the process of setting up a new one as proof that they are experienced and know what they're doing. In fact, if the marketplace allows it, they will usually unite their stores under the same account. By contrast, if you find stores that are selling very similar things, accessed by the same IPs, run by accounts accessed at similar times of day, and sending money to the same accounts when they're taking it out of the platform, but which appear to have nothing to do with one another, are apparently connected to different accounts, owned by different people…. Well, more investigation might well be worthwhile.

In terms of identifying scams more generally, a common feature with scam sellers is that they'll often build up fake good reviews so that they can emulate a good reputation, making customers more likely to order from them. They will do this initially, but also likely keep it up as the business attracts more customers so that they can drown out bad reviews with a flood of good ones. Often, these reviews will be very short, perhaps only one word long, and entirely unimaginative, because they'll be posted by a bot or by a fraud gig worker given a short list of options to post multiple times. All this means that the same word, or words, will usually be used over and over again—which means, in turn, that running tests for word frequency on feedback or reviews is a great way to flag suspicious accounts.

Here's a Python example using FreqDist and StopWords from the NLTK (Natural Language Toolkit) library (*https://oreil.ly/8qd5R*) to count the frequency of words in your sample. Note that, importantly, it's designed to ignore words that are very common in English, such as "and" and "the":

```python
from nltk.tokenize import wordpunct_tokenize
from nltk.probability import FreqDist
from nltk.corpus import stopwords


nltk.download('stopwords')

with open('customer feedback for sellers.txt', 'r', encoding='utf8') as f:
    text = f.read()
```

```
# ignore frequent English words e.g. 'the', 'and'
fd = FreqDist(
    [
        word
        for word in wordpunct_tokenize(text)
        if word not in set(stopwords.words("english"))
    ]
)
fd.pprint()
```

The same technique can work for identifying cases of "product not as described," when customers make very much the same sort of complaint about a particular product. It won't be as clear cut, since the irate customers may not use precisely the same language, but often there are strong correlations between their complaints, and this can be a good early warning sign to help marketplaces identify these scams before they trick too many customers.

Though running analyses like this can help you identify accounts that need to be looked at more closely, you can't treat the discovery of word frequency as an instant sign of guilt. Some sellers encourage their legitimate customers to leave similar sorts of reviews, and these are often simple and repetitive as well (to make it easy for the customers so that they're more likely to actually go and leave that review). Figure 18-1 shows a real-life example of a case that popped up due to word frequency flagging, which proved on investigation to be a legitimate seller whose customers really did think his baked goods were "yummy."

Finding evidence that points to either fraud or legitimate use in these cases is generally a job for manual review. Encourage fraud analysts who engage in these sorts of reviews regularly to take time once each quarter or so to think of ways in which the flagging process can be made more accurate, if there are certain signs in the cases they have reviewed that point consistently to fraud or legitimacy.

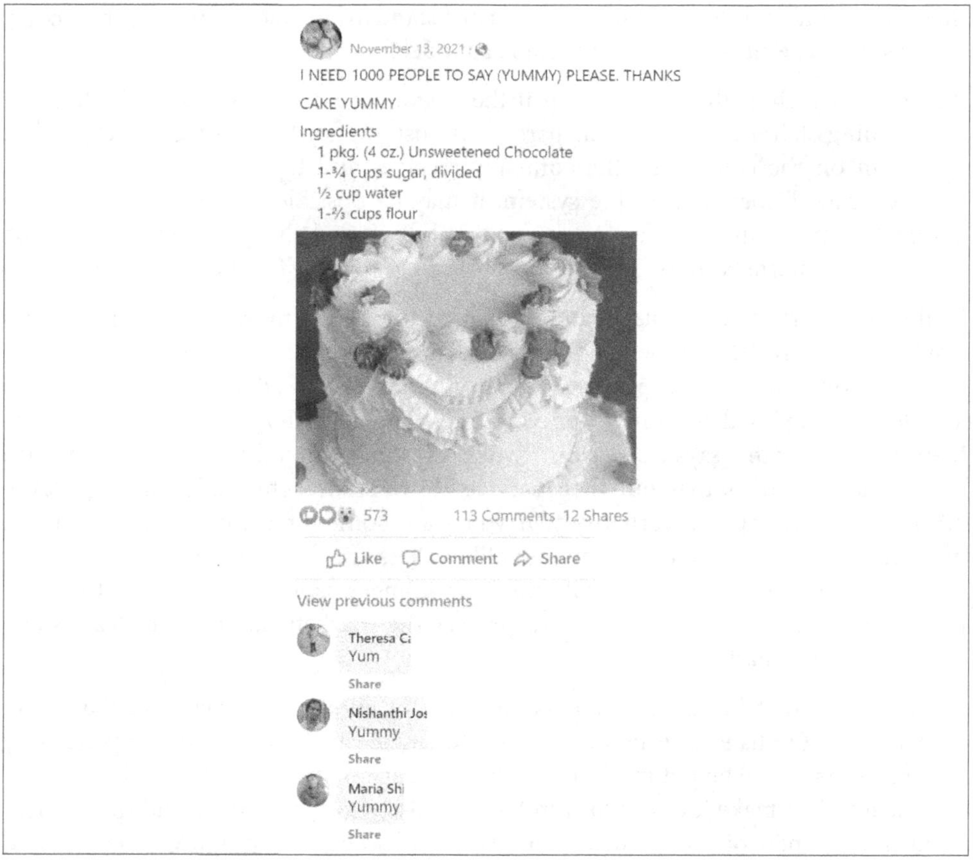

Figure 18-1. A local baker asking for 1,000 followers to comment with the same text: "Yummy"!

Dubious Goods

As with scams, some of the best ways to deal with the challenge of dubious goods is to put processes in place to make it easier for consumers to understand what they're getting, and for brands to make it easier to protect their real goods. There are a range of such processes, targeting different challenges. One might be to require sellers to provide documentation showing that they are licensed to sell products from a particular brand, or that they have legitimately obtained original goods from the brand or an authorized distributor. A similar system can be put in place for trademarks or copyrighted content.

Or you can make it easy for the customer to do their own due diligence, mandating that sellers provide accurate details regarding things like manufacturing date, location, and materials and ingredients. The blockchain solution (*https://oreil.ly/6B8TD*) being trialed by Louis Vuitton, Cartier, and Prada is an interesting development along these lines, and if it does become an industry standard, it may help with the luxury goods sector as well as potentially become a model for other industries.

Approaches such as these won't help if the customer is being willfully blind, but it makes things fairer and more transparent for customers who do care, which should cut down on the complaints the company receives and the fraud department has to investigate. Depending on the system, it may be possible for the marketplace to automate some of this comparison, protecting buyers and also good sellers, who lose out when counterfeits are sold more cheaply than is possible for the real thing.

In the same sort of vein, sellers can be required to provide more business identification, such as tax ID number and bank account information (even if they choose to take money out of the platform using an electronic wallet). You can also use a seller's rating to determine your withdrawal policies. For example, you might institute a policy that says a seller can't withdraw funds immediately unless they have a full year of ratings that put their service above some achievable but high level: 4.8 stars, for example. Alternatively, if you want something more targeted than a blanket approach, you can say something like sellers are able to withdraw funds from sales only after receiving confirmation of a customer's satisfaction with that specific purchase (something that should also protect the marketplace from at least some instances of first-party fraud).

It's important that fraud departments be aware of all such policies, and that fraud teams who often handle related issues be encouraged to think of further policies or programs that could be put in place to help. Once again, interdepartmental collaboration doesn't just make it easier to stop fraud, it also shows that the fraud department is an integral part of the business and aware of a range of complex issues beyond those for which they're directly responsible.

Regarding goods that are dubious by the nature of the product itself, such as bogus certificates or essays being sold for the purchaser to pass off as their own, the easiest way to keep on top of these sorts of problems is to search for specific terms, in the same way we described in "Scams." Precisely which goods fall in or out of policy for your marketplace may be a discussion you'll need to have with Legal; essays being sold "as models which students may be able to use as a basis on which to write their own essays" fall into a gray area that fraud teams don't usually want to dive into. Once again, though, you can't assume that other departments are aware of the challenges you're facing. Communication is key.

Dubious goods may seem like an area that shouldn't be part of a fraud team's mandate. Fraud fighters, after all, have enough to worry about. The trouble is that both the reputational risk and the financial risk from these sorts of goods has become substantial: a 2020 report by the Department of Homeland Security found that counterfeit goods have become a $509 billion issue (*https://oreil.ly/3AsI7*). The scale of the problem means many departments in a marketplace get pulled into solving it, and a fraud department, with its ability to identify suspicious behaviors, connections, and patterns, is a good partner in this process.

Fraud teams are sometimes asked to make recommendations about where to focus resources when it comes to preventing the sale of dubious goods. As so often is the case, analysis is the answer here; you want to know which kinds of dubious goods are causing the most problems and complaints on your marketplace. Beyond that, you'll want to know what each type costs; there may be a significant gap between the cost to the marketplace if you're comparing essays and copyright infringement, for instance. More than that, there's the reputational damage involved; accidentally selling counterfeit blankets will likely not result in coverage as damaging as the discovery that sellers are successfully peddling cosmetics with perilous levels of dangerous ingredients. Legal or finance departments may not be aware of all of the components of this tricky problem, so the more on top of it your department can be, the better—assuming this is an issue in which you're involved, of course. But it is very much a collaborative process; the legal department will be aware of issues that would not be part of a fraud analysis, such as which country takes which issue more seriously (e.g., some countries spend considerable time and energy on copyright protection, while others focus on health and safety threats).

Laws are under discussion in a number of countries in an attempt to cut down on counterfeit goods. If this is an issue your fraud team sometimes gets drawn into to help with, it's worthwhile having a regular check-in with the legal team to see if anything has changed on that front, and, most importantly, whether there's anything coming that your team needs to know about. Other departments may forget the impact that alternations in their areas of expertise could have on fraud fighters' work; it's a fraud prevention professional's job to remind them and make it easy for them to keep you up to date.

Summary

This chapter discussed the complexities of various types of fraud attacks carried out against online marketplaces by fraudulent sellers on the marketplaces. Broadly speaking, the types of attacks were divided into three categories: seller slipups segueing into fraud; scams; and dubious goods. The chapter explored identification and mitigation strategies for all three cases. We'll keep that "exploitation of an ecosystem" mentality as we move to a different kind of problem: money laundering.

## PART V

AML and Compliance Analytics

The chapters in this part of the book focus on money laundering and anti–money laundering (AML) efforts. AML and fraud prevention are closely related in some important ways; notably, they often face the same criminals or criminals who are part of the same wider crooked organization. It was important to us to reflect these two similar problems in the book.

The chapters largely refer to banks in their examples, because banks are required to make robust investments in AML and compliance, and these operations are relatively similar among all banks. Most relevant regulations also reflect, in one way or another, the assumption that the main players in this field are banks and other financial institutions. However, it is increasingly true that other, newer players on the scene, such as those in the fields of cryptocurrency (*https://oreil.ly/vnBgq*), electronic wallets, and other alternative payment methods, must also grapple with AML and compliance responsibilities. The chapters that follow are as relevant for these companies as they are for banks, though their internal organizational structure may be different from those we habitually refer to as being common to banks.

With regard to ecommerce, compliance is also an important factor, but it's relatively more manageable because many of the relevant actions, restrictions, and so forth are built into the payment services used by ecommerce companies. So, compliance is something to check out when choosing payment services rather than something that sits entirely within the ecommerce company.

Some compliance areas do remain the direct responsibility of the ecommerce company, such as General Data Protection Regulation (GDPR) requirements. Maya Har-Noy, one of the leading fintech strategists in the industry, noted that "It's very difficult to estimate the ROI of the immense effort needed by an organization to achieve PCI compliance." After accompanying several ecommerce operations as they were jumping through all the hoops necessary for PCI compliance (*https://oreil.ly/2eYPi*) alone, Har-Noy said she would confidently recommend that young ecommerce companies partner with a service that would save them the hassle: compliance as a service, so to speak. More mature ecommerce companies will often place compliance in the hands of data security or cybersecurity teams, perhaps working hand in hand with DevOps teams. So, these chapters have relevance in the ecommerce field as well, though perhaps to a lesser extent than in relation to banking or payments.

Finally, there are a number of areas where many of the AML and compliance experts we talked to agree that change is needed to enable them to do their jobs more effectively, and to improve the level of protection for the financial services industry as a whole. Many of these areas are, regrettably, beyond the scope of this book, such as breaking down data silos within organizations, standardizing data definitions, and creating a golden format for how data is shared and which data is shared. All of these improvements would streamline processes and make automation far easier.

Also frequently mentioned as "wish list" items are finding new ways for institutions around the world to collaborate, including over specific data points, in a way that doesn't harm privacy and regulatory requirements. Experts note that in a sense, diverse financial institutions are in fact partners, part of a complex network that moves money around the globe, enables money to impact the world, and tries to ensure that criminals are kept out of that loop. Many of those we spoke to while writing this book reference valuable relationships they have developed with other financial institutions around the world, which have come in handy on many occasions in solving problems or catching fraud or money laundering attempts—and many wish that more structure existed to enable such relationships and interactions more commonly with a greater diversity of institutions.

These elements are certainly important to the industry and its future development and success in combating financial crime. However, we don't deal with these kinds of considerations in this book, because any process to improve the situation would be a long-term project carried out by many different financial institutions. Discussion in this book would not be valuably actionable for individual professionals or teams, which means that although the topics are very important for the industry, they're not relevant for this book.

That said, you should keep all of these issues in mind as you read these chapters. Each chapter focuses on a different aspect of scenarios that AML or compliance teams (or, perhaps, both, if the two are working together in some capacity) must be able to identify and, depending on policy and the relevant regulatory rules, either track and report, or ban and stop.

## CHAPTER 19

Anti–Money Laundering and Compliance: Wider Context

As I went down in the river to pray, studying about that good ol' way...
—"Down in the River to Pray," traditional folk song

The motivation for fighting money laundering is different from that for fighting fraud. As Nikki Baumann, a Fraud Principal at Farfetch who also has experience in both banking and cryptocurrency, pointed out, money launderers might also be fraudsters: "It's all the same way of thinking, where the criminal works out what the bank or the merchant is doing and tries different ways to circumvent that, often using the same tactic to conceal money laundering as to conceal fraud." Indeed, there are notable similarities between certain aspects of fraud fighting and AML, and we encourage AML professionals to read Parts I and V and Chapters 12 and 15 of this book in particular, as they are especially relevant to their work. Despite the considerable overlap, however, the purpose of the fraud prevention teams and the AML teams working against the criminals is different.

Fraud prevention is fundamentally about mitigating loss, both from successful fraud and from false positives or dissatisfied customers. Anti–money laundering (AML), on the other hand, is about being compliant, and being able to show that your business is compliant, with the relevant regulations. A close relationship with legal and compliance officers is absolutely essential, since the legal landscape is dynamic and AML efforts must reflect that. In the same way, a close relationship with AML teams may be very valuable for compliance teams working to prevent the sale of prohibited goods or block sanctioned individuals, countries,[1] or entities from transacting, since

---

1 The Financial Action Task Force (FATF), a global money laundering and terrorist financing watchdog, keeps a list of high-risk countries (*https://oreil.ly/InFg3*).

AML teams often have insight into which tricks and individuals are "hot" right now. There's frequent overlap in the criminal group that each department is interested in stopping.

An organization can gain enormous benefits by developing strong working relationships between the fraud prevention and AML teams. As Maximilian von Both, senior vice president of Compliance at Paysafe, pointed out:

> In a very real sense, fraud fighting and AML are two sides of the same coin. For fraud, you need to follow the money. For AML, you need to know where it's coming from. If you silo, you lose a lot of intelligence, and that has a real negative impact on your ability to combat financial crime in both directions. That can hurt the business on so many levels: financial, your reputation with other banks, your reputation with customers, with merchants…and that, ultimately, can become further financial loss. Long term, you lose trust, and you lose the ability to offer a wide range of services. Ultimately you lose customers. Having fraud prevention and AML teams working closely together, or even integrated into a single team, is far more effective.

AML Challenges and Advantages

In a sense, being regulation based is an advantage for AML as a profession; the regulations give very clear rules as to what you need to do and aim for. It's not like fraud, where finding the right balance between antifraud and friction can be challenging depending on your business's priorities and loss.

On the other hand, it's more difficult to measure day-to-day success in AML and compliance, because there isn't the same regular feedback of chargebacks flowing in to validate decisions or show where mistakes were made. This in turn makes it more difficult to judge internal processes; should your team be manually reviewing 1% of daily transactions? 10%? How fast should you optimize for, especially given the necessity to include holding funds in your calculations in some cases? All of this is difficult for any individual team to determine alone; discussions and comparisons with AML and compliance teams in other similar businesses are valuable in helping teams see where they fall within industry norms.

AML and compliance teams also have the challenge that their key work is to ensure that their company can show it is taking appropriate steps to be compliant. Businesses are not always supportive of investing in resources to go beyond the letter of the law. This is, to an extent, in contrast to Know Your Customer (KYC) efforts, which include the regulatory aspect in a similar way to AML, but which also protect the business from financial loss if done well and done beyond the letter of the law. KYC by itself won't protect you from the fraud that the regulations are also trying to stop; further effort is required, and is easy to justify, because the extra work prevents financial loss that would otherwise occur. AML and compliance efforts, in contrast, protect the business from loss only insofar as being able to prove that all responsible steps have been taken protects the business from heavy fines. That is certainly very important, especially given that AML fines more than doubled (*https://oreil.ly/v1kNy*) between 2019 and 2020, but management may lack incentive to invest beyond the steps needed to guard against fines.

As the public becomes more aware of and more sensitive to issues surrounding money laundering and the reputation of businesses comes into play, the easier it is for AML and compliance teams to build a case for investing beyond the letter of the law, especially since the law is, by nature, always a few steps behind the criminals. As one of the experts we talked to for this section commented dryly, "If people find out Al-Qaeda has been using your company to launder their money, well, that's not a good look."

AML and compliance teams do have one other advantage. Customers using services that require such scrutiny usually anticipate or understand the need for answering questions, or even taking a little time to ensure everything is above board. An exception to this is cryptocurrency, which has a number of unique challenges (see Chapter 22).

Additionally, AML and compliance efforts carried out after KYC typically occur post-transaction, taking a little of the pressure off the need for speedy decisions, in comparison to ecommerce fraud decisions. That said, the customer is still waiting, and teams can't afford to add too much delay into the process.

AML and compliance teams, in common with fraud prevention teams, often find themselves in an ongoing dialogue with departments focused on operations or business growth. Frequently, the topic under discussion is the knotty one of false positives. Especially where avoiding sanctioned individuals, companies, or vessels may be concerned, false positives are likely to be a painful problem. Even where sanctions are not an issue, patterns that denote legitimate transfers can be unfortunately similar to those that reflect dubious activity, and false positives are a continual challenge.

Signals that indicate whether a team is finding the right balance in their work between robust money laundering identification and friction and false positives often come from sources external to the AML team, and it's important to be aware of that and the value of this feedback. As von Both noted, "Every financial institution is part of a network of other institutions, and if many of those other organizations are regularly sending you requests for information about transactions or transfers, then you might have an issue you need to look into; something is getting through." In the same way, if the fraud prevention team uncovers fraudulent activity associated with an account, and the AML team has never flagged any issues with transfers made or received by the account, it might be worth investigating. On the other hand, if Customer Success is complaining they're being called day and night by customers being blocked or frustrated by AML policies, the bar might be set too high.

AML, Compliance, and KYC

Throughout this section we frequently mention Know Your Customer (KYC) processes, and of course KYC is an important part of AML and compliance protection for a business. But it is crucial to bear in mind two important distinctions between AML and compliance on the one hand and KYC on the other.

First, KYC takes place at onboarding, when a customer or company is attempting to open an account. Sometimes it happens at certain stages afterward, if a bank is taking a staggered approach to KYC so that customers don't have to go through the whole process at once. AML and compliance operations, however, need to take into account the entire lifecycle of an account, for reasons we will get into shortly.

Second, the motivation behind KYC, and AML and compliance, is not quite the same, although they are closely related and play a regulatory function. KYC processes seek to establish the identity behind the account. Identity is an important part of AML and compliance, largely from a functional perspective, in that problematic or recurring identities can be a good hint that money laundering is perhaps being attempted. The scope of AML and compliance is broader, encompassing the various topics outlined in coming chapters.

Although regulatory requirements are the driving force behind AML and compliance operations, it is also important to consider that many banks and financial institutions have their own internal knowledge of types of individual profiles, or business profiles, which may be suspicious, and that much of this knowledge may be in the hands of the employees who carry out manual reviews of transactions or transfers on a daily basis. It is important to enable these employees to feed their insights back into the system as a whole, refining it over time. In some cases they can be empowered to do this personally, using relatively simple rules tools. In others it can be done through regular communication sessions with those responsible for AML or compliance strategy. AML and compliance may intuitively appear to be top-down areas, and in many ways they are, but as discussed in Chapter 4, it is equally crucial to enable bottom-up improvements as well.

In the same way, although individual investigation is important, just as manual review and research are necessary in fraud prevention, successfully integrating machine learning in AML and compliance systems can dramatically speed up pattern recognition and reduce the need for additional and unnecessary levels of human review. AML has to some extent lagged behind the fraud prevention world in this regard, but Chapters 4 and 5, which deal with this, are just as relevant to AML and compliance teams and should be read in that light. The same is true for automatically incorporating additional data sources, for data enrichment, also discussed in Chapter 4, to make scoring and decisioning faster and more accurate.

Summary

This chapter has laid the groundwork for the chapters ahead, which dive into different forms of money laundering and other problematic money transfer scenarios, including funds being sent to sanctioned organizations and funds being used to purchase prohibited items. With the right context established, we can now move on to looking more deeply at the different forms these issues can take.

## CHAPTER 20

Shell Payments: Criminal and Terrorist Screening

You're just too good to be true, can't take my eyes off of you…
—Frankie Valli[1]

Shell payments are payments carried out through a *shell* company or account—that is, one that exists only on paper, though it may own passive investments. There are plenty of legitimate use cases for shell companies, generally involving protecting individuals or parts of a company from liability. But there's no doubt that in the public mind, there are also dubious associations with the term, notably tax evasion and money laundering.

How Shell Payments Work

From the anti–money laundering (AML) perspective, shell payments are similar in a sense to synthetic identity accounts (discussed in Chapter 15); they're set up to carry out actions from which the criminals can benefit, by leveraging an entity that appears to be substantial but in reality is just, well, a shell.

The motivation for using shell payments from the criminal side is generally either to conceal the illegal source of the funds being transferred and ultimately laundered, or to assist in a tax evasion scheme. In either case, there may be some telltale signs hinting toward the fact that more investigation is required, but as with synthetic identities and some other kinds of fraud, it's often difficult to catch the patterns on the first attempt. Once the operation is attempted at scale, though, the patterns start to emerge.

---

1 Frankie Valli, "Can't Take My Eyes Off You," written by Bob Crewe and Bob Gaudio, Phillips, 1967.

Organized crime organizations are often responsible for this problematic behavior, frequently working through money mules—often, a chain of them. (Money mules, also sometimes called *smurfers*, are links in a fraud or criminal chain—they're people who transfer money acquired illegally on behalf of someone else. You can learn more about how money mules are recruited in this piece (*https://oreil.ly/A8AVN*) from Vice.) As we discussed in Chapters 7 and 17, it has become even easier for criminals to find mules to work with due to the rise of the fraudster gig economy, where people offer supportive small services to criminals. This gig economy got a boost during the COVID-19 pandemic that caused many people to search for jobs they could do from home.

All of this is just as true for money mules as it is for shipping mules, and as with shipping, it is valuable to criminals to be able to hire money mules in different states and countries around the world to increase the scale and spread of their operations. Doing so makes it more difficult to pinpoint a pattern linking the activities of the mules working for a single criminal organization. In the same way, the COVID-19 pandemic meant that a wider age range of mules was available, further confusing attempts to profile and identify money mules.

These mules use either their own identity or a synthetic identity (one that has been created using at least some legitimate details so that the elements likely to be checked do check out) to set up a bank account to use as a shell. Sometimes they do this by walking into a physical bank. The risk is slightly greater for the mule, but it's more difficult to reject someone in person, and usually a decline will not result in an arrest because suspicion is not enough to justify the spectacle of calling in the police and the risk that the person will turn out to be legitimate. Sometimes, of course, the accounts are set up online, dodging through KYC processes as successfully as possible.

As we discussed in Chapter 12, fraudsters who attempt to set up an account and fail initially may try again, learning from their mistakes every time. So, watching out for repeated patterns of device, location, and behavior can be very effective in preventing these attempts.

Funds are entered into the account. If the account is set up in person, it will typically be with cash received as part of illegal trade, and if it's online, it will of course be a transfer. Organized crime groups are often careful to leave the funds in place for some time, often longer than whatever period is required by the bank at the beginning of an account. They have even become conscious of the need to randomize the period slightly so that a pattern in their movements is harder to trace. There will, however, frequently be a set range of time within which the money is moved, and when this is identified it can be helpful in identifying these cases.

From the mule's account, the funds will often take several further hops to confuse the trail. These may include the following:

- More mule accounts.

- High-volume purchases of easily monetized goods such as cryptocurrency, gift cards (see Chapter 9 for more information), or prepaid cards, especially those bought with cash. Several EU countries have seen organized crime operations that translate their earnings from cash to the banking system using prepaid cards obtainable in the post office.

- Shell payments. These may be made via a fake ecommerce site that was built as a cover. To achieve this, the criminal would need to successfully pass the vetting of a payment service provider (e.g., sign up successfully as an eBay seller, PayPal merchant, Amazon store, etc.). This requires investment, but once the process has been worked out, it can be done over and over again more easily. And since larger criminal enterprises are usually involved with shell payment schemes, the resources are there and can be justified by the effectiveness of this method in terms of money laundering.

- Account handover. This involves a similar process to the fake ecommerce site, except it uses an existing site with a good reputation. It's just as common to see criminals buying existing merchant accounts from businesses that are about to go under as it is to see them setting up "shop" themselves. The advantages of account handover are that the criminal doesn't need to go through the process of establishing the store, and they can leverage the existing reputation of the business, making at least initial payments made through it look more legitimate. Payments can even be made to mirror the past history of the store so that the new owners are less apparent. Account handovers are sometimes offered to businesses that are close to failing, and sometimes are carried out more forcibly. In general, the original owner will receive payment in exchange for handing over access to their site. Sometimes the deal will be that the original owner will continue to use the site as before, with that use helping to mask the behavior of the criminals who have also begun to use it. This can make a new pattern of payments difficult to identify, though it does leave open the likelihood that new IPs and devices, often from a very different geographical location from the original owner, may be visible accessing the account, and isolating their transactions may show a pattern.

- Dropshipping operations. This method of working is identical to the triangulation/dropshipping scheme outlined in Chapter 7, except that instead of orders coming in from legitimate customers and payments being made with stolen cards, the orders are fake and there are no chargebacks, since the aim is not to steal but to launder tainted money.

In many cases, money being laundered will be cycled through several stages of one or a mix of these schemes, before finally being transferred out of the mule's account and reaching the account of the criminal organization involved.

The Real Risks of Money Muling, for the Mules

Unlike shipping mules, money mules bear significant risks. Few money mules realize these dangers, which are concealed or skated over by the criminals who recruit them. Moving a little money around, and getting a cut of it, seems harmless enough. Until it goes wrong, at which point the mule ends up looking a lot more like another victim of fraud: one with little recourse, since their problems originated from a criminal act.

As Ben Russell, deputy director at the UK's National Economic Crime Centre, told us:

> If you're a money mule you can get arrested, you can get prosecuted, you can end up in prison. But I think the issue that we're really worried about in terms of consequences is that, if you agree to take part in money laundering, and the bank spots it, and they seize the money, and they freeze the money, you might quickly find that you owe a nasty criminal group a lot of money—and they're not going to take no for an answer. So, what looks like an easy way of making money, for the mule, turns into a situation where they owe debt to a criminal group, and that debt often comes with interest. We spend our time hearing victims' stories, and we get people who've lost their homes, and their livelihoods. Even cases where people commit suicide, because they've lost their life savings or are so heavily in debt and so scared they can't see a way out.

Identification and Mitigation

In the eyes of regulators, money laundering is the realm of due process and KYC/KYB (*https://oreil.ly/ZUPjZ*). In the eyes of fraud fighters, money laundering is more about transaction pattern identification. The best approach is a strong combination of KYC and monitoring. As discussed in Chapter 19, this benefits both AML and fraud prevention teams in the long term, and can also get best results in specific cases being reviewed or in identifying new emerging trends.

Online businesses of all kinds do worry about and try to avoid enabling money laundering on their platform, but in general, if you're an ecommerce retailer, it's enough to have a rule-based system that can and should be designed to alert your risk or compliance team about relevant abnormalities. It's a concern, but not a burning issue.

But if you're a fintech operation, particularly if you're licensed to practice any form of banking, you fall into the "banks and financial institutions" category, and that means a robust KYC process and several safeguards against the manipulations mentioned so far. Failing to institute sufficiently robust AML efforts risks fines and ultimately

---

the loss of the license to practice, which can incline teams toward a conservative attitude. This makes sense, but should be tempered with caution, since false positives may be a particular pain point with shell payments: as mentioned earlier, identifying a shell company doesn't mean you've automatically identified an attempt at money laundering. Over time, teams can find the right balance between automation and manual review to ensure that manual reviewers are not burdened with more examples than they can cope with.

As Maximillian von Both, senior vice president of Compliance at Paysafe, told us, a deep assessment of your risks within the context of your customers, business model, and priorities results in a realistic and grounded understanding of the weaknesses, strengths, and opportunities of your business as it relates to risk management. Such processes are time consuming and resource intensive, but valuable. "Risk assessment is often seen as a regulatory necessity (and the hassle involved in this is so huge that it often obscures the point!), but the actual exercise is crucial," von Both said.

> If you don't understand your risk—which includes understanding your product and your customers and how they use the product, and the tech (because otherwise you don't know how you're vulnerable) and the bad actors involved—then you can't define your risk, and if you can't define, you can't defend against it. Real, in-depth, meaningful risk assessment is one of the most difficult, most unnerving, but most vital tasks you have.

Once a real understanding of your risk landscape is established, you can use that to find the right balance between efforts to prevent money laundering and avoiding false positives.

As Chapter 12 points out, there are excellent options today for using both vendors and automated internal processes as part of KYC efforts. Notably, many vendors offer online document validation augmented by AI, in conjunction with selfie and liveness checks to ensure that the individual using the device matches the person in the photograph of the ID. Forms included in the sign-up process can also include questions that provide valuable fraud-fighting information. This is valuable because they can be checked against multiple third-party data sources, and automated systems can be taught which kinds of answers are internally coherent and which seem to pull in different directions.

Additionally, many identity verification vendors are doing a lot of work to keep records up to date and free of manipulation so that phone-based verification is possible and reliable, making multifactor authentication (MFA) an important part of the process as well.

As with account takeover (ATO) prevention (Chapter 13), what is crucial here is a layered approach. No single factor will be enough to either protect your business from money launderers or show regulators you are doing appropriate due diligence. A number of overlapping approaches must be combined to protect the business from many different angles, and the results need to be looked at holistically so that breaks in the coherent pattern can be detected.

Much KYC work is of overlapping relevance to both AML and fraud prevention teams, and having these teams work together closely to pool resources, information, and trends is highly recommended. Some banks have dedicated KYC or customer/business onboarding teams for this purpose, including both fraud fighters and AML professionals. Though this structure may not be right for all companies, close collaboration on KYC work benefits all involved.

KYC is an essential step in the AML process, but it cannot be relied upon to prevent shell payments. First, mistakes happen, and a fraudulent shell account may slip through the cracks. Second, accounts that were initially set up with legitimate and substantial information may over time become corrupted with fraudulent data, either through adding more information to the account, ATO, or the suborning of an employee, either consciously, through bribery or blackmail, or through social engineering. Just imagine the damage that could ensue if a skillful social engineer persuaded a bank employee to add a fraudster's phone number to the account's trusted credentials list, for example.

For this reason, staying vigilant against shell payments is important long after the account has been set up. It's more effective in preventing AML, and it's also good practice in terms of demonstrating that your business takes AML seriously and works hard to remain in line with its regulatory requirements.

One common step to take as part of this process is to sample and monitor cases of users who are employing identity anonymizing tools. Customers who are using obfuscation may have something to hide.

On the other hand, and bearing in mind the danger of false positives, there are also a number of legitimate scenarios in which customers might reasonably prefer to conceal their identity. Some users are simply very concerned about their privacy, which is not unreasonable after so many years of data breaches and the promotion of their dangers. And with tools such as Apple's Safari15/iOS 15 IP masking services becoming better known and easily available to ordinary consumers, those who are privacy conscious may not have to go to much effort to hide their identities anymore. Some users are very sensitive to spam and take steps to avoid it. Others may want to access content or services that cannot be reached from their location and so habitually make an effort to appear to be from somewhere they are not.

To provide a very simple example of bringing together KYC and transaction monitoring in order to track potential money laundering, consider the query in Example 20-1, which generates a report that is designed for your monitoring team to use.

Example 20-1. Query to track potential money laundering

```
SELECT
    customers.occupation,
    AVG(payments.trasaction_amount) / AVG(customers.credit_score),
    COUNT(customer_id)
FROM
    customers
    INNER JOIN
        payments (USING customer_id)
GROUP BY 1
ORDER BY 2 ASC, 2 DESC
```

Table 20-1 shows the output from Example 20-1.

Table 20-1. Output from query in Example 20-1

customers.occupation	avg(payments.trasaction_amount)/ avg(customers.credit_score)	count(customer_id)
Teacher	10.43	100
Retired	0.5	200
State worker	0.53	150

 As shown in Table 20-1, this type of analysis is a useful tool to zoom in on a possible population currently operating as mules in your system. Break this down into states, genders, age buckets, or any other hunch you have on the data and you'll get a sense of the norms and averages in your customer base. Then you'll be able to identify those few cases that deserve a deeper manual inspection.

Criminal and Terrorist Screening

Within the context of shell payments, it is appropriate to also discuss criminal and terrorist screening, because some of the entities most likely to try to hide their actions behind shell payments are criminal or terrorist entities. We will be talking about standard criminal and terrorist screening based on lists of known problematic entities. We won't be delving into what to do against the exception to every rule: North Korea, a country that fields an elite team (*https://oreil.ly/8Z3LW*) of cybercriminals (*https://oreil.ly/Zmzar*) whose job, among other things, is to steal from banks and financial institutions. In general, nation-state actors are a problem for cybersecurity teams, not fraud prevention or compliance, and this more or less remains the case with North Korea even though its cybercriminals aim for theft. At the least, this is an issue in which the cybersecurity team would lead and other departments contribute assistance as appropriate. You can always chat with your own cybersecurity department if you're curious about this intriguing problem and what your organization is doing to protect against the threat.

Teams entrusted with screening need to be able to prove they make appropriate efforts to identify, flag, and prevent actions being taken by entities on specific lists of sanctioned or prohibited individuals, companies, groups, or countries. In 2021 the Office of Financial Sanctions Implementation (OFSI) imposed a $25.4 million fine on a UK bank for Russian sanctions violations. The team responsible for preventing sanctions violations is the one protecting their company from fines on this kind of scale. Though this section is written primarily with teams from banks or financial institutions in mind, fintechs are increasingly finding themselves needing to be sensitive to and compliant with regulations and demands of this sort; in July 2021, PayPal announced a project designed to prevent transactions that fund hate groups (*https://oreil.ly/0cbCn*).

You can approach the challenge of finding sanctioned entities in a number of ways. Traditional banks are likely to invest considerable effort into identifying the problematic terms associated with the entities, and are likely to be conservative about what potentially problematic entities are allowed to do. Fintech companies, on the other hand, may take a more creative approach: banning any cards with an Iranian BIN from being used on the site, for instance. Yet they may be willing to give the customer the information about why the card was rejected, which subtly nudges them toward procuring a non-Iranian credit card. (In this case, Iranian users will probably shift toward using virtual private networks [VPNs], foreign credit cards, or prepaid credit cards, and perhaps false billing addresses, so a policy is needed for that as well.)

In terms of identifying specific names on the relevant lists, the greatest challenge is probably false positives. As one of the experts we spoke to during our research for this section put it, "You have to remember that if all you're doing is looking for 'Iran' you're going to find 'hair and nail salon' as well—and probably you'll find far more hair and nail salons than you'll find references to Iran!" A team of analysts tasked with sanctions compliance for their company did in fact have exactly this problem, and many others like it, and had to refine their system to ensure that a flood of false positives didn't create an unreasonable burden on the team, for whom time is a key metric.

The problem came about, of course, because if you remove the spaces between the words, the last two letters of "hair" and the first two letters of "and" when put together spell "iran"—and you can't rely on spacing to protect you from this sort of issue because that's far too easy a trick for criminals or terrorists to use. As with fraudsters, sanctioned entities will take advantage of any loophole they find. That makes fuzzy string matching and phonetic matching crucial, simply to block off the obvious ways around which sanctioned entities might otherwise take. At the same time, it increases the challenge of false positives. One expert noted that giving reviewers the ability to make changes and institute new rules to adjust to evolving trends can help reduce false positives, and regular biweekly meetings to discuss new trends and see whether work can be done to reduce false positives related to them can also be very impactful in this regard.

Much of the work of looking for matches can fortunately be done with automated rules designed to filter bad or dubious cases through to a human review team. It's particularly fortunate that automation has become more popular in this area since the volume of material to be screened has increased so much in recent years. Many people forget that when they're making a payment using alternative payment methods such as electronic wallets or fintech applications, the traditional banking system is still a part of the infrastructure that supports those payments. The more payments or money transfers there are overall, the more work there will be for sanctions teams.

One advantage that sanctions teams have is that although the volume they're dealing with is huge, a lot of repeat payments are generally seen within that volume. For example, someone might be sending more or less the same amount of money from the same account to the same account, at more or less the same time every month. Perhaps they're sending money home, or subsidizing a child who is currently a student, or contributing to a particular cause, or making a payment to a business for a regular service. Ensuring that your automated system can do repetitive pattern matching can take a lot of the load off your team. If the payment is identical and very regular, with a solid history of previous checks behind it, you may want to clear or block it automatically. Or if it's still early for that pattern, you can send it to two team members, and if both agree it's part of the same pattern, the previous decision can be repeated without further action. Since experienced reviewers in this field can often review cases in seconds, or certainly well under a minute, this is an efficient way to keep things moving quickly.

For cases that are not obvious and require investigation, the investigation and analysis process is very similar to that required to prevent ecommerce fraud: details are checked with third-party data sources or consortiums, history is delved into, and if escalation is required the remitting bank can be contacted, or even the customer.

Searching for sources of information from within your own organization's data set is also important. For example, there are certain organizations with ethnic (or cultural) origins that mean certain names are more likely to be found in the organization than in the population at large. If you're trying to prevent those organizations from moving money through your organization, some work on name origin can be helpful in identifying these individuals.

Predicting origin (and gender) based on names can be achieved with the help of several popular APIs from companies such as Namsor (*https://namsor.app*) and Name-API (*https://www.nameapi.org*) (a helpful review (*https://oreil.ly/WeIpE*) of these services is also available, thanks to the work of Santamaría and Mihaljević, of the

University of Applied Sciences in Berlin and the Amazon Development Center in Berlin). Another option is to build your own classifier. There are some brave open source attempts (*https://oreil.ly/IYF2J*) at achieving this with Naive Bayes models, but unlike gender guessing (which already has its own Python library (*https://oreil.ly/wzEB7*)), name origins are often not that easy to predict.

Research of this kind is valuable in ensuring that any gray areas are covered, strengthening your system's ability to catch problematic entities and proving your business's seriousness in preventing transactions connected to prohibited entities. It can also help you expand the nexus of entities so that you can catch ones that are connected to already-sanctioned entities. This puts you ahead of the next list and protects your company from criticism should the connections be obvious.

Nikki Baumann, who during his career has been the team leader of FinCrime (AML/CTF) at Revolut, head of fraud and security at CoinPoker, and senior operations manager at Deutsche Bank, noted that work that goes above and beyond the minimal needs of the sanctions list is the most valuable in protecting the business's reputation and proving the business's reputation in fighting against terrorist or criminal transactions. It shows genuine dedication to preventing sanctioned entities from using your system—something that is important in proving to regulators and customers that your company is taking its responsibilities seriously. Baumann said this work, like fraud prevention efforts, involves a lot of pattern detection and analysis, and that in this context investing in educating customer support and operations teams about relevant details can be enormously important, so that they can flag anything suspicious for further review. That might include suspicious subject lines, which can, when discovered, be a good word cloud project so that future instances are caught automatically. (See Chapter 10 for a word cloud example.) Baumann further pointed out that making sure a range of languages are screened is important in making sure this work is really effective.

Finally, close collaboration with the compliance team, and with other financial institutions around the world, can also help improve screening efforts and streamline the process. As one expert told us, "There are hundreds of financial institutions around the world, most of which invest great effort into screening and AML efforts. When a transaction is made, a number of those FIs are usually involved. Even in a simple case of international money transfer, several banks might be involved. If each of those is screening, then you have a kind of safety net effect." Since teams from different banks and different countries are traditionally good at collaborating over suspicious transactions and sharing trends, this effect is amplified. The more this becomes institutionalized through established forums, conferences, meetups, and roundtables, the greater the impact of collaboration in this area is likely to become.

Summary

This chapter explored the issue of shell payments, which often play a role in money laundering schemes, and discussed different approaches to tackling this challenge, both through KYC processes and beyond. AML work in this context is vital for regulatory reasons, of course, but can also play an important role in preventing bad actors from exploiting the bank's systems and in guarding against reputation damage from successful misuse. The next chapter looks at preventing abuse around prohibited items, which also has this dual role of both regulatory compliance and business protection.

Summary

## CHAPTER 21

Prohibited Items

No soup for you!
—Seinfeld[1]

In the same way that shell payments (Chapter 20) are used to conceal the *source* of funds, with prohibited items the trick is to conceal the *nature* of the item sold. The topics covered in Chapters 9 and 22 are very relevant in considering prohibited items as well. Cryptocurrency is often used to purchase prohibited items because of the increased anonymity associated with cryptocurrency, and some of the stages that might get added into money laundering attempts in order to confuse the trail, as discussed with shell payments (Chapter 20), may be used in this context as well. Account takeover (ATO) or account handover, in particular, can play a role in selling prohibited items because when you're trying to fly under the radar with illicit goods, it's very helpful to be selling them from a business that already has a good reputation and has really been selling legitimate goods for some time.

In terms of prohibited items, it's particularly common to see the type of account handover/takeover whereby a deal is reached to allow the criminals to gain access to the backend of the store in order to use it as a front, while at the same time the legitimate business continues as normal. The business owner is often a willing accomplice, or an unwilling but conscious accomplice (as in communities where it is very hard, and probably unwise, to say no to the local crime organization), but from time to time this scenario also pops up in cases where ATO has occurred. In these cases, the hidden hand of the hacker will usually access the account at different times of the day than the real owner to help conceal their presence, and will sometimes go

---

1 *Seinfeld*, Season 7, Episode 6, directed by Andy Ackerman, written by Spike Feresten, NBC, aired November 2, 1995.

so far as to set up temporary "deals" on their prohibited merchandise, which will be over and archived by the time the real owner is likely to log back in.

As discussed in Chapter 17, for the successful sale of prohibited items you need an element of collusion between the buyer and the seller. That is to say, you need someone who wants to sell forbidden goods, and also someone who wants to purchase them. Both ends of this arrangement are problematic for banks, financial institutions, and the marketplaces used to make the sale.

New entrants to the field of fraud prevention or anti–money laundering (AML) often ask why people who want to buy and sell prohibited items don't simply stick to the dark web. There are plenty of forums and marketplaces there, and no shortage of sales of illicit goods—stolen information, arms, drugs, and more. Cryptocurrency transfers can be anonymous (Monero and Zcash are favored for this use case), and chargebacks aren't possible, protecting both buyer and seller. It seems like an ideal solution.

There are a number of reasons why this wasn't always the method of choice even before steps began to be taken (*https://oreil.ly/V7kF9*) to regulate cryptocurrency to make precisely this misuse more difficult. For one thing, it's important to remember that in cases of prohibited items, you may not always be dealing with career criminals, at least on the buying side. Some goods, while illegal in many countries, are still popular among people who live normal lives and are not typically part of the criminal fraternity outside the specific area of the prohibited items. Drugs, and to a lesser extent, weapons, are the main examples here. Someone who lives an otherwise irreproachable life but has an affinity for the effects of psychedelic drugs may want to purchase them online, and is unlikely to be comfortable with the dark web and relatively unlikely to be knowledgeable about cryptocurrency. They'd much rather go onto an online marketplace they're familiar with and make the purchase there, or head over to what looks like an ordinary online store, armed with the knowledge of which "special products" to order, and pay using whatever method they're most comfortable using online. Accommodating these customers expands the customer base that those selling the prohibited items can appeal to—in some cases, considerably.

Additionally, although professionals in the payments space often rail against the complexity of the system and the intricacies of navigating it successfully, from the perspective of a simple seller and buyer online, buying and selling on the internet is pretty easy. Setting up an account on an existing marketplace is very easy, since the payment structure is all in place there and integration is made extremely simple, and even setting up an online store and setting up payments for it is relatively intuitive nowadays. Especially if you're doing it multiple times, which a large criminal organization may be doing. Easiest of all, of course, is the account handover scenario described earlier, which is one of the reasons it's so popular in this context.

The way it works in terms of transactions is simple. As an example of an account handover, say the site that's being used sells baked goods; it could be a seller on a marketplace or a standalone site. In this example, the original owner still makes and sells delicious and entirely drug-free breads, cakes, cookies, cupcakes, and so on, but at the same time, the criminals also have a presence on the backend, using the legitimate store as a front. Those who are interested in purchasing drugs know to click on the "special brownie" product, and to order "1000 special brownies" if what they really want is, say, x grams of cocaine. Good customers won't be ordering 1,000 special brownies, and the customers who are don't want brownies. But the payment goes through as normal, and everyone is happy—except the compliance team, who are responsible for preventing exactly these sorts of interactions.

The exact same scam works for money laundering, except with the variation that no product is ever actually delivered. Collusion is always a money laundering sweet spot, and is yet another example why AML and compliance teams would do well to pool insights and keep in close touch with one another.

Of course, it isn't always dangerous, nor does it need to involve physical items. Prohibited items can also include pirated content being sold online, both on respectable marketplaces who fight against the flood of piracy and on more dubious websites that don't mind being part of the pirate party. In these cases, the goods tend to be available more naively and openly—far less effort is put into concealing what's really going on. Regardless of the question of IP infringement and brand protection, which can quickly escalate into a civil lawsuit from the owner of the IP, fintech and ecommerce operations are expected to have and enforce a policy of what can and cannot be sold using their service, and it's this angle that compliance teams need to have covered. Here the legal situation, and what companies are required to do about it, is critical, and for this it's generally best to draw up guidelines in conjunction with the company's lawyers, who remain vigilant for changes to the law that require updating the guidelines. This area is far more complex than other regulatory areas, because what companies are required to do is usually far more open to interpretation. A close relationship with Legal is essential.

Similarly, it's worth bearing in mind in this context that there are some items or industries that aren't necessarily prohibited but that fall into a complex gray area, such as sweepstakes. If a product like this is relevant for your business, it's important to raise the delicacy of the issue with management so that a policy can be developed about how to handle it. Compliance teams are likely to see the risks or complexities earlier than other departments, and can save the business hassle and potential trouble later on by raising it early, before any legal or regulatory issues force attention to it.

Identification and Mitigation

Unlike with money laundering—where considerable effort is invested by both criminals and their mules to conceal the origin of the funds, often involving many steps in the concealment process—with prohibited items it's not uncommon to see a less sophisticated approach, especially from the buyers' side. The fact that they're buying illicit goods doesn't mean they're technically competent or even aware of some of the giveaways that might indicate that they're up to something suspicious. In some cases—as in our "brownie" enthusiasts, for example—they might use their real name. If the sale is through a well-known marketplace rather than a dedicated site, they may even use their real account. From their perspective, this transaction ought to look entirely aboveboard. There's nothing to raise an eyebrow about if all they're doing is purchasing baked goods on a reputable site.

Sellers often invest just a bit less thought and work into their end too, perhaps influenced by their knowledge of their customers. From their side it's a relatively safe operation, after all. Their customers already know what to do, the sale is in the bag, and there's nothing overtly problematic about the setup. Moreover, unlike with fraud attempts, there won't be any chargebacks coming through to tip the site off to the fact that something dodgy is happening.

When it comes to detection, this relative lack of caution can be a significant advantage, and it's worth investing in automation and research to make sure you're catching the careless cases. For example, make sure your system is detecting items that are way off their normal price tag. Sometimes it could be really simple to do—for example, with something like this:

```
SELECT
    product,
    AVG(price),
    MIN(price),
    MAX(price),
    MAX(price) - MIN(price) AS price_change
FROM
    store_prices_log
WHERE
    dayid BETWEEN {min_day} AND {max_day}
GROUP BY 1
ORDER BY price_change DESC;
```

Illustration of results:

Product	AVG(price)	MIN(price)	MAX(price)	PRICE_CHANGE
Blondies	$51	$2	$100	99
Brownies	$2	$1	$3	2

Notes:

- While any type of increase in cookie price should be considered a crime, it's easy to see here that something suspicious happened to the price of "blondies" in this store, especially if people are willing to pay these prices.

- If the store does not keep a historical log of prices, the same figures can be retrieved from the sales table (assuming there's a record of how many cookies were purchased in each order, to derive the price per item). In fact, using the sales records can also add a metric of the item's median price, which could help with evaluating the scale of the potential shell payment operation (i.e., the closer the median price is to the highest price, the more incidents of overpriced cookie sales there are in your system). If the median aggregate function isn't supported in your database, consider using PERCENTILE_CONT.

- A third option, probably only for cases in which you suspect that many products are being used for prohibited activity, is to compare your entire catalog against a competitor or a historical benchmark data set; see, for example, this price comparison by Vikrant Yadav (*https://oreil.ly/bLcI1*).

Sadly, not every criminal is considerate enough to leave a red flag, like a $101 cookie (although many do, which is why it's worth looking for). They might put more thought into it, working out which products would more or less match the price tags they're putting on their goods, and perhaps even choosing items that can be bought in bulk or by appropriate weight so that customers can indicate amounts without triggering any alarms. In that case, you'll need to go one better as well.

Moreover, the account half-handover case that we discussed, in which the original business goes on operating as normal with the original owner and the criminals simply run their additional sales on the side using the store as a front, is more difficult to catch. There will be very mixed signals from this store—it's mostly legitimate business, which drowns out the suspicious signs. That's part of why the criminals like to do it this way, after all.

These last scenarios can be identified using the following analysis of anomalies in the popularity of certain products against the general population/benchmark. This can be used to find a suspicious product that is suddenly becoming "too popular to be true" on a certain week:

```
WITH suspected_products_table as (
  SELECT sale_id, product
  FROM
  --Population: choose a day range where you suspect shell payments
    sales_table as S
  WHERE
    day_id BETWEEN {min_day} AND {max_day}
) --choose suspected period
```

```
SELECT
  sales_aggregated_table.product (
    count_sales - count_suspected_sales
  ) / count_suspected_sales AS benchmark_rate,
  count_suspected_sales / count_sales AS suspected_sales_rate
FROM
  (
  SELECT
    product,
    COUNT(sale_id) AS count_sales,
    SUM(
      CASE
          WHEN sales.sale_id = suspected_products.sale_id
          THEN 1
          ELSE 0
      END
    ) AS count_suspected_sales
  FROM sales_table
    LEFT JOIN suspected_products_table USING (sale_id)
  WHERE
    day_id BETWEEN {min_day} AND {max_day} --choose benchmark period
  ) AS sales_aggregated_table
HAVING
  suspected_sales_rate > 0.05
ORDER BY
  suspected_sales_rate DESC;
```

Illustration of results:

Product	Benchmark_rate	Suspected_sales_rate
Brownies	9.00%	14.88%
Blondies	5.00%	23.94%
Cheesecake	11.00%	11.64%
Danish	5.69%	5.00%

When charting the results of this query, we find in Figure 21-1 that "blondies" seem to be our potential "crazy cookie" of the month, since their popularity is currently spiking well above the benchmark.

RMSE (root mean square error) is a helpful visualization for many use cases of deviation. Pricing anomalies for shell payments could also be easily obtained with Python (*https://oreil.ly/UParG*).

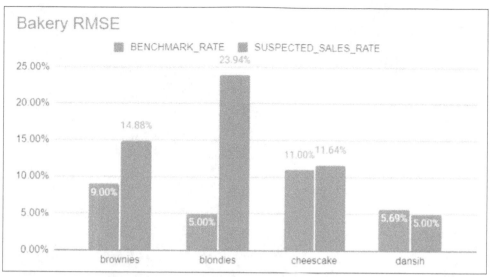

Figure 21-1. Graph showing the results of the baked goods analysis

By taking all these overpriced cookie scenarios with a cautious grain of salt, you'll be able to ensure that your ecommerce operation remains compliant and that no prohibited items are being laundered through your system.

Summary

This chapter discussed the challenges of identifying the sale of prohibited items, a topic that typically falls into a compliance mentality rather than fraud prevention. Customers do usually make real payments for prohibited items, since to do otherwise draws attention to the forbidden activity. It is crucial for businesses to be able to show that they are taking appropriate steps to prevent the sale of prohibited items, as otherwise they run the risk of being seen as complicit. The next chapter looks into a form of anti–money laundering that comes with the same sort of burden: companies must be able to prove they're taking all appropriate steps to prevent cryptocurrency money laundering, or they'll face serious fines and censure.

## CHAPTER 22

Cryptocurrency Money Laundering

How do you hold a moonbeam in your hand?
  —Rodgers and Hammerstein[1]

It wasn't that long ago that when someone mentioned anti–money laundering (AML) work, they implicitly referred to the world of banking. Now, though, some of the greatest AML challenges are those faced by professionals trying to prevent money laundering through cryptocurrency. The basic crime is the same as in the ordinary financial system: moving money gained through criminal activity around enough times, and with sufficient obfuscation, that it comes out looking "clean" or as though it hadn't been gained illicitly. However, many of the solutions tailored over the years to fit the traditional banking world aren't effective, or aren't as effective, against cryptocurrency money laundering attempts, meaning teams need to get creative about how to remain compliant. That's especially true if they want to follow not just the letter of the law, but also its spirit.

Cryptocurrency: More Regulated Than You Think, and Likely to Become More So

Many consumers aren't aware of the extent to which cryptocurrency is increasingly governed by the same sorts of regulatory considerations as traditional banking, but the increasing regulatory environment is something no company involved in cryptocurrency, or in services related to it, can afford to ignore. In fact, in the United States, FinCEN has had regulation in place for a number of years now. In Europe it

---

1 Richard Rodgers and Oscar Hammerstein, "How Do You Solve a Problem Like Maria?" in *The Sound of Music*, music by Richard Rodgers, lyrics by Oscar Hammerstein, book by Howard Lindsay and Russel Crouse (1959).

was the 5th Anti-Money Laundering Directive that mandated AML requirements for cryptocurrencies, something that impacts the UK as well. And recently the European Commission announced that it would be extending AML rules (*https://oreil.ly/3Qafy*) so that companies facilitating crypto transfers must collect information identifying both sender and recipient, check whether the information is misleading, and avoid allowing transfers to or from anonymous crypto-asset wallets, in the same way that anonymous bank accounts are prohibited under EU AML rules.

These laws may take some time to be confirmed and take effect, but they are a strong indication of the way the industry is moving, at least in countries that traditionally take AML regulation seriously.

Cryptocurrency players themselves are getting involved in influencing the regulatory game: Coinbase has called for the creation of a new US regulatory body to over-see digital assets (*https://oreil.ly/reVFM*). This makes sense, taken in context: one report found that the prevalence of theft and crime within decentralized finance is largely due to the untested and immature nature of the technology available.[2] The prevalence is no joke, and is growing as the cryptocurrency market does; in 2021, cryptocurrency-related crime hit a new high (*https://oreil.ly/IA0ch*). A 2021 MIT paper found that 3% of transactions in bitcoin are illegal activity.[3] It's ultimately to the benefit of companies in the field to make that technology, and the industry, safer and more trustworthy.

The Challenge of Cryptocurrency Money Laundering

Even with these regulations, however, cryptocurrency AML can represent a minefield of hazards. To start with, of course, there are all the usual tricks that money launderers or mules try against traditional banks, as discussed in Chapters 19 and 20. But beyond that, cryptocurrency has its own unique challenges. For one thing, crypto companies are often licensed in countries such as Malta where regulations are more relaxed, which can cause impact farther down the chain as well; the ecosystem as a whole is not covered by consistent protections. Additionally, cryptocurrency is by nature international—that's part of the appeal—which means that dealing with multiple regulatory environments is inevitable and often confusing.

Beyond that, the customer base most attracted to cryptocurrency is a diverse one that often doesn't show the same characteristics associated with good customers in traditional banking. Customers may have variable credit scores or no credit scores, come from a range of backgrounds and countries, and expect to be able to move

---

2 "DeFi Fraud and Theft Losses Reach $10.5 Billion in 2021" (*https://oreil.ly/tOPBj*), Finextra, November 19, 2021.

3 Betsy Vereckey, "Bitcoin: Who Owns It, Who Mines It, Who's Breaking the Law" (*https://oreil.ly/6e3t9*), MIT Sloan School of Management, October 14, 2021.

money around as though international borders didn't exist. High-volume activity is also common in cryptocurrency, even with ordinary customers. It's common for customers to open a new cryptocurrency address for every transaction, making it harder to see when lots of steps are being taken on purpose to conceal money laundering.

Essentially, your average, legitimate crypto customer looks a lot like the persona who'd be under suspicion of money laundering if you were working in a traditional bank. In addition, a significantly influential chunk of your legitimate customers are people who hold controversial notions about the need to obey any form of regulation or law. The notion of "code is law" (*https://oreil.ly/uiOrM*) is generally accepted among many "whales" (*https://oreil.ly/U2Lch*) of cryptocurrency. This situation poses many challenges and, naturally, attracts many fraudulent actors. Some of these actors would even argue that "code is law" should protect them from consequences of any AML or fraud activity; at least, this is what was claimed by the 18-year-old math prodigy who hacked the decentralized finance (DeFi) protocol and refused to return the $16 million (*https://oreil.ly/6oyvI*) he obtained through the attack.

At the same time, the suspicions of the AML team are likely heightened, because the fact is that cryptocurrency is a great vehicle for money laundering, and criminals know that. Dark web forums and marketplaces and dodgy Telegram channels frequently reference cryptocurrency of various kinds as the preferred payment method, for ease of transfer and relative anonymity. In fact, Nikki Baumann, a Fraud Principal at Farfetch who also has previous experience in both banking and cryptocurrency,, noted that mixing personal and business accounts along the trail of money laundering is particularly common in this context, which can further confuse things. Since anonymity comes with many kinds of cryptocurrency as part of the offering—privacy is a key part of the product—too much friction or demand for identification defeats part of the value and promise of the product. This means the steps that KYC and AML teams at a bank can take are far more challenging within the cryptocurrency context; users are likely to be offended and angered by attempts to pin down their identity, and may try to move to a different option.

Cryptocurrency mixers add to the problem. A *mixer* (also called a *tumbler*, or sometimes referred to as *CoinJoin*) is a service or app that mixes different streams of potentially identifiable cryptocurrency. You could think of it as something like taking a dollar into a store, and asking the cashier to break it into pennies. Those 100 pennies are shown to you, but are then mixed back in with all the other pennies in the cash register. At the end of the process, you get a dollar's worth of pennies back, but the actual coins you get are selected at random, and probably don't include any of the coins you saw when your dollar was first broken for you. You've got a dollar, but the journey of any particular coin would be hard to trace. And you can request the cashier to repeat the process of mixing the pennies in with those in the cash register and drawing out new ones as many times as you like. That's more or less how it works with cryptocurrency mixing, except as it's digital rather than physical, it's a lot easier and faster. (And it doesn't annoy a hapless cashier.) All this makes ownership of specific "coins" harder to trace, considerably increasing the anonymity of the transactions and transfers. You can consult the ledger, for cryptocurrencies that have open ledgers, but if a user has gone in for a lot of mixing, you might be facing a decidedly uphill battle.

Something that people who don't work or deal frequently in cryptocurrency often fail to realize is that, by default, blockchains typically encourage transparency, meaning even more than in the fiat world, data about transactions is at the fingertips of any user who cares to look for it. That's why privacy lovers and fraudsters go to such lengths to disguise their activities.

Due to the severity of the challenges we've described, some banks are so wary of cryptocurrency that they do not permit turning cryptocurrency into fiat or vice versa. This is understandable, particularly given that cryptocurrency is still relatively new, and so extreme caution may seem the best approach. But given the increasing normalization of the use of cryptocurrency, this hardly seems like a long-term solution. If Sotheby's is willing to take bitcoin for a rare diamond, it's probably past the time to wonder whether cryptocurrency will ever find a home in traditional transactions. As Aite Group's Colin Whitmore puts it, "It is about risk assessment and mitigation— financial institutions need to assess and manage the risk, whether they are directly or indirectly involved; they cannot turn a blind eye to it."[4] Even Warren Buffet, who has made no secret of his negative feelings toward cryptocurrency, isn't staying completely clear (*https://oreil.ly/KFdLM*) of the burgeoning crypto economy.

Opting out simply isn't going to be an option forever, if you're a part of the financial ecosystem. Given that, finding effective strategies for the identification and mitigation of money laundering within cryptocurrency becomes increasingly urgent.

Identification and Mitigation

When talking about identification and mitigation, it's important to understand two distinct kinds of challenges. First, there are the difficulties faced by exchanges, which have little insight into identities or accounts. All they do is exchange one form of cryptocurrency for another. Often, all an exchange sees is cryptocurrency addresses— not which country the coin is coming from. Second, there are the challenges faced by services that convert fiat to cryptocurrency and vice versa. These services have access to more information: where the money is coming from and going to, which locations

---

4 Alin Popa, ed. "Anti-Money Laundering and Cryptocurrencies – Safe or too Risky to Touch?" (*https://oreil.ly/ 9OBLb*) The Paypers, July 27, 2021.

are involved, the IP address, and so on. On the other hand, they have to operate more within the world of traditional banking since, by definition, fiat is involved.

For consumers who want to change crypto into fiat or vice versa, there are two obvious paths to take. Some traditional banks will do it, generally charging a particularly high rate for the privilege. AML teams dealing with this use case will likely be under orders to ensure each transfer undergoes considerable scrutiny.

A second method is for consumers to use a service like Coinbase, Binance, Kraken, Gemini, Wirex, Metal Pay, or others that have become credit card issuers. Sometimes these credit cards may connect directly to e-wallets, as in the case of Coinbase cardholders topping Google Pay up with crypto. A similar approach to this is taken by UK neobank Revolut, which allows its customers to use cryptocurrency and convert it to fiat, as long as the coin isn't from an external source; it must have been bought in-app or received from another Revolut user. This is an ingenious way to facilitate growing consumer interest in crypto while still keeping transactions within the Revolut ecosystem, which ensures the AML team has good visibility into account ownership and identity.

With all these options, Know Your Customer (KYC) processes at onboarding mean the AML team has both filtering power at sign-up, and valuable information to draw on when investigating a transaction. KYC in this context often involves both typical KYC elements, such as a selfie and liveness check to match an ID, often using AI to check the match, and questions such as asking about the source of the funds and what the individual plans on doing with them. In general, with cryptocurrency, *investment* is a common answer to both questions. Where more cryptocurrency-specific answers appear, such as "the source of the funds is cryptocurrency mining," more investigation can be done—for example, in one case we heard about, asking for utility bills to show the electricity cost of mining, which is an energy-intensive process.

Going down to this level of detail—and we suspect asking for utility bills is more detail than most AML teams will go to—is more relevant in cases of deposit than withdrawal, due to the necessity to ensure that the source of the funds is legitimate. In all these cases, enabling such transfers is a crucial part of business, so the work of the AML team in protecting the company's future and its current transactions is vital.

As an example for what mitigation in this field should look like, we can take a typical product offer of a blockchain intelligence service, aiming to de-anonymize crypto transfers. The "crypto personas" shown in Figure 22-1 demonstrate the way crypto money movements can be tagged as high risk (or scored according to their relative risk level). As discussed in Chapter 9, using rich data to build up customer personas in this way can be valuable in fighting fraud.

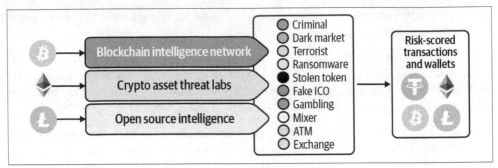

Figure 22-1. Risk analysis for cryptocurrency personas[5]

There may be many nuances in the personas suitable for your population. For example, you might want to make the distinction between general exchanges and *high-risk* exchanges—ones favored by criminals, such as BTC-e, which was seized by US authorities in 2017. Mixing and ATMs could be completely legit in the context of your audience; dubious ICOs (Initial Coin Offerings (*https://oreil.ly/62oRi*)) may be irrelevant to you from the AML perspective and more interesting for the purpose of social engineering fraud. It would be quite a lot of work to create this type of risk-score mechanism in-house, so consider using a third-party vendor such as Chainalysis, CipherTrace, or Elliptic. The third-party route may be especially helpful for banks, which don't necessarily deal with crypto on a daily basis.

KYC: Combating Money Laundering from the Start

Exchanges vary considerably in their approach to AML, both in terms of the regulatory requirements they're mandated to fulfill, which vary depending on where they're located, and in how seriously they take the problem of money laundering beyond the needs of regulatory requirements. We assume, for the purposes of this section, that we're writing this for someone who does care about preventing money laundering and that therefore measures such as KYC, which may not be mandated but which can be very valuable in preventing money laundering, are relevant. Fiat-to-crypto services are more likely to need KYC by default.

As mentioned, exchanges have limited information available to them that could help determine whether a given transfer or transaction is legitimate or a step in a money laundering scheme. For this reason, finding alternative ways of getting relevant information from customers is all the more important.

For both exchanges and fiat-to-crypto services, implementing a robust KYC process so that anyone wanting to use the service has to provide at least some information

---

5 Image adapted from CipherTrace (*https://oreil.ly/GxRpz*).

about who they are is invaluable. Customers only need to go through the process once, and it can shed light on every action thereafter. Certainly, friction is a concern, and as a market, cryptocurrency users are not enthusiastic about either delay or the need to provide information about themselves. As with setting up bank accounts, it's possible to stagger a KYC process so that some questions or requests for information are delayed until a customer wants to take a particular step—transferring money, for example. This can assuage some concerns about friction. With exchanges, as well, the process can be limited to the information that is most useful in preventing money laundering; it doesn't have to include all the steps and checks that a full KYC process might usually include.

Using a vendor that provides document verification checks, combined with selfie and liveness checks, may be the easiest way to insert friction in a way that doesn't feel too burdensome for the customer. People using cryptocurrency are more likely than the average customer in a traditional banking context to be comfortable with the technology involved, and the speed of these mechanisms is another point in their favor with this audience. If this step throws up some red flags, further friction can be inserted, such as a request for proof of a physical address.

 Nikki Baumann noted that the value of KYC goes beyond KYC itself. If an account passes KYC, but does so in such a way that you're even slightly suspicious of it, it can be flagged so that its activities are actively monitored on an ongoing basis. This can dramatically reduce the chances of later problems.

It's not popular to say this, but the best way to prevent cryptocurrency being used in money laundering is probably to treat customers more in the way they would expect to be treated in a traditional bank, as discussed in Chapter 12. It may not be popular initially, but in time the added legitimacy this gives to the industry should benefit everyone working with cryptocurrency. This is a silver lining to regulations such as those planned by the European Commission.

Beyond KYC

Though cryptocurrency has unique challenges when it comes to preventing money laundering, it also has unique services that can help mitigate the challenges to some extent. One example is the ability to use websites such as Bitcoin Who's Who (*https://bitcoinwhoswho.com*), a site that lets users enter a bitcoin address, keyword, name, screen name, and so on associated with a transaction they're contemplating so that they can see whether that data point has come up in previously reported scams before they send money to it. It's like a community for reporting scams, and it can be a useful signal of whether something suspicious is going on. It's not entirely reliable, because it's run by users, for users, and sometimes users malign one another for personal reasons or out of resentment if there was a noncriminal problem with their business (think of customers leaving bad reviews on sites for sending them 22 duplicates of an item when they wanted two, even though the reason is that the customer added an extra digit by mistake). That said, Bitcoin Who's Who and sites like it can be useful as an indicator that more investigation is needed or, if there are already red flags, it can serve as supporting evidence.

There are also services like Chainalysis or CipherTrace that leverage the potential of open ledgers and the immutable, traceable nature of most blockchain transactions to create a picture of what's going on with different accounts, addresses, and coins—in some cases a visualization of the network, using a graph database such as the Neo4j example shown in Figure 22-2. They also, where possible, link cryptocurrency activity to real-world identities, resulting in something like a risk score for an identity or address. These can help AML teams by presenting relevant connections, and by mapping the landscape in a way that feels more manageable than the kinds of individual investigations discussed in this chapter.

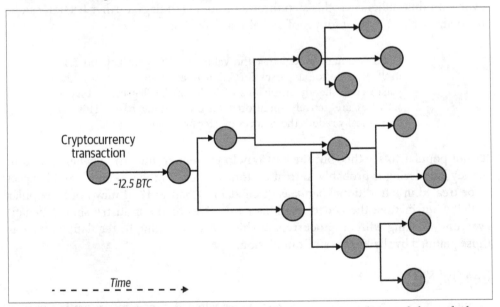

Figure 22-2. What connections might look like when trying to understand the path that cryptocurrency has taken[6]

There's an inherent limitation to the extent of the mapping that can be done, since cryptocurrency addresses are so much more dynamic than comparable data points

---

6 Claudio Bellei, "The Elliptic Data Set: Opening Up Machine Learning on the Blockchain" (*https://oreil.ly/ XvtOd*), Elliptic (blog), August 6, 2019.

in traditional banking or ecommerce efforts, such as credit card numbers or bank accounts. Additionally, at least for now, cryptocurrency users are far more likely than average consumers to be very conscious of privacy concerns; they're more likely to engage in device, browser, and IP obfuscation, and to move their money around through additional steps or even use a mixer.

Nonetheless, what many people don't appreciate is that even with cryptocurrencies that specifically offer and advertise their privacy functionality, the overwhelming majority of users don't actually take advantage of it, even if they're more comfortable knowing they could. Researchers from Carnegie Mellon University found that 99.9% of transactions involving Zcash and 30% involving Monero (another so-called privacy coin) were traceable, and reports from Chainalysis suggest similar results.[7] In the same way, though mixing adds considerable confusion, it relies on users being able and willing to find and trust one another in order to carry out the process, which is an extra step many users just don't take. So, when there is evidence of mixing, those may be the cases that are worth extra investigation.

Having said that, the social nature of cryptocurrency makes it extremely sensitive to the popular fleeting trends. Mixing may be a cause for concern today, but it could become a consensus tomorrow; Zcash/Monero may become as popular as Ethereum (the spikes in Ether for 2021 are already beginning to resemble the early days of bitcoin), or alternatively have a temporary spike like Dogecoin. One must always remember how easy it is to drown in the noise of a booming, viral trend.

All of this gives AML teams a real advantage, in a sense, even over AML teams working on regular fiat transactions, because if it's possible to leave privacy mechanisms aside, cryptocurrency is by nature more transparent in terms of tracking the flow of money than fiat. It seems likely that as cryptocurrency becomes more established over time, more and more services will grow up to leverage this factor. Crypto enthusiasts may complain that it detracts from the libertarian dream many found embedded within the early days of the industry, but it will make it easier for more consumers, and more regulators, to take it seriously and safely.

Summary

This chapter examined the elements that make preventing cryptocurrency money laundering so challenging, and discussed some of the tools and techniques developed to overcome them. That mindset will serve us well in the next chapter, which focuses on ad fraud, another field where the built-in challenges sometimes seem to favor the fraudster side more than seems entirely fair.

---

7 Claire Ye et al. "Alt-Coin Traceability" (*https://oreil.ly/sCzZn*), May 18, 2020.

## CHAPTER 23

Adtech Fraud

Bots! Bots everywhere!
—Lil Robotussin[1]

 Full disclosure: Gilit Saporta, the author of this chapter, currently acts as director of fraud analytics for DoubleVerify, a leader in measurement services for the advertising industry.

Adtech was a bit late to the game of online fraud. Fraud in this realm only began to flourish from the early 2010s, when it became obvious that the spend by advertisers was growing rapidly enough to make it really worthwhile for "top-notch" fraudsters to get in on the game. Its status in the world of fraud is still evolving, which is one of the reasons we have placed it within the compliance section. Whichever industry ad fraud belongs in, it's certainly a compliance issue, in the sense of abusing terms and conditions and expected practice.

In addition to the high potential gain, many fraudsters have found that the relatively young ecosystem of adtech is vulnerable to manipulation. This is especially true if traffic is transacted through real-time bidding (RTB), also called programmatic buying, which is a method of selling and buying online display advertising in real time. This way, the inventory for presenting an ad to a user (also called an impression) is not sold directly from a publisher (such as CNN News) to an advertiser (such as Coca-Cola). Instead, it is channeled and masked through various platforms and often changes several hands along the way, as seen in Figure 23-1. Aggressive practices or even malicious code can easily hide in several corners of this young industry.

---

1 Lil Robotussin, "Bots Everywhere," Boomy Corporation, 2021.

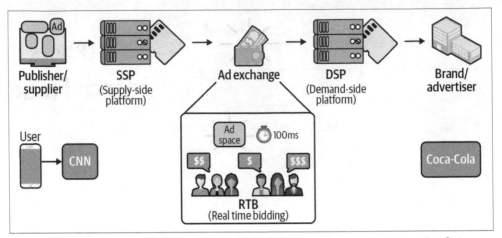

Figure 23-1. The complex ecosystem behind the ads appearing to consumers on their devices

Over the past decade, ad fraud has expanded dramatically in both scale and sophistication. To use a popular culture analogy: adtech fraudsters compared to ecommerce/fintech fraudsters are like comic book writers compared to classical authors—they're not necessarily inventing a new type of "art" in their fraud practice, but they do find an innovative way to translate several old fraud techniques into a medium that is both massive and lucrative.

Just like comic books, ad fraud became even more popular via television. More specifically, what lured the best fraudsters into this industry was the introduction of video ads, with an emphasis on streaming (otherwise known as connected TV content, whether on smart TVs or on any other device). Video ads are far more expensive than display ads; to quote SpotX, a leading video advertising platform: "Industry executives estimate that video ads on a niche website can command as much as $30.00 eCPM [effective cost per thousand impressions], compared with just $0.20 eCPM for static display ads. This helps to explain why fraudsters go to such lengths to insert themselves in the arena and take a piece of the pie."[2]

Other than the fun of comparing ad fraud to comic books, it's no coincidence that we're talking about adtech fraud in the context of mass entertainment, since one of its victims is the quality of online content. Adtech fraud snatches away the potential earnings of true content providers—websites, blogs, apps, podcasts, streaming channels—targeting anything that relies on showing users advertisements in order to provide free or cheap content.

---

2 SpotX, "Fraud and the Irresistible Allure of Ad Dollars" (*https://oreil.ly/OepO0*), blog post, December 17, 2014.

Fraudsters who operate bots that "watch" huge numbers of ads create impossible competition for legit content publishers, who don't have a bot to visit their website. This kind of competition sets up problematic incentives even for well-meaning content providers. An online content writer or journalist, forced to the realization that the survival of their website depends on being able to present extremely high volumes of entries (and/or ad clicks) to their website, is incentivized to choose virality over quality. Clickbaits, inflammatory topics, and fake news are the result. The days of the mild-mannered reporter are a thing of the past (if you don't recognize the reference, it's time to catch up on some good old comic book classics) and some of that can be laid at the door of adtech fraudsters.

Just like the cryptocurrency revolution had (and still has) to overcome the surge of pyramid scams to stay alive, so does the adtech industry need a committed fraud-fighting campaign to build a better industry. Regulation over this industry has been in the works since 1996, when the Interactive Advertising Bureau (IAB) was formed, but only really kicked in once the IAB founded its tech lab in 2014 and, together with the Media Rating Council (MRC) and the Mobile Marketing Association (MMA), began issuing standards and guidelines for the adtech jungle.

This chapter offers a glimpse into what's under the hood of teams who work to guard the internet from ad fraud. At the same time, it's a good opportunity to explore the problem of bots and how to identify them, which is relevant far more generally than in ad fraud.

Sites combating resellers or protecting particularly hot items such as sneakers or tickets for popular shows, which sell out extremely quickly, all spent resources combating the menace of bots. Similarly, bots are used to perform credential stuffing, running through stolen data or guessed passwords at tremendous speed to gain access to accounts or attempt the use of stolen payment methods. Bots attack password reset processes, set up new accounts that are later used for fraud, and generally make a nuisance of themselves anywhere that performing simple repetitive tasks at great speed and scale (*https://oreil.ly/XQ9TU*) can be useful as part of a fraud operation.

The Ultimate Money Maker

Without going too deep into the definitions of invalid/fraudulent traffic in the eyes of the regulating/accrediting bodies (IAB/MRC/MMA), adtech fraud is mostly about identifying and uprooting the weeds of bot traffic from the good, strong growth of legitimate traffic in the context of a website or app. Proper bot protection is crucial for any website/app operator, considering that cybersecurity researchers have begun warning about "the internet being mostly bots" (*https://oreil.ly/KGYsa*) since early

2017. While more recent research suggests that about 25% of 2020 traffic was bots, that's more than enough to indicate a serious problem.[3]

Identifying bot traffic is hardly an issue reserved for adtech fraud. Blocking bot traffic has been the bread and butter of many services in the industry, such as PerimeterX, Akamai, CloudFlare, Imperva, and more. There's plenty of bot fraud to go around for the many services in this business: as per CloudFlare, "Bots comprise roughly 50% of all Internet traffic. As much as 20% of websites that serve ads are visited exclusively by fraudulent click bots."[4] As we mentioned, looking beyond the context of ads, many companies track and in some cases block bots for other reasons as well. Bots are often created by infecting and thus co-opting victims' machines through malware (for more on this aspect of the problem, see Chapter 14).

Fraudsters (and sometimes the websites/apps that gain from fraud) have extremely high motivation to keep their operation going. The industry is rapidly evolving, and fraud labs need to level up their game both in catching the more elusive techniques of bot masquerading and in developing transparent communication with clients who may need to make tough decisions about where they choose to spend advertising dollars.

Fraudsters who are new to adtech might be upgrading to adtech from spam spreading schemes, brute-force operations, or any other attack involving bots. As with the types of fraud discussed throughout this book, there's a lot of overlap between fraudsters attacking across industries and types of fraud. If your home PC or mobile device seems to be acting up, losing battery power, or burning through its data plan very quickly, it could be that you are, as SpotX puts it, one of the many[5]

> [H]ome users who remain completely unaware their machines are performing automated tasks over the internet to do all kinds of malicious things like monetize fraudulent sites, monetize legitimate sites with fraudulent traffic, send out spam and spread viruses. Using a fully automated browser, a hijacked device will make HTML or ad calls on a browser hidden from the user's view. With session hijacking, additional html or ad calls are made independently of the content being requested by the user. The malware running on the device inserts ads and redirections into the user experience to achieve its goal—making money.

Within adtech, rookie fraudsters often opt for routing inhuman traffic through a couple of servers (often using proxies, hosting servers, and cloud services) rather than investing much effort in mimicking real users. Only when they see that their inhuman data center traffic isn't passing as true impressions (i.e., events of a human

---

3 Erez Hasson, "Bad Bot Report 2021: The Pandemic of the Internet" (*https://oreil.ly/sGQph*), Imperva (blog), April 13, 2021.

4 "What Is Click Fraud?" (*https://oreil.ly/41ej2*) CloudFlare, Inc., accessed March 10, 2022.

5 SpotX, "Fraud Series Part 3: Botnets & Hijacked Devices" (*https://oreil.ly/5ZOnb*), blog post, January 15, 2015.

viewing/hearing an ad) will they begin to craft increasingly sneakier methods of impersonating a human being.

The value of ad fraud, and therefore the incentive of fraudsters to perpetrate it successfully, increased substantially once connected TV (CTV) devices became part of our lives and many users began streaming content regularly. This shift signaled to sophisticated fraudsters that it was worth investing in ad fraud. Advertisers are willing to spend 10X or 20X higher rates for ads that are stitched to the episode a viewer is watching on a streamer, in comparison to a banner shown on a website or an app. This means a successful attack can net the fraudsters behind it millions of dollars monthly, especially if they can also manipulate the programmatic advertising platform to think the ad is being played on a premium CTV channel (also called a CTV app or bundle) broadcasting a popular show.

When fraudsters are able to dupe ad exchanges and networks (and by proxy, advertisers) into thinking that a certain ad is presented on a popular show, when in fact it can be presented on completely unrelated content, they're creating a risk to the brand that goes far beyond the direct financial loss. Brand safety is a consideration that many high-end advertisers would protect with vigilance, to ensure that their brand is never shown in the wrong context. In this aspect, guarding display ads is just as important as guarding video ads, even if the latter are the most expensive. Domain laundering (aka spoofing or masking), illustrated in Figure 23-2, is a prevalent technique in adtech fraud, one that clarifies the need for transparency in this industry.

Figure 23-2. URL masked by an apparent, cloaking URL

As with all other forms of fraud, it's all about return on investment (ROI) for the fraudsters involved. The more lucrative the industry became, the better fraudsters got at spoofing or falsifying both the details of the alleged user who is watching the ad and the details of the channel/app where the ad is allegedly being shown. Paired with malware and device hijacking techniques, some of the fraud schemes began to demonstrate extremely high levels of sophistication, taking advantage of every loophole of this fairly young industry. For example, server-side ad insertion (SSAI) technology, used to "stitch" ads to CTV content, was manipulated by several fraud schemes. (For those interested in the details of an example of this kind of SSAI attack, where traffic is designed to mimic real SSAI events, look up white papers released on fraud schemes ParrotTerra (*https://oreil.ly/BvJFW*) and LeoTerra (*https://oreil.ly/megMd*), as well as a more elusive variant called SneakyTerra (*https://oreil.ly/EhFT6*).)

Beyond Bot Detection: Looking into Invisible Ads

Part of what makes adtech fraud tricky is that website owners aren't necessarily interested in blocking bot traffic. On the contrary, some website operators will go for monetization schemes offering them higher revenues from ads, while turning a blind eye to the fact that their traffic is rapidly spiking with no plausible explanation. For that reason, some of adtech fraud prevention focuses on identifying websites/apps that willingly invite bot traffic to their gates, then informing advertisers or adtech networks that they may wish to reconsider spending their advertising budget on that specific app/website.

A typical example of sites/apps that are worth avoiding would be ones that knowingly incorporate invisible or hidden ads on their page. To paraphrase SpotX (*https://oreil.ly/84RWl*), hidden ads are exactly what they sound like. They're on the page, but displayed in a manner such that they'll never be viewable by a user. They often use iframes, but other methods are known as well. Some examples of ways an ad might be hidden include:

- Making the visible part of the ad really tiny, perhaps 1×1 pixels (see Figure 23-3).
- Making the ad invisible, with zero opacity. If the opacity is set to zero, there's nothing to see, as far as the viewer is concerned.
- Stacking the ads. When many ads are layered on top of each other in a single spot, the viewer only sees the one on top.
- Having an ad clipped by an iframe so that the viewer will never see the video.

Adding complexity to the issue, these strategies aren't always used in isolation. By deploying a variety of creative tactics and then hiding behind bogus domain registrations, masking their digital tracks and working out of hard-to-trace regions, perpetrators can be extremely difficult to catch. While botnet fraud is most prevalent because it scales well and captures high-value ad spend, fraudsters will often create real human traffic using click farms (hordes of low-paid workers rapidly clicking on ads). With their browsers sufficiently stuffed, fraudsters clone those human cookies and use bots to scale their operations.

Figure 23-3. A tiny ad hiding almost invisibly in a web page

For all these reasons, adtech fraud prevention presents a particularly interesting challenge. To work effectively, fraud prevention in this industry has to be done in real time. Whenever possible, adtech fraud aims to isolate only the inauthentic traffic and flag it in real time so that advertisers are not paying to show their ads to a bot. The real-time aspect is intrinsic to the nature of the product. This challenge is what makes adtech fraud so interesting currently. It's tied to one of the holy grails of fraud fighting: to be effective, mitigation needs to be both surgically accurate *and* fully automated.

Bot Identification in Adtech and Beyond

Before adtech fraud became a serious issue, bot management was largely left to chief information security officers (CISOs), who would in turn advise fraud prevention teams facing bots attacking on the credential stuffing, account sign-up, card testing, or promo abuse side. User friction, in these use cases, was both relevant and effective.

As noted by Forrester, bot management solutions were used against the following major types of scenarios:[6]

- Distributed denial-of-service (DDoS) attacks and malware spreading
- Credentials stuffing, account takeover (ATO), and stolen card testing
- Shopping cart fraud and inventory hoarding
- Web scraping, web recon, competitor aggregators, and scrapers

---

6 Sandy Carielli and Amy DeMartine, *The Forrester New Wave™: Bot Management, Q1 2020* (*https://oreil.ly/ofZkf*), Forrester, January 29th, 2020.

Many of these attacks could be mitigated through traditional friction filters such as CAPTCHA (or Google's reCAPTCHA, or the later hCAPTCHA). However, the cost in user insult was severe—good users don't necessarily have patience to choose all the buses in your CAPTCHA images—and it was only one step in the arms race. Soon enough, bots evolved until they could solve CAPTCHA filters more efficiently than most humans (*https://oreil.ly/oW0JC*). When organizations began looking for suspiciously fast CAPTCHA solutions or suspiciously uniform solutions, the bots evolved again to mimic human speed and patterns of behavior.

This bot evolution, together with a general surge of ATO trends, led many fintech operations to opt for multifactor authentication (MFA; see Chapter 13) and other strong auth solutions. These remain popular and can be effective, but many companies continue to seek more frictionless alternatives to keeping bots and ATOs at bay. Much of the latest development in such alternatives comes from the adtech fraud prevention industry.

It makes sense that adtech would lead the way when it comes to frictionless bot fighting. CAPTCHA has never been a relevant solution for adtech: you wouldn't expect anyone to solve a CAPTCHA in order to watch an ad, right? There's a good chance they don't want the ad to begin with. They certainly won't jump through hoops for it. Subtle tech had to be developed to determine whether a particular banner/image/video ad being presented on a website/app was being watched by a human or a bot.

This is why adtech became a leading industry when it comes to bot identification and bot management more generally. While many other solutions can focus on "just" spotting cases where an IP is suddenly generating large volumes of allegedly unrelated browsing sessions, adtech fraud prevention services will often need to take this to a higher resolution. For example, if a bank wants to protect its website from DDoS attacks, it makes sense that any IP generating more than 10,000 login attempts per day would be blocked. However, for an adtech company, an IP with this volume might be a completely legitimate server that's connected to a screen at the front desk of a hotel, which may be playing ads 24/7 on the hotel's home page. The delicacy of IP intelligence and traffic analytics had to evolve to solve these sensitive use cases and ensure bot prevention could stay at least one step ahead of bot fraud.

For example, if a virtual private network (VPN) used to be a helpful classification that allowed risk organizations to decide whether the IP address represented an authentic user or not, nowadays a VPN IP address is not enough in its own right to justify a decision. There are many valid reasons for VPN usage that would not justify a fraudulent-bot traffic diagnosis. Likewise, there are many fraudulent actors who realize that hiding behind the right type of VPN would be a good way for them to stay under the radar.

Crawlers Aren't Necessarily Creepy

Web crawling bots are used by search engines (e.g., Google, Baidu) to visit as many web pages on the internet as possible, as often as possible, and index them in the database based on their keywords. If a certain website spots an IP that seems to be visiting the site excessively, it may very well be a legitimate crawler.

Bear in mind that adtech fraud prevention also has to be able to separate between fraudulent bots and legitimate bots such as these crawlers. Your site should be able to welcome crawlers in order to be properly indexed. If some of them become too excessive, as is often reported for Baiduspider (the crawling bot for Baidu.com), it is possible to block it from visiting your site, but this would have a negative impact on your visibility in the Asia-Pacific region.

All of this means that within adtech, bot solutions of all types realize and reflect the importance of analyzing traffic spikes in the context of their device types, connection types, audience, and flow. Adtech continues to push the envelope on even the trickiest anomalies, which is why staying abreast of developments in this field is valuable for any fraud fighter or fraud prevention team interested in or working to prevent bots in any context.

Very often, what the latest research shows is the need to continue investing in research, especially to find new tricks and anomalies. A classic example would be an automated detector released by DoubleVerify's Fraud Lab in May 2021, following intense deep dive research. The detector and the fraud scheme it was catching were named *SmokeScreen* (*https://oreil.ly/8JmBa*). The name derived from the fact that one of the ways the scheme operated was through a screensaver that users had installed on their CTV devices.

It's a simple and ingenious trick. After a viewer downloads a screensaver on their CTV, SmokeScreen hijacks the device and generates fake impressions en masse using falsified data—even when the screen is turned off. This works because the CTV devices are not built into the TV and have an independent power source. The TV may be off, but the CTV device and SmokeScreen remain active.

By looking at an hourly breakdown of SmokeScreen traffic, shown in Figure 23-4, we can see the fraudulent activity next to normal CTV benchmark activity.

From midnight to 5 a.m., while most people are sleeping, we expect to see CTV traffic decrease—as indicated in the green line on the graph. Then, after 6 a.m., traffic gradually begins to increase. But on devices hijacked by SmokeScreen, the impression volume remains stable—almost flat.

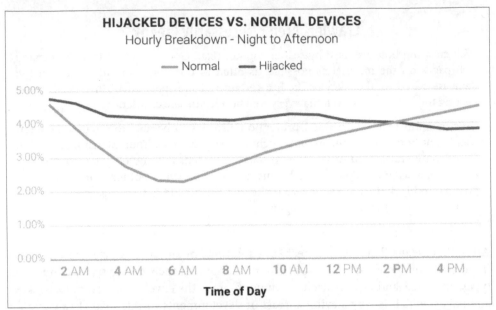

Figure 23-4. Chart showing the daily activity of hijacked devices versus normal devices

Flagging the hijacked traffic and ensuring that advertisers are protected from buying ad time as part of it (as well as protecting publishers' reputations from being associated with fraudulent traffic) is technologically challenging, but not impossible. It is doable thanks to strong modeling, which enables the fraud team to identify the anomaly and work out its context, and thanks to strong infrastructure, which can use this knowledge to avoid bad traffic in real time.

In the same way, it continues to be vital that fraud prevention teams in all contexts be willing to set time aside for in-depth research into new trends—who had even heard of CTVs five years ago?—and how those trends might play into both fraud and fraud prevention.

Summary

This chapter discussed ad fraud and focused on the bots that drive a large portion of it. A fast-evolving field, adtech is challenging because it has to combat ad fraud in real time, and without friction. In this sense, it's valuable for fraud fighters in diverse industries to keep an eye on the developments within adtech. Many of the innovations developed to prevent ad fraud can be adapted to prevent bot traffic and malicious activity in many other contexts as well.

## CHAPTER 24

Fraud, Fraud Prevention, and the Future

We shall overcome...
  —People's Songs, Bulletin No. 3[1]

An old Israeli joke, written for a popular 1976 film *Halfon Hill Doesn't Answer*, comes to mind whenever one tries to interview a fraud fighter about their work. The setting of the joke is a small Israeli military reserve force, stranded in the middle of the desert, struck by sun and boredom. When a high-ranking officer tries to hold an inspection of their vigilance, he asks an approximately 50-year-old veteran to describe what he would do if he saw the Egyptian army approaching (the film predates the Egypt–Israel peace treaty of 1979). The soldier replies that if he sees the Egyptians, "We would do the same thing as we did in 1956." To this the officer replies, "What did you do in 1956?" and the soldier answers, "Oh, the same thing we did in 1948." "What did you do in 1948?" demands the officer. The soldier replies, "It was 30 years ago...who can remember?"

Apart from the fun chance to butcher a joke with translation, it's helpful to remind people of this popular joke when they're being asked about their fraud prevention methodologies. So many risk analytics methodologies have been shaped by decades of playing "cat and mouse" (or, to be more accurate, "cops and robbers") with fraudsters. So many underlying working theories have been buried in years of practice that teams are reluctant to question a piece of heuristic or code in their system, even if it seems to be obsolete.

Moreover, many fraud-fighting teams are understandably cagey about their practices, because they fear the consequences of exposing the "secret sauce" not only to bad

---

1 "We Shall Overcome," gospel song, lyrically derived from a hymn by Charles Albert Tindley, 1901, adapted by Pete Seeger, 1947.

actors, but also to competitors (and sometimes to auditors). Trust and safety teams and/or risk teams are ready to willingly admit that their approaches to fraud are based on their numerous years of experience, but when you try to dig into specifics, you'll hear that familiar reply, "It was years ago…you can't expect me to remember."

Indeed, many misconceptions in the field are rooted in what fraud attacks looked like 10 or 20 or even 30 years ago. Letting code and heuristics age is seldom graceful, and for fraud prevention outdated practices could be absolutely devastating. A strong antidote to stagnation is a continuous flow of new ideas and perspectives. If there's a single bottom line to this book, it's the call to all fraud fighters to broaden their horizons and be willing to recalculate their route on a daily basis. Fraud is always evolving, and therefore, fraud fighters can never afford to rest on their laurels.

The way to keep the industry strong is to boost everyone's contribution to the shared know-how. In the words of Paddington Bear, "if we're kind and polite" and willing to share from our experience, we make the entire ecosystem safer from the slightly less "good and polite" offenders out there. After all, fraudsters aren't shy about sharing their tips and tricks; therefore, if fraud fighters fail to join forces, the whole industry will be at a disadvantage.

The message of collaboration that has echoed so loudly throughout this book—more emphatically than we expected at the start, to be honest—is inspired both by grass-roots movements such as Risk Salon (*http://RiskSalon.org*) meetups in San Francisco, Tel Aviv, and Seattle, and by established conferences such as the RSA Conference in San Francisco, MRC Flagship Conferences in Las Vegas and Europe, and FraudCon and CyberWeek in Tel Aviv.

It's usually so much easier to share know-how between work-level teams on such events than it is to try to push authorities and upper-level decision makers to collaborate. Professor Itzhak Ben Israel, chair of CyberWeek (*https://oreil.ly/ePZmM*), as well as chair of the Israeli Space Agency and the National Council for R&D, head of the Blavatnik Interdisciplinary Cyber Studies Centre, head of the Security Studies Program, and head of the Yuval Ne'eman Workshop for Science, Technology and Security at Tel Aviv University, noted that it's almost against our human nature to share data.

"We know that knowledge is power because Francis Bacon told us so in the 17th century," Itzhak said.

> Bacon, by the way, had to resign from the Queen's Court for charges of corruption and embezzlement, so luckily for us he became a philosopher. Thanks to him we learn that to overcome nature, one needs to study its laws through observation. This was a great inspiration to one of his students, Isaac Newton, who mentions Bacon's influence in his *Philosophiæ Naturalis Principia Mathematica*.
>
> However, both Newton and Bacon forgot that our human nature is to save power—and by proxy, knowledge, or data—for ourselves. This is what makes fraud fighting and

cybercrime fighting so tricky, since it is very often a cross-border and cross-company attack that will succeed due to the lack of cross-border or cross-company collaboration.

We tend to think that technology will solve the problem, but tech solutions to human problems can only take you so far. In most of the issues I know in cyber today, unless you address the mass psychology aspects, legal aspects, ideology conflict aspects (e.g., privacy versus security), it's unlikely that you have actually solved anything.

To counter the somewhat pessimistic notion that humans don't like to collaborate, the industry of fraud prevention has been buzzing in the past decade with meetups, conferences, webinars, publications, and most of all, many, many private discussion groups of various types, including the work of the Merchant Risk Council. It's also reflected in the growth of collaborative networks, like Identiq's network for anonymous identity validation, which is a good example of active collaboration. Fraud fighters around the globe hold a shared goal of keeping the digital ecosystem safe from fraud. Collaboration in the fraud-fighting ecosystem is often perceived as a service to the greater good. Add this sense of camaraderie to the fact that untangling impersonification schemes is pretty much super cool and you have a true hub for knowledge sharing.

As mentioned earlier, a shining example of open discussion among fraud fighters was the activity of Risk Salon, a nonprofit community active in the San Francisco Bay Area from 2016 to 2020. Reading the manifesto of Risk Salon (*https://oreil.ly/BESjf*) makes it clear that the founders saw the value in collaboration:

> It's hard to talk about the sensitive issues in modern trust & safety, yet at the same time it's critical to work together to beat the attackers. Risk Salon facilitates collaboration across the tech industry using the Chatham House Rule to protect everyone's information. We come from diverse functional areas (engineering, product, data science, operations, legal, and more) and we share best practices and success stories to help protect everyone's platforms and users.

We sat down for a Risk Salon talk with Sardine.ai CEO Soups Ranjan, who co-founded the community with Nate Kugland, to learn about the inspiration that led to the formation of a forum to encourage open discussion on sensitive fraud topics:

> The fraudsters are always meeting up on dark web forums, sharing tips and tricks. Meanwhile, crypto/fintech companies don't ever meet to share high-level ideas. That's why we started the Risk Salon community. When Risk Salon just began, we were about 15 people or so, getting together in a roundtable format, which was inspired by data science meetups (that were gaining popularity at the time). We ensured people would be comfortable sharing, knowing that what they say wouldn't be attributed to their company [using the Chatham House Rule (*https://oreil.ly/yerap*)]. We would read from a list of questions submitted in advance by the attendees and then break into groups to discuss. It was very innovative at the time and it was a smash hit for beginners looking to educate themselves. The rest is history: the forum grew rapidly and became important to beginners and experts alike. We had three successful yearly events [Deflect Conference (*https://oreil.ly/F3Z92*), 2017–2019], we branched out to

Seattle and Tel Aviv, we made a difference. If we as fraud fighters are able to effectively collaborate, payments will get cheaper and faster for all.

The Fraud and Identity Forum online roundtable discussions currently run by Identiq, also using Chatham House Rules, take inspiration from this open format and focus on the real challenges fraud and risk professionals face today. Being online, they bring together people from a range of countries and time zones. The Risk Salon model showed what's possible when fraud fighters work together, and it is unsurprising and encouraging that it started a trend.

There are a lot of messages we hope you take away from this book. The importance of educating other departments in your organization—and especially upper management—about crime, fraud, and fraud prevention is a key one. It's not a nice extra, it's a key part of the job, necessary to ensure your team's work is respected, taken into account in plans and strategy, and rewarded. Then there's the value of linking; the importance of layering forms of identification, and of using dynamic friction to adapt to the level of risk involved; remembering to view identities as a whole, in the context of the story in which they're appearing, rather than disparate data points that can be labeled "good" or "bad"; building relationships with colleagues from different departments; and looking after your fraud team as people, and working to ensure they feel positively about their jobs and the impact they're having on the company and the ecosystem more broadly.

Ultimately, though, if you only remember one thing when you think about what you've read—next year, or the year after, or even in 10 years' time—we want you to remember the importance of collaboration, both internally with other departments and externally with fraud or AML teams at other companies. We heard it again and again from the experts we talked to while we were researching the book, and it was borne out over and over as we compiled the examples to illustrate chapters. No one can fight fraud alone, as effectively as they could if they were working with other fraud fighters. Working together makes us all stronger and more likely to succeed. All of us except the fraudsters, that is—but then, really, isn't that the point?

Collaboration in the Era of "The New Normal"

We began writing the proposal for this book during the first COVID-19 quarantine. It felt like a way to preserve some sanity by planning ahead and envisioning our post-pandemic future. We're submitting this book to print, nearly two years later, from our nth quarantine. (We've pretty much lost count.)

The concept of fraud fighter collaboration was something that shifted in our minds over the course of writing the book. Its importance became clearer than ever to us, partly because we heard the same theme repeated from so many of our interviewees. At the same time, the nature of what collaboration can or should be changed as well, as it became clear that the pandemic is becoming a constantly moving particle in the matter of our professional and personal lives. Many conferences took a hit in 2020–2022, including RSA, MRC, Money20/20, MPE, CyberWeek, Risk Salon/Deflect, Defcon, BlackHat, Transact, CNP Expo, Paris Fintech Forum, ACFE, and more (not to mention so many technology-focused meetups and workshops that are often even less suitable for virtual/hybrid formats).

Without the classic expos and events, which used to be a strong stimulator for cross-organization exchange of best practices, fraud prevention practitioners turned to private channels, one-to-one Zoom calls, and the occasional virtual meetup/webinar, until we all got a bad case of Zoom fatigue.

We're hopeful that by the time this book goes public, COVID-19 concerns will be a thing of the past and this section will seem outdated. Just in case, we'll add our two cents about how to keep learning effectively, despite any new COVID variant or mutation that's plaguing our (exhausted) society, and despite all the distractions of daily life and current affairs that will be a feature of life even after the pandemic is over.

First and foremost, we want to share a wish that every reader of these words will aim to become a thought leader, by writing and sharing from their experience of fraud prevention. The excellent thinkers who were quoted within the chapters of this book have set a superb example, in many cases over more than a decade of sharing ideas and experiences. Now it's time to stand on their gigantic shoulders and speak up via blogs, LinkedIn posts, roundtable discussions, speaking opportunities, and whatever else you can imagine.

Sharing from experience is almost always impactful, even if it doesn't serve your short-term purposes (yes, we understand that you may feel too busy in the day-to-day fight against fraud, so you can't imagine finding the time to tell your "war story"). You might be surprised to discover that when you make a fraud trend public, its volume starts to diminish. One person being open really can have that much impact, because the result is that more fraud teams quickly realize they suffer from the same fraudster or attack. More teams then fight to defuse the attack, until the fraudster becomes discouraged and goes back to their drawing board.

The motivation to collaborate needs to become more of a grassroots movement, stemming from research teams rather than from marketing, business development, and upper management. Traditionally, and with MRC an honorable exception, conferences and meetups have often been attended mostly by marketing folk (and some C-level managers dragged in by the marketing team), and by people who were considering their next career move. To some extent, these audiences disappeared, because the pandemic made it harder to network over the coffee break. We sincerely hope these words will nudge you into sharing your work with the community, even if it doesn't directly serve any immediate networking purpose. Making fraud-fighting techniques available for the greater community is simply doing something good for the world.

Eventually, writing (or speaking, tweeting, posting, miming, singing, whatever, we won't judge) about your work will deepen your analytic understanding. If there's one common ground we've seen among all the people who contributed to this book, it's that they all appreciate the philosophy of this industry. Being able to cherish the intellectual sport of "solving the puzzle" and explaining the "how" and the "why" of each fraud pattern is a strong sign that you belong in this field of thought. So, share that buzz, and feel it all over again by contributing to outlets like About-Fraud (*https://www.about-fraud.com/news*), Dark Reading (*https://www.darkreading.com*), or the *Fraudology* podcast (*https://oreil.ly/kEq8e*).

We opened this book by including a reference to the curiosity of Lewis Carroll's Alice. Now, we wish for you—our brave fellow fraud fighter—that in addition to Alice's curiosity, you'll also be blessed with the White Rabbit's energy (see Figure 24-1). There's no need to run around worried, looking for your gloves. Instead, pick up the glove and join the community today. Be active. Share. Suggest. We hope we've helped you feel ready to do so. If you'd like to reach out with further questions, we welcome them. Good luck, and Godspeed.

Figure 24-1. "The White Rabbit," from Alice's Adventures in Wonderland[2]

---

2 Sir John Tenniel, *The White Rabbit* (*https://oreil.ly/nwMPz*), in *Alice's Adventures in Wonderland* by Lewis Carroll, illustrations by John Tenniel (London: Macmillan and Co., 1865), via Wikimedia Commons.

Index

Symbols

2FA (two-factor authentication)
    account takeover mitigation, 210
    bot generator defense, 30
3-D Secure (3DS), 44, 181
5th Anti-Money Laundering Directive (EU), 311

A

abuse versus fraud, 15-17
    account creation, 15, 16
    click fraud, 17
    content abuse
        adtech fraud, 322
        fake reviews, 16, 277
    friendly fraud, 15, 169
        tolerance for abuse, 169
    promo abuse, 15
    refund abuse, 171
    reseller abuse, 170
account creation
    abuse versus fraud, 15, 16
    anti–money laundering, 18
    online account opening fraud, 191-201
    open banking, 198
    residence outside US, account in US, 197
    shell payments, 292
account handovers, 204
    account piggybacking, 234, 274
    prohibited items for sale, 303, 304
        identification and mitigation, 307
    shell payments, 293
account takeovers (ATO)
    about, 203
    account handovers versus, 204
    account testing by fraudsters, 14
    account versus transaction, 39
    advantages of, 208
    attack stages, 206-208
        time involved, 208
    behaviors associated with account, 208
    BOPIS and BORIS mitigation, 143, 144-147
    bot mitigation via friction filters, 328
    business email compromise fraud, 186, 214
    COVID-19 pandemic, xvii, 49, 205
        phishing spike, 50, 205
    data related to, 206, 209
    example: identifying a trusted session, 218-220
    gift card fraud, 155
    identification and mitigation, 210-220
        about, 210
        biometrics, 210-212
        customer knowledge, 216
        device fingerprinting, 215
        dynamic friction, 217
        multifactor authentication, 212-215
        network context, 215
        overlay attack identification, 216
    malware
        data theft, 207
        overlay attacks, 209
    online account opening fraud, 192
    overlay attacks, 209
        identifying, 216
    percentage from social engineering, 225
    porch piracy of package interception, 128
    prohibited items for sale, 303

connected TV (CTV)
    adtech fraud, 322, 325
    attempted attacks, 46
    server-side ad insertion, 326
    SmokeScreen hijacking device, 329
consortium model of fraud prevention, 59-63
    data enrichment tools versus, 62
    providerless consortiums, 62
        credit and lending fraud collaboration, 252
        Identiq identity validation network, 63
    using consortium data, 61, 237
conspiracy versus collusion, 258
content abuse
    adtech fraud, 322
    fake reviews, 16
        seller scams, 277
context
    about importance of, xxii
    bot attacks, 12
    customer behavior
        crises causing shifts in, 50
        mule similarity, 49
    domain expertise importance, 21
        research analytics team, 63
    identity behind transaction, 3
    pop quiz, 34
    velocity, 12
cookie-cutter fraudsters, 24
    data theft, 205
    instead of bots, 207
    organized crime fraudsters versus, 31
copyright infringement in marketplace, 274
    prohibited items for sale, 305
cost justification of fraud prevention, 68
    fraud tech strategy, 73
counterfeit goods, 274, 280
courier convinced to manipulate address, 130
COVID-19 pandemic
    collaboration in era of "new normal", 334
    curbside product delivery fraud (see BOPIS (Buy Online, Pick up In Store))
    customer behavior shifts, 50
        chargebacks, 34
    fraud rate increase, xvii, 49
    friendly fraud increase, 52
    gift card purchases, 154
        victim-assisted fraud, 156
    gig economy fraud, 25

lessons learned, xvii, 13
    (see also crisis planning and response)
    money mules, 191, 292
    new accounts spike, xvii, 51, 205
    phishing attacks, 205
    refund fraud, 172
    seller slipup turning into fraud, 272
    stimulus fraud, 247, 248, 250
crawlers (web crawling bots), 329
credential stuffing malware attacks, 223
credit and lending fraud
    about, 245
    Buy Now Pay Later fraud, 248
    identification and mitigation, 249-253
        badlists or decline lists, 251
        collaboration, 251
        email domains favored by attackers, 252
        habitual loan fraudsters, 251
        machine learning systems, 249
        manual review, 250
        organized crime coercing, 251
    nonprofessional fraudsters, 246
        accountants and opportunists, 246
    professional fraudsters, 246-248
        no intention of repaying, 246
        social engineering, 247
        synthetic or stolen identity, 246
        website or app for identity theft, 247
    stimulus fraud during COVID-19 pandemic, 247, 248, 250
    synthetic identities, 246
credit card fraud
    3-D Secure, 44
    card skimming, xvi
    card testing by fraudsters, 14
    chargeback thresholds, 66
    machine learning training, 91
    online attacks predominant, xvi
    organized crime sophistication, 32
    stolen cards
        about, 103
        defining stolen credit card fraud, 104
        email analysis definitions, 105
        identification of fraud, 107-116
        IP address information sources, 108
        IP analysis reliability, 113-116
        IP masking overview, 108
        masked IPs, 111-112
        mismatched IP, 108